SOUNDINGS IN
THE RELIGION OF
JESUS

SOUNDINGS IN THE RELIGION OF
JESUS

Perspectives and Methods in Jewish and Christian Scholarship

Edited by Bruce Chilton, Anthony Le Donne, and Jacob Neusner

Fortress Press
Minneapolis

SOUNDINGS IN THE RELIGION OF JESUS
Perspectives and Methods in Jewish and Christian Scholarship

Cover image: Fragment of a mosaic from the synagogue of Maon. Talmud epoch, before 538 CE, Snark / Art Resource, NY
Cover design: Tory Herman
Book design: PerfecType, Nashville, TN

Library of Congress Cataloging-in-Publication Data
Soundings in the Judaism of Jesus : perspectives and methods in contemporary scholarship / Bruce Chilton, Anthony Le Donne, and Jacob Neusner, editors.
    p. cm.
  Includes bibliographical references.
  ISBN 978-0-8006-9801-0 (hardcover : alk. paper) — ISBN 978-1-4514-2429-4 (ebook)
  1. Jesus Christ—Jewishness. 2. Jesus Christ—Jewish interpretations. 3. Jesus Christ—Historicity. 4. Christianity and antisemitism. 5. Judaism—Relations—Christianity. 6. Christianity and other religions—Judaism. I. Chilton, Bruce. II. Le Donne, Anthony, 1975– III.
Neusner, Jacob, 1932–
  BT590.J8S628 2012
  232.9—dc23
                          2012008045

Manufactured in the U.S.A.
16 15 14 13 12   1 2 3 4 5 6 7 8 9 10

in memory of
Alan Segal (1945–2011)

Contents

Illustrations

Figures

Contributors

Bruce Chilton is Bernard Iddings Bell Professor of Religion and director of the Institute of Advanced Theology at Bard College. He wrote the first critical commentary on the Aramaic version of Isaiah (the Isaiah Targum) and is the author of a number of academic studies situating Jesus in his Judaic context, including *A Galilean Rabbi and His Bible* (1984), *The Temple of Jesus* (1992), *Pure Kingdom: Jesus' Vision of God* (1996), *Rabbi Jesus: An Intimate Biography* (2002), and *The Way of Jesus: To Repair and Renew the World* (2010), among others. He is co-author of *Studying the New Testament: A Fortress Introduction* (2010). An Anglican priest, he is rector of the Church of St. John the Evangelist in Barrytown, New York.

Michael J. Cook is professor of intertestamental and early Christian literatures and holds the Sol and Arlene Bronstein Chair in Judeo-Christian Studies at Hebrew Union College, Cincinnati. A rabbi, his recent publications include *Modern Jews Engage the New Testament: Enhancing Jewish Well-Being in a Christian Environment* (2008) and articles in *The Jewish Annotated New Testament* (2011), *The Wiley-Blackwell Companion to Jesus* (2010), and *The Jewish Jesus: Revelation, Reflection, Reclamation* (2011).

James D. G. Dunn is Emeritus Lightfoot Professor of Divinity at the University of Durham and a fellow of the British Academy. He is the author of more than twenty monographs in New Testament studies, including *Jesus, Paul, and the Law* (1990), *Christology in the Making* (1996), *Jesus Remembered:*

Christianity in the Making (2003), *New Perspectives on Jesus* (2005), *Did the First Christians Worship Jesus?* (2009), and from Fortress Press, *The Living Word* (2009). He is a Methodist Local Preacher.

Leonard Greenspoon holds the Klutznick Chair in Jewish Civilization and is professor of classical and Near Eastern studies and of theology at Creighton University. An internationally recognized expert on the history of Jewish Bible translations, he has also published numerous studies in Jewish history and areas of popular culture in the series Studies in Jewish Civilization; he is a co-author of *Jesus through Catholic and Jewish Eyes* (2000). He writes a column on the use (or misuse) of the Bible in the daily press for *Bible Review* and is editor of the Society of Biblical Literature *Forum*.

Anthony Le Donne is author of *The Historiographical Jesus: Memory, Typology, and the Son of David* (2009) and *The Historical Jesus: What Can We Know and How Can We Know It?* (2011) and is co-editor of *The Fourth Gospel in First Century Media Culture* (2011). He is a member of the Presbyterian Church (USA) and a founding member of the Jewish-Christian Dialogue and Sacred Texts consultation for the Society of Biblical Literature. His home on the web is anthonyledonne.com.

Amy-Jill Levine is University Professor of New Testament and Jewish Studies, E. Rhodes and Leona B. Carpenter Professor of New Testament Studies, and professor of Jewish studies at Vanderbilt University Divinity School and College of Arts and Science. She is also affiliated professor at the Woolf Institute, Centre for the Study of Jewish-Christian Relations, in Cambridge, U.K. She is the author of numerous scholarly essays and books, including *The Misunderstood Jew: The Church and the Scandal of the Jewish Jesus* (2006); editor of the Feminist Companion to the New Testament and Early Christian Writings series; and co-editor of *The Jewish Annotated New Testament* (2011). A self-described Yankee Jewish feminist, Professor Levine is a member of Congregation Sherith Israel in Nashville, Tennessee, an Orthodox Synagogue, although she is quite unorthodox in many ways.

Anne Lapidus Lerner is the founding director of the Jewish Feminist Research Group and assistant professor of Jewish literature at The Jewish Theological Seminary. She has played both a scholarly role as a pioneer in Jewish women's studies and an activist role in the struggle for women's rights in Judaism. Like her most recent book, *Eternally Eve: Images of Eve in the Hebrew Bible, Midrash, and Modern Jewish Poetry* (2007), her current research brings together her interests in both Jewish women's studies and the ways in which classic Jewish texts and traditions relate to contemporary readers.

Joel N. Lohr is currently a visiting scholar at the University of Toronto, soon to become the Director of Religious Life and Multifaith Chaplain at the University of the Pacific. His recent books include *Chosen and Unchosen: Conceptions of Election in the Pentateuch and Jewish-Christian Interpretation* (2009), *The Torah: A Beginner's Guide* (coauthor, 2011), *A Theological Introduction to the Pentateuch: Interpreting the Torah as Christian Scripture* (coeditor, 2012), and *Making Sense in Religious Studies: A Student's Guide to Research and Writing* (coauthor, 2012). Lohr is a Licensed Lay Reader in the Niagara diocese of the Anglican Church of Canada.

Jacob Neusner is the Distinguished Service Professor of the History and Theology of Judaism and a senior fellow of the Institute of Advanced Theology at Bard College. He has written or edited more than 950 books on Judaism and Jewish history, including *The Mishnah: A New Translation* (1991), *Introduction to Rabbinic Literature* (1999), *Theology of the Oral Torah* (1999), and *A Rabbi Talks with Jesus* (co-author, 2000), and from Fortress Press, *A Short History of Judaism* (1992), *Recovering Judaism: The Universal Dimension of Judaism* (2000), and, with Bruce Chilton, *Jewish-Christian Debates: God, Kingdom, Messiah* (2000). He was a Conservative rabbi for decades and has recently returned to Reform Judaism.

Eyal Regev is associate professor and chair of the Department of the Land of Israel and Archaeology at Bar-Ilan University, Israel. His books include *The Sadducees and Their Halakhah: Religion and Society in the Second Temple Period* (2005) and *Sectarianism in Qumran: A Cross-Cultural Perspective* (2007). He has authored more than eighty scholarly essays, including "Were the Early Christians Sectarians?" in the *Journal of Biblical Literature*. He is an Orthodox Jew.

Adele Reinhartz is professor in the Department of Classics and Religious Studies at the University of Ottawa. She is the author of numerous articles and several books, including *"Why Ask My Name?": Anonymity and Identity in Biblical Narrative* (1998), *Befriending the Beloved Disciple: A Jewish Reading of the Gospel of John* (2002), *Scripture on the Silver Screen* (2003), *Jesus of Hollywood* (2007), and *Caiaphas the High Priest*, and co-editor of *Jesus, Judaism, and Christian Anti-Judaism* (2002). She is currently completing a book on the Gospel of John and the "parting of the ways" with support from the Social Sciences and Humanities Research Council of Canada. She was elected to the Royal Society of Canada in 2005 and named General Editor of the *Journal of Biblical Literature* in 2012.

Donald Senior, C.P., is President and Professor of New Testament at Catholic Theological Union in Chicago. He is the author of *Jesus: A Gospel Portrait* (1992) and *The Gospel According to Matthew* (Interpreting Biblical Texts, 1997) and co-author of *The Biblical Foundations for Mission* (1983) and *Invitation to the Gospels* (2002). He is a member of the Pontifical Biblical Commission and Vice President of the Council of Religious Leaders of Metropolitan Chicago and has been active in interreligious dialogue, particularly with Jewish and Muslim communities.

Gerd Theissen is Professor of New Testament Theology at the University of Heidelberg and an ordained pastor of the United Church of Baden (Lutheran and Reformed Congregations). His books include, from Fortress Press, *The Shadow of the Galilean* (1987), *The Religion of the Earliest Churches* (1999), and *The New Testament: A Literary History* (2011); as co-author, *The Historical Jesus: A Comprehensive Guide* (1998); and as co-editor, *The Social Setting of Jesus and the Gospels* (2001).

Dagmar Winter is an Anglican parish priest in rural Northumberland, Northeast England, and Diocesan Rural Affairs Officer. She is the author of *The Quest for the Plausible Jesus: The Question of Criteria* (2002) and *In the Footsteps of Jesus: Explorations and Reflections in the Land of the Holy One* (2005). Areas of her research include the implications of Jesus' rural ministry for sustainability in the rural context today.

Foreword

This book poses a deceptively simple question: Can a consideration of Jesus' Jewishness benefit Jewish-Christian dialogue? The answer seems obvious: yes, of course. The very notion of a Jewish Jesus signals the significant common ground shared between Judaism and Christianity. Acknowledgment of this common ground should enhance the mutual understanding and respect that dialogue is intended to foster.

As the essays in this volume illustrate, however, neither the question nor the answer is as straightforward as it may appear. What does it mean to say that Jesus was Jewish? That he was born into a Jewish family? Would that also include everything that flows logically from that one fact—that he lived within a Jewish society and therefore observed Jewish law to the same extent and in the same ways as those around him, that he shared his community's sensibilities, values, and concerns? If so, what happened to transform him from a Galilean carpenter to the focus of worship of a world religion which has shaped the lives of countless individuals and the history, culture, and laws of numerous countries? Was it something he did or said? Or the things that were said about him and done in his name? Some combination of these and other factors?

Further, what does Jewish-Christian dialogue entail, and what does it accomplish? Participants in dialogue groups often discuss the beliefs and values that Jews and Christians have in common. They may study with and learn about their Jewish or Christian counterparts, and perhaps most important, they may develop friendships and a sense of comfort with those who come from different points of view. But anyone who has participated in Jewish-Christian dialogue groups or activities will attest that they do not attract either Jews or Christians from across the full spectrum of their respective faith communities. While there are many Jewish and Christian clergy and laypeople who are committed to Jewish-Christian dialogue, it remains an activity that is marginal to the lives of most Jews and Christians. In addition to the personal benefit and enhanced knowledge that dialogue participants may experience, might one also wish for a broader impact on the relationships between Jews and Christians, Jewish and Christian leaders, and Jewish and Christian organizations?

Lurking beneath the question of whether Jesus' Jewishness can benefit Jewish-Christian dialogue are two important observations. The first is that the symmetry implied in the very term *Jewish-Christian dialogue* is misleading, at least to some extent. The fact that Jesus was Jewish is not germane to many of the ways in which Jews live out and express their Jewish identities, including the beliefs and practices of Judaism as a religious system. Nor do Jews "need" to understand Christianity in order to understand the Jewish Scriptures, Jewish practice, or Jewish law. But where Jews do need to engage with Christians is in the understanding of Jewish history and in coping with the dominant, Christian-influenced culture in which many Jews live. Without understanding something about Christians and Christianity, Jews and other non-Christians in the Americas, Europe, and many other parts of the world are unable to understand their neighbors, their public holidays, their movies, and their presidential debates.

The second observation is more pointed: whether overtly acknowledged or not, the subject that matters most to most participants in Jewish-Christian dialogue is anti-Semitism. It is the history of Christian anti-Semitism and, most urgently, the role that Christian anti-Semitism may have played over many centuries in laying the groundwork for the Holocaust that most often drives Jewish-Christian dialogue. This in itself creates another asymmetry. Jews and Christians are not equal partners in the dialogue. There is often a perceived need for Christian participants not only to understand the powerful impact of anti-Semitism on Jewish identity and experience but also to apologize for it; this is matched by the perceived need for the Jewish participants to hear out and accept the apology.

This dynamic is evident not only anecdotally but also in published manifestos. The 2002 document "A Sacred Obligation: Rethinking Christian Faith in Relation to Judaism and the Jewish People," published by a group of prominent Christian scholars and clergy from a range of Christian denominations, acknowledges that "For most of the past two thousand years, Christians have erroneously portrayed Jews as unfaithful, holding them collectively responsible for the death of Jesus and therefore accursed by God."

The document rejects this accusation, and "repent[s] of this teaching of contempt."[1] The 2002 declaration *Dabru Emet* ("speak the truth"), by a group of prominent Jewish rabbis and scholars, acknowledges the recent "dramatic and unprecedented shift in Jewish and Christian relations" brought about by the statements by "official Church bodies, both Roman Catholic and Protestant" expressing remorse for Christian mistreatment of Jews and Judaism and pledging to reform "Christian teaching and preaching . . . so that they acknowledge God's enduring covenant with the Jewish people and celebrate the contribution of Judaism to world civilization and to Christian faith itself." *Dabru Emet* absolves Christianity of responsibility for the Holocaust but acknowledges that "Without the long history of Christian anti-Judaism and Christian violence against Jews, Nazi ideology could not have taken hold nor could it have been carried out."[2]

The difficult matter of Christian anti-Semitism underlies not only the enterprise of Jewish-Christian dialogue but also the matter of Jesus' Jewishness. Jesus' Jewishness would not be a controversial topic were it not for the fact that for centuries he was understood as standing over against Judaism and as the universal divinely sent savior, the Son of God, who by definition cannot be attached to any particular ethnic group, let alone the Jews, who refused to believe in him and whose leadership opposed him unto death. Although Jews and Christians have been in conversation with one another in various eras and locations over the past two millennia, sometimes even harmoniously so, modern Jewish-Christian dialogue very likely would not have come into existence were it not for the Holocaust and the recognition among some Christian churches of a level of complicity, whether intentional or not.

It is not surprising, then, that the question of Christian anti-Semitism is addressed, usually directly, in some cases indirectly, in each of the essays in this volume. The volume has two underlying assumptions: that Jesus was a Jew and that Jewish-Christian dialogue is a good thing. Historically speaking, the first point is incontrovertible. Ethically and morally, the second point also seems assured; any activity that leads to mutual respect, understanding, and cooperation between Jews and Christians is worth fostering. In both cases, the issue of anti-Semitism must be raised, not only with respect to recent events, but in the very sources for the life of Jesus himself: the New Testament.

One approach is to suggest that the anti-Semitism or anti-Judaism arises in the interpretation of Scripture, not in Scripture itself. Joel Lohr, for example, argues that the parable of the sheep and the goats in Matthew 25 is not about the division between Christians and non-Christians, as it is often read, but between gentiles who have met Jewish standards and those who have not. In this case, negative perceptions of Judaism can be attributed not to the Gospel writers but to the history of interpretation; this approach excises the problem, neatly and without bloodshed, using the sharp knife of historical-critical exegesis.

But what to do about the passages that more directly put Jews and Judaism in a highly negative light? One obvious example can be found in the Passion narratives, which portray the Jewish leadership and/or the Jewish crowds as morally if not literally culpable of Jesus' death, thereby engendering the threatening chant of "Christ-killers" to which many Jews are exposed even today. Michael Cook addresses this point by arguing that some aspects of the Passion accounts have no basis in history, in which case the deicide charge itself is also unhistorical. Cook's is a minority view, even among interpreters highly sympathetic to Judaism, as Dunn's response in this volume shows. But even if Cook is right, what is one to do with these passages? One might be inclined simply to ignore them were it not for the fact that they are translated into virtually every language known to humankind. In their contributions to this volume, Leonard Greenspoon and Amy-Jill Levine measure the gains and losses of translating the New Testament in ways that draw attention to the Jewishness of Jesus, his family, and his earliest followers. Both attempt to eliminate or at least attenuate anti-Jewish/anti-Semitic readings. Whether translation should play down the problem, or draw attention to it, remains a difficult question.

Although the "quest of the historical Jesus" (Albert Schweitzer's famous term) is most often attempted as an exercise in objective historical scholarship, reconstructions of Jesus' life and message often project onto this first-century Jew the ideals and aspirations of times and places far removed from his own. As Anthony Le Donne's essay notes, in eras when anti-Semitism was acceptable, or at least tolerable (and even when it was not), lives of Jesus have often betrayed an anti-Jewish bent. This point is reinforced by the essays by Dagmar Winter, who explores the role of anti-Semitism in the attempts of Protestant scholars to disassociate Jesus from Judaism, and Gerd Theissen, who focuses on the presuppositions and agendas of Jesus research in Germany during the Nazi era.

Anti-Semitism, however, is a painful topic, and important as it is to Jewish-Christian dialogue, it should not become the sole item on the agenda. It is no wonder that in the effort to promote harmony and mutual respect, dialogue as such, and many of the essays in this volume, strive to find the common ground between Jews and Christians. But, as Donald Senior notes, Jewish-Christian dialogue needs not only common ground but also honest recognition of difference, including theological difference. Senior comments that while the Jewish identity of Jesus reminds us of the historical bonds between Christians and Jews, there is no way to smooth over one crucial difference: Jesus' christological identity. In addition to the acknowledgment of difference between Jews and Christians, dialogue must also include painful

conversation within each group. Anne Lapidus Lerner's study of the Canaanite woman in Mark 7 and Mark 15 from the perspective of modern Jewish
women's studies points to the need to accept that each of our religious traditions includes texts and ideas that fail to affirm the humanity of the other.

Stripping Jesus of his Jewish identity was a disservice to Jesus, and to
Christianity; to the extent that this destructive act both served and promoted
anti-Semitism it was also a disservice—to put it mildly—to Jews and to
Christians as well. By drawing attention to the question of Jesus' identity,
the texts from which we construct that identity, and the complex history of
Jewish-Christian relations, this book does indeed achieve its goal, which is
"to model a dialogue that deals honestly and reflectively with the distinctive
and (sometimes) analogous characteristics of our tradition" (page 7). If it can
spur more people to engage in thoughtful dialogue, all the better.

Introduction: Allowing Historical Study to Serve Interfaith Dialogue

Anthony Le Donne

In his book *Jesus the Jew,* Geza Vermes begins chapter 1 with these words:

> Most people, whether they admit it or not, approach the Gospels with preconceived ideas. Christians read them in the light of their faith; Jews, primed with age-old suspicion ... Yet it should not be beyond the capabilities of an educated man to sit down and with a mind empty of prejudice read the accounts of Mark, Matthew and Luke as though for the first time.[1]

These words, first written in 1973, were among the very first of the so-called "Third Quest" of the historical Jesus. Already, fifteen years before N. T. Wright would coin the phrase that marked the phase, a consensus had been reached that Jesus' Jewishness was historical fact.[2] An entire generation of Jesus scholars (the most productive generation in history—if measured by publications) would nuance, debate, marginalize, and reframe Jesus' Jewishness. But the fact of Jesus' ethnicity and religion was no longer a matter of debate among serious historians. Vermes was far from the first with this program, but it was his voice that set the tone for this generation.

So it is with the greatest respect that I offer the following criticism: not only is it beyond the capability of any person to read any narrative empty of prejudice, Jews and Christians cannot and should not attempt to do so with narratives that are so laden with the baggage of misinterpretation. This is not to suggest a resignation to hopeless subjectivity; neither do I suggest that we

1

abandon the rigors of historical discipline. My point is that the closest we can come to reading the narratives of Jesus "objectively" is when we acknowledge our prejudices, including those related to our religious heritage. Christians and Jews cannot check their religious identities at the door on their way to the roundtable discussion of history. Moreover, they should not be asked to do so.[3]

Jon Levenson has helpfully argued that objectivity is "a necessary ideal," even if it cannot be achieved absolutely.[4] To an extent, personal biases (including those that stem from our faith commitments) can be bracketed. We must be willing to follow our research to conclusions that have not been pre-scripted by our faith communities. Although, according to Levenson, such "bracketing" must not be confused with the illusion that these prejudices do not exist.[5] The primary obligation of the historian is honesty, with both the data before us and the impact that our choices make in shaping our collective identities.

Generation after generation of Christians and Jews has chosen different histories to remember. Even when these histories have overlapped, we have repeatedly selected our memories divergently.[6] We have employed these memories in service to distinctly different rituals and calendars—often to the detriment of the other. Because memory shapes identity, by choosing to remember differently Jews and Christians have become aliens in this process. With this in mind, Jewish and Christian historians will do well to lay bare our prejudices and be willing to question which of them have the potential to harm. Conversely, historians must retain those commitments that reinforce the collective identities of their people, especially when our collective identities are met with the crises of cultural amnesia. According to Yosef Hayim Yerushalmi, this is nothing short of a moral obligation:

> The burden of building a bridge to his people remains with the historian. I do not know for certain that this will be possible. I am convinced only that first the historian must truly desire it and then try to act accordingly [. . .] What historians choose to study and write about is obviously part of the problem. The notion that everything in the past is worth knowing "for its own sake" is a mythology of modern historians, as is the lingering suspicion that conscious responsibility toward the living concerns of the group must result in history that is less scholarly or "scientific."

Confronted with the problem of the loss of collective memory (and thus the loss of collective identity), Yerushalmi asks, "Who, then, can be expected to step into the breach, if not the historian? Is it not both his chosen and appointed task to restore the past to us all?"[7] Perhaps this description aggrandizes the task of the historian. But—and this is especially true of the history between Jews and Christians—there is a greater danger in belittling the damage done by misinterpretations of Jesus over the centuries.

Some of our prejudices are survival mechanisms that protect the boundaries of our collective identities. We will do well to ask whether these serve a purpose in the modern world. Perhaps yes, perhaps no. Some of our prejudices represent the very heart of our collective identities. It is the historian's responsibility to have an eye to such decisions and realize that we are not isolated arbiters in this endeavor.

For this reason the authors of this book write not only as scholars of the history and legacy of Jesus but also as Jews and Christians. Each author has been asked to illuminate an aspect of Jesus' history or legacy and suggest talking points for Jewish-Christian dialogue. You will see that these authors represent the finest and most disciplined of their field and that they have not sacrificed any rigor in service to this project.

Educating Ourselves about the Jewish Jesus

Jesus research now represents something of a common ground between Jewish and Christian scholarship. While the name of Christ has long been wielded as a divisive force, we now see Jesus situated in the religion and culture of his birth, in conversation, debate, and polemic with fellow Jews. Remarkably, there has been very little use of this consensus for contemporary Jewish-Christian dialogue.

In her recent essay, "Jesus from a Jewish Perspective," Sybil Sheridan claims that "this [scholarly] trend has made no impact at all on the beliefs and practices of the Jewish faithful." While acknowledging that Christianity has shaped Judaism significantly since its inception, her claim is that "Judaism exists—or at least, thinks it exists—without reference to the person of Jesus, and that studies that show the opposite are rare and recent."[8] Sheridan's assessment is indicative of two related rifts that have had tragic consequences: (1) that between Jews and Christians and (2) that between Christian history and doctrine.

While the so-called "historical Jesus" of scholarly construction is almost entirely unknown to non-academic Jews, the phrase "Christ Killers" is notorious.[9] For many Jews and Christians, the name Christ is set in antithesis to Judaism. The average person may know that Jesus was Jewish, but when this fact is treated trivially, it does very little to reframe two thousand years of anti-Jewish Christology.[10]

Modern Judaism (of all ilks) has, in large part, retreated from religious contact with Christians. Fear of sinister motives has led to a history of ignorance on both sides. Sheridan's claim that Judaism "thinks it exists" without reference to the person of Jesus is telling. Ironically, Jesus may be the most influential historical figure in western history, but Jews and Christians alike know very little about him: Jews because of disinterest, and Christians because Jesus is deceptively familiar. In either case, the charge of ignorance is only helpful when heard internally. Peter Ochs writes, "This veil of ignorance may once have served the purposes of Jewish self-definition. It is no longer wise or tenable."[11] As a Christian, I must echo a similar indictment of general Christian ignorance.

Christians need to hear from recent research that Jesus was not a Christian. He never converted to Christianity. His Judaism was not his "cultural background," as if he was raised a Jew but then became something else. Nor is Jesus' relationship to Judaism simply a matter of ethnicity. From a historical perspective, Jesus' actions are only intelligible once he is understood as a Jew who remained a Jew. It is equally important for Christians to hear that such affirmations do not in any way degrade Christianity. There must be some continuity between the "historical Jesus" and the figure venerated in the New Testament.[12] Importantly, one of the most obvious continuities here is that the Jesus of the New Testament—the Son of God—is Jewish.

For all of the tension that existed between Jews and gentiles in the New Testament, Jesus was never portrayed as a Roman, or a Greek, or an Egyptian gentile. From the very beginning of Christian worship, Jews and gentiles were called to recognize and venerate a Jewish messiah. New Testament scholars believe that Rom. 1:3-4 (cf. 2 Tim. 2:8) contains our earliest surviving Christian creed. This creed is generally considered to be a pre-Pauline creed taken from primitive Christianity.[13] Here Paul confesses that Jesus "came from David's seed according to the flesh; who was established the Son of God with power by the resurrection from the dead." The fact of Jesus' flesh and blood identity within Israel is at the very heart of Christianity. Even the episodes that are most doubted as historically plausible portray Jesus as a Jew.[14] Finally, as Jesus walked and talked among his contemporaries, he was chiefly concerned for the welfare of the people of Israel. Those of us who take Jesus' "Lordship" seriously must take seriously the concerns of the human Jesus.

Good interfaith dialogue seeks to replace ignorance with education. To this end, Jews and Christians who are open and interested in authentic dialogue will be helped by discussions of Jesus' Jewishness. The goal here is not to find common ground at the expense of our many religious differences. The goal is simply to allow this education to inform our dialogue. Both sides must ask difficult questions both of themselves and of the other. Thus we must be well equipped with informed talking points.

Chapters at a Glance

This book is divided into four parts: (1) the New Testament Jesus and exclusionary boundaries, (2) early Jewish and gentile perspectives of Jesus,

(3) Jesus research before and after German National Socialism, and (4) Jesus in Jewish-Christian dialogue. The first three of these parts consist of chapters written with particular topics in mind and conclude with talking points. Part four responds to the previous chapters and concludes with a jointly written reflection.

Leonard Greenspoon's chapter explores the gains and losses of translating the New Testament in ways that eliminate anti-Jewish/anti-Semitic readings. By analyzing recent attempts to do so, he demonstrates that once the anti-Semitic elements are erased from the tradition, Jesus' original ethnicity, religion, and worldview (indeed, his very identity) are further obscured. Greenspoon ultimately suggests that translators must continue to keep the problems of anti-Jewish readings present to mind but must do so cautiously.

Joel Lohr's chapter discusses Jesus' eschatological portrait of sheep and goats in Matthew 25. He argues that the best reading of this oft debated passage is one that situates it within the concerns of first-century Jewish eschatology in general and a Jewish election ethic in particular. Within these milieux, Lohr argues that this vision of judgment describes the division of "gentiles" who have met Jewish standards of charity and those who have not. Thus his reading stands contrary to many traditional Christian readings that see this division as that between Christians and non-Christians. This reading, argues Lohr, suggests a more nuanced and perhaps less uniform New Testament soteriology, one that might help Christians to appreciate their indebtedness to Jewish visions of the world to come.

Anne Lapidus Lerner's chapter offers a close reading and literary analysis of Jesus' episode with the Canaanite/Syrophoenician woman (Matt. 15:21-28; Mark 7:24-30). Reading from the concerns of modern Jewish women's studies, Lerner analyzes the stories presented by Matthew and Mark side by side. She calls attention to the dismissive, derogatory, and dehumanizing words of Jesus in Mark that become still harsher in Matthew. Moreover, Lerner observes that these stories diminish the voice of this nameless woman and enclose hers with the frame of the man's voice. At the same time, this woman occupies a remarkable exception within the Gospels and becomes the "hero of the story" for Lerner. Lerner carefully and respectfully suggests that interfaith dialogue requires honest criticism of one's own faith texts, especially those that fail to affirm the humanity of the other.

Michael Cook's chapter addresses ten anomalies in Mark's treatment of the Jewish leaders (chief priests, scribes, elders, Pharisees, Herodians, Sadducees), and argues that all can be resolved simultaneously by a single hypothesis. His determination that Mark's portraits of these groups are artificial raises the sobering problem of their impact on Matthew, Luke, and later Christian writers and preachers, and thus also on the well-being of Jews throughout the ages.

Donald Senior's chapter suggests that while Matthew must be understood as a Christian narrative written for a Jewish-Christian audience, it provides glimpses of the life of Jesus before he was venerated as Christ. Moreover, Matthew's agenda to situate Jesus within his Jewish context is an overt redaction of the Markan Jesus, but perhaps (at times) a more plausible reconstruction of the historical Jesus. Senior suggests that the Jewish identity of Jesus reminds us of the historical bonds between Christians and Jews. Ultimately, however, it is Jesus' christological identity that remains most problematic for Jewish-Christian dialogue. Matthew's Jesus is at once (paradoxically) Christ of Christianity and Jewish Jesus. It is the faith-appropriation of this (these) identity (identities) that provides both the common ground and the honest recognition of differences needed for Jewish-Christian dialogue.

Eyal Regev's chapter argues that Jesus' arrest and trial was due to his action in the temple coupled with his saying about the temple's destruction. He argues that these elements, seen from Roman and Sadducean perspectives, would have provided sufficient warrant for Jesus' arrest and trial. In light of this, Regev rejects the idea that Jesus was arrested and tried as a result of any messianic claims. Moreover, such claims probably do not reflect the historical claims of Jesus.

My chapter argues that while it is common for Jesus historians to attribute the "First Quest" to Hermann Samuel Reimarus, critical evaluations of the life of Jesus began much, much earlier. I argue that recent surveys of the Jesus "Quests" have made a misstep in following the lead of Albert Schweitzer in this respect. Moreover, I suggest that we commonly see the topic of Jesus' Jewishness emerge from Jewish-Christian dialogue in late antiquity and medieval periods. My chapter also explores the influences on anti-Judaism and anti-Semitism on modern Jesus historians.

Dagmar Winter's chapter explains four (sometimes overlapping) motives of Protestant scholars to disassociate Jesus from Judaism. She demonstrates that the history of Jesus research from Luther onward both consciously and unwittingly painted the portrait of a Jesus dissimilar to Judaism. This agenda, she argues, is fourfold. Winter argues that the historical Jesus became dissimilar to first-century Judaism in the minds of nineteenth- and twentieth-century historians because of the aims of (1) European anti-Judaism and anti-Semitism, (2) Protestantism's projection of Reformation disputes onto first-century Judaism, (3) the focus of European and British historiography on "genius" in history, and (4) Dialectical Theology's emphasis on the Christ of Faith at the expense of Jesus of History.

Gerd Theissen's chapter provides a window into the presuppositions and agendas of Jesus research in Germany leading to and through the years of National Socialism. He distances his historical method both from the "German Christians" who attempted to create an Aryan Jesus and from others who attempted to show Jesus as a Jew who transcended Judaism. Theissen argues that Jesus must be located in the very center of Judaism with regard to his message but might also be called "A Marginal Jew" with regard to his radical lifestyle.

The responses by James Dunn and Amy-Jill Levine dialogue with some of the points raised in the previous chapters and reflect on these topics. Dunn's response deals with each chapter's contributions, critiquing the exegetical, historical, and dialogical contributions of each one. He does so as a committed participant of historical Jesus research and Jewish-Christian dialogue from a Christian perspective. Levine's response critiques the parameters delineated and assumed by the authors and editors of the project. She does so as a committed participant in historical Jesus research and Jewish-Christian dialogue from a Jewish perspective. These responses model Jewish-Christian dialogue in at least three ways: (1) both approach the topic with informed questions and self-awareness; (2) neither equivocates the important differences between Jews and Christians; (3) both are attentive to the literary details, historical context(s), and practical impact of their study; they expect this from themselves and from the other participants in this dialogue.

Bruce Chilton and Jacob Neusner round out this book with a jointly written conclusion. They helpfully move the discussion beyond "Jesus" and widen the scope to the traditional truth claims of Judaism and Christianity. Rather than attempting to find simplistic or superficial commonalities between the two, they highlight the ways in which these two traditions have parted ways. Chilton and Neusner then offer a way forward for recognizing and analyzing the many analogues between Judaism and Christianity.

The authors and editors of this book hope to model a dialogue that deals honestly and reflectively with the distinctive and (sometimes) analogous characteristics of our traditions. The choice of Jesus as an entry point, we readily acknowledge, is only one avenue for mutual understanding. It is one, however, that requires much more exploration. We hope that this book will be a step closer to historical, exegetical, and theological study done side by side and to mutual benefit.

Part One

The New Testament Jesus and Exclusionary Boundaries

CHAPTER ONE
Translating *Jesus* and *the Jews*: Can We Eradicate the Anti-Semitism without Also Erasing the Semitism?

Leonard Greenspoon

Most readers of the New Testament are, I would imagine, Christians. And for many, if not most, of these readers, the modern-language version of the New Testament they read is, or at least functions as, their New Testament.

In a sense, this is as it should be. After all, the heart of the New Testament, the sayings attributed to Jesus, is translation: Jesus spoke in Aramaic and perhaps a bit of Hebrew; his words are preserved, with very, very few exceptions, only in translation—Greek translation. So it is not completely unexpected that his words can be as easily cited, quoted in a modern language, as they were in ancient languages not his own.

Moreover, and perhaps in part reflecting this distinctive linguistic circumstance, there are relatively few efforts, especially in the modern world, to instruct Christian laity in the languages of the Bible. If my experience is at all representative, it is not unusual for even clerics to have little more than a smattering of proficiency in these languages and to make only occasional use of them in preparing sermons and educational materials for their congregations.

We may, if only briefly, contrast this circumstance with the situation in Judaism, where, for example, even the most nontraditional synagogues continue to house Torah scrolls in Hebrew and to expect their youngsters, in preparing for a bat or bar mitzvah, to have mastery, however halting, over at least a bit of biblical and liturgical Hebrew. Hebrew schools remain a staple of synagogue organization and communal life, and Hebrew expressions regularly appear in the sermons and pedagogical documents of rabbis. Thus it is that Jewish translations or versions of the Bible, for which there is a history of well over two millennia, are not intended to replace the original text of the Hebrew Bible, but rather to point to it—as is characteristically indicated, among other ways, by having the modern language and the Hebrew on facing pages.[1]

This digression, slight as it was, serves to highlight the unique place Scripture in translation occupies for Christians. It also helps to justify the considerable attention given to translations of the New Testament in this essay. Our primary interest is the Jewishness of Jesus, as evidenced in the New Testament. To appreciate this portion of Jesus' personality, if you will, we cannot ignore what the Greek text of the New Testament says. But, for our purposes, these data form the platform upon which we construct our edifice and not the edifice itself.

In short, we will be looking at how translations of the New Testament, specifically English-language translations, portray Jesus' Jewishness. In general, our emphasis is on passages that have, in the opinion of one or more critic, been mishandled so as to separate Jesus from the first-century Jews and the first-century Judaism of which he was authentically a part. Such renderings may have been deliberate and well thought out or random and unconscious—on this point opinions differ. Whatever the case, corrections and improvements have been suggested, and we will also look at and evaluate them. All of this is offered as an exercise that is valuable in itself and moreover as a contribution toward furthering profitable dialogue among faith communities.

We first look at the handling, that is, the rendering, of the proper names of major New Testament figures; specifically Jesus, his family, and his followers. The literary critic and translator Willis Barnstone has emerged as the principal spokesperson in bringing this issue to the fore. He sets out his agenda in this regard forthrightly: to correct one of the great enigmas and distortions of religious and intellectual history, how through the manipulation and intentional falsification of translation, Jesus, in the eyes of Christians and even Jews, ceased to be one of "our guys"; that is, how Jesus, through the translator's deft, authorizing hand, ceased to be a Jew.[2]

He continues: many translators of the Bible into the vernacular, beginning with the Vulgate, have conducted sectarian, combative missions to change the recognizable identities of people in the Bible. This is distortion of identity by means of translation.[3] Elsewhere, he speaks of this process as a "grand identity theft."[4] By sleight-of-hand translating, only certain figures of the Christian Scriptures remain clearly identifiable as Jews: not John the Baptist, not Mary, not Jesus, nor James and Paul. Even their names are not biblically Jewish.[5]

This makes it possible for Christians to hate Jews, yet not hate Jesus (Yeshua) as a Jew, nor his mother Mary (Miryam) and father Joseph (Yosef), or his followers.[6] These translators succeeded in creating a book, the New Testament, about Jews in which the main figures, "good Jews," are not perceived as Jews at all.[7]

As Barnstone observes, the results of this deception (or rather this history of deception) are as shameful as they are predictable: those seen to be Jews are depicted deplorably and always as guilty. Jews, as the enemies of Jesus, must be punished for all generations to come. In the New Testament, all the good people are Christians and the evil ones are Jews.[8]

Moving from general statements to specifics, Barnstone sets forth a number of examples to buttress his case. In this connection, Barnstone observes that in the genealogy of Jesus, Jacob's Hebrew name *Ya'aqob* is transliterated in the Greek text as *Iakōbos*. To be consistent, English translators use "Jacob," a name familiar from the Hebrew Bible. Thus, this form is found in English-language versions at Matt. 1:2 and in Luke 3:34.

Thereafter, however, a divergent form appears, as Barnstone notes: after the genealogy in Matthew, Greek *Iakōbos* becomes "James" in English, when referring to an apostle, a brother of Jesus, or the author of the Letter of James. Why, Barnstone queries, is "James" used to refer to these new Christians? His response: it was done precisely and deliberately so as not to associate any of these individuals named James with Jacob, one of the patriarchal figures of Judaism. In order to keep Jews separate from Christians, Greek *Iakōbos* is Jewish "Jacob" in the Old Testament and Christian "James" in the New.[9]

Barnstone then asks this question: which of Jesus' associates retains his association with Jews? His answer: only one, the traitor Judas Iscariot. There are others with the Greek name *Ioudas* in the New Testament. But only one of them, Judas Iscariot, is known as Judas—with clear connections to Judah, Jacob's son. It is Barnstone's contention that the decision to invent new names for the other Judases (from *Ioudas*)—Judah, Juda, and Jude—lies entirely with the translators of the Greek text, who are, in his words, "as faithful in their religious mission as they are faithless as translators."[10]

For Barnstone, the most inspired and fundamental name change in the New Testament occurs in connection with its main character. His name is not translated from the original Hebrew (Joshua), but rather is represented by making the Greek version of his name sound English or German or Italian. For this process, Barnstone makes use of one of the strongest terms of opprobrium possible: as a result of "the *ethnic* cleansing" of his name through double translation, the name has become absolutely disconnected from its Hebrew original.[11]

In Luke's genealogy (3:29), Greek *tou Iēsous* is translated as "Jose" in the King James Version, and other renderings are also found (including Joshua), but very rarely "Jesus." The source of this practice is absolutely clear to Barnstone: it is, he writes, as if the translators could not stomach "Jesus as the translation for the 'Iesous' who was an Old Testament progenitor of Jesus." In so doing, such translators insured that no reader of their versions would associate Jesus by name with any Hebrew Bible Jew.[12]

In summarizing the practices of translators and the effects such practices had, Barnstone is unequivocal: in all of these instances, translation faithlessness obeys a higher order of faith, demanding that the translation extirpate all evidence suggestive that Jesus was a Jew or came from an ancient family of Jews. As a result, few think of Jesus as a Jew or of his early followers as Jewish Christians. Jesus has not been accorded the dignity of truthful acceptance of who he was.[13]

Barnstone closes this section of his book, titled "How through False Translation into and from the Bible Jesus Ceased to Be a Jew," with this "dream": imagine if the Christian Scriptures were retranslated today, and instead of encountering Jesus and James; Mary, Peter, and Paul, we found Joshua and Jacob; Miryam, Kepha, and Saul.[14]

Barnstone has been fortunate enough to live out, as it were, his dream. In several successive projects he has formulated an English-language version that, in his estimation, carries out his goals, one of which, in keeping with the theme of this essay, is to restore probable Hebrew and Aramaic names and so frame the Jewish identity of the main characters, including Yeshua (Jesus), his family, and his followers.[15] The most recent of these is his *Restored New Testament: A New Translation with Commentary, Including the Gnostic Gospels Thomas, Mary, and Judas,* which appeared in 2009.[16]

An examination of this "Restored" New Testament is instructive. At Matt. (*Mattityahu*, in Barnstone) 1:2 and Luke (or *Loukas*) 3:34, Greek *Iakōbos* appears as *Yaakov*. In this, Barnstone appears to be reflecting some of the same concerns as Everett Fox in his *Schocken Bible.*[17] With respect to the other figures named *Iakōbos*, Barnstone has *Yaakov* for the apostle (as at Matt. 4:21, with an explanatory footnote), *Yaakov* for the brother of Jesus (as at Mark [Marcos] 6:3), and *Yaakov* for the eponymous author of the Letter of Yaakov (James). At least in this instance, Barnstone has followed through on his earlier observations.

For Judas Iscariot, Barnstone has *Yehuda of Keriot* or *Yehuda the man of Keriot* in the gospels of Matthew and John. When the name *Ioudas* occurs elsewhere in the Greek of the New Testament, with reference to another individual, *Yehuda* also appears in Barnstone's version. One example of this is the document usually rendered as the Letter of Jude; in Barnstone it is the Letter of Yehuda (or Judas). In his introduction to this Letter, Barnstone writes, "Scholars agree that 'Jude' came into English naming in order to dissociate Judas of this letter from Judas Iscariot. . . . Hence the unparalleled

King James Version translates a common name found in Hebrew and its Greek version eight hundred thirteen times as "Judah," and thirty-three times as 'Judas,' reserved for the Iscariot. In eight hundred thirteen occasions, its version precludes association of other biblical Judases with Judas the betrayer. Hence, today we have the Letter of Jude rather than the Letter of Judas."[18]

In accordance with Barnstone's expressed concerns (see above), the "Old Testament" *Iēsous* of Luke 3:29 is rendered by *Yeshua*, which replicates the name of the New Testament's main character. Jesus' parents, Mary and Joseph, are banished, replaced in Barnstone's version by *Miryam* and *Yosef* (at Matt. 1:18, these forms are explained in the endnotes). For the apostles (for which Barnstone prefers the term *messengers*, as in Activities of the Messengers instead of the traditional Acts of the Apostles), familiar names are "restored" (to use a term of which Barnstone would surely approve): *Shimon Kefa* for Simon Peter; *Andreas* for Andrew; and the brothers *Yaakov* and *Yohanan* and their father *Zavdai* for James and John, sons of Zebedee (Matt. 1:18-21). As illustrated by these last examples, Barnstone is as concerned about originally Greek names (e.g., "Andrew") as he is about the many names of Semitic origin that have been transmitted in the Greek of the New Testament.

Barnstone's efforts in this regard are not limited to the proper names of individuals. Especially instructive here is his handling of the term *Pharisees*. His rendering is *Prushim* or *Perushim*, which, as he explains it in his introduction (in a section titled "Should Paul's Letters Precede the Gospels?"), comes from the Hebrew form meaning "separatist" and "deviant." Barnstone's use is intended, among other things, to counteract "the cartoon version of Pharisee as 'hypocrite' [which] persists in the dictionary."[19] For Sadducees, Barnstone uses the term *Tzadokim* (as at Matt. 3:27, with a footnote explaining both terms discussed in this paragraph).

Although we have merely sampled the many changes wrought by Barnstone, it nonetheless seems appropriate at this point to consider whether or not Barnstone's version is likely to have the effect on readers that he desires.

Prior to an assessment of this issue, we should at least briefly raise a question about a related topic. With regard to proper names, Barnstone considers the changes he enumerates—and, in his version, "corrects"—the result of a concerted, deliberate scheme to de-Judaize all of the positive characters in the New Testament, separating them from their Old Testament forebears and placing them within the new and highly praised category Christians. Is it in fact the case that the names Barnstone highlights are the result of this sort of effort?

In the works I consulted, Barnstone does not provide any detailed support for this characterization of the motivation(s) of many generations of translators. Even without such analysis, it is difficult for a fair-minded observer to exclude such factors as an impetus, perhaps a primary impetus, for some translators. However, I am wary about implicating all, or even most, translators in such subterfuge. Rather, I suspect that many translators and an even higher percentage of revisers simply replicated these names in the forms that were already well known in their communities and among their intended audiences. Laziness, if that's what this is, is surely no excuse, but it lacks the implications of malice with which Barnstone tends to characterize the entire process of Christian Bible translating.

Even granting that the names Barnstone targets may not be the result of a large-scale conspiracy, they are the ones that appear, in one form or another, in almost every translation of the New Testament. And in this regard, as in several others, Barnstone does present a New Testament that diverges from the familiar. Do these changes construct an environment, if I may use that term, in which users of the New Testament (that is, those who listen to, as well as those who read) can more easily detect the essential Jewishness of Jesus, his family, and his earliest followers? In the absence of any empirical or even anecdotal evidence, it is not prudent to draw many, if any, conclusions in this regard. We are of course permitted, or even encouraged, to hope that Barnstone's approach yields positive results.

Beyond this very tentative observation, we may note three other considerations. First, the changed names that Barnstone presents, especially when they involve major characters such as Jesus, Peter, or Paul, are bound to make some impression on all but the most casual of readers or hearers. However, as a second point, we cannot be at all certain that such readers or hearers will make the connections that Barnstone is looking and hoping for. Since, for many (most?) New Testament readers, the "Old Testament" has ceased to be understood as a "Jewish" work, they may appreciate names such as "Yeshua" and "Miryam" as somehow more authentic, but not necessarily as more Jewish. It is not difficult to imagine comments like this: "That's really interesting. Jesus' name used to be Yeshua, and Mary was Miryam." In this and related ways, Barnstone's version may succeed in teaching history, but it will not be the theological "game-changer" that he seeks.

Finally, we need to take into account how people today encounter—perhaps, interact with—the New Testament. For some, the context is a study group, but the subject matter, unless under some sort of academic leadership, is not likely to center on names, even changed ones. For others, the Bible is something heard at church. Lectionaries or preaching guides based on Barnstone's text might make an impression, even a lasting one, as part of liturgy or a service, but it strikes me as unlikely that Barnstone's version will be widely adopted for such purposes, if at all. Alas, for large numbers, the Bible has simply become an assemblage of verses, either read rather mechanically one-a-day or sampled randomly via smart phone or computer.

Of course, I may be unduly pessimistic or cynical about the ability of a version of the Bible to effect change, especially widespread change. Such a charge would almost certainly be leveled against me by David H. Stern, the translator of the *Jewish New Testament,* a product of Jewish New Testament Publications, based in Jerusalem. Stern, a well-known "messianic" Jew, later expanded his reach to include the Old Testament in the *Complete Jewish Bible.*[20] In my experience, works like Stern's do not often figure in scholarly analyses. Certainly, neither he nor his version has the weight that we are accustomed to attribute to Barnstone and his translations.

Nonetheless, it would be a mistake, perhaps a serious one, simply to dismiss Stern's efforts. For one thing, they are widely available. Of greater significance for our purposes, his text incorporates many of the same changes that Barnstone proposed and adopted. For example, the names of two of the Gospels in Stern's edition are given in Semitic forms: *Mattityahu* and *Yochanan,* where Barnstone has *Mattityahu* and *Yohanan.* Arguably, Stern has done the better job of reflecting the presumed original name of the author of the fourth Gospel. On the other hand, he leaves untouched the originally Greek names, Mark and Luke, who are, for Barnstone and his readers, Markos and Loukas.

Throughout Stern's edition the main character is Yeshua, his mother is Miryam, and his father is Yosef, exactly as in Barnstone. Also like Barnstone, Stern has Ya'akov in Jesus' (Yeshua's) genealogy, as the name of one of Jesus' brothers and apostles, and as the author of a Letter. Again, we might observe that Stern's representation is slightly more accurate than Barnstone's, with Yaakov. Shim'on Kefa and Zavdai are found in Stern's version of Matthew 4, but for Barnstone's Andreas, Stern's readers must make do with the traditional Andrew. For Pharisees and Sadducees, Stern's *P'rushim* and *Tz'dukim* are quite close to Barnstone's language.

This is not to say that the experience of reading Stern's "Jewish" New Testament is the same as perusing Barnstone's "restored" text. Barnstone seeks to present a fully literary rendering that exposes the often poetical qualities of the Greek that are largely, if not entirely, absent from the mostly pedestrian versions of modern times. Stern has no such aspirations. But they are, as it were, united in their efforts to bring to the fore the essential Jewishness of Jesus and his environment. In fact, the subtitle of Stern's work is *A Translation of the New Testament That Expresses Its Jewishness.* So, Stern observes in his introduction, the New Testament is in fact a very Jewish book.[21] Much of what is in the New Testament can be comprehended only within its Jewish context.[22] Unlike Barnstone, Stern does not believe that the translators of the New Testament were or are themselves antisemites;

rather, they have absorbed substantial elements of anti-Semitic theology and thereby produced anti-Jewish translations.[23]

Further, Stern writes, the *Jewish New Testament* brings out the New Testament's Jewishness in three somewhat overlapping ways. Especially relevant for this essay are the changes he groups under a single description as cosmetic (or superficial). Such cosmetic changes from the usual renderings are, he continues, the most frequent and obvious: names like Jesus, John, and James, and terms like *baptism* (replaced by *immersion*; for example, at Mark 1:4 in Stern's edition we meet Jochanan the Immerser; in Barnstone, it is Johanan the Dipper) and *apostle* (replaced by *emissary*). Although any one of these changes is superficial, the sheer quantity of them produces a true and genuine effect that is not superficial.[24]

So far, so good, I suppose. But Stern goes further: his version also draws on "Jewish English," which is defined here as "Hebrew and Yiddish expressions which English-speaking Jews incorporate into everyday speech." With at least some degree of reflection, Stern acknowledges that some readers may find this aspect of the translation anachronistic. Nonetheless, the translator appeals for tolerance of the inclusion of such elements as, for example, *tsuris* instead of troubles and to do *tzedakah* instead of to give to charity.[25]

I consider myself among the most tolerant of readers and researchers. However, I have no sympathy for Stern's practice here: simply put, to place Yiddish expressions in Jesus' mouth is not just anachronistic, it is bizarre. Whether it works for Stern's target audience, consisting I suppose of members of "Messianic Judaism" and those with at least some sympathy toward their point of view, I do not know. But, unlike the "restoration" of names, I can see no serious point to this aspect of Stern's edition.

Although in this essay I chose to discuss issues relating to proper names first, there is another aspect of New Testament translation that has, over the past decades, come up with greater frequency in regard to Jesus' Jewishness or, perhaps more broadly, Jews and Jesus. This issue of translation arises from a feature of the Gospel of John and, to a lesser extent, of the Acts of the Apostles. As characterized by Barnstone, who is far from unique in this perspective, John is the most fiercely anti-Jewish Gospel in its pattern of engendering hatred for those whom John identifies as Jews, and the word *Jew*, meaning "enemy," appears on almost every page of the Gospel. People who are allied with Jesus are simply people. Those who are kin, friends, or disciples of Jesus have ceased to be addressed as Jews. The word is used as an epithet to malign enemies of the Christ, particularly those who do not accept his divinity. Thus is created a Jesus whom an overwhelming number of Christians perceive as a gentile among gentile friends and Jewish enemies, a Christian in the land of Israel.[26]

Not unexpectedly, there are a number of exegetes, generally grouped among the more conservative biblical interpreters, who would deny that the author of the Gospel of John was himself anti-Jewish or anti-Semitic. But there is no one, or virtually no one, who would deny that John's language, however it was initially intended, became a major rhetorical weapon in the mouths of generations of individuals and groups opposed to Jews and Judaism—and the impetus for "real" weapons in the hands of such opponents on lamentably numerous occasions.

Among those who disagree with Barnstone on the intent of the author of the Gospel of John is Barclay Newman, who is best known as the editor-in-chief of the Contemporary English Version (CEV).[27] Newman is thoroughly convinced that it was never the intention of any New Testament writer to perpetuate anti-Jewish sentiments. And, he firmly states, the goal of the CEV translation was a faithful rendering of the *intent* of the Greek text. Nothing more, nothing less.[28]

The Greek term that has traditionally been translated "the Jews" is *hoi Ioudaioi*. According to statistics presented by David Burke, this expression occurs one hundred ninety-two times in the entire New Testament, more than one hundred fifty of which are in John and Acts. Especially in those books the term carries an inherent bias: the opponents are systematically, broadly, and negatively cast, by this bias, as "the Jews."[29]

If it is correct to render *hoi Ioudaioi* with "the Jews" and if this rendering has currency within over four hundred years of English-language versions, why should translators not retain this expression? As Burke sees it, the problem with "the Jews" deals primarily with the implications the term presents to "poorly informed modern readers." The modern reader, he writes, is not equipped to be able to sort out that "the Jews" as opponents are in fact just other Jews who did not accept Jesus' identity as Messiah—whether these are individuals, groups, local leaders, religious or political authorities, or the like. Given the way the overall picture is painted, it is very difficult for modern readers to think this through in terms of such ambiguities.[30]

Or, as Newman puts it, in many New Testament passages (especially in Acts and John) where the phrase "the Jews" occurs, a literal rendering has historically resulted in arousing negative reactions that were not intended by the authors. The cumulative impact of a literal rendering of "the Jews" in negative contexts signals something significantly different to readers today than was originally intended by New Testament writers. It is exegetically inaccurate to retain this inclusive phrase when not every Jew is intended.[31]

It is not simply a matter of exegetical accuracy or inaccuracy. As we observed above, the Gospel of John, as translated into many languages, served as a proof text for the eternal enmity between Jews and Christians. The term *the Jews*, particularly with the definite article in English, carries wide-sweeping implications that would cover all Jews of Jesus' time (or worse, all Jews of all time). Because these New Testament passages provide "fuel" for continuing contemporary expressions of anti-Jewish hatred, the question of how to translate this term (and related expressions) is a critical one.[32]

Both Barclay Newman and David Burke are closely associated with the American Bible Society. It is clear, on the basis of the statements provided here (as well as many others), that Burke shares Newman's concerns and is in complete agreement with Newman's, and CEV's, resolution or solution: throughout most of the New Testament, "the Jews" is best understood to mean "the other Jews" or "some of the Jews" or "a few of the Jews" or "the Jewish leaders" or "some of the Jewish leaders" or "a few of the Jewish leaders." And it is on the basis of this understanding that the phrase is to be translated. Never does it refer to the nation as a whole of that time; even less does it refer to all Jews of all times.

A truly faithful translation of the New Testament, Newman contends, requires that the translator constantly seek ways in which false impressions may be minimized and hatred overcome. As a result of the CEV's basic concern to produce a faithful and stylistically appropriate translation of the meaning of the Greek text, the CEV contains fewer passages in which the phrase "the Jews" can be wrongfully understood as a reference to the entirety of the Jewish community, past or present.[33]

David Burke has collected the data that most clearly demonstrate the thoroughgoing manner in which the CEV has carried out Newman's directive. The CEV is the most sensitive English-language version when it comes to nuancing its renderings of *hoi Ioudaioi*;[34] an earlier translation brought out by the American Bible Society, Today's English Version (also known as the Good News Bible), already exhibited a considerable degree of such sensitivity, with its handling of *hoi Ioudaioi* becoming ever more nuanced in successive editions.[35] It was a surprise, at least to me, to learn that the Living Bible also came out rather well on this issue; moreover, its earlier advances have largely been followed by the New Living Translation or NLT and in many places improved.[36]

In order for readers of this essay to make their own assessment as to the effects on this strategy, I have reproduced below John 7:15 in three English-language versions. The first, the New American Standard Bible (NASB), was selected because of its close adherence to the Greek. Second is the NLT; third, the CEV (I have put the key phrases in bold type for emphasis):

NASB

John 7:1 And after these things Jesus was walking in Galilee; for He was unwilling to walk in Judea, because **the Jews** were seeking to kill Him.
John 7:2 Now the feast of **the Jews**, the Feast of Booths, was at hand.

John 7:3 His brothers therefore said to Him, "Depart from here, and go into Judea, that Your disciples also may behold Your works which You are doing.

John 7:4 "For no one does anything in secret, when he himself seeks to be known publicly. If You do these things, show Yourself to the world."

John 7:5 For not even His brothers were believing in Him.

John 7:6 Jesus therefore said to them, "My time is not yet at hand, but your time is always opportune.

John 7:7 "The world cannot hate you; but it hates Me because I testify of it, that its deeds are evil.

John 7:8 "Go up to the feast yourselves; I do not go up to this feast because My time has not yet fully come."

John 7:9 And having said these things to them, He stayed in Galilee.

John 7:10 But when His brothers had gone up to the feast, then He Himself also went up, not publicly, but as it were, in secret.

John 7:11 **The Jews** therefore were seeking Him at the feast, and were saying, "Where is He?"

John 7:12 And there was much grumbling among the multitudes concerning Him; some were saying, "He is a good man"; others were saying, "No, on the contrary, He leads the multitude astray."

John 7:13 Yet no one was speaking openly of Him for fear of **the Jews**.

John 7:14 But when it was now the midst of the feast Jesus went up into the temple, and began to teach.

John 7:15 **The Jews** therefore were marveling, saying, "How has this man become learned, having never been educated?"

NLT

John 7:1 After this, Jesus stayed in Galilee, going from village to village. He wanted to stay out of Judea where **the Jewish leaders** were plotting his death.

John 7:2 But soon it was time for the Festival of Shelters,

John 7:3 and Jesus' brothers urged him to go to Judea for the celebration. "Go where your followers can see your miracles!" they scoffed.

John 7:4 "You can't become a public figure if you hide like this! If you can do such wonderful things, prove it to the world!"

John 7:5 For even his brothers didn't believe in him.

John 7:6 Jesus replied, "Now is not the right time for me to go. But you can go anytime, and it will make no difference.

John 7:7 "The world can't hate you, but it does hate me because I accuse it of sin and evil.

John 7:8 "You go on. I am not yet ready to go to this festival, because my time has not yet come."

John 7:9 So Jesus remained in Galilee.

John 7:10 But after his brothers had left for the festival, Jesus also went, though secretly, staying out of public view.

John 7:11 **The Jewish leaders** tried to find him at the festival and kept asking if anyone had seen him.

John 7:12 There was a lot of discussion about him among the crowds. Some said, "He's a wonderful man," while others said, "He's nothing but a fraud, deceiving the people."

John 7:13 But no one had the courage to speak favorably about him in public, for they were afraid of getting in trouble with **the Jewish leaders**.

John 7:14 Then, midway through the festival, Jesus went up to the Temple and began to teach.

John 7:15 **The Jewish leaders** were surprised when they heard him. "How does he know so much when he hasn't studied everything we've studied?" they asked.

CEV

John 7:1 Jesus decided to leave Judea and to start going through Galilee because **the Jewish leaders** wanted to kill him.

John 7:2 It was almost time for the Festival of Shelters,

John 7:3 and Jesus' brothers said to him, "Why don't you go to Judea? Then your disciples can see what you are doing.

John 7:4 "No one does anything in secret, if they want others to know about them. So let the world know what you are doing!"

John 7:5 Even Jesus' own brothers had not yet become his followers.

John 7:6 Jesus answered, "My time hasn't yet come, but your time is always here.

John 7:7 "The people of this world cannot hate you. They hate me, because I tell them that they do evil things.

John 7:8 "Go on to the festival. My time hasn't yet come, and I am not going."

John 7:9 Jesus said this and stayed on in Galilee.

John 7:10 After Jesus' brothers had gone to the festival, he went secretly, without telling anyone.

John 7:11 During the festival **the Jewish leaders** looked for Jesus and asked, "Where is he?"

John 7:12 The crowds even got into an argument about him. Some were saying, "Jesus is a good man," while others were saying, "He is lying to everyone."

John 7:13 But the people were afraid of **their leaders**, and none of them talked in public about him.

John 7:14 When the festival was about half over, Jesus went into the temple and started teaching.

John 7:15 **The leaders** were surprised and said, "How does this man know so much? He has never been taught!"

Well-known New Testament scholar James Sanders is sympathetic to the approach taken by the CEV and the NLT. Further, he observes that the NRSV, which frequently abandoned the Hebrew and Greek texts in order to sponsor inclusive translations of words and phrases dealing with human gender, is quite literal in translating *hoi Ioudaioi* and even followed KJV in adding "the Jews" in English where it does not occur in Greek (Acts 23:30).[37] Sanders would go further than the CEV in connection with the expression "scribes and Pharisees," which, he notes, has become a pejorative term because of the Gospels and has been used in Christian propaganda or apologetics against so-called "Jewish legalism." The CEV translates "Pharisees" literally in all of its occurrences, but twice nuances "scribes" with "teachers of the law." Sanders's contention is that we might translate "scribes" as "Scripture scholars" and "Pharisees" as "religious experts," context permitting.[38]

With reference to the CEV and the NLT, I think that it is fair to assess the former as mainstream in its theological orientation and its intended audience, with the latter (the NLT) appealing to a more theologically conservative base, as can be seen by the affiliations of its translators and publisher. Both of these versions, especially the CEV, have been the beneficiary of Irvin J. Borowsky, a philanthropist and founder of the Philadelphia-based American Interfaith Institute. Although some bloggers have made much— all of it negative—of Borowsky's Jewish faith, insinuating that he has been propelled by his Judaism to dilute the truth of the New Testament, no one has successfully demonstrated how he has been able to seduce a broad range of Christian leaders spanning the CEV and the NLT, among others.[39]

Beyond questions of marketing and the not unexpected sniping from the far right, there are substantive objections to the approach taken by the CEV and the NLT. Characteristic of what I would term mainstream criticism are the remarks and observations by Joseph Blenkinsopp, who says the intention behind the CEV is fully understandable, even if some of its translations are questionable. But can the New Testament be purged of anti-Judaic sentiment by changing the way in which *hoi Ioudaioi* is translated?

For Blenkinsopp, there are many instances in the CEV where the task of translator is confused with that of commentator. The task of translation, he asserts, is to render a text as faithfully as possible, not to massage or coerce it into saying what we want it to say, however praiseworthy our intentions may be. Anti-Jewish attitudes in the New Testament should not be sanitized, but they should be explained. Blenkinsopp concludes, "I am under no illusion that explanation by itself will prevent people from abusive appeal to these early Christian texts. . . . But we do not remedy the situation by retranslating the texts to make them say what their authors had no intention of saying—and in fact did not say."[40] In short, we must render the text as it is, warts and all. Giving the text a face-lift is commentary and thus belongs in the notes. Or so Blenkinsopp avers.

Barnstone is at least as critical as Blenkinsopp. As part of his criticism, Barnstone notes another possible weakness of the CEV/NLT approach; namely, that in removing the "Jews" as Jesus' opponents, we also remove Jesus from Judaism. Or, in Barnstone's words, a number of new versions have changed the word *Jew* to *opponent*, *Judaean*, or some euphemism. Such changes are inaccurate to the New Testament texts as we have them and actually reinforce a much more significant misconception, namely that Yeshua and his family and followers were somehow not Jews.[41] Returning to a familiar theme, Barnstone continues that such a misconception—whereby the central figures of the New Testament lose their Jewish identity, in a "grand identity theft"—is already perpetrated through the "tradition" of using in translation largely Greek names for the Hebrew and Aramaic names of these NT figures.[42]

As Barnstone notes in passing, some translators have adopted, or urged the adoption of, the rendering *Judaean* for *hoi Ioudaioi*, giving the term a primary designation of geography (essentially *Judaean* as opposed to *Galilean*) rather than religion. Another option, proposed by Gerald Sloyan, among others, is to leave *hoi Ioudaioi* untranslated, especially in public settings and in preaching. He believes that this untranslated Greek heightens awareness of the tendency to make inaccurate assumptions about Jews and Judaism.[43]

I find myself torn, and not for the first time, by the various proposals made by translators and commentators concerning the most appropriate rendering for *hoi Ioudaioi*. At one level, and this the broadest, it raises substantive and substantial questions about the nature of translation—all translation. Because, I suspect, all translators (even subversive ones) want to be thought of as faithful, we are brought forthrightly to differing understanding of what "faithful" means and to whom/to what a translator should be faithful. Is it to what the text says? What the text means? How the text has traditionally been understood in our community? How an intended audience is likely to perceive our words? Of course, the possibilities are almost endless.

Within this endlessness lies despair, but perhaps also a way (or, better, ways) out. If it is the case that a translation can be understood as more or less faithful, then we can choose to allow for these multiple valences—provided that a given translator clarifies what it is that he or she is faithful to. Along these lines, we can also choose to follow Sloyan, at least in his appreciation of the fact that different audiences may have their valid needs best met by different versions. This would, of course, go beyond the question of transliteration.

When it comes to the best way to educate Bible readers about concerns with the traditional rendering, "the Jews," the issue is sometimes, as we saw above, framed as a feud between translators-as-translators and translators-as-interpreters. But this does not seem to be the most productive way to look at this issue. All translation, as we know is, to a greater or lesser degree, interpretation. When the issue is as highly charged as this one, we can easily forget that our approach to this one phrase should be consistent with the approach we take in general.

Again, I do not pretend to have "the" answer, but I do have a relevant observation, in the form of a query: if we want readers to pick up on a point that we consider of central importance, will we more likely get their attention in the text itself or in the notes and annotations? It is not difficult to discern, even in the way I phrased this question, that I do not find marginal or bottom-of-the-page notations to be beneficial purveyors of knowledge. Not only do the frequency and contents of notes vary considerably in the printed editions of Bible translations, but electronic versions typically dispense with notes altogether. This observation, assuming that it is accurate, does not permit translators simply to enlarge their texts through the insertion of all sorts of interpretive materials (something of this sort did, I suspect, happen in the earlier Targums); at the same time, it should caution translators and editors against the tendency to refrain from making tough decisions about the text under the allusion that all "problems" can be dealt with in the notes.

To return once more to the specifics of "the Jews," I would ask readers of this essay to consider their own reaction(s) to the three versions of John 7:1-15 that I included above. Is there a marked difference in the perception of this passage when read in the "literal" NASB as opposed to the "nuanced" NLT or CEV? If there is, is the difference more in the way "the Jews" are portrayed or in the manner in which Jesus is seen as apart from/as part of the Judaism of his day? Perhaps it's both; or neither. Moreover, even if readers of this article find little, if any, substantive difference between these three versions, can they nonetheless imagine an audience among whom such differences might be perceived and for whom such differences might matter?

This essay began by stressing the crucial importance of scriptural translation within the Christian context. It is probably worth adding one additional point to what was said above: Christian translations of the Bible continue to appear with some frequency, especially those versions aimed at conservative and/or evangelical Protestants. There is no reason to expect any diminution in the number of future new/revised/improved editions; in addition, the advertising and marketing of Bible translations are likely only to increase with new formats becoming available on an almost daily basis. With this in mind, I affirm the value of submitting such versions to the type of analysis we have applied here.

We looked at a select number of English-language translations of the New Testament with a primary emphasis on how they rendered proper names and/or how they represented the phrase *hoi Ioudaioi*. In particular, we were interested in changes from traditional renderings that aimed at restoring Jesus to his historically (and, we might add, theologically) correct position as a first-century-CE Jew within a first-century-CE Jewish community. The translators and editors whose work we carefully examined were all motivated, or at least claimed to be motivated, by a sincere desire not only to correct misunderstandings about Jesus, but to counter the disastrous effects such misunderstandings have had on Jewish-Christian relations over the past two thousand years.

Thus it is that, in the view of these translators and editors, very large changes can be effected by what might appear, at first glance, to be relatively small changes. In describing and evaluating these modern-language texts, I have attempted to apply a variety of criteria that, in my view, are relevant. Nonetheless, we do not have, to my knowledge, anything even approaching a systematic study of how actual individuals or groups of individuals have reacted to, or interacted with, these versions.

We do, on the one hand, have some bitter denunciations of the CEV and NLT on the part of what I would term far-right bloggers. Their criticisms cover the issues we've raised in this essay, but they also go beyond them. On the other hand, we can find a good deal of promotional material, compliments of their respective publishers, attesting to the wide audience appeal of the CEV and the NLT. Such endorsements typically cover a range of issues, in which the rendering of *hoi Ioudaioi* may play little if any role.

This is not at all unexpected. For example, among the major "selling points" of the CEV is that it avoids the use of technical or difficult-to-understand "Bible English," in favor of words, phrases, and grammatical structures that can be understood by a person with an average reading level. So, the "ark of the covenant" becomes "the sacred chest"; alas, Noah's ark sinks, in my view, as (simply) "the boat." Because the CEV is intended to be spoken as much as, if not more than, it is read, words that might cause confusion in this regard are not used. Among those specifically mentioned are "synagogue" and "manger." Moreover, the CEV's Old Testament, unlike its New Testament, is in my view decidedly not "Jewish-friendly." Capitalizing the first letter of the word *spirit* (thus, "Spirit") is in line with a Trinitarian reading of Hebrew Scripture, and use of the term *virgin* (rather than the more lexically and contextually correct "young woman") at Isa. 7:14 is evidence of reliance on the text of the New Testament (in this instance, Matt. 1:23). In short, a full evaluation of the CEV must take into account all of the goals that its editors and sponsors had in mind. The same surely holds true for the NLT.

This essay may be the first in which Barnstone and Stern receive, as it were, equal billing. For this, I do not apologize. At the same time, I hasten to add that a full reckoning of these editions must take into account far more than we have had the opportunity to discuss here. For Barnstone, there is the issue of poetry; for Stern, the appeals to "Messianic Judaism." To state the obvious: simply because they both find traditional English renderings of proper names to be wrong, dangerously wrong, and they both resolve this matter by "restoring" the names to their Semitic (and, in the case of Barnstone, also their ancient Greek) forms does not make these translations equivalent in any other ways.

Having made these and myriad other observations and set up abundant caveats, I finally address the question that is implicit in this essay: are these efforts, as commendable as they are, worth the effort? My response, based as much on my hopes as on my research, is "yes." These versions of the New Testament can indeed bring knowledge and, of perhaps greater importance, sensitivity to Christian audiences. They may also enable Jews to read the New Testament in greater numbers and with enhanced interest. And, finally, these translations may provide something of the common ground so often lacking when Jews and Christians attempt to discern shared values as well as different emphases. If these editions, as imperfect as each is, enable and enhance positive relations between and among faith communities, then, yes, it's all been worth it.

CHAPTER TWO

A Jewish Teaching:
Jesus, Gentiles, and the Sheep and the Goats (Matthew 25:31-46)

Joel N. Lohr

If a consensus of scholarship on the interpretation of this pericope were to be sought, it would support the view that the saying is, in large part, from the historical Jesus.[1]

Few Matthew scholars today would agree with what Lamar Cope could claim about Matt. 25:31-46 a mere forty years ago. While some might agree that the core of the sheep and the goats passage goes back to Jesus himself, moderately few scholars hold such a position today.[2] Most Jesus scholars view Matt. 25:31-46 to be an ecclesial creation. As Cope went on to argue in the piece cited above, the authenticity of this passage is suspect due to a number of factors, not least for its identification of Jesus with the Son of Man but also for its suggestion that final judgment will be determined based on one's treatment of the disciples.[3]

In this chapter I will not focus on this question directly but instead investigate related matters: the Jewishness of this passage, how it has functioned within Christian theology, and how it might contribute to Jewish-Christian dialogue and relations today. In a nutshell, I hope to show that this passage, even if it cannot be plausibly explained as an early memory of Jesus' own teaching, is one deeply grounded in a first-century Jewish worldview. Moreover, I will suggest that this passage contributes significantly to our understanding of Matthew's Gospel as a whole, a gospel that in many ways reads like a treatise on the author's perceived divine rejection of the scribes

and Pharisees, perhaps the Jewish people as a whole. However, in coming
to understand the Jewishness of this passage, it seems more likely that apart
from those who opposed Jesus directly (the Jewish leaders), Matthew probably understood all Israel (all Jews, whether or not they were associated with
Jesus) as part of the elect who belong to God, and the Sheep and Goats story
involves the judgment of gentiles apart from that people in a way very similar
to Noahide law. I will conclude by suggesting that this passage has much
to contribute to contemporary Jewish-Christian relations and dialogue; for
Christians who seek to make bridges to and engage with contemporary
Judaism, the story of the Sheep and the Goats is an often overlooked, but
important passage.[4]

In what follows, I first briefly trace a picture of Jewish judgment ideas
in antiquity. I then move to examine *who* and *what* Matt. 25:31-46 might be
about before I explore how this passage has been an embarrassment to the
church. I then provide a short survey of Matthew's Gospel in order to place
our pericope within it contextually. I conclude with some reflections on our
passage as it relates to Jewish-gentile relations, the historical Jesus, as well as
Jewish-Christian dialogue.

Jewish Judgment in Antiquity

My goal in what follows is not to present an exhaustive survey of Jewish
judgment texts or to uncover new material that shows Matt. 25:31-46 to be
Jewish in orientation. Few scholars today would disagree that the passage
reflects at least a basic Jewish ethos. However, it may be instructive to recount
briefly some features of Jewish judgment in antiquity in order to set the stage
for how Matthew 25 might have been understood in the first century.

The first thing to note, and it is a key point, is that there was a wide variety of Jewish judgment ideas in antiquity. Marius Reiser, in his monograph
Jesus and Judgment, surveys judgment in Jewish eschatological thought of the
Second Temple period, and his conclusions are many.[5] Despite the variety of
judgment motifs in this period, it seems clear that a few principles guide this
literature. First, judgment is a central idea of Judaism, and in fact it might be
said that a final judgment is a defining characteristic of Jewish thought. Such
judgment usually takes one of two forms: Israel's enemies are judged at some
point in history, as a turning point in Israel's existence (as in a "day of the
Lord" or a "day of visitation"), or a judgment involving all people takes place
in the hereafter, usually after death. Sometimes, however, these two are combined. Second, there is usually a division of Israel and the gentiles or of the
righteous and the wicked. It is typically assumed that Israel belongs to the
righteous and the gentiles to the wicked, but at times there is crossover from
each group. In other places there are two judgments, one of Israel, and one

of the gentiles. Third, the judgment usually, though not always, has God as its judge. This is typically unambiguous, though at times the judge is unidentified and God is assumed, or sometimes divine representatives judge for God, such as the archangel Michael, but also Melchizedek, the son of man, Abel, or "the messiah."[6] Fourth, the standard for final judgment is most often related to fidelity to the Torah. At the risk of oversimplification, salvation is obtained through obedience, while judgment comes as the result of infidelity to its teachings.[7] In some places, "the Torah is apparently replaced by general ethical norms, but they are not concretely described."[8] Lastly, the function of the final eschatological judgment is to create "the precondition for Israel's salvation by subjugating the gentile nations to Israel, or eliminating them entirely. . . . Only the God-fearers among them are spared; they then come to Zion, together with the scattered members of Israel, to live there forever in peace according to God's law."[9]

One problem that arises, as is apparent from the previous paragraph, is the lack of coherence and at times competing views of judgment. Based on our summary, should we speak of a final judgment in the hereafter or simply a judgment "here and now" that changes Israel's history? Is it Israel that is judged by God, or is it just Israel's enemies? Can gentiles be included among the righteous, or are they most often automatically punished, or damned? Reiser discusses the problem of multiple Jewish views of judgment and concludes:

> Most of the writings and authors we have treated use not just one, but several eschatological conceptions and traditions in combination. . . . This phenomenon cannot simply be explained as the result of the compilation of different literary units and traditions. . . . A search for concretization of imagery and internal consistency, coherence of ideas, motifs, and conceptions, is foreign to the apocalyptic authors. That is clear from every one of their eschatological descriptions and may never be forgotten in interpreting them.[10]

We might add to Reiser's words here the problem of reading ancient eschatological judgment texts in a reifying and linear fashion when these are mythic and nonlinear in orientation.[11] Whatever the case, we will see from Matthew's Gospel that a multilayered and complex judgment teaching is at work. Before we address that, however, we look to analyze some of the specifics in the passage under study itself.

Who and What Is Matthew 25:31-46 About?

The passage initially seems straightforward enough. When the son of man comes in his glory, an activity already mentioned in Matt. 24:29-31, he will sit on his throne of judgment to determine the fate of "all the *ethnē*" ("nations," or "gentiles," translation to be discussed). The criterion for judgment of the *ethnē*, and thus their ultimate fate, is directly related to their treatment of people in need, those with whom the judge identifies. The story makes clear that persons on each side of the judgment are surprised in that they appear not to have known that their serving the needy was in fact in service of the judge himself or that their failure to care for those in need was to his neglect. The problem is that it is not entirely clear exactly who is being judged, who the needy are, and how the author of Matthew intended this teaching to be understood in light of the larger judgment discourse and the gospel as a whole.

At the risk of repeating what will already be familiar to many readers, the problems may be summarized under two main heads: (1) who are "all the *ethnē*" in verse 32, and (2) who are the needy with whom the judge identifies? These matters are important in that they not only affect who is being judged, but also how one understands the needy in this passage could significantly affect how the judgment is determined. If the needy are Jesus' disciples, then the ethical demands of this passage become much narrower and potentially reduced. If the passage speaks of any person in need, the demands are intensified. Further, if the judgment is only of non-Jews and those outside the Christian community (that is, "gentiles"), then the passage may well contribute to a larger theology of Jewish-Gentile-Christian relations in the book of Matthew, something many scholars overlook in interpreting it.

It is instructive to begin by noting that when Franz Delitzsch made his translation of the New Testament into Hebrew, he translated the words *panta ta ethnē* in Matt. 25:32 as *kal ha-goyim*.[12] *Goyim*, the Hebrew term that most closely resembles the English word *gentiles*, usually indicates (according to the Hebrew Bible and Second Temple literature) all non-Israelites or non-Jews, without distinction (thus, "all the gentiles").[13] Of course the trouble is that *ethnē*—and *goyim* as well—can also simply mean "nations" and could possibly be universal in outlook, and thus include Israel. The debates regarding the use of the term *ethnē* in Matt. 25:32 (and 28:19) are heated, especially because Matthew does seem to use *ethnē* most commonly as a term for gentiles, or non-Jews (or perhaps better, all those outside Israel). Does this imply that the judgment in Matt. 25:31-46 speaks only to the fate of non-Jews (or those outside Israel, however defined)? And, if applied to Matthew 28, does the so-called Great Commission speak only of making disciples of gentiles, and not Jews?

The most substantial and sustained argument for translating *ethnē* as "gentiles" everywhere in Matthew came from Douglas Hare and Daniel Harrington in a 1975 journal article.[14] In this work, concerned in the first instance with the use of the term in the Great Commission (Matt. 28:16-20), Hare and Harrington work through ancient Jewish usage of *ethnē* as well as in Matthew and argue that the term always, virtually without exception, means "gentiles."

They rightly point out that if Matthew had meant "all people" (including Israel) *ethnē* was surely an unfortunate choice of terms; why, they ask, would the author not use *pantas tous laous* (all the peoples) if that was what was meant? One might also ask why, if Matthew used another perfectly useful descriptor for all people, Jew and gentile, in the previous chapter, does he not use the same one here? In that passage, the author speaks of the son of man appearing to "all the tribes of the earth" (*pasai hai phylai tēs gēs*) before he gathers his elect from out of them (Matt. 24:30). At a minimum, Hare and Harrington are correct to point out that much confusion results if Matthew did not mean gentiles here and in Matt. 28:19—the meaning implied elsewhere in Matthew and most regularly throughout the rest of the New Testament.

Hare and Harrington's interpretation of *ethnē* as "gentiles" everywhere in Matthew has not gone unchallenged. The strongest opposition to their work came from John Meier, who, although in agreement that ancient Jewish use of *ethnē* and *goyim* was unambiguously in their favor, and that most instances of *ethnē* in Matthew do point to gentiles, argued that Matt. 21:43 is the exception that proves the rule and thus *ethnē* could (and should, according to Meier) be read as "nations"—inclusive of Israel—in our passage and elsewhere.[15] In 21:43, the Matthean Jesus tells his listeners, particularly the chief priests and Pharisees, that the kingdom will be taken from its rightful heirs and given to an *ethnei*, which Meier translates as "people." I remain unconvinced overall for a number of reasons.[16] Whatever the case, the matter is still under debate. However, it is interesting to note that many of those interpreters who agree that *ethnē* probably means "gentiles" in Matthew 25 and 28 seem, probably out of respect to Christian tradition, reluctant to translate the term as such and usually opt for the more inclusive alternative of *all the nations* (thus permitting Israel's possible inclusion).[17] It is also clear that for some interpreters a translation of *gentiles* brings about significant theological discomfort. If it is only gentiles that are judged here, and their destiny is based on acts of charity to the needy, would not such a translation mean that there is another way to salvation for gentiles, one that is not by way of explicit faith in Jesus? Lutheran interpreter R. C. H. Lenski is troubled by just this prospect. In his mind, "This would, indeed, be a new way of salvation, and one that would contradict everything else that is said in the Bible in regard to it."[18] To get around this apparent problem, some interpreters seem prepared to make misleading statements about the semantics of the Greek word itself. While one might possibly grant that *ethnē* does not *always* mean *only* "gentiles," surely Leon Morris misleads his Christian readership when he states that those who translate *ethnē* as *gentiles* in Matt. 25:32 "seem to contradict the meaning of the Greek."[19]

How we translate the term, if I am correct, is of tremendous importance to our understanding of both Matt. 25:32 and 28:19, and to the overall relationship between Jews and gentiles in Matthew. I would suggest, for now, that a translation of *gentiles* not only makes the most sense based on the Greek, ancient Jewish usage, and Matthew's usage of the term elsewhere, but it makes the most sense for the passage under study in the larger context of Matthew. Before we get to that, however, we will briefly consider who "the least of these my brothers [and sisters]" are in Matt. 25:40.

Who Are the Least of These My Siblings?

Although there is debate concerning the identification of "all the *ethnē*," such debate seems relatively tame when compared to that which revolves around the identity of those who are needy in Matt. 25:31-46. Are these "least of these my brothers [and sisters]" simply all people in need, in any place, at any time? In other words, is the phrase to be understood universally and thus one's treatment of any person in need counts at the time of judgment? Or are the terms *brothers* and *least ones* cryptic catchphrases that point to the disciples of Jesus, those who are predicted by Matthew to be poor, hungry, persecuted, put in prison, and so on?

For some, this matter is "the watershed of the entire discussion," *the* issue for the interpretation of the passage.[20] A great many scholars conclude, based on the way the word *brother* is used elsewhere in the gospel, and the way Jesus speaks of his followers being "little ones" (*mikroi*) in Matthew, that the text refers to the followers of Jesus, specifically his disciples.[21] In this reading, those who welcome and care for Jesus' disciples are admitted into the kingdom while those who reject, ignore, or are apathetic toward these Jesus followers will be punished. Given Matthew's apparent concern to explain the difficulties and sufferings of those in his community (or minimally Christian missionaries),[22] such a reading fits reasonably well, it seems, and would console a persecuted church. Further, it would appear that such a reading coheres well with other Jewish judgment ideas whereby one's final destiny is bound up with one's treatment of the people of Israel (compare Gen. 12:3), something Matthew now connects to Jesus followers, the "true Israel."[23] Moreover, such an interpretation appears to be the dominant one of the church down through the ages, at least until the 1800s.[24]

Despite these strong supporting arguments, a number of factors suggest we should be cautious in making conclusions of this sort too hastily. First, it is not clear that all references in Matthew to "brothers" (*adelphoi*) point to disciples. Snodgrass nicely summarizes things this way:

> Matthew uses *adelphos* ("brothers" or "brothers and sisters") thirty-eight times, of which twenty refer to literal [biological] brothers. At least eight of the eighteen metaphorical occurrences do not have the sense "disciple" but

are used generically in the sense of one's neighbor (e.g., 5:22: ". . . everyone angry at his brother or sister . . ."). The most important occurrences that suggest that "brothers" does refer to the disciples are 12:46-50; 23:8; and especially 28:10. Are these occurrences sufficient by themselves to elevate "brothers" to the level of a title for the disciples so that the mere appearance of the word in 25:40 indicates that the issue is the reception of Christians or more specifically of Christian missionaries? Does "brother" have in view only Christian brothers and sisters? Metaphorical uses such as 5:22 surely argue against such constriction of the word.[25]

Second, for those who would suggest that it is in the combination with "the least" (*tōn elachistōn*) that this term finds its meaning as "disciples," again, caution is necessary. Snodgrass addresses this issue as well, this time by pointing out that although *mikroi* ("little ones") is used of the disciples in Matthew's gospel, that specific term is *not* used here and *elachistōn* ("least ones"), the term that is used, is essentially used only once elsewhere in Matthew, not in direct reference to the disciples, but in a negative sense for those who might lead people astray (Matt. 5:19).[26] Some ancient versions of the gospel have added *tōn micrōn* to Matt. 25:40, or have changed *tōn elachistōn* to *tōn mikrōn* in an attempt to make a connection to the disciples clearer, suggesting, to my mind, that the identification of this group as disciples is *not* clear and was thus clarified.[27] As for the related idea that the reading of the disciples-as-the-least is the most prominent in the history of interpretation, we should allow for the very real possibility that once the church emerged as a largely gentile entity, reading Matt. 25:32 and 28:19 as "gentiles" would have lost its initial significance. In other words, an early passage with Jewish specific concerns began to be read with ecclesial questions in mind regarding the acceptance of the church and its message.

However, the greatest reason for caution in identifying "the least of these my brothers" with Jesus' disciples is that such a reading sits at odds with a straightforward reading of the text. In short, it reduces its rhetorical power. This powerful judgment tale is rhetorically strong precisely because of its surprise factor, in that those on both sides of judgment are astonished to find that their good or poor treatment of the needy was in service or neglect of Jesus himself. Making the needy followers of Jesus affects this "punch line" and climax dramatically. Francis Watson argues along these lines and suggests that understanding "the least" as disciples runs counter to the natural thrust of the text:

> No one, reading Matt. 25.31-46 in isolation, would suppose that its subject is the treatment of Christian evangelists. Within this text, the "brothers" are characterized only as hungry, thirsty, homeless, naked, sick and imprisoned; nothing is said about their either making disciples (cf. 28.19) or

being disciples (cf. 19.28). Yet, in the conventional exegetical procedure, the apparent literal sense of this text has to be subordinated to other texts scattered throughout the Gospel, a procedure justified by appeal to authorial intention understood as a means of imposing relative unity on apparently heterogeneous material.[28]

Watson later concludes,

[So] who are [the least]? All we know is that they are victims of deprivation and injustice and that they are universally present to be either assisted or neglected by all peoples of the world, at every time and in every place. Their universality indicates that they are, quite simply, all victims of deprivation and injustice; no other distinguishing characteristic is given, and no other is needed.[29]

My suggestion here overall, again, is that caution should be observed in this matter and that it is ultimately difficult to conclude definitively. Both readings have some merit. However, I am suspicious of the least-as-disciples reading also because it seems to be used by many interpreters to serve a particular theological end. This leads us into our next section, one that explores the embarrassment this passage has brought to the church and the creative attempts over the years to domesticate it. In short, a good deal of Christian interpretation shows a discomfort with this text precisely because it speaks of apparent non-Christians entering the kingdom of heaven without ever having directly encountered the risen Jesus in faith.

Matthew 25:31-46: An Embarrassment to the Church

After I have spent a good deal of time in the literature surrounding this passage, one thing has become clear. For many interpreters, if Matt. 25:31-46 teaches that people can inherit the kingdom of heaven apart from faith in Jesus, we must be misunderstanding it. It seems that for some Christian interpreters the way to alleviate this tension is by insisting that "the least" in this passage are the disciples, and thus those who treat them kindly are in fact—in some way or another—responding to the gospel, through faith in Jesus himself. Consider, for example, the following string of conclusions drawn regarding this passage, based on a disciples-as-the-least reading. The first is by Ramsey Michaels, from a 1965 *Journal of Biblical Literature* article, who concludes:

The *ethnē* that are gathered for judgment in Matt 25 can thus be understood as those to whom the gospel has been proclaimed; they are judged on the basis of their response not only to the message but also to the messengers, who serve as Jesus' representatives on earth. There is nothing here about how gentiles who have never heard of Jesus will be judged; the theme is rather the standard of judgment for those who *have* heard the gospel.[30]

Somewhat similar is Morris, who is conscious to stress that grace is the ultimate source of salvation, not one's deeds. He states, "That grace is not part of the present picture does not mean that it is any the less significant. . . . Jesus is not saying that these are people whose good lives have earned them salvation as their right. He is saying that God has blessed them and . . . he proceeds to cite evidence that shows that they do in fact belong in that kingdom."[31]

In both of these readings, a move is made in which, because the needy are in fact Christian disciples, the ones being welcomed into the kingdom have consciously responded to the gospel or the disciples' message (presumably in *faith*), not simply performed acts of charity. Some scholars, however, still wish to emphasize that serving the needy is important. They do this even while they can conclude, because the passage is *really* about treatment of the disciples and the acceptance or rejection of their message, that Matt. 25:31-46 says nothing at all about a larger universal ethic. As Graham Foster states:

> It is no part of the purpose of this paper to . . . criticise specifically Christian concern for those who . . . are burdened with physical or material need. . . . The point is that this particular passage simply does not bear upon these issues. Rather than press it into the service of something for which it was not intended either by Matthew or by Jesus we should instead attend to its distinctive teaching.[32]

One can readily recognize in the above interpretations of Michaels, Morris, and Foster a genuine and understandable concern to demonstrate that faith, not works, is the primary criterion in the final judgment. This is understandable given the emphasis this idea received in the Reformation and later Protestantism. However, it is difficult not to conclude that each interpreter reads the passage according to a predetermined theology and not strictly according to the concerns of the passage itself.

Matthew 25:31-46 within the Larger Context of Matthew

We are still left with the larger problem of determining what this passage is actually about and how it might relate to the book of Matthew, the historical Jesus, and Christian theology. Is this passage concerned primarily with Christian suffering, or is it about the fate of the gentiles? What I will propose is that readers will inevitably be confused and misunderstand this passage if the first-century Jewish nature of it is diminished, or if we fail to read it in light of the larger gospel as a whole.

The passage likely is about gentiles, as much as Matthew's dreadful "woes" in chapter 23 are about the scribes and Pharisees. In fact, the two ideas are interrelated, and I will argue that Matt. 25:31-46 is connected to a larger theme—one of the key themes in Matthew—of Jewish-gentile-Christian relations, which ultimately culminates in the "Great Commission." In order to make that case, however, we need to address briefly some of the development of this in the gospel and how these details relate to Jews and gentiles more generally. I do so, in what follows, by drawing from a helpful study by Ulrich Luz on anti-Judaism in Matthew.

In an important article now translated from the German, Luz reflects on the problem of anti-Judaism in Matthew, and in particular focuses on the overall development of this as it culminates at the end of the gospel.[33] For Luz, it is not a coincidence that the prologue of Matthew tells of the Jewish-born Jesus beginning in Bethlehem and travelling to Galilee of the gentiles (Matt. 4:14-16). According to Luz, this anticipates the story that Matthew is about to tell. For Matthew, Jesus is a Torah observant Jew whose first order of business is to teach that he did not come to abolish the Law or the Prophets; rather, one's righteousness must surpass that of the scribes and Pharisees through strict obedience to it, properly understood. These words, speaking of scribes and Pharisees as those whom followers of Jesus must outperform, hint at the coming conflict that will permeate the rest of the gospel. Already near the end of Jesus' first sermon, Matthew's Jesus is warning his listeners of seeming insiders who appear in sheep's clothing but are actually ravenous wolves (7:15-23). Immediately following this is a key story of a gentile—not Jew—about whom Jesus proclaims:

> Truly I tell you, in no one in Israel have I found such faith. I tell you, many will come from east and west and will eat with Abraham and Isaac and Jacob in the kingdom of heaven, while the heirs of the kingdom will be thrown into the outer darkness, where there will be weeping and gnashing of teeth. (Matt. 8:10-12)

Here Matthew is not content to present the story of the centurion as it is found in Luke's parallel version (7:1-10). Rather, Matthew adds Q material into this context (compare Luke 13:28-29) to serve his larger goal of judging Israel, particularly the scribes and Pharisees. This theme only intensifies as Matthew's Gospel continues.

In chapter 9, virtually every miracle Jesus performs is challenged by the scribes and Pharisees who are methodically put in their place by the Matthean Jesus. Jesus becomes disheartened not only that "the workers are few" but that the Jewish people are "like sheep without a shepherd" (9:36-37). In light of this, Jesus immediately lays out a mission for his disciples, a mission that is explicitly *not* to the gentiles, but to "the lost sheep of Israel"

(10:5-6). This seems to be a recipe for disaster in that Matthew's earlier stories have already established a bitter conflict between Jesus and Israel's leaders. Jesus makes clear to his disciples that they are being sent out as sheep in the midst of wolves, and that these people will "hand you over to councils and flog you in their synagogues" (10:17). However, this will serve "as a testimony to them and the Gentiles" (10:18).

The conflict only gets stronger as Matthew continues to tell his story. When compared with the other gospels of Mark and Luke, Matthew's versions of the same stories always seem to have an added edge that serves to condemn the Jewish leaders and, at times, whole Jewish cities (Matt. 11:20-24). Examples abound. To take one characteristic example, note how Matthew adds to Mark and Luke's account of the Pharisees' challenge to Jesus' Sabbath observance (Matt. 12:1-8; Mark 2:23-27; Luke 6:1-5). In Matthew's version, Jesus must make clear that he (or minimally, "something") is "greater than the temple," and the Pharisees are indicted for not understanding the Scriptures or what mercy (*hesed, eleos*) means.

It is not long before the Matthean Jesus makes plain that the Jewish leaders (minimally the Pharisees) are beyond redemption. According to Matthew, this evil-speaking "brood of vipers" commits a sin that is unpardonable in their attributing Jesus' power to Beelzebub, a fatal transgression not to be forgiven in this age or the next (12:22-32). Although Mark (3:2-30) and Luke (11:14-28) contain a similar story, it is in the detailed additions of Matthew that the Pharisees receive a stronger, seemingly fatal, condemnation. Following this, and being told that Jesus' disciples will judge the twelve tribes of Israel (19:27-28), Jesus is involved in a series of stories which make plain that these leaders are no longer heirs of the kingdom. "No fruit shall ever come from you again!" (21:18-19) states Matthew's Jesus; further, Jesus makes clear that "[God] will put those wretches to a miserable death . . . the kingdom of God will be taken away from you and given to a people (*ethnei*) that produces the fruits of the kingdom" (21:41, 43). In case there was any reason for doubt, these wretches are then identified, "When the chief priests and the Pharisees heard his parables, they realized that he was speaking about them" (21:45).

Matthew's extended and exceptionally vicious woes against the scribes and Pharisees follow, and in enters what is probably the New Testament's most vitriolic condemnation of the Jewish leaders. It is not without some warrant that David Levenson has titled this section "To Hell with the Pharisees."[34] Although Luke's version contains harsh condemnations of the leaders as well (Luke 11:37-53), when compared Matthew's woes are particularly sharp and angry, leaving little room for turning, or repentance.[35] Although Jesus longed to gather up the children of Israel as a hen does her chicks, they were unwilling (23:37-39). Their house will be made desolate and judgment is coming. That judgment is now to be uncovered and explained in Matthew 24–25.

All of the above implies, if I read the book correctly, that Matthew is as much about Jesus vis-à-vis the Jewish leaders (and perhaps people) as it is about Jesus and a message of salvation. This picture does not change in Matthew's passion narrative but only intensifies, something Luz reflects upon with particular despondency. Here the Jewish leaders plot Jesus' death (26:1-5), Pilate ritually washes his hands of Jesus' blood (27:11-26; a "particularly grotesque" image),[36] blame is placed squarely upon the Jewish people for Jesus' death ("his blood be on us and on our children"; 27:25), and the Jewish leaders, in the end, deceitfully conspire to cover up Jesus' resurrection by paying a guard to fabricate a lie, which "is still told among the Jews to this day" (28:11-15). All of this leads directly into the conclusion of Matthew, its very climax, found in no other gospel. Here Matthew concludes his story with Jesus giving a final command to his disciples to go "to all the gentiles" to make disciples of them. Given that Jesus in Matthew admonished his disciples *not* to go to the gentiles because the mission was to "the lost sheep of the house of Israel," one cannot help but think that this is essential to Matthew's plotline and things have now changed drastically. Even if the mission still does include the Jewish people, which I think is doubtful for the author, the lost sheep of Israel are certainly—at a minimum—no longer the focus.[37] Matthew has built his case against the Jewish leaders and has explained why he and his community have turned to the gentiles. His gospel is complete. How does this contribute to an understanding of our passage, the story of the sheep and the goats?

Reading the Sheep and the Goats as Gentile Judgment

The sheep and the goats story must be understood in light of the above context—Jewish-gentile relations—as well as the immediate context of the judgment narrative of chapters 24–25. This narrative discourse tells of a coming judgment, and it first focuses on those who will hear these words, namely, the Matthean community. For these listeners, those who are understood by Matthew to be the true heirs of Israel, the message is simple: Be ready. The coming of the son of man will be witnessed by "all the tribes of the earth," and the elect will be taken out from them (24:29-31). The parables that follow encourage these listeners to prepare for their master's return. Just as a servant keeps his master's house in order in case the master returns unannounced (24:45-51), just as the five virgins are prepared for a delayed bridegroom, and just as the wise workers are productive with what their master entrusted them (even though his return is long in coming), so too should all those who hear these words be diligent and prepare for the coming of the great judge, the son of man.

But what of those who cannot prepare, because they have not heard Jesus' words? What of those outside this community? Although Matt. 24:14 speaks of the gospel being preached to all the gentiles (*ethnesin*) as a testimony, there seems to be a need, as in other Jewish judgment texts, to determine the fate of the gentiles apart from the people of God. What of those outside of Israel, those that do not hear the message of Jesus? What of the gentiles? Will they be judged as "we" are, in other words, as Israel is judged?

I think it is fundamental to remember that ultimately the Matthean community did not see themselves as non-Jews, or non-Israelites, or somehow a group that was not linked to Israel. They surely understood themselves *not* as gentiles, but as the true heirs of the kingdom, those who would eventually dine with Abraham. They are, from their perspective, Israel. It is likely that Matthew understood the scribes and Pharisees to have committed unpardonable sins, but it is not entirely clear that Matthew viewed all Jews, even "unbelieving" ones (with reference to Jesus), to be outside this group or damned despite their disagreements. There is a degree of separation between the Jewish leaders and the Jewish people in the gospel.[38] Some sins against the son of man are apparently permitted, and those Jews who do not follow Jesus might, we can deduce from this and ancient Jewish election theology more generally, still be included based on their heritage as Abraham's children. They are the elect, presumably included in those gathered by the son of man in 24:29-31.[39] However, according to Matthew they must not blaspheme the Holy Spirit, and it is only those leaders who persistently opposed Jesus and deemed his work to be that of Belezebub, it seems, that are condemned forever. Those who speak against the son of man can be extended mercy ("Whoever speaks a word against the Son of Man will be forgiven"), but the fate of the scribes and Pharisees is apparently sealed: "whoever speaks against the Holy Spirit will not be forgiven, either in this age or in the age to come" (12:31-32).[40]

In Matt. 25:31-46, the author explains that the gentiles, those outside the people of God (or Israel), will also stand in judgment before the son of man, the one who will judge them based on one criterion: love in action, or selfless acts of charity. That a judgment of different persons is in view—the gentiles, as opposed to those who should have prepared—is supported by the fact that the immediately preceding parable teaches that the wicked, lazy servant knew better and should have done more with his talent: the master replies "You *knew* that I reap where I do not sow . . . *you should have* . . ." (Matt. 25:24-28). In Matt. 25:31-46, however, we are dealing with persons who apparently *do not know the master*. That this story speaks of these people as *ethnē*, or gentiles, and that they are *surprised* in judgment is significant.

The contrast to those who know what the master is like, and should have prepared for his return based on their knowledge of him, is readily apparent once noticed. The story of the sheep and the goats clearly moves in a different direction from the parables that preceded it. No longer are we dealing with those "in the know" who are to prepare for the return of their lord. This account rounds off the longer judgment discourse of Matt. 24-25 in that we now have all people accounted for, Jews and gentiles. It finishes the discourse by explaining what will happen to those who do not know the master: they too can partake in the kingdom by acting charitably to the needy, something seen to be in service of the unknown master. The placing side-by-side of these parables appears strategic, and they make best sense in that light.

It is no coincidence that this judgment ends positively regarding gentiles, provided they exercise love in action. A positive view of gentiles has been building throughout the gospel and culminates here and in what follows in the Great Commission.[41] Further, positive views of gentiles, even those who are outside of Israel at the time of judgment, are not necessarily out of step with Judaism in this period.[42] Although gentiles entering the kingdom apart from the church may not be entirely congruent with later Christian theology, it seems to be an idea at work here, one that has precedents in ancient Jewish thinking that continues into the modern period.[43]

Matthew 25:31-46 and Jewish-Christian Dialogue

Despite some agreement here between early Christian teaching and historic Judaism on gentile judgment, there are still multiple ways that Matthew is a problem for the church and Jewish-Christian relations. The first and most important problem comes when contemporary Christian readers construct their understanding of Jews today upon descriptions from the book of Matthew. Matthew's rhetoric is extremely charged, and it should not be taken as a definitive statement on either what first-century Pharisaism (or Judaism more generally) was like or what Judaism is like today. Not only does his work reflect a particular Jewish setting and locale, but his picture is invariably shaped by his agenda and circumstances. The writer is likely a leader in a less dominant, mainly Jewish group that was expelled from local synagogues, and this surely tainted his view of his Jewish contemporaries. Further, the fact that his message regarding Jesus was largely rejected by this particular group of Jews certainly affects the tone and potentially the accuracy of his descriptions.

It is also clear that Matthew wrote for a community in the first century, and it is always difficult to read such literature as if it applies directly to modern religious settings. As noted by many, Matthew likely writes as a Jew for a (largely) Jewish community, *against another Jewish community*. Luz is especially helpful here in his engagement with conflict theory in the social sciences. He shows just how deeply Matthew's family break from the Pharisees would have affected his writing.[44] Luz deems portions of Matthew's words not to be based on reality (for example, the vicious woes in chapter 23), and various sections thus have limited relevance for life in the church today. It is a family conflict of which we have little knowledge, and we might wish to keep in mind that in "family conflict, many things are permitted and possible which would be unacceptable in a conflict between strangers."[45] However, we must go one step further to add that some of the things Matthew says of his family are not necessarily things that should have been said or should be repeated (especially by non-Jews). Even if Matthew's rhetoric was not out of step with other inter-Jewish polemics of its time, I agree with others that it is time to acknowledge that such rhetoric is damaging and thus needs not only to be read carefully, but needs to be read in a spirit of repentance, in the same way (for example) many Christians today read Paul's words on the role of women in the church.[46] At a minimum, Christian readers today need to address how well Matthew's teachings and rhetoric here square with Jesus' teachings on forgiveness and love of enemy.

The Historical Jesus, the Sheep and the Goats, and the New Testament

Does Matt. 25:31-46 reflect a saying remembered by Jesus' earliest disciples, one spoken by their master? Perhaps not entirely, or not at all, but there is little doubt that it is a deeply Jewish teaching, similar to other Second Temple Jewish teachings on gentile judgment, and probably one that would not have been out of line with what Jesus taught more generally. I think the criterion of embarrassment comes into play here, and if it is not a Jesus saying it is certainly one that sits in considerable tension with later Christian theology, teachings like *Extra Ecclesiam nulla salus* ("outside the Church there is no salvation") and some New Testament texts that imply the same (for example, John 3:36; Acts 4:12). We need to keep in mind, however, that the New Testament is very much like other Second Temple literature in that there is no one unified teaching on final judgment. Further, Matt. 25:31-46 is not necessarily at odds with everything the New Testament teaches on judgment or gentile salvation, and we might argue that Paul himself taught something similar. Paul's words in his letter to the Romans are certainly not far from Matt. 25:31-46 with regard to gentile judgment:

> When Gentiles, who do not possess the law, do instinctively what the law requires, these, though not having the law, are a law to themselves. They show that what the law requires is written on their hearts, to which their

own conscience also bears witness; and their conflicting thoughts will accuse or perhaps excuse them on the day when, according to my gospel, God, through Jesus Christ, will judge the secret thoughts of all. (Rom. 2:14-16)

There seems to be in Matt. 25:31-46, as well as in Rom. 2:14-16, a concern to make sense of what happens to the *ethnē*, the gentiles, and this concern is one that has had a long Jewish history. Although many Jewish judgment texts equate gentiles with the unrighteous, there are also multiple Jewish texts that suggest gentiles can take part in the world to come if they obey a basic set of ethical standards, at times called Noahide laws, or what David Novak calls a "partial Torah."[47] This is true of Judaism in the past as well as in the present, and I can't help but think it is time for Christians to allow this undervalued New Testament teaching to permeate the Christian tradition more fully. It is a Jewish idea that has largely been lost, particularly outside modern Catholicism.[48] Part of this, no doubt, is due to fears that other Christian teachings will be underemphasized or excised entirely, most importantly the command to missionize the gentiles. However, the book of Matthew is instructive in this matter. It is significant that the author climaxes his Gospel with a mission to the gentiles, given as the final command of the risen Jesus, even while he can at the same time teach that gentiles, those not missionized, can partake in the world-to-come if they lived lives that demonstrate charity toward the needy. The teaching of gentile judgment in the sheep and the goats story need not diminish the significance of the Great Commission.

For Christians and for Jews, this text opens up a significant area for discussion. Like others, I view genuine dialogue not simply as the attempt to find commonalities or to emphasize similarities between the religious groups involved but as the opportunity for each group to work through their deepest particularities with the other. Further, real dialogue is only possible if both parties involved are willing to end up somewhere other than where they first began. This passage is of tremendous value because it provides much by way of commonalities between Jews and Christians (for example, judgment of the gentiles based on a basic ethical standard), but it also has a host of difficulties for the two groups to work through together (most prominently vehement Matthean anti-Judaism as part of its presentation). It also provides a great deal of space for both groups to be changed in the process in that its teachings as presented above are likely to be unknown to many practitioners in both religious groups. The prospects for fruitful dialogue are strong.

Conclusion

It seems clear that the sheep and the goats story in its context of Matthew 24–25 shares many of the things that make for a Jewish judgment text in antiquity: the judgment of all people, Israel and the gentiles; God as judge or judgment through his representative (here, the son of man); fidelity to torah or an ethical standard as the foundation for judgment (even while the "elect" hold a special position provided they do not "unelect" themselves); and seemingly conflicting, nonlinear judgment images placed side by side (in this case, gentiles can be saved apart from Israel, even while they are encouraged to join the people). It is lamentable that the profound Jewishness of this passage has not been explored with seriousness in Christian interpretation. It may be that because scholars are predisposed to see this as a creation of the early church they are less inclined to explore its Jewishness. It is difficult to be sure, however.

In any event, although we cannot suggest that the Jewishness of this passage implies its "authenticity" as a Jesus saying, it is clearly an early teaching of Jewish-Christianity, perhaps one that reaches back to the time of Jesus himself, conceivably built upon or derived from other popular Jewish judgment ideas of that time—now with Jesus as judge. It holds out hope for those gentiles who do not know the master directly but live charitably, an idea with much in common with traditional Judaism, one that might be recovered as a Christian teaching even if Christianity has a distinct mission to them.

I hope my modest contribution to this discussion, if nothing else, spurs readers—especially those who stand, in one way or another, within the Jewish and Christian traditions—to fruitful dialogue, deeper appreciation of the other, and long-lasting peaceable relations.

CHAPTER THREE

A Dogmatic Jesus[*]

Anne Lapidus Lerner

A First Reading

As an observant Jew whose scholarly expertise lies in modern Hebrew literature and Jewish women's studies, rather than in New Testament studies, I find myself both troubled and encouraged by the story of the Syrophoenician woman that appears in Mark 7:24-30[1] and its parallel in Matthew 15:21-28.[2] As an outsider, I bring to the task an "alien" perspective, as well as a scholarly interest in the close reading of sacred texts and in the portrayal of women in them.

This story seems to center on a depiction of Jesus the Jew whose ministry is to the Jews, not the gentiles. But even more striking to me than Jesus is the unnamed foreign woman whose determination and intelligence resound through her words and her actions.

At first glance the story is of a piece with the healing tales that abound in the opening chapters of Mark. This unnamed woman is not the first parent to ask Jesus to cure a child,[3] although she is the first mother; she is not the first woman to approach Jesus for a cure,[4] nor is her child the first gentile to be cured of a demon by Jesus.[5] Thus, the reader who encounters the story in its biblical context has every reason to believe that Jesus will accede to the woman's request. Although in Mark's telling Jesus is hiding out in a house in an unspecified location in the Tyre region, perhaps trying to get some

[*]I would like to acknowledge the knowledge and support generously shared with me by my son-in-law Dr. Adam L. Gregerman, Jewish Scholar, Institute for Christian and Jewish Studies, Baltimore; the errors are all mine.

"down time," he cannot really hide as his reputation consistently precedes him. Sure enough, this woman, who is clearly identified as both a foreigner and a gentile, "immediately" heard about Jesus and approached him. Based on Jesus' well-known reputation and record of achievement, the reader also anticipates that Jesus will grant the request with alacrity. Given Jesus' willingness to heal supplicants and the relatives of supplicants, his rejection of this petitioner is unexpected.

The woman does not merely ask Jesus for help in casting the demon out of her daughter; she falls at his feet, begging for his assistance. Jesus is an expert at casting out demons. Mark 1:32-34 records that in the Galilee Jesus has effected wholesale demon removal. Surely granting this woman's urgent request would not prove onerous to Jesus; his cures are easily accomplished.

Jesus' response comes as a shock: "Let the children first be satisfied; for it is not right to take the children's bread and throw it to the dogs" (Mark 7:27). Not only does he refuse the woman's request, but he also demeans her. Further, he does not address her directly at all but rather responds by means of an allegory.

The terms of the allegory are as clear to the woman as they are to modern readers. The woman is not perceived as an individual but as a member of a group. Jesus sets up a binary opposition between children and dogs vying for food. The supplicant woman is a dog who has come seeking help for her own child who is, perforce, also a dog. Jesus literally turns the table on her by introducing a hierarchy among categories of humans and indicating that his interest lies with the "children" at the table, not with the "dogs" beneath it.

But the woman, impelled perhaps by her beloved daughter's desperate situation, does not retreat like a dog with her tail between her legs. This quadruply marginalized Greek, Syrian, Phoenician woman turns out to be a careful listener who, discovering a fallacy in Jesus' statement, quickly responds: "Lord, even the dogs under the table eat from the children's leftovers" (Mark 7:28). Her retort neither challenges Jesus' assumptions, nor questions his canine allegory. She picks up his argument, continuing to use his categories, but takes it one step further to maintain, reasonably enough, that dogs eat the crumbs that the children let fall to the floor. She has heard in Jesus' use of "first" the possibility of the dogs' receiving something, but she does not use it to draw him into an argument; she stays with his analogy. The woman also emphasizes his high status, the hierarchical distance between herself and Jesus, calling Jesus "lord."[6] She is willing to be a lowly hound if that's what it takes to save her child.

Surprisingly enough, the woman's strategy succeeds; Jesus' response is positive: "Because you said this, go—the demon has gone out of your daughter." Ultimately, of course, Jesus' response is cryptic. Is it her tenacity or, perhaps, her humility that wins him over? Might it be that she has bested him in a rhetorical joust? She certainly has no interest in his grounds for effecting the cure, only in the outcome. The woman does indeed return home to find that her daughter has recovered.

On first reading this story I was struck by what I saw as a reversal of roles between the supplicant and the healer. In my reading, the hero of the story is the woman who apparently teaches Jesus a lesson. She trounces him in a rhetorical argument and ends up achieving her goal. She is widely acknowledged to be the only person who bests Jesus in an argument in the Gospels.[7]

Jesus' negative attitude towards gentiles is not nuanced here. Clearly he sees the Jews as his primary audience with a focus so exclusive that it precludes his healing a non-Jew and leads him, by extension, to denigrate all non-Jews. That seems at odds both with the general impression of Jesus as a kind and caring healer and with the ready acceptance subsequently accorded him in the gentile world.

A Closer Look

Structure

The structure of the Markan story, a mere seven verses in length, is straightforward: the opening three verses introduce the time, place, and actors. Three more verses convey the dialogue between the woman and Jesus. The final verse is the empirical confirmation of Jesus' healing power. Mark uses a structure that highlights the two-part dialogue between the woman and Jesus.

Matthew's introduction is but a single verse, even more enigmatic than Mark's. Matthew's final verse does not really close the scene as it leaves all the characters where they were without sending the woman home. Only the narrator testifies to the miraculous healing without citing a source. Matthew's focus is on the woman's extended three-part dialogue with Jesus.

Location

Mark's opening and closing of the story provide the frame for the dialogue between Jesus and the woman. Despite its length the opening conveys only a small part of what the reader would like to know. The first verse takes Jesus from "there" to "the region around Tyre" (Mark 7:24). Since Jesus had been previously located in the region of the Sea of Galilee, he has gone a significant distance north northwest to reach Tyre.[8] The reason for his journey, specifically whether he is heading for Tyre or away from the Galilee, is not given, but it is not a casual trip, so it must have had some purpose. His immediate and circuitous return to the Sea of Galilee, which is the setting for the next story, makes this brief foray into gentile territory all the more puzzling.[9]

The specific location of Mark's Jesus at the time of the story is provided only in a nonspecific way—as a house that he entered. We do not know whose house it was, its size, or its precise location, but are told that he "didn't want anyone to know it" (Mark 7:24). Jesus' attempt to hide failed as "he could not escape notice," but we do not know whether many people or only this woman detected him.

The *mise-en-scène* in Matthew is similar, but not identical. Again, the place from which Jesus started out and the reason for his trip are unclear. In fact, the text in Matthew is even vaguer than Mark. Mark tells us that Jesus "got up and went away" (Mark 7:24), perhaps implying that Jesus wanted to leave Galilee, while Matthew states simply that he "went out" (Matt. 15:21). Further, the place to which he goes is referred to in Mark as "the region around Tyre"; in Matthew, as "the region of Tyre and Sidon" a larger area and an idiom used for Phoenicia.[10] It is the only instance when Jesus is reported to have traveled beyond the Land of Israel in his ministry.[11] The writer of Matthew, generally dated as later than Mark and assumed, by most scholars, to have had access to Mark,[12] provides the reader no information about the specific setting, which might be public,[13] in sharp contrast to Mark's placing the scene in a private home, a detail that has led many to point to the possibility of a secrecy motif.[14]

Characters

Given the lack of specificity about the place and the journey, it is not surprising to have the characters initially introduced without precise details. Jesus is clearly the "he" of Mark's story, although the narrator refers to him only through pronouns; Matthew uses the name Jesus only in the opening and closing verses (Matt. 15:21, 28). The woman is first introduced as "a woman whose daughter had an unclean spirit" because that was the reason that she sought Jesus out. The Markan story is so focused on these two that we have no indication of whether or not any other people, such as disciples or other followers or the householders, were present. A verse generally viewed as parenthetical (Mark 7:26) provides further information about the woman. She is "a 'Greek' a Syrophoenician by race."[15] There must be some significance to this elaborate additional statement about her provenance. Marcus suggests that it is "the functional equivalent of Gentile" and may indicate that she, as a Greek speaker, belongs to the upper class.[16] The meaning of the Syrophoenician descriptor is less clear, but definitely marks her as someone who is not Jewish.[17] Matthew suggests that she is a local Canaanite. Both versions of her story make clear that she is not a Jew without mentioning the word but by defining her as something else.

Dialogue

Curiously, unlike Matthew, Mark does not record the woman's opening statement. This leaves the reader unable to assess whether or not Jesus' sharp, negative response is appropriate. We can ponder whether or not she introduced the food analogy, whether she was deferential or dominating, timid or confident, but we have scant evidence. The most that we can know is that she is a woman who has intruded on Jesus and has lain down at his feet. Those two pieces of evidence are, at best, contradictory.

Matthew's description of the place omits some of Mark's details, while adding specifics to the character descriptions to present a fuller picture of what transpired between the woman and Jesus. Matthew amplifies the Markan text, interpolating an additional dialogue between the woman and Jesus and recording that the woman "came out, cried and said, 'Have mercy on me, Lord, Son of David. My daughter is severely demon-possessed'" (Matt. 15:22). We hear the woman's voice clearly, contrasting with the absence of her own voice in Mark.[18] Indeed, hers is the first woman's voice we encounter in the Gospels.[19] Her cry has three parts. Whereas Mark's woman is focused entirely on her daughter's welfare, Matthew's seems to see the situation at first as something affecting her, initially asking for mercy for herself. The second element in her articulate cry is the apostrophe identifying Jesus both as lord, using both *Kyrie*, the Septuagint's translation of the Hebrew tetragrammaton, which might also mean "sir," and "son of David," a descriptor that probably implies messianic status.[20] Only in the third element of her request does the woman indicate that the problem is that her daughter has been possessed by demons. As Luz remarks, there is "a great deal of literary artistry" in the Matthean story.[21]

Although this story as it appears in Mark anticipates Jesus' rejection and the allegory of the children and the dogs, in Matthew, the articulated response is slow to come: "But he answered her not a word" (Matt. 15:23). In Matthew, as in Mark, "but" counters the expectation that Jesus will respond positively to her plea. Jesus' silence is not explained.

According to Matthew, the silence is broken neither by Jesus nor by the unnamed woman but by his disciples, who are entirely absent from the Markan narrative. "And his disciples came and asked him and said, 'Send her away, for she is crying after us'" (Matt. 15:23). Just as she puts her own discomfort before her daughter's so do they think of themselves rather than the woman. They assume that Jesus will not respond positively to her request, for, if they thought otherwise, they would have asked him to effect the healing rather than to send her away. They know well that Jesus sees his ministry as directed to the Jews, not the gentiles. They simply ask him to dismiss her. From the context it appears that Jesus' response confirms and intensifies the disciples' rejection of the woman.[22] Although he says to them: "I was sent only to the lost sheep[23] of the house of Israel" (Matt. 15:24), he prob-ably intended that the woman hear his words, for the disciples needed no reminder that Jesus was not interested in helping non-Jews.[24]

In what is probably a continuation of the adaptation of Mark, Mat-thew has the woman respond briefly to Jesus' "lost sheep" statement. "But she came, fell down before him, and said, 'Lord, help me!'" (Matt. 15:25). Faced with what Luz terms a "massive rejection," the woman repeats only the essence of her request.[25] Although she understands that she is not among the "lost sheep of Israel," she addresses Jesus again, this time using only the term *Kyrie*. From her hierarchically self-abased position of kneeling she simply asks Jesus for help. The specifics of her appeal fall away. She needs help, and Jesus is in a position where he might yet be persuaded to offer it.

The somewhat puzzling scene with the disciples and the woman's dou-bled request is not found in the text of Mark. The Markan narrator picks up the thread of the story at the point where the reader anticipates Jesus' posi-tive response, or perhaps it is when the narrator anticipates that the reader will expect a positive reply to the woman's narrated predicament. However, the "but" that introduces Jesus' words indicates that the anticipated positive response will not be forthcoming.

In Mark, Jesus' response is not addressed directly to the woman, whose voice we have yet to hear. It is an apodictic statement, which actually neither approves nor denies the request. It does warrant careful examination: "Let the children first be satisfied; for it is not right to take the children's bread and throw it to the dogs." Jesus is presenting an allegory here. The children represent the Jews who are the objects of Jesus' ministry; the woman and her daughter are likened to dogs, not humans. That identification is obvious from the context, but, Marcus notwithstanding, Jesus does not invoke God here and thus does not claim that the Jews are God's children, or God's only children.[26] The woman is concerned for her child, the person with whom she has a special relationship; Jesus is concerned for the Jews, a group with whom he has a special relationship.

With limited resources, how does one determine who has priority? A later rabbinic text that appears in a discussion of the allocation of loans to help the poor may well represent earlier practice as well. It offers a system for triaging legitimate requests for help. "The poor of your house[hold] and the poor of your city, the poor of your house[hold] take precedence."[27] When allocating limited resources like money and food, one needs a system for making hard decisions. It makes sense to take care of those closest first.

Although Jesus' analogy seems to work at first glance, it is actually seri-ously flawed. While food and money are finite by their nature, the power to heal, as exercised by Jesus, seems to have no such limits.[28] There have been numerous reports of hundreds being healed at the same time. While Jesus' energy may have ebbed, surely he can muster the strength to perform one more healing miracle.

Jesus seems to present a binary choice between feeding the Jews ("children") and feeding the gentiles ("dogs"). There are other possibilities. Do the children have to be entirely satisfied before moving on to others in need? Could not the children be left a bit hungry? Further, humans and dogs are not equally deserving of priority treatment. Although the rabbinic dictum envisions concentric circles of caring, they are all for humans, not animals. Jesus creates two categories of humans, not based on consanguinity, demeaning some by comparing them to dogs, even domesticated dogs that wait by the table. Although Marcus proposes that New Testament comparisons of dogs and gentiles further develop an existing "Jewish association between dogs and Gentiles,"[29] Mark D. Nanos argues that there is no pre-Pauline evidence for this.[30] Further, no mention of dogs in the Mishnah is linked to gentiles, leading me to suspect that it is a canard.[31] Most significantly, whatever its provenance, this is a gratuitous denigration of the supplicant; "strangers" would have served Jesus' purposes just as well as dogs.[32]

Matthew has introduced some changes in the Markan story. Jesus' response, "It is not good to take the children's bread and throw it to the dogs" (Matt. 15:26) is almost identical to the text in Mark, but Matthew's omission of "first" gives it the air of an absolute refusal that is missing in Mark. It is of a piece with Matthew's strong emphasis on Jesus' ministry to the Jews.[33] Further, it follows the woman's absolute plea that is almost wordless. Matthew has Jesus present two contrasting animal analogies. Matthew's eloquent presentation of the care to be lavished on the one strayed sheep out of the flock of one hundred is yet to come,[34] but his meaning is clear. Either all the Jews are lost sheep or some of them are lost sheep,[35] but no gentiles are sheep at all; gentiles are dogs.

Once more, Mark's narrator introduces "but" as if to signal that the action is not proceeding in the direction the reader or listener has probably anticipated. In other words, while there may have been no response expected of the woman, only her retreat, she does in fact respond. The woman's words are introduced with the formulaic "she answered and said to him" (Mark 7:28), which, according to Joel Marcus, is "a formula that often expresses the main point of the passage."[36]

As indicated above, the woman stays within the scene that Jesus has set—the children's dining table where dogs are awaiting their scraps. Ignoring Jesus' hint that patience might yield "food" for the "dogs" after the children are satisfied, the woman retorts: "Lord, even the dogs under the table eat from the children's leftovers" (Mark 7:28). Like Jesus' statement to her, the woman's response to him is ambiguous. She does not respond by begging or by weeping. She maintains the dispassionate tone that Jesus uses, as though they were involved in a debate with no practical outcome. Her description of canine behavior rings true. When the dogs are allowed to approach the table while the humans are eating, they do not have to await the end of the meal to be fed but partake of the inadvertent droppings of those at the table. Generally speaking, children manage to drop more food than do adults. Luz adduces a wide range of classical and rabbinic texts to prove that this was so in ancient times.[37] Thus, in the situation under discussion, there is no reason that curing the supplicant's daughter has to be postponed until after the healing of all the suffering Jews.

The most significant word here may, however, be her first. As Marcus suggests, *Kyrie* might be translated either as "sir" or as "lord," in the divine sense.[38] Does the woman win her daughter's healing by implying that she accepts Jesus' divine status? Like so much of this story, this, too, is ambiguous.[39]

Matthew removes from the introduction to the woman's response the "but [*de*]" that indicates a reversal. By this point, having twice heard the insistent voice of the woman and having had her unceasing crying reported by the disciples, there is no surprise in her continuing demands. She does what is expected, that is, she retorts with practically the same words that appear in Mark. The exception is, however, instructive. Her first word, as reported in Matthew, is "certainly [*nai*]" and it is followed by *Kyrie* (Matt. 15:27). She next makes explicit her apparent acceptance of the allegory of the children and the dogs before using it to challenge Jesus' conclusion. Although she presents herself initially as submissive, and, indeed, humility has often been read into her story, her words belie that assessment.[40]

Unlike Jesus' original statement and the woman's retort, Jesus' response is not introduced by "but." This may well indicate that it will accord with the reader's expectations, rather than counter them. "And [*kai*] he said to her, 'Because you have said this, go—the demon has gone out of your daughter'" (Mark 7:29). It is a clear statement that does not imply any empathy on Jesus' part.[41] It does clarify that the daughter is not present, making this the only instance of Jesus' curing someone at a distance recorded in Mark.[42] But the ambiguity of Jesus' statement: "because of this word [*logos*]"[43] leads one to question which word or words, which aspect of her statement, might have been the key to unlocking the healing power. Faced with making a choice, one can hardly select anything other than *Kyrie*.

Closing

The closing verse of Mark's story serves simply to provide confirmation that the exorcism has indeed been accomplished. Jesus effects this without seeing, much less touching, the woman's daughter. Also, in the Markan story the daughter's cure is quick because by the time her mother returns home, her daughter has been cured.

Matthew's story ends a bit differently because Jesus specifies the reason for the cure: "Then Jesus answered and said to her, 'Woman, your faith is great. Let it be to you as you wish.' And her daughter was healed from that hour" (Matt. 15:28).[44] Of course, looking for the indications of her faith, one would likely settle on both her use of possibly messianic language and her perseverance, indicating that she really believes that Jesus can cure her daughter. As Amy-Jill Levine maintains, the precise object of her faith "is never made explicit."[45]

But there is another significant aspect to the ending of this story: Jesus has the last word. As Elisabeth Schüssler Fiorenza puts it: "the authority of the text rests with the 'master' voice of Jesus."[46] The openings of the two versions of this tale both focus on Jesus, and he is the last speaker in each. The woman's story is enclosed, literally defined, by the man's. This intriguing and powerful biblical woman has her moment on the stage, but it is just that, a moment before she becomes invisible once more.

The concluding comment of Matthew's narrator is also a little different from the close of the story in Mark. The cure is instantly effected, leaving one to consider whether the daughter is a silent presence during this encounter. Mark's version explicitly leaves the sick daughter at home to be acknowledged as healed by her returning mother. So the daughter is either a silent absence, as she surely is in Mark, or silent, whether or not she is present, in Matthew. On one level the dispute between Jesus and the foreign woman is all about the sick daughter—and she is not a presence.

This anonymous woman is not without precedents. There are a number of women in the Hebrew Bible whose situations and actions find an echo in her story. Amy-Jill Levine links her identification as a Canaanite in Matthew with Rahab, the Canaanite prostitute who shelters Joshua's spies (Josh. 2; 6:16-25) and is mentioned in the Matthean genealogy as an ancestor of Jesus.[47] Levine also points to Tamar as another Canaanite woman listed in Matthew's genealogy, who uses her intelligence to protect herself from Judah without publicly shaming him (Genesis 38).[48] Another Hebrew Bible precedent is the story of Elisha and the Shunamite (2 Kings 4:8-37), which presents another nameless woman, identified only by geography, who acts to ensure that her son, whose conception had been a miracle, recovers from what appears to be death. Although she does not exhibit the Syrophoenician woman's rhetorical prowess, she acts with speed and intelligence to bring Elisha to her son's side so that he may revive him.

Insofar as these verses can be read as a story, rather than as an allegory relating to the issue of mission to gentiles, the outcome is clear. Despite his hesitation, Jesus has been swayed by the "word(s)" or the "faith" of this articulate, persistent woman to use his healing powers on behalf of her daughter who is likely, like her mother, a foreigner of Syrophoenician origin. The woman displays a high level of rhetorical skill in responding to Jesus. Although Mark does not allow the reader to hear her voice initially when she makes her request, we hear it loud and clear in her retort to Jesus. She is a woman to be admired.

A Personal Afterword

As I confront this story, I find myself pulled between the two main characters, each of whom faces issues that are paramount to me. For me, Jesus is a Jew confronting a boundary issue.[49] He is trying to negotiate what he perceives as a conflict between the demands of belonging to a particular group and those of humanity as a whole, his responsibility to his people and his responsibility to those beyond his own group. His vision of himself is a person whose mission was exclusively to the Jews. We all face this question to a lesser or greater extent. Do we focus on our families, our friends, our coreligionists? Where do we invest our time and money? Do we give more of ourselves to outsiders or to our own families, extended families, local needs, or international needs? Do the earthquake victims, the tsunami victims, or the local unemployed command our attention? When can we simply say, in good conscience, "I am over-extended and can't take this on"?

My empathy for Jesus' dilemma stops with the dogs both because he denigrates the "other" and because he does not attempt to negotiate a compromise in an emergency situation. Particularly in Matthew, where his first response to the distraught petitioner is to enunciate a disembodied principle, rather than to look in her face, Jesus is diminished in my eyes. He never so much as addresses her in response to her humbly calling him "*Kyrie*." Not only does he not ask her name, but he omits any form of direct address.[50] The Matthean Jesus leaves little room for Levinasian human interaction, especially if the other human is treated like a dog. Further, Jesus does not repent, does not openly and honestly say that his initial reaction was wrong, or that he has learned a lesson.[51] The first step in repentance is to acknowledge what one has done wrong. Although Jesus heals the daughter, he does not apologize for his initial refusal or for his egregiously comparing the woman's daughter with a dog.

My identification with the woman comes to the fore. She is articulate and quick-witted enough to offer a swift and biting rejoinder to Jesus' canine comparison. Most of all, she is persistent and persuasive. She is a woman, undefined in most areas, except for the only one that matters to her at this time—motherhood—and the one that matters to Jesus—otherness. She is totally alone, with no man to support her in this difficult situation, most likely without even the desperately ill daughter for whom she seeks a cure. She will try anything, even the somewhat risky Markan irruption into the retreat of the unknown healer, to save her daughter's life. She has my empathy.

What could we learn from this text for inter-faith encounters? The most important thing is to appreciate the position of the other. Another is to listen attentively, as it is careful listening that empowers the Markan woman. Finally, I would suggest humbly and as an outsider, that when we find a text in our tradition that troubles us—and every tradition has them—we need to confront that text and honestly face its flaws, rather than hiding the text or explicating the flaws away. When we willingly hear the perspectives of those outside our faith traditions as well as those within, we better understand each other and the multifaceted nature of our traditions.

Part Two

Early Jewish and Gentile
Perspectives on Jesus

CHAPTER FOUR

The Distribution of Jewish Leaders in the Synoptic Gospels: Why Wariness Is Warranted

Michael J. Cook

Over many centuries, the well-being of the Jewish people has been jeopardized by Gospel traditions—especially about the Passion—blaming the Jews for Jesus' death. Here, Jesus is presented as arrested by *Jewish* conspirators, condemned by a *Jewish* court, and charged with blasphemy, a *Jewish* crime. The aroused *Jewish* mob opts to free not the innocent Jesus but Barabbas, a murderer as well as an insurrectionist. Pilate has Jesus crucified so as to quell clamoring by this *Jewish* crowd. This complex of accusations generated an intensely anti-Jewish mentality that, applied throughout the ages, resulted in death for many thousands of Jews and an abiding sense of insecurity for literally millions of others. Only in the modern day has voluminous scholarship successfully challenged, to varying degrees, the accuracy of each of the foregoing Passion allegations.

The current essay focuses on a second, partially overlapping, complex of passages that has served to buttress the anti-Jewish animus of the Passion texts: namely, traditions of Jesus in controversy (often vitriolic) with various groups of Jewish opponents: chief priests, scribes, elders, Pharisees, Herodians, Sadducees. Scholars often refer to the content of such controversies to help define various modes of pre–70 CE Judaism and to distill essentials of Jesus' ethics and theological outlook. Yet these episodes are also routinely mined by historians bent on tracing the escalation of hostility between Jesus and his opponents that culminated in his execution. With respect to this last venture, I believe that, because certain methodological problems usually go unrecognized, findings here have been misleading, thereby only reinforcing the anti-Jewish orientation of the Passion framework itself.

In assessing the historicity of these "controversy" traditions, this essay will focus on a series of literary oddities that have received scant attention. Each of these ten is a function of one basic problem: the curious *pattern* in which the *titles* of those cast as Jesus' opponents are *distributed* throughout the Synoptic traditions. Here the Gospel of Mark is especially determinative if, as most scholars agree, Matthew and Luke drew upon Mark as their primary narrative source.

Disturbingly, Mark himself—likely a gentile writing in Rome around 71 CE[1]—appears unclear about who some, or even all, of these Jewish elements had been at the time of Jesus' ministry. By Mark's day, none of the six groups was still meaningfully functioning in the holy land except the Pharisees (soon to become the early rabbis). Nor is it likely that any of these elements had been particularly familiar to gentiles in diaspora regions. From where, then, did Mark himself secure information on these groups, how did he integrate them, and why are they distributed in the fashion we find them in his Gospel? Further, to what degree should we be skeptical of those parallel controversy traditions that Matthew and Luke inherit from Mark and often then embellish on their own?

Ten Anomalies

In identifying, and taking my cue from, ten stylistic anomalies *internal* to Mark's presentation of the Jewish leaders, I contend that all can be resolved simultaneously by but one and the same hypothesis. In our canvassing now these ten anomalies, some may strike readers as more consequential than others. I construe them all, however, as *equally* important in my reconstruction of how these Synoptic traditions originated.

Anomaly #1—Amorphous Titles?

Some of Mark's Jewish leader titles are so imprecise, even elusive, as to seem but general constructs, virtually literary devices. Is "elders," for example, more than a generic label? The meaning of "Herodians" has eluded scholars. What ancient Jewish sources employ "chief priests" as a technical name (or is this simply Mark's expedient to denote the *more important* priests)?

Mark's parenthetical comment on a definitely known group, the "Pharisees" (7:3-4), explains for gentile readers in *his* day Jewish ceremonial washing: "the Pharisees, and all the Jews, do not eat unless they wash their hands, observing the tradition of the elders; and . . . many other traditions . . . they observe, the washing of cups and pots and vessels of bronze."[2] In clarifying the contextual verses at hand (7:1-2), Mark was not obligated to be more expansive. Nonetheless, since in Mark's day the Pharisees were the new native personnel whom Rome had installed over the holy land, it seems odd that Mark conveys nothing more substantive concerning them. Also, the phrase "and *all* the Jews" impedes readers from distilling the Pharisees' distinguishing profile in *Jesus'* day. Is it correct to say that Mark "does not appear to be familiar . . . with Jewish customs," and that he "over generalizes about the Jews . . . from whom he seems to distance himself"?[3]

Mark's sole explanation of the "Sadducees"—who "say that there is no resurrection" (12:18)—is accurate but presents no other dimension of their identity or platform. Also, Mark peculiarly fails to cast the Sadducees as seeking Jesus' execution, a goal he is careful to specify for each other group. Since this single Sadducee episode sets up the Scribe's striking inquiry about Jesus' Great Commandment (12:28), did Mark perhaps find 12:18-34a as a single unit? That is to say, because Mark seems all but disinterested in the Sadducees, perhaps their mention in this unit is incidentally attached to an episode that Mark has included due to his interest in "the scribes" (representing the group that Mark mentions by far the most frequently)?

Anomaly #2 — Two Different Profiles for "Scribes"?

As for Mark's "scribes," they peculiarly radiate two radically different profiles. One is bland, imparting nothing as to who they are or what they do in their own right (Mark 8:31; 10:33; 11:18, 27; 14:1, 43, 53; 15:1, 31). The other profile, however, advances them as teaching with authority (1:22), overbearing in demeanor (12:38-40), and formidable in doctrine—for example, in their insistence that the Messiah be preceded by Elijah's coming (9:11-13) and be a Davidic descendant (12:35). When Mark brackets the impersonal scribes with chief priests—as in "chief priests, *scribes*, and elders"—are these scribes *Sadducean* despite displaying no overt sympathy with priestly interests? Are the other scribes, then, *Pharisaic* as when (in 12:28) the Scribe applauds that Jesus "answered . . . well" the Sadducees on resurrection (a defining Pharisaic precept) and effusively praises Jesus' Great Commandment, whose two components are consistent with Pharisaism: the Shema (Deut. 6:4-9) and Golden Rule (Lev. 19:18)?

Anomaly #3 — Artificial Compartmentalization?

While chief priests, scribes, elders, Pharisees, and Herodians are each committed to Jesus' destruction, they seem precluded from merging their forces. For Mark rigidly compartmentalizes them into two distinct camps (Figure 4.1):

FIGURE 4.1: COMPARTMENTALIZATION INTO DISTINCT CAMPS

Judea-Based Camp	Galilee-Based Camp
Chief Priests (+ Scribes + Elders)[4]	Pharisees (+ Herodians)[5]

In the former, the chief priests hold sway, with the scribes and elders silent tagalongs. The latter camp depicts the Pharisees as dominant, with the Herodians their occasional silent tagalongs. Never do the Judean-based chief priests encounter either the Galilean Pharisees or Herodians. The same is true of the Judean elders.

"Scribes" are again the exception. When linked with the chief priests, they never encounter the Pharisees or Herodians. But the second profile scribes (not so linked) do connect with the Pharisees—albeit only twice (2:16; 7:1, 5).

Anomaly #4—Only Two Encounters of Scribes and Pharisees?

In 7:1, we read of Galilean "Pharisees . . . with some of the scribes who had come from Jerusalem."[6] Some scholars argue that the scribes' presence here is "historically unlikely,"[7] even that it is ridiculous when "scribes from Jerusalem come [down into Galilee] simply to see the disciples eat"[8] (they "came down" also in Mark 3:22)! The other exceptional text, 2:16, presents "scribes *of* the Pharisees" and a variant, "scribes *and* the Pharisees." In the more than fifty mentions of leadership groups by Mark, no Judean member encounters anyone of the Galilean camp except on these two occasions (2:16; 7:1, 5), when the *dynamic* scribes link up with the Pharisees.

Anomaly #5—Lack of Independence?

Most of these groups seem unnaturally restrained from behaving independently. The Herodians are always harnessed to the Pharisees, as the elders and the bland scribes are always tied to the chief priests.[9] Even when the chief priests *appear* to be on their own, they turn out to be implicitly bracketed with scribes or elders, or both.[10] The Pharisees and second-profile scribes, however, do often act independently. Why this disparity?

Anomaly #6—Absence of Pharisees from the Passion Narrative?

The Pharisees and the Herodians plot Jesus' death as early as 3:6 yet strangely play no role in the Passion (chapters 14–15). Instead, "the hierarchs and the scribes take up what the Pharisees and the Herodians were the first to plan."[11] Apologists for the Pharisees' successor-rabbis may insist, if not trumpet, that the Pharisees' absence exonerates the rabbis from any "inherited" taint of culpability in Jesus' death. Yet why deem the Pharisees exonerated if 3:6 shows them determined "to destroy" Jesus?

Anomaly #7—Difficulty Differentiating between Scribes and Pharisees?

Mark usually distinguishes between the scribes and Pharisees yet appears actually unable to specify exactly *how* they differ—a deficiency leaving Matthew and Luke similarly puzzled (see below).

Anomaly #8—Disproportionate Frequency of Scribal Appearances?

Since the chief priests and the Pharisees propel the Markan plot, why do appearances of the scribes dwarf those of the others—twenty-one times versus fourteen for chief priests, eleven for Pharisees, five for elders, two (or three) for Herodians, and only one for Sadducees?[12]

Anomaly #9—Odd Segues, Placements, Seams?

The premature crescendo of hostility in Mark 3:6 ("the Pharisees . . . immediately held counsel with the Herodians . . . how to destroy him") fits better near the story line's *end* than beginning. Moreover, inexplicably the intensity of Pharisee/Herodian rage diminishes after 3:6. Luke, sensing the incongruity, dilutes Mark's words to read merely (Luke 6:11): "they were filled with fury and discussed with one another what they might do to Jesus."[13]

Incongruous also is Mark 12:34b, concluding the Great Commandment (12:28-34a) with "no one *dared* to ask him any question." Yet this has been the sole cordial exchange by Jesus with any Jewish leader. Why here of all places are listeners cast as *shrinking* from posing follow-up questions?

Anomaly #10—Clustering of Leadership Appearances?

Figure 4.2 reveals that the most prominent mentions of Mark's Jewish leadership groups seem unnaturally concentrated. Chief priests + scribes + elders are clustered primarily in chapters 14–15, the Passion Narrative. Chapter 12, meanwhile, clusters scribe pericopes (here limited only to the dynamic scribes independent of the chief priests). Further, another scribe episode, 9:11-13 (asking "why . . . the scribes say that first Elijah must come"), seems akin to "how can the scribes say that the Christ is the son of David?" (12:35). Might Mark himself have shifted this Elijah episode from the scribal litany in chapter 12 now instead to chapter 9, so that it would juxtapose *Elijah's* presence at Jesus' transfiguration (9:4ff.)?

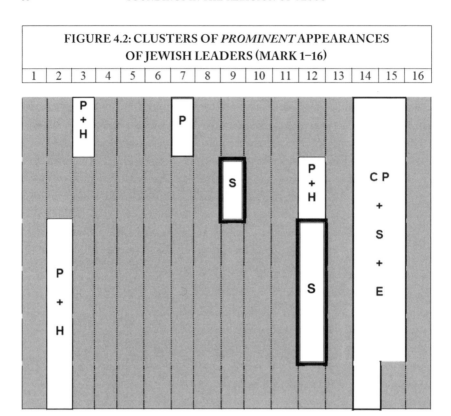

FIGURE 4.2: CLUSTERS OF *PROMINENT* APPEARANCES
OF JEWISH LEADERS (MARK 1–16)

	PRIMARY CLUSTERS	*Editorial* touches outside the clusters? (Not pictured)
CP + S + E	Chief Priests (+ Scribes + Elders) in 14:1—15:32, passim	8:31; 10:33; 11:18,27
S	*(Dynamic)* Scribes alone in 9:11-13; 12:18-40	1:22; 2:5b-10,16; 7:1,5; 8:31; 9:14;10:33; 11:18,27
P + H	Pharisees (+ Herodians) in 2:15—3:6; 7:1ff; 12:13-17	8:11,15; 10:2

As for the bulk of Pharisee (including Herodian) material, this in turn is clustered in chapters 2–3, 7, and 12. Yet affinities between those materials in chapters 7 and 12 with the concentration of episodes already in chapters 2–3 suggest that there may originally have been a single block of material—the core still underlying chapters 2–3—two episodes of which Mark parceled out to the other locations (7:1ff.; 12:13-17).

Still additional mentions of Jewish leaders, but here outside the clusters, look to be wholly editorial improvisations, that is, not originally rooted in the clusters but improvised by Mark separately. Figure 4.2 tentatively labels these: "*editorial* touches outside the clusters?" (to be explained shortly).

Source Theories: Help or Hindrance?

Is there a single reconstruction that could compellingly account for all ten anomalies? Most scholars drawn to our subject circumvent these idiosyncrasies if indeed, to repeat, they even notice them. Instead, they gravitate toward *source theories* to explain Mark's configuration of traditions residing within the clusters. This is understandable since, in the case of similar swaths of Markan material, source theories have been a favored solution: for example, regarding the cluster of Kingdom parables (4:1-34); of the miracle catenae (6:[30]34—7:37; 8:1-26); and of the "Little Apocalypse" (chapter 13). On our subject as well, from the early 1900s scholars have proposed Mark's co-option of blocks of written traditions some of whose original contours are claimed to remain discernible in the canonical text.

Source theories, however, can be fraught with methodological problems. A circularity can assume control, with a presumption of sources soon "confirming" their existence, then even defining their scope and content. Such preoccupation can also divert attention from the Evangelist's own editorial creativity, including adaptations of whatever his underlying materials are claimed to have been.

These pitfalls explain why, by contrast, this essay will cautiously set, front and center, not a presupposition of hypothetical sources but instead the challenge of resolving the ten anomalies. At the same time, given Mark's apparently nebulous treatment of these groups, we must be open to his having accessed material from outside his personal experience, prompting the question: is it possible to *reason backwards* from the ten anomalies to envision what kind of source theory, if any, could compellingly resolve them all?

Thus, while I will emphasize the anomalies, some possible combination of these two approaches may ultimately be needed. Let us, then, sample three classic source theories on this problem: the paradigms offered, respectively, by Martin Albertz, Burton Easton, and Paul Winter[14]:

1. *Martin Albertz's Two-Source Theory* posited a first pre-Markan source set in Galilee, incorporated by Mark virtually intact, and underlying Jesus' clustered controversies with various opponents in 2:1—3:6:
- 2:1-12   the Paralytic and Forgiveness
- 2:13-17   the Call of Levi; Eating with Tax-Collectors and Sinners
- 2:18-22   Fasting

- 2:23-28   the Sabbath (Gathering Corn)
- 3:1-6   the Sabbath (Healing the Man's Withered Hand)

Albertz proposed also a second source, this underlying 11:15—12:40 and encompassing seven episodes:
- 11:27-33   Authority
- 12:13-17   Tribute to Caesar
- 12:18-27   Resurrection
- 12:28-34   the Great Commandment
- 12:35-37   David's Son

—introduced by the "Temple Cleansing" (11:15ff.), and concluded by a warning against the scribes (12:38-40).

2. *Burton Easton's Single-Source Theory* trimmed Albertz's two proposed pre-Markan collections into one of eight pericopes only:
- 2:13-17   the Call of Levi; Eating with Tax-Collectors and Sinners
- 2:18-22   Fasting
- 2:23-28   the Sabbath (Gathering Corn)
- 3:1-6   the Sabbath (Healing the Man's Withered Hand)
- 12:13-17   Tribute to Caesar
- 12:18-27   Resurrection
- 12:35-37   David's Son
- 12:38-40   Warning against the scribes

Easton argued that Mark bisected this source, assigning the first four components to the Galilean ministry, the remaining four to Jerusalem. (Easton dismissed the Great Commandment—12:28-34—from inclusion.[15]) Seminal was Easton's contention that, originally, in the single pre-Markan collection, the Tribute to Caesar (12:13-17) *directly followed* the Healing of the Man's Withered Hand (3:1-6). The current nine-chapter hiatus between them is due to Mark's bisection of this once single litany of traditions.

3. *Paul Winter's Strata Approach* was uniquely predicated on the group *titles* to distinguish the contours of once separate pre-Markan strata:
- Passages where Jesus' foes are chief priests + scribes + elders reflect the earliest stratum
- A later stratum underlies passages presenting scribes *alone*
- The latest stratum advances passages featuring Pharisees + Herodians

Are Winter's proposed stratification and sequence plausible? As for the *Earliest* stratum, yes—Christianity could indeed first have required some succinct Passion tradition narrating the week that brought Jesus' death; here enemies such as "chief priests + scribes + elders" would serve to support the flow of such a story line. For the *Intermediate* stratum there could well have congealed thereafter another stratum of episodes featuring "scribes" alone and in the main challenging Jesus' messianic credentials; here exchanges presenting words by Jesus to the "disciples" would model proper Christian responses to objections lodged by "scribes" (here literally cast simply and primarily as Jewish skeptics). For the *last* stratum, the anti-Pharisee material, focusing primarily on *legalistic* matters, could well reflect the later impact of Paul's missionary agenda or preaching.

I find Winter's hypothesis vital because, in taking its lead from the *distribution of the group titles*, it alone offers at least the potential of resolving *all* of the ten anomalies—although, paradoxically, Winter himself appears not to have noticed many of them. Severely compromising matters, however, is that in other respects Winter's proposal is porous. Accordingly, we cannot readily apply it to our problem without first shoring up his methodological respectability.

To start with, while the distribution of group titles is the key to Winter's differentiation among his three proposed source strata, he peculiarly overlooks what Mark himself—surely more than a mere "cutter-and-paster"—might have contributed *redactionally*. If this editor, on his own, devised *new* material replicating the very same group titles that Winter claims Mark co-opted from the proposed strata, then Winter, in effect, would be allocating Mark's own *editorial* touches to pre-Markan sources! Second, what is to say that Mark did not himself resequence individual pericopes that he lifted from his presumed source strata or parcel them out to other locations in the Jesus story line?

Third, artistically but nonetheless artificially, Mark schematized his Gospel first into Jesus' *Galilean* ministry (chapters 1–9), followed by Jesus' last days in *Judea* (chapters 10–16). But Winter leaves unclear why Mark apportioned the various leadership groups to *either* Judea *or* Galilee—are we to suppose that the alleged strata dictated such, or did Mark himself so decide? This is important since, after committing himself to this bifurcation, Mark strenuously labored to camouflage it (see below). Fourth, Winter's eagerness to defend the Pharisees impeded his judgment as to why Pharisees are absent from Mark's Passion and induced Winter categorically to deny all commonality between the Pharisees and the scribes—both of which conclusions, we shall see, run expressly counter to the very logic of Winter's strata theory.

In shoring up Winter's proposal, I will need to conjecture at least rough contours for each of his three proposed pre-Markan source strata. Otherwise, there will be no basis for differentiating group titles reflecting Mark's editorial hand from those titles that he presumably lifted from his strata. I will also need to clarify the geographical problem as well as to neutralize Winter's pro-Pharisee apologetic.

Revamping Winter's Theory of Three Proposed Strata

The following recasts Winter's theory of three pre-Markan strata and suggests what each stratum might essentially have conveyed:

Winter's EARLIEST proposed stratum, revamped: a skeletal primitive Passion tradition set in Jerusalem that conveyed at least the plot against Jesus, his arrest and delivery to Pilate, and his consignment to the Cross. (There are scores of analogous but more detailed scholarly reconstructions.[16]) From this stratum Mark became introduced, among other matters, to the chief priests + scribes + elders. Later, Mark would expand this originally succinct nucleus into 14:1—15:32. Figure 4.3 lays out the basic rough contours of the pre-Markan stratum proposed (the possible contents are here severely abridged):

FIGURE 4.3: PROPOSED CONTOURS OF WINTER'S EARLIEST PRE-MARKAN STRATUM—FEATURING CHIEF PRIESTS + SCRIBES + ELDERS (ABRIDGED)	
Plot and arrest	. . . the **chief priests** and the **scribes** were seeking how to . . . kill him. . . . Came the **chief priests** and the **scribes** and the **elders** . . . and . . . led Jesus to the high priest; and all the **chief priests** and the **elders** and the **scribes** were assembled.
Consultation, delivery, accusation, mockery	And as soon as it was morning the **chief priests**, with the **elders** and **scribes**, . . . held a consultation . . . and delivered him to Pilate. . . . The **chief priests** accused him of many things. . . . So also the **chief priests** mocked him . . . with the **scribes**.

Winter's INTERMEDIATE proposed stratum, revamped: this consisted of material other, and later, than the rudimentary Passion, and presented Scribes *alone*—but here solely the dynamic type. This source need not have assigned scribes to Judea, but Mark himself could have inferred the need for such an assignment because his first (the Passion) stratum situated *in*

Jerusalem the chief priests + *scribes* + elders. Figure 4.4 abridges the basic rough contours proposed.[17]

FIGURE 4.4: PROPOSED CONTOURS OF WINTER'S INTERMEDIATE PRE-MARKAN STRATUM— FEATURING "SCRIBES" *ALONE* (ABRIDGED)		
9:11-12a, 13	Elijah's coming	"Why do the scribes say that first Elijah must come?" . . .
12:18-34a	Resurrection and Great Commandment	Sadducees . . . who say that there is no resurrection. . . asked. . . . One of the scribes, . . . seeing that [Jesus] answered them well, asked . . ., "Which commandment is the first of all?" Jesus answered . . . The scribe said . . ., "You are right, Teacher. . . ." . . . Jesus . . . said . . ., "You are not far from the kingdom of God."
12:35-37	Son of David	35 . . . "How can the scribes say that the Christ is the son of David? . . ."
12:38-40	Against Scribes	38 . . . "Beware of the scribes, who . . ."

Winter's LAST proposed stratum, revamped: this material, presenting Pharisees + Herodians, need not have assigned the Pharisees to *Galilee*, but Mark could have inferred such because here he found them linked with Herodians whom Mark would have associated with Herod Antipas, tetrarch—even "king" (6:14, 25-27)—of *Galilee*. Figure 4.5 abridges the basic rough contours proposed.[18]

FIGURE 4.5: PROPOSED CONTOURS OF WINTER'S LAST PRE-MARKAN STRATUM—FEATURING "PHARISEES + HERODIANS" (ABRIDGED)		
7:1-2, 5	Washing hands	The **Pharisees** . . . saw that . . . his disciples ate with hands defiled. . . . The **Pharisees** asked . . ., "Why do your disciples not live according to the tradition of the elders, but eat with hands defiled?" . . .
2:15-17	Eating with tax-collectors and sinners	. . . The **Pharisees** . . . said to his disciples, "Why does he eat with tax-collectors and sinners?" . . .
2:18-22	Fasting	. . . "Why do John's disciples and . . . the disciples of the **Pharisees** fast, but your disciples do not . . . ?" . . .
2:23-27	Gathering corn	The **Pharisees** said to him, ". . . why are they doing what is not lawful on the Sabbath?" . . .
3:1-5	Healing on Sabbath	[The **Pharisees**] . . . watched . . . to see whether [Jesus] would heal him on the Sabbath. . . . His hand was restored.
12:13-17, 34b	Tribute to Caesar	They sent . . . some of the **Pharisees** and . . . **Herodians** to entrap him. . . . "Is it lawful to pay taxes to Caesar . . . ?" . . . "Render to Caesar. . . ." . . . They were amazed at him. . . . And after that no one dared to ask him any question.
3:6	Resolve to destroy Jesus	The **Pharisees** went out, and immediately held counsel with the **Herodians** against him, how to destroy him.

A Reconstruction: How Did Mark Knit Together Winter's Proposed Strata?

A profound divide inheres in this Gospel between the early plot against Jesus by *Galilean* "Pharisees + Herodians" and Jesus' ultimate condemnation instead by *Jerusalem* "chief priests + scribes + elders." I propose that, in struggling to soften this divide, Mark himself composed a number of passages, primarily *outside the clusters*, replete with the same group leadership titles. Such a possibility Winter, focusing solely on pre-Markan strata instead of also on Mark's editorial role, appears not to have contemplated. What Mark appears to have done is (1) to *retroject* Jerusalem's chief priests + scribes + elders toward, and into, "Galilee" chapters (earlier than what are now 14–15); and (2) to *project* Galilean Pharisees + Herodians toward, and into, "Judean" chapters (later than what are now 2–3).

Retrojecting Jerusalem Groups toward, and into, Galilee

Mark needed to address why the "chief priests + scribes + elders," who were co-opted originally from the first stratum—a primitive Passion tradition restricted to Jerusalem—wished the execution of a Jesus figure whom, ostensibly, they had yet to encounter! Mark's response was a reverse-thrust editing,[19] using chapters 10–13 as his staging arena.

First, Mark composed 11:27-28, which supplied a compelling motive for their taking action against Jesus: "the chief priests and the scribes and the elders . . . said . . . , 'By what *authority* are you doing these things . . . ?'" (This "authority" motif, as shown below, enabled Mark to shift scribes, in particular, even as early as 1:22 and 2:10.) Then Mark, working further backwards, added 11:18: "the chief priests and the scribes . . . sought a way to destroy him; for they feared him, because all the multitude was astonished at his teaching." By "sought a way to destroy him," Mark here creatively paralleled this passage to 3:6, where the counterpart "Pharisees + Herodians" likewise had taken counsel "how to destroy him."

Mark could not "bodily" shift the Passion triad, as a *unit*, any earlier than chapter 10 because on what plausible basis could their head group, the chief priests, be shown roaming the Galilean countryside far from their Jerusalem temple base? Yet Mark could easily manufacture four *predictions* by the all-knowing Jesus: 8:31; 9:12b; 9:31; and 10:33-34. The fourth he placed soon after Jesus first set foot into Judea; the other three while Jesus *was still in Galilee*. Collectively, these foretold the evil designs that, supposedly, the three Passion groups had long been harboring toward Jesus, as in 8:31: "the Son of Man must . . . be rejected by the elders and the chief priests and the scribes, and be killed. . . ." In these details and others, the predictions correspond so precisely to the culminating Passion as to expose them as crafted only after the fact by Mark himself (even the uncharacteristic sequencing of "elders" *first* in 8:31 suggests origination from Mark's own hand).

Additionally, Mark could push (what he assumed were) *Judean* scribes into Galilee earlier still since about them alone Mark had a *second* stratum with colorful details that he could co-opt and embellish (compare this with the nondescript elders). Indeed, as long as Mark specified that these (active) scribes had come down from Jerusalem (3:22; 7:1) he could introduce them anywhere in Galilee besides assigning them whatever words or deeds he wished.

Mark even inserted scribes into material drawn from his "Pharisee + Herodian" source stratum! Accordingly, in 2:16, those protesting Jesus' eating with tax collectors and sinners were originally neither "scribes *of* the Pharisees" nor "scribes *and* the Pharisees" but *solely* Pharisees—scribes were only secondarily grafted in by Mark himself. (Did this irregularity contribute to the variant readings in 2:16?) Likewise, in 7:1 (cf. 7:5), those originally complaining that Jesus' disciples ate with unwashed hands were not Pharisees "with some of the scribes, who had come down from Jerusalem," but rather Pharisees *alone*. Scribes here came down from Jerusalem solely because Mark himself *brought* them (the same in 3:22)! Recall also the likely detachment and shift of the Elijah pericope to (what is now) chapter 9 from what may have been its original Jerusalem mooring in chapter 12—matching Mark's technique elsewhere of retrojecting scribes from Judea into a Galilean backdrop.

Mark's most consequential (also transparent) intrusion of scribes involves the Healing of the Paralytic as far back as 2:1-12 (Figure 4.6). This twelve-verse pericope is uncharacteristically long (for oral transmission) because Mark himself has inserted five to six extraneous verses.

FIGURE 4.6: SAMPLE MARKAN INTERPOLATION OF "SCRIBES" (2:5B-10), ABRIDGED

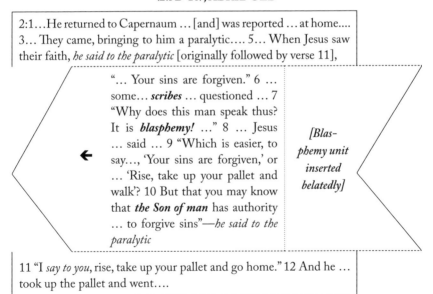

2:1…He returned to Capernaum … [and] was reported … at home…. 3… They came, bringing to him a paralytic…. 5… When Jesus saw their faith, *he said to the paralytic* [originally followed by verse 11],

"… Your sins are forgiven." 6 … some… **scribes** … questioned … 7 "Why does this man speak thus? It is **blasphemy!** …" 8 … Jesus … said … 9 "Which is easier, to say…, 'Your sins are forgiven,' or … 'Rise, take up your pallet and walk'? 10 But that you may know that **the Son of man** has authority … to forgive sins"—*he said to the paralytic*

[Blasphemy unit inserted belatedly]

11 "I *say to you*, rise, take up your pallet and go home." 12 And he … took up the pallet and went….

Note the tell-tale splice marks: first, Jesus' interrupted speaking part (end of verse 10); second, Mark's awkward switch of those whom Jesus addresses from the scribes to the paralytic; and, third, the double appearance of "he said to the paralytic" (ending both v. 5 and v. 10). All these signal an interpolation.

When we remove the evident insertion, the *short* original tale reappears uninterrupted (read consecutively vv. 1-5a, 11-12).

Mark's purpose here in inserting 2:5b-10 was not only, again, to bridge Jerusalem Jewish leaders from the Passion chapters with the *Galilean* locale—here as early as chapter 2—but also to introduce Sanhedrin personnel ("some . . . scribes") condemning Jesus for "blasphemy." This was to foreshadow the Sanhedrin verdict, in 14:64, "you have heard his *blasphemy*." Mark also here, in chapter 2, has Jesus arrogate to himself "authority" (2:10; cf. 11:27-28) as the Son of Man, thereby foreshadowing Jesus' strident response to Caiaphas a dozen chapters later, in 14:62 ("you will see the Son of Man seated at the right hand of Power"). Because Albertz did not recognize here the interpolation of the verses concerning the scribes, he misconstrued 2:1-12 as leading off his first proposed pre-Markan controversy source—whereas the *original* Paralytic episode was devoid of Jewish leaders altogether! All these foregoing editorial maneuvers would enable Mark to clarify why the Passion triad—lifted from the earliest stratum Winter proposed—had sought Jesus' demise.

Projecting Galilean Groups toward, and into, Jerusalem

Mirroring Mark's shift of Passion personnel (from chapters 14–15) into earlier chapters (1–13) is his propelling of the Galilean Pharisees + Herodians (from chapter 2–3) into later chapters in Galilee, then into Judea, and ultimately Jerusalem proper. Easton, accordingly, was correct that the Jerusalem Tribute to Caesar episode in 12:13-17, involving Pharisees + Herodians, had originally extended the Galilean episode of chapter 3 (Healing the Man's Withered Hand). For Mark himself severed and shifted far later the Tribute to Caesar, in Winter's terms originally the last story of the Pharisee + Herodian stratum. This explains why the Galilean Pharisees + Herodians suddenly surface in Jerusalem *this one time only*. As for why Mark did not likewise transfer 3:6—"the Pharisees . . . held counsel with the Herodians . . . how to destroy him"—to chapter 12, since he could not easily storm the *imminent* and already packed Passion stage (chapters 14-15) with still more villainous personnel (Pharisees + Herodians), it was better to leave 3:6 quietly unfulfilled far back in chapter 3 than glaringly unfulfilled as late as chapter 12.

At Luke's corresponding juncture, he capitalized on Mark's move here of Herodians to Jerusalem (in Mark 12:13) by fancying that none other than Herod Antipas "was himself in Jerusalem at that time" (Luke 23:7). This is why, among the Synoptists, Luke alone locates here a vignette of Antipas pronouncing Jesus innocent.

Another Markan shifting of a Pharisee episode later on may be the material opening chapter 7 ("when the Pharisees . . . saw that some of his disciples ate with hands defiled"), whose content, eating, is akin to what *now* opens Pharisee material in 2:15-16 ("when they saw that he was eating with sinners and tax collectors"). Did the chapter 7 pericope originally commence Winter's third pre-Markan (the Pharisee + Herodian) stratum, as displayed in Figure 4.5? Conceivably, then, from an original continuum encompassing what are now traditions from 7:1ff; 2:15—3:5; 12:13-17, 34b; 3:6, Mark severed both the first episode and the Tribute to Caesar, allocating them to chapters 7 and 12, respectively (albeit retaining 3:6 in its original placement).

Matters become far more conjectural with the pericope on divorce opening chapter 10 ("he . . . went to the region of Judea . . . and Pharisees came . . . to test him"). In interweaving his sources, did Mark likewise here propel this *entire* episode involving the Galilean Pharisees just barely across the Judean border (in 10:2)? Or did Mark here instead simply insert solely "Pharisees" into this Judea story—mirroring his insertion into 7:1 of scribes who came "down from Jerusalem [into Galilee]"? For like scribes, Pharisees "are always present when the editor needs them . . . as typical participants in debate,"[20] meaning that Mark could himself have introduced Pharisees into the divorce pronouncement (along with their characteristic aim "to test" Jesus; cf. 8:11) just as Mark introduced scribes into 9:14: "they saw a great crowd . . . and *scribes* arguing with them."

More taxing still is how to assess 8:11, 15, replete with Jesus' caution to the disciples to "beware . . . the leaven of the Pharisees and the leaven of Herod" (or "the Herodians"). All these miscellaneous texts, just noted, I label (in Figure 4.2) "*editorial* touches outside the clusters."

Solving All Ten Anomalies

Only Winter's theory—once it is upgraded in the fashion proposed—contributes to the resolution of all ten idiosyncrasies, our core concern.

[1] *Explaining the Amorphous Titles*—Mark, c. 71 CE, was not himself sufficiently familiar with who the Jewish leadership groups had been during Jesus' own day. Some titles that he received from the three earlier strata were amorphous constructs that he simply drew into his Gospel and left undefined.

[2] *Explaining the Two Profiles for "Scribes"*—Mark had two discrete strata for "scribes" that, respectively, offered radically contrasting profiles—which Mark dutifully incorporated but without attempting to reconcile them.

[3] *Explaining the Groups' Artificial Compartmentalization*—Mark imported a primitive Passion stratum bequeathing him *solely* chief priests + scribes + elders and a later collection bequeathing him *solely* Pharisees + Herodians. He left these camps unintegrated.

[4] *Explaining the Two Links of Scribes and Pharisees*—The irregularities in 2:16 and 7:1, 5 arose from Mark's introduction of scribes into what originally were solely Pharisee pericopes. The variant readings in 2:16 (scribes "*of the* Pharisees"; "*and* the Pharisees") resulted from this conflation, possibly from copyists' own confusion over Mark's odd departure from his rigid compartmentalization elsewhere. Evidently himself confused, Matthew simply dropped "scribes from Jerusalem" in his parallel 9:11 text—presenting Pharisees alone!

What, then, of Acts 23:9: "some of the scribes *of the Pharisees' party*" at Paul's trial? If Luke here (likewise in Luke 5:30) was relying on a "scribes *of the* Pharisees" reading from his primary source, Mark 2:16,[21] then our recourse to Acts 23:9 is circular reasoning. The same is true with claims, likewise predicated on Acts 23:9, that scribes were the Pharisees' intellectual elite or that Sadducees also had scribes. Further, we can readily surmise *why* Luke invented his odd Sanhedrin formulation.[22]

[5] *Explaining the Groups' Relative Lack of Independence*—This is a byproduct of the groups' being hemmed in by their radically compartmentalized camps; also of their lack of independence in the source strata themselves.

[6] *Explaining the Absence of Pharisees from the Passion*—Mark's early Passion tradition featured chief priests + scribes + elders but *not Pharisees*. Solely this factor accounts for the Pharisees' absence from Mark's Passion. Although Winter's strata theory fully solves this problem, in a lapse of judgment Winter instead capitalized on the Pharisees' absence to absolve them from involvement in Jesus' death.

[7] *Explaining How to Differentiate between Scribes and Pharisees*—scribes and Pharisees never appeared *together* in any one of Mark's three strata. The two earlier strata on "scribes" (the primitive Passion tradition and scribes-alone material) never mentioned "Pharisees"; the last stratum featuring "Pharisees" never mentioned "scribes." Thereby Mark passed on to Matthew and Luke *two* groups that could essentially even have been one-and-the-same societal element. (Is the following analogy apt: certain rabbinic traditions similarly seem to preserve *sopherim* ["scribes"] as an earlier term for *perushim* ["Pharisees"]?[23])

This would also explain first why Matthew so regularly bracketed "scribes, Pharisees, hypocrites!" (chapter 23); namely, he could not determine *from Mark* how these two elements differed. Second, it explains why Matthew, when copying Mark, sometimes omitted scribes altogether.[24] Likewise stymied, Luke at least opted for what both groups seemed to share *in common*—they were "lawyers" (10:25; 11:46, 52); "teachers of the law" (5:17; Acts 5:34). Winter's zeal to defend the Pharisees precluded his acceptance of Luke's solution: Mark's use of scribes implied their commonality with Pharisees, not divergence from them.[25]

[8] *Explaining the Disproportionate Frequency of Scribal Appearances*—
Scribes are the only group whom Mark accessed from *two* strata, this alone
perhaps explaining their inordinate frequency of appearance in his Gospel.
Further, of the primitive Passion triad, scribes were the only Judean element
(cf. the nondescript elders) affording Mark leeway to maneuver them into
Galilee by the simple specification (3:22; 7:1) that they "came down from
Jerusalem." Such editorial additions increased further the scribes' relative fre-
quency of appearance.

[9] *Explaining Odd Segues, Placements, Seams*—Mark 3:6 and 12:34b
betray Mark's untidy editorial intersecting and interweaving of two source
strata (Winter's Intermediate and Last). Sensing that something was
amiss with 3:6, Albertz mistook its premature crescendo ("the Pharisees
. . . held counsel with the Herodians . . . how to destroy him") as exposing
the *end* of an underlying pre-Markan collection. But Easton processed the
matter correctly: the Healing of the Man's Withered Hand was originally
continued by the Pharisee + Herodian episode of the Tribute to Caesar
(12:13-17).

Yet Easton himself did not realize how the Tribute pericope must originally have ended with 12:34b ("no one dared to ask him any question"). For
here, blatantly, Mark had two more "questions" he wanted to *slip in* before
he ended the Tribute pericope with the content of 12:34b. Since Mark had
"questions" by the Sadducees (12:18-23) and by the scribe (12:28), he put
12:34b *on hold* until it could end the Great Commandment pericope even
though *there* it is glaringly unsuitable—depicting listeners as not *daring* to
ask more questions despite the unique air of camaraderie pervading this
single tradition. Easton also did not recognize that 3:6 could originally
have culminated all these matters as now loosely sequenced by Figure 4.7
(abridged).

FIGURE 4.7: VERSES AS ORIGINALLY SEQUENCED?

3:5 . . . his hand was restored. 12:13 And they sent to him some of the Pharisees
and some of the Herodians, to entrap him in his talk. . . . He said . . . , 12:17 . . .
"Render to Caesar the things that are Caesar's, and to God the things that are
God's." And they were amazed at him. 12:34b **And after that no one *dared* to
ask him any question. 3:6 The Pharisees . . . held counsel with the Herodians
against him, how to destroy him.**

---

[10] *Explaining the Clustering of Group Appearances*—This circumstance
is consistent with Winter's thesis that the leadership groups were drawn
from different pre-Markan strata identifiable by the group titles employed.

Sobering Ramifications for Jewish-Christian Relations

This essay, while necessarily speculative, should nonetheless give readers cause for pause, for it proposes what may be the only reasonably plausible reconstruction that can account for all ten Markan anomalies in presenting the Jewish leaders vis-à-vis Jesus. The foregoing effort is further justified because of the far-reaching historical ramifications of the topic: early Christian traditions of Jewish enmity toward Jesus, a *fellow* Jew.

I do not deny that Jesus engaged in controversies with Jewish authorities. Assuredly, however, we cannot confidently accept as historically accurate the disputations as Mark himself narrates them, for he inspires no confidence that he knows enough about any of the six Jewish leadership groups as they functioned in Jesus' day but, instead, appears to co-opt materials that he does not fully enough command.

To the extent that Matthew and Luke depend on Mark for these narrative materials, they perpetuate Mark's fundamental rendition, and likely—by adding their own improvisations—even further contort Mark's own questionable reportage. Historians should thus realize that what Mark set into motion contributed disproportionately to horrendous consequences for the Jewish people extending even into the current day. This essay, then, extends and deepens my contention (in other studies)[26] that we must deem Mark *the* pivotal Gospel if we are most fundamentally to comprehend the generative process of Christian anti-Judaism.

CHAPTER FIVE

Viewing the Jewish Jesus of History through the Lens of Matthew's Gospel

Donald Senior, C.P.

In July 2009, I had the pleasure of presiding at the Colloquium Biblicum Lovanienses, the venerable international biblical meeting that each year brings scholars from around the world to the Catholic University of Louvain, Belgium, to explore biblical topics of interest. The theme of the 2009 meeting was "The Gospel of Matthew: At the Crossroads of Early Christianity."[1] The term *crossroads* referred primarily to the intersection of Jewish and Gentile Christianity in the first century of the Christian era. Observers have long noted paradoxical features of this Gospel: while portraying the Jewish leaders in an aggressively hostile light, Matthew also portrays Jesus in strongly Jewish tones.

A conviction of many of the participants at the colloquium was that a new paradigm was now guiding research on this Gospel. Matthew was no longer viewed by most interpreters as having definitively cut its ties with Judaism and turned to the gentile world, but was a Gospel emanating from a community still self-identifying with Judaism, even if experiencing strained relations with dominant Jewish groups because of its views about the religious authority of Jesus. Some, in a related position, would claim that Matthew's Gospel originated in a community that seemed to stand astride two worlds, maintaining deep and abiding roots in Judaism, yet now was entering more deeply into the gentile world. Donald Hagner describes well part of that ambivalence. Although Hagner believes that Matthew's community had already severed its ties with Judaism, he finds evidence that Matthew's Christians were still caught "between two loyalties, like people simultaneously holding passports from two countries at war. They were torn between their Jewish kinfolk on the one hand and Gentile Christians on the other, wanting to reach back for continuity with the old and at the same time to reach forward to the new work God was doing in the largely Gentile church—answerable at the same time, so to speak, both to Jews and Gentiles."[2] Similarly Dennis Duling has used the notion of "marginality" to describe Matthew's situation. One experience of "marginality" is that of the person who is "condemned to live in two different, antagonistic cultural worlds, but does not fully belong to either."[3]

One fundamental conviction of virtually all the participants was that, while Matthew's interaction with its Roman context is an interest of some recent scholarship, the relationship of the Gospel to Judaism remains its fundamental and essential context.[4]

At the outset, it must be conceded that Matthew's Gospel is a thoroughly Christian document, written to a Christian community or a series of communities[5] whose membership was probably a majority Jewish Christian with a minority of gentile Christians joining in increasing numbers, possibly in a major Greco-Roman city outside Palestine such as Antioch (although other interpreters prefer a Palestinian Jewish origin), and probably written sometime after the cataclysmic events of the Jewish revolt and the subsequent destruction of the Jerusalem temple in 70 CE.[6]

The most plausible scenario from my point of view—one shared with many other students of this Gospel—is that the traditions forming this Gospel developed in a Jewish Christian setting originating in the Galilee region and moving north and east along the Syro-Palestine corridor, not unlike the community that would have produced the collection of Jesus' sayings now identified as the Q source.[7] Then at a key juncture in its evolution, Matthew's community, with its emphasis on the teachings of Jesus, would have encountered Mark's Gospel with its strong focus on the narrative of Jesus' deeds and, especially, its focus on the Passion of Jesus. From this developing tradition would emerge what was in effect a new "edition" of Mark's Gospel, what we now call the Gospel of Matthew, which blends the narrative focus of Mark with the rich teaching tradition of the Q source. All of this would be taking place during a turbulent and dynamic period in the life of the early Church, when it, along with emergent rabbinic Judaism, was dealing with the trauma of the Jewish revolt, the loss of the temple, and the collective effort to forge a new form of Judaism in the wake of the loss of both priesthood and temple and the leading elites who had dominated pre-70 Judaism.

Therefore the encounter with Judaism in Matthew's Gospel represents the polemical context of post-70 as much as it does the context of Jesus' own times and context. The contents of the Gospel in both its portrayal of Jesus and his teaching as well as his sharp critique of the Jewish leaders was part of an effort to establish the legitimacy of its Jewish Christian perspective by emphasizing Jesus' continuity with Jewish history and tradition, on the one hand, and by an attempt, on the other, to de-legitimize opponents of Jesus as lacking integrity (even as Matthew has to acknowledge their authority! See Matt. 23:1-2).

Yet, at the same time, I am convinced that there is much to learn about the historical Jesus through the lens of Matthew's Gospel. Matthew's portrayal of Jesus in such emphatic Jewish tones, the subjects of the controversies over interpretation of the law between Jesus and his opponents, the passing descriptions of Jewish life and customs that are part of the Gospel narrative—all of these and more offer contact points with the historical circumstances of Jesus in his own context. It is some of these leads that I would like to focus on in this chapter.

The Jewish Context of the Gospel Narrative

We can note at the outset that Matthew's Gospel and the traditions that stand behind it provide background information about first-century Judaism and its geographical and historical context.[8] Matthew's Gospel provides us with a fairly complete roster of the major characters and geographical and institutional settings in play in the early part of first-century Palestinian Judaism. We learn of the general topography of Israel: the northern region of Galilee and the significant role of the "Sea" of Galilee in the life and economy of the area and its contrast with Jerusalem and Judea with the dominant role of the temple and its priests and elders; we get glimpses of the Judean wilderness and the Jordan river, the scene of the ministry of John the Baptist. We become aware of other areas beyond the boundary of Israel such as the region of Tyre and Sidon and the region of the Decapolis on the eastern side of the lake. We learn of the presence of villages and towns, including the key role that Capernaum played in the public ministry of Jesus (Matthew, like the other Gospels, has no reference to larger cities such as Sepphoris or Tiberias in connection with Jesus' mission). We learn of travel down the Jordan valley, through Jericho and up to Jerusalem.

While some of the views ascribed to Jesus' opponents may be anachronistic (for example, the stereotyping of the Pharisees as uniformly hypocritical and hostile), we nevertheless learn about Herod and his sons, Herod Antipas and Herod Phillip (including the cruel and ill-fated Archelaus), as well as Roman officials such as Pilate and military figures such as the centurion of Capernaum. We meet Pharisees, Sadducees, priests (including the high priest Caiaphas), elders, lawyers, and synagogue administrators. We see a picture of the ordinary population: farmers, village dwellers, unemployed day laborers, fishermen, toll collectors, soldiers, wedding guests, and banquets. We get glimpses of the ordinary diet: wine, grain, fruits, and vegetables. We also encounter a long list of maladies that affect the people: blindness, deafness, paralysis, chronic fevers, mental illness, and childhood death. We hear of synagogue life in the villages and sense great reverence and awe, along with some ambivalence, about the magnificent Jerusalem temple build by Herod the Great.

While this cultural matrix might not directly illumine our understanding of Jesus the man, it should not be ignored. It confirms that the roots of the Gospel narrative originated not in some vaguely defined part of the Greco-Roman world but in the land of Israel and in a thoroughly Palestinian Jewish social, economic, and political context of the first half of the first century and therefore gives us some idea of the circumstances of Jesus' life and mission.

There are other features of Matthew's Gospel that may enable us to glimpse further aspects of the historical Jesus in his Jewish setting.

Restoring the Jewish Context of Jesus' Mission

Under the assumption that Matthew used the Gospel of Mark as a major source—an assumption still widely subscribed to in contemporary gospel studies—there is clear evidence that Matthew "re-introduces" Jewish perspectives missing in Mark's account. Admittedly this may be because Matthew's own community had a more Jewish character than that of Mark's Gospel, which may have had a Roman provenance.[9] While Matthew's Gospel uses Mark's account as a primary source, this does not mean, however, that the community that stands behind Matthew's Gospel did not have access to traditions that would antedate Mark's account. The so-called "Q" source, for example, would almost certainly be prior to Mark and would have deep roots in Palestinian Judaism.

The net effect is that Matthew's account in effect provides a more historically probable setting for Jesus' teaching and ministry.

Several examples come to mind. In the keynote text of Matt. 5:17, for example, the Matthean Jesus affirms that he has not come "to destroy the law or the prophets but to fulfill them." This text as it stands within the setting of the Sermon on the Mount is probably a Matthean creation, yet Matthew emphasizes on more than one occasion that Jesus' disputes about law over Sabbath observance or purity laws are not about whether the law is valid or not—an inconceivable position for a first-century Jew—but rather are disputes about the *interpretation* of the law. Furthermore, the Jesus of Matthew's Gospel exhibits reverence and respect for Jewish institutions even as on another level he directs criticism toward them. For example, while excoriating the Jewish religious leaders for their hypocrisy, the Matthean Jesus admonishes his disciples to respect and obey the leaders "because they sit on

Moses' seat" (Matt. 23:1-3). And even though Matthew depicts Jesus disrupting the temple activities, it is clearly presented as a defense of the sacredness of the temple. Matthew also omits Mark's enigmatic reference to Jesus' stopping all activity (Mark 11:16), a reference that in Mark's perspective may signal the end of temple sacrifice.[10] In the trial before the high priest Caiaphas, Matthew once again subtly alters Mark's version of the accusation against Jesus, omitting Mark's reference to a "temple made by hands" and substituting the more reverential "the temple of God" (Matt. 26:61).

The Primacy of the Mission to Israel

Here is another example where Matthew's narrative restores a more Jewish perspective on the narrative of Mark. In Mark's account, Jesus clearly and intentionally extends his mission beyond the boundaries of Israel to encounter gentiles, as in the story of the Syrophonecian woman where Jesus goes to the region of Tyre and Sidon and encounters this gentile woman and her sick daughter (Mark 7:24-30)[11] or in the extended story of Jesus' crossing over the Sea of Galilee to the region of Decapolis where he encounters a tormented gentile demoniac (Mark 5:1-20). In contrast, Matthew mutes both of these instances consistent with the Gospel's clear affirmation of the historical priority of the mission to Israel.

For example, at the beginning of the mission discourse in 10:5, the Matthean Jesus instructs his twelve apostles "Go nowhere among the Gentiles and enter no town of the Samaritans, but go rather to the lost sheep of the house of Israel." This emphatic statement is repeated in the story of Jesus' encounter with the Canaanite woman (Matt. 15:21-28; the woman is designated a "Greek, a Syrophoenician, a Greek" in Mark's version). Here the Matthean Jesus, in contrast to Mark's version, appears not to cross over into the region of Tyre and Sidon and instead this gentile woman comes out to him (Matt. 15:22). And in the encounter itself, the Matthean Jesus is much more emphatic about the primacy of the mission to Israel than in Mark's version ("I was sent only to the lost sheep of the house of Israel," 15:24) before finally giving way to the active faith of this woman on behalf of her child.

Similarly, in Mark's narrative of the Gadarene demoniac, the movement of Jesus across the sea of Galilee to the Decapolis region is a dramatic presentation that includes an encounter with the man named *Legio* living among the tombs, the presence of a herd of pigs, and Jesus' commissioning the man freed from the demon to go among his own people and proclaim the gospel (see Mark 5:1-20)—making this in effect the beginning of the mission to the gentiles embedded within the Gospel story itself. In Matthew, although some of the dramatic elements remain, the story is much briefer and greatly muted (see Matt. 8:28-34) with no mention of the Decapolis or any commissioning of or even any exchange with the two demoniacs who are liberated by Jesus.

In Matthew's Gospel there are indeed hints or anticipations of the mission to the gentiles (see, for example, the magi who come to honor the infant Jesus, the centurion of Capernaum, and the Canaanite woman) and the Gospel will conclude with the risen Christ commissioning his disciples to go "to all nations" (28:16-20). Matthew's Gospel, therefore, clearly endorses the gentile mission in which his community was beginning to engage, but he also makes clear that during his lifetime, in his own setting, Jesus' mission was to his own people Israel—a portrayal that is historically probable and one that has the effect of reinforcing the Jewish context of Jesus' mission.[12]

Jesus' Interpretation of Law

There is no doubt that the historical Jesus' relationship to the Jewish Law is a complex question. In the fourth volume of his massive study of the historical Jesus, *A Marginal Jew*, John Meier tackles this question, and I would like to use his work as a way of entering into this formidable topic.[13]

Meier focuses on several key law issues—each of them, by the way, found prominently in Matthew's Gospel: divorce, oaths, Sabbath observance, purity laws, and the love commandments. He notes at the outset that a major part of the difficulty is not only determining the position of the historical Jesus on these issues but also determining, as it were, the positions of the "historical Torah", that is, what was the prevailing interpretation of law on these questions in the first part of the first century of the common era?[14] Meier's study tackles both questions in an attempt to come to conclusions that are not influenced by later Christian theological concerns.

In the instances of Jesus' interpretation of the law concerning Sabbath observance or purity laws presented in Matthew's Gospel, Meier finds Jesus' view fully compatible with that of his contemporaries. Clearly the Jesus presented in the Gospel of Matthew does not speak disparagingly of Sabbath observance. Matthean Jesus tells his disciples to pray that in the chaos of the endtime that they would not have to flee "in winter or on a Sabbath" (Matt. 24:20). The conflicts in the Gospel about Sabbath observance have to do, in Matthew's versions of the stories, with interpretation of what might constitute a violation of the Sabbath—not the fundamental command to revere the Sabbath. For example, in the controversy about plucking grain on the Sabbath (Matt. 12:1-8), Jesus defends his disciples' actions by appealing to the text of Hosea 6:6. Similarly, in the story of the healing of the man with a withered hand on the Sabbath, Jesus defends his action by claiming it is "lawful to do good on the Sabbath" (Matt. 12:9-14). Meier believes that most of the disputes between Jesus and his opponents depicted in these stories should be attributed to the early church and its conflict with rabbinic

Judaism and that Jesus himself conformed fully with Sabbath observance in his own setting.[15]

In the instance of the purity laws, most of Jesus' conflicts with his opponents in the Gospel of Matthew have to do with accusations about their "hypocrisy" and lack of integrity rather than a rejection of the purity laws themselves. In Matthew's version of Jesus' conflict with the Pharisees and scribes about observance of tradition concerning the purity laws concerning food, Jesus lashes out at his opponents for their disregard of the law of God and their insincerity, but Matthew omits the sweeping declaration found in Mark 7:19: "Thus he declared all foods clean." It is likely that Matthew's Jewish Christian community continued to observe the purity laws regarding food. The sharp polemics in these stories, as Meier concludes, also stem from the tension between Matthew's post-resurrection Jewish Christian community and the dominant majority Jewish majority led by the Pharisees.[16] But when all is said and done, Matthew's portrayal of a Jesus who respects these basic Jewish institutions is historically accurate.

However, in the case of Jesus' prohibition of divorce and remarriage found in Matt. 5:31-32 and repeated in 19:3-9, Meier believes this is an instance in which the teaching of the historical Jesus—accurately retained in Matthew's Gospel—is more rigorous than the prevailing interpretation of the law in Judaism contemporary to Jesus or, put more bluntly, contravenes a step permitted by the law.[17] The apparent exception phrase "except for unchastity" (Matt. 5:32 and 19:9) is, in the view of many interpreters, not a pastoral adaptation in the case of infidelity but a Matthean reference to marriage within forbidden bloodlines which rendered the marriage invalid in the first place. Such a warning may have been directed particularly at gentile converts who were entering the community in such circumstances and who would be required to sever their invalid marriage ties to conform with Jesus' teaching. Here the prophetic and eschatological tone of Jesus' teaching requires conformity in this lifetime to the condition that would prevail in the age to come—a condition established by God at creation. But because the Israelites were wounded by their "hardness of heart," Moses was led to permit divorce (see Matt. 19:8).

Meier finds a similar case of departure from the prevailing view of the law in Jesus' absolute prohibition of oaths (Matt. 5:33-37; see also 23:16-22).[18] However, in this instance Jesus' prohibition is in harmony with the concern about frivolous oaths found in some post-exilic Jewish traditions and in Philo.[19] Similarly, there are other instances in which the apparently singularity of Jesus' rigorous moral stances, such as the teaching on lust in Matt. 5:27-30, where looking at a woman with lust is equivalent to a man "already committing adultery with her in his heart," or the danger of anger and alienation for human relationships and the need for reconciliation (Matt.

5:21-26), resonate with exhortations found in other rabbinic literature on the dangers of a wandering eye or unbridled anger if not expressed with the same rigor as Jesus' teaching.[20]

Meier spends considerable time on the question of Jesus' teaching about the love commandment. There are several instances of this in Matthew's Gospel. Meier rules out the famous "Golden Rule" in Matt. 7:12 as an authentic saying of Jesus ("In everything do to others as you would have them do to you; for this is the law and the prophets"), considering it a traditional proverb found already in Greek culture. Matthew adapts the saying to the Gospel context by the addition of the phrase "for this is the law and the prophets."

However, in two instances Meier detects in Matthean texts the authentic sayings of the historical Jesus concerning the love commandments. The first of these is the well-known and often discussed "love of enemies" text found in Matt. 5:43-48: "You have heard that it was said, 'You shall love your neighbor and hate your enemy.' But I say to you, Love your enemies and pray for those who persecute you, so that you may be children of your father in heaven; for he makes his sun rise on the evil and on the good, and sends rain on the righteous and on the unrighteous." After combing through various segments of ancient literature (the Old Testament; Qumran; Greco-Roman moral philosophers; Philo; rabbinic texts; etc.), Meier concludes that no clear parallel exists to this saying of Jesus in ancient literature and, therefore, on the principle of "discontinuity" believes that this saying should be attributed to the historical Jesus. Meier also notes that its blunt, provocative style harmonizes with the rhetorical style of other authentic teaching of Jesus.[21]

It should be noted that Matthew's Gospel places this saying in a climactic position within the Sermon of the Mount. It comes at the end of the series of so-called antitheses or preferably "contrast statements" found in 5:21-48, which in effect illustrate the meaning of Jesus' teaching about the "greater righteousness" demanded of the disciples (5:20) and contrast Jesus' teaching with other more traditional or alternate interpretations.[22] After a number of such contrasts dealing with anger, alienation, lust, divorce, oaths, and retaliation for injury, Jesus' teaching about righteousness culminates in the love of enemy command. Love of one's enemy brings one's actions into harmony with God's own manner of acting, which is benevolent even to the evil and unrighteous. Thus the disciple is asked to become "perfect . . . as your heavenly Father is perfect" (Matt. 5:48).[23]

One other prime example of the love command is found in the conflict story of Matt. 22:34-40. In an encounter with a lawyer belonging to the Pharisee party, Jesus is "tested" with a question about which commandment in the law is the greatest. Matthew draws this story from his primary source, Mark, but changes it significantly. In Mark's version (Mark 12:28-34) it is not a story of Jesus' conflict with his opponents; rather, a "scribe" who is taken with Jesus' teaching during a dispute puts to Jesus a sincere question, "Which commandment is the first of all?" Jesus then responds with the twofold commandment of love of God and love of neighbor, to which the scribe—in agreement with Jesus' teaching—adds "this is much more important than all whole burnt-offerings and sacrifices" (Mark 12:33), an answer that is commended by Jesus.

In Matthew's version, however, the challenge offered by the lawyer who is testing Jesus draws from him the teaching on the twofold command—similar to that found in Mark—but Jesus concludes not with a reference to sacrifice as the scribe in Mark does but with the legal principle: "On these two commandments hang all the law and the prophets" (Matt. 22:40). Although Matthew has framed Jesus' teaching as a conflict story in a manner typical of his Gospel, Meier believes that the core teaching of the controversy reflects a saying of the historical Jesus.[24] Drawing on fundamental texts of the Hebrew Scriptures, for example, the command to love God from Deuteronomy 6:5 and the command to love one's neighbor from Leviticus 19:18, the distinctive contribution of Jesus was to bind these two commandments together as the single fundamental principle of law interpretation. Once again, Meier draws on the principle of "discontinuity" to make his case. While the two components of the love command are based on Old Testament texts, these texts are not cited again in the whole of the Old Testament nor are they ever bound together in other parallel literature such as Qumran, Philo, or early rabbinic literature. Meier also observes that both these distinctive expressions of Jesus love commandments (for example, love of enemies and the twofold love commandment) are not repeated as such in the rest of the New Testament as well![25]

Throughout his multi-volume study of the historical Jesus, Meier is extremely hesitant to assign to Jesus' mission some grand synthesis or overarching motif. The fragmentary evidence we have about the historical Jesus, he claims, does not permit such a synthesis. Moreover, Meier believes that Jesus was a prophetic and charismatic figure rather than a systematic or philosophical one. His teaching was provocative and intuitive rather than deduced from a grand principle. Yet in the instance of the love commandments Meier believes one comes as close as possible to what was the fundamental stance of Jesus' overall teaching. Love, mercy, and compassion as expressions of how Jesus understood the nature of God's own relationship to Israel is a basic feature of the historical Jesus' teachings and actions—a feature not in any way antithetical to the broader stream of Jewish tradition yet pressed with singular intensity and force by Jesus of Nazareth.[26]

Such a conclusion fits into Meier's overall assessment of the historical Jesus as a "marginal Jew"—someone thoroughly within the broad range of first-century Judaism yet whose prophetic teaching, intense healing activity, and personal claims to unique moral authority placed him on the margins of the dominant perspectives of his contemporaries. While, as I will note below, Matthew's Gospel has its own post-resurrection theological perspective, at the same time its portrayal of Jesus' interpretation of the law substantially coincides with the carefully nuanced conclusions that Meier and others have drawn concerning the relationship of Jesus' teaching to more mainline Jewish teaching contemporary with Jesus.

Encountering the Difference

Our focus to this point has been on demonstrating the fundamental Jewish character of the Jesus portrayed in Matthew's Gospel and that, in many instances, this portrayal is likely to give us at least a glimpse of the historical Jesus in his Jewish setting.

However, on another fundamental level the portrayal of Jesus in Matthew's Gospel seems to sharply diverge from its Jewish moorings. Matthew's Gospel has a "high" Christology, portraying Jesus as bearing an exalted and unprecedented identity and religious authority. For example, the Gospel ascribes to Jesus an array of traditional titles drawn in most instances from the Hebrew Scriptures and Jewish tradition but taking on new meaning in the confessional context of the Gospel and the Christian faith that underlies the Gospel.

At the outset of Matthew's Gospel, Jesus is proclaimed as "Son of Abraham" and "Son of David" (1:1), reaffirming through these titles and the genealogy that follows (1:2-18) his profound roots in Jewish history. But the reader soon learns that Jesus' conception is not by human means but through the power of the Holy Spirit, as announced to Joseph by an angel (1:20). Matthew clearly identifies Jesus as the "Christ" throughout the Gospel narrative (see, for example, the opening verse 1:1 and Peter's dramatic confession of Jesus in 16:16), but in the Gospel's perspective his identity exceeds the messianic expectations of Israel. He is given the name "Jesus" because he will save his people from their sins and the name "Emmanuel" because he is "God-with-us" (1:21, 23). He is declared to be the "Son of God" in a manner that both subsumes the traditional royal understanding of this term in the Jewish Scriptures (see the enthronement Psalm 110—"You are my son, this day I have begotten you") and transcends it. Jesus as Son of God rejects the assault of Satan in his desert test (4:1-11), is able to walk on the water and calm the force of nature (14:22-33; 8:23-27), enjoys unique intimacy with the Father (11:25-27), and at the moment of his triumph over death is acclaimed as Son of God by the Roman soldiers who oversee his crucifixion (27:54). Jesus is also the "Son of Man," a designation drawn from the apocalyptic literature of Judaism (see, for example, Dan. 7:13) but used in the Gospels to describe both the humiliation of Jesus in his sufferings and death and the promise of his triumphant return at the end of time as judge and savior (Matt. 24-25; 28:16-20). Among the array of confessional titles used by Matthew to describe the religious identity of Jesus is also the term *Lord* (*kurios*) which, drawing on the Septuagint translation for the divine name, is found in the confession by Peter and the disciples of Jesus' divine power (see especially, Matt. 14:28).

Through this array of titles and additionally through the extraordinary exorcisms, healings, and other miracles of Jesus (including the multiplication of the loaves, healing at a distance, and his power over nature in calming the storm and walking on water), Matthew and his community ascribe to Jesus a unique identity, one unprecedented in Jewish tradition. While miracles are ascribed to Elijah and Elisha, they do not match the profusion and marvelous character of the wonders ascribed to Jesus in the Gospels (see the array summarized by the Matthean Jesus in 11:4-6). Jesus is, in the confessional assertions of Matthew's Gospel, a human being imbued with the divine presence; he is Emmanuel, God-with-us, upon whom "all power in heaven and on earth" has been bestowed (28:16-20). For Matthew—as well as for early Christianity as a whole—it is this identity of Jesus that is the basis for his authority as teacher. The Jesus who ascends the mountain in Matthew's Gospel to deliver the Sermon on the Mount (4:23—5:1) is not simply an extraordinary prophetic teacher in the manner of a Moses or Elijah but the longed for Messiah and Savior of Israel and, even more, the embodiment of the divine presence. The Jesus who defends his interpretation of the Sabbath law is not simply a wise and compassionate teacher but the "Lord of the Sabbath" (12:8).

Clearly this theology, or Christology, of Matthew's Gospel represents a post-resurrection perspective, the context in which the Gospel was written and the fundamental purpose of the Gospel's message to the Christian community. We are obviously dealing here with the Christ of faith and not simply the Jesus of history. But a key question—particularly for a Christian audience—is to what extent one can find continuity between the person and mission of the historical Jesus and the profound religious identity ascribed to him by Christian faith as in Matthew's Gospel? One key element within the perspective of Christian faith is belief in the resurrection of Jesus, a reality that is by definition meta-historical even though belief in the resurrection has had profound historical consequences (for example, the creation of the Christian church). Beyond that is there some degree of compatibility between what can be glimpsed of the historical Jesus and the identity ascribed to him in the post-resurrection Christian community?

This is a question that takes us beyond the scope of this work but it remains a question of importance not only for Christian faith but also for the implications of the search for the historical Jesus. Those Christian interpreters who do believe that there is a level of continuity between the historical Jesus and the Christ of faith—as I do—would find suggestive points of contact in such aspects of the historical Jesus as the cogency and beauty of his ethical teaching, his unquestioned integrity, his power as a charismatic healer, his apparent sense of personal authority, the intensity of his piety, his prophetic role and spiritual intuition, the impact that he had on his followers, and the sharp resistance to his teaching and appeal by some religious authorities and by the Romans themselves that ultimately led to his death.

In this array of characteristics should also be added what appears to have been the historical Jesus' association with those on the margins of society— the sick, the poor, the socially despised (for example, tax and toll collectors, what Matthew's Gospel calls "the lost sheep of the house of Israel"; 10:6; 15:24), and even the occasional gentile (e.g., the Centurion of Capernaum; the Canaanite woman). This at once inclusive and expansive dimension of Jesus' mission not only appears in the Gospel stories of such encounters but is a recurring motif of Jesus' parables and sayings.[27] This should not be seen as a point of negative contrast with Jewish tradition—one that in fact classically emphasizes compassion toward the "widow, the orphan, and the stranger"—but nevertheless as an emphatic quality of the historical Jesus. Later Christian reflection, including that of Matthew's Gospel, would see in this the foundation of the later post-Easter Christian mission to the gentiles already anticipated or signaled in the mission of Jesus himself.[28] This is especially emphasized by Matthew's Gospel, as noted above. Matthew's narrative intentionally confines the mission of the earthly Jesus to Israel, with only occasional encounters with gentiles; it is only the Risen Christ at the dramatic conclusion of the Gospel who commissions his apostles to bring the message of Jesus to "all nations" (see Matt. 28:16-20).

While Matthew's Gospel portrays Jesus in profound theological and christological hues, nevertheless I believe it is possible to detect through the lens of this Gospel points of contact with the historical Jesus (such as those described above) whose personal history and the impact of his mission provoked in some of his contemporaries a credible basis for subsequent Christian faith.[29]

Conclusions and Reflections

Our review of Matthew's Gospel suggests some conclusions that I believe are of consequence for the ongoing dialogue between Jews and Christians concerning the historical Jesus.

First of all, Matthew's Gospel gives strong testimony to the thoroughly Jewish character of Jesus and to the abiding Jewish context of early Christianity. While conceding that Matthew's Gospel is a Christian document written from the perspective of Christian faith and addressed to a Christian audience, at the same time a careful reading of this Gospel provides leads to the historical circumstances of Jesus and his mission within the context of first-century Palestinian Judaism. The human Jesus glimpsed in Matthew's Gospel is a devout Jew whose life and mission were confined to the land of Israel, whose origin was in Galilee, who reverenced the Jerusalem temple even as he may have been critical of some of its attendant activities and ultimate destiny, who drew his inspiration from the Jewish Scriptures and the examples of great Jewish historical characters, whose mission was directed to the renewal and reform of his own people, a mission that began in the shadow of John the Baptist (himself a historically attested Jewish prophet), who was an eloquent teacher in the rabbinic style (parables, stories, wisdom sayings), who was viewed by many of his contemporaries as a prophet and charismatic healer, whose claims to authority and the provocative nature of his teaching (particularly some aspects of his law interpretation) and mission undoubtedly produced some degree of conflict with other religious factions of his day, and who, in the tension of Judean Roman rule, ultimately came under scrutiny of the Roman authorities and was arrested and executed by crucifixion.

Matthew's community, written later from the vantage point of Christian faith in Jesus as the risen Christ and Son of God, views Jesus as much more than this bare historical sketch. Yet, at the same time, Matthew's Gospel firmly maintains the Jewish character of Jesus and his mission, stresses continuity with the traditions and history of Judaism, and defends its convictions as a legitimate—indeed the most valid—expression of Jewish faith. Even as the Matthean community finds itself at a profound transition point in early Christian history, with increasing numbers of gentiles entering the community, it presents a brand of Christianity that retains a strong Jewish character. And although this is debated by some interpreters, I believe that the turn to the gentiles at the conclusion of Matthew's Gospel ("Go to all nations. . . ." Matt. 28:19) did not negate on Matthew's part the ongoing mission to Israel. Although being the object of the Christian mission may not be a welcome affirmation of Matthew's Gospel for contemporary Judaism, it nevertheless indicates the continuing attachment to his Jewish roots and community on the part of the first-century evangelist.

The context in which Matthew's Gospel was written, that is, at a turbulent time of transition in the wake of the Jewish revolt and the destruction of the Jerusalem temple—and the impact that these events had on both Judaism and early Christianity—helps put into context the hostility found in the Gospel concerning the religious authorities. The sharp polemic of Matthew's Gospels, such as the condemnations of the scribes and Pharisees found in chapter 23 or the assigning of major responsibility for the death of Jesus to the Jerusalem religious leaders, stem as much from this context of tension between early Jewish Christianity and emergent rabbinic Judaism as it does from the conflicts the historical Jesus may have had with his contemporaries. In some traditional interpretations of the Gospel of Matthew (as well as of other New Testament texts), the negative portrayal of the Jewish religious leaders and Jesus' condemnation of them were seen as driving a wedge between Jesus and his Jewish context, and led to a caricature of first-century Judaism. Biblical scholarship over the past few decades has made major strides in correcting such stereotypes of first-century Judaism, appreciating its diversity and varied contexts as well as rethinking the complexity of its relationship to the emergence of Jewish Christianity.[30]

Finally, focusing on the Jewish character of the historical Jesus through the lens of Matthew's Gospel, which is the focus of this essay, also lays bare the strong christological perspective of this Gospel. Dialogue between Judaism and Christianity that takes place in a spirit of mutual trust and respect has to contend with our differences as well as with our commonalities. When all is said and done the fundamental difference between contemporary Judaism and Christianity is not a dispute about the Jewish character of the historical Jesus but the ultimate identity and mission attributed to Jesus by orthodox Christian faith.[31] Understanding this gives the proper perspective, it seems to me, to the dialogue between contemporary Judaism and Christianity. The intended goal cannot be conversion of the dialogue partner by either party nor can its ultimate goal be to mask or mute our fundamental differences for the sake of mutual serenity. Genuine friendship and close collaboration on the issues of mutual concern are all compatible with honest recognition of what makes us different from each other.

At the same time, the figure of the Jewish Jesus in his historical context also serves paradoxically to remind us of the deep bonds between Judaism and Christianity. Both contemporary Judaism and Christianity emerged from the same biblical roots and share a common historical backdrop as well as many fundamental theological convictions, ethical values, and even religious practices.[32]

All of this has been acknowledged in a recent document of the Pontifical Biblical Commission, the body that serves as an advisory council on biblical interpretation to the Vatican's Congregation for the Doctrine of the Faith and ultimately to the Pope himself.[33] The document describes in detail the debt that the Christian Scriptures owe to Judaism and charts the array of fundamental theological convictions we share, as well as the differences that separate the two religious traditions. It acknowledges the anti-Jewish potential of some of the New Testament materials and insists, as mentioned above, that these types of texts should be put in their historical context in order to be properly interpreted.

The text concludes with a reflection that can also serve as the conclusion to this essay: "This discord [i.e., the differing viewpoints between Judaism and Christianity] is not to be taken as 'anti-Jewish sentiment', for it is disagreement at the level of faith, the source of religious controversy between two human groups that take their point of departure from the same Old Testament faith basis, but are in disagreement on how to conceive the final development of that faith. Although profound, such disagreement in no way implies reciprocal hostility. The example of Paul in Rom. 9-11 shows that, on the contrary, an attitude of respect, esteem and love for the Jewish people is the only truly Christian attitude in a situation which is mysteriously part of the beneficent and positive plan of God. Dialogue is possible, since Jews and Christians share a rich common patrimony that unites them. It is greatly to be desired that prejudice and misunderstanding be gradually eliminated on both sides, in favor of a better understanding of the patrimony they share and to strengthen the links that bind them."[34]

CHAPTER SIX

The Trial of Jesus and the Temple: Sadducean and Roman Perspectives

Eyal Regev

Throughout Jesus' trial before the Jewish high priest and Pontius Pilate in Mark 14:53—15:20, two accusations are presented: that he is guilty of committing a sacrilege against the temple, and that he is a false messiah regarding the charge that led to Jesus' arrest and execution.[1] In this article I would like to (briefly) question the former accusation and argue for the latter one. I will present several reservations concerning the historical credibility of the false messiah charge. My main concern, however, is twofold: to stress the historical credibility of the temple charge based on the evidence found in the gospels and to point to its possible effect on both the high priests (that is, the temple authorities) and the Roman authorities. This requires a further look at the religious worldview of the Sadducean high priests and the political-cultural aspect of the cult and cultic resistance in the Roman Empire. My argument is that Jesus' so-called cleansing of the temple and the saying attributed to him about destroying the temple were sufficient grounds for his arrest by the high priests and crucifixion by the Pilate, his actual intentions and other sayings and deeds notwithstanding.

Questioning the Historical Credibility of the False-Messianic Charge

According to the Gospels, the final charge against Jesus that led to his execution by Pilate was his self-claim as a messiah, which was also regarded as blasphemy (Mark 14:61—15:2 and par.; John 10:24-38; 18:33—19:16). Most modern commentators have not followed the gospels in viewing the historical Jesus as an actual messiah and have not thought that he presented himself as such to his followers and outsiders.[2] Nonetheless, numerous modern scholars accepted the historicity of the evangelists' claim that he was executed as a false messiah. They argued that since Jesus was an eschatological prophet, the Jewish (and consequently Roman) authorities understood his eschatological mission as threatening and outrageous. That is, his apocalyptic-eschatological message made him a would-be messiah in the eyes of both his followers and opponents.[3]

While this partly reflects the belief of all four evangelists as well as Paul (1 Cor. 15:3), it cannot be accepted at face value by the historian. This is because the mere historical source upon which the false messiah charge is based—the Passion Narrative—is historically dubious. The Passion Narrative was composed some time after the crucifixion and probably incorporated into Mark somewhat later,[4] in order to demonstrate the belief in Jesus' being Christ and his resurrection from the dead (for example, Mark 15:29; 16:19). It is a theological and apologetic composition lacking many historical characteristics.[5]

The questionable historical value of the Passion Narrative is demonstrated by the following arguments.

(1) The high priest's question "Are you the Messiah, the Son of the Blessed One?" and Jesus' announcement "I am; and you will see the Son of Man seated at the right hand of the Power and coming with the clouds of heaven" (Mark 14:61-62) coheres perfectly with Markan (and partly also Pauline) Christology, containing the markers of Jesus being Christ, Son of Man and Son of God, following Ps. 2:2, 7. It therefore probably resulted from a later reworking.[6]

(2) The scenes of Jesus' "trial" by the high priest and Pilate bear literary reworking apparent in a structure of two questions in each, in which one is answered by Jesus while in response to the other he remained silent. In each scene Jesus is verbally and physically humiliated after the "trial."[7]

(3) The conversations between Jesus and the high priest and Pilate were not witnessed by Jesus' followers. Their contents remained a mystery that the Passion Narrative aimed to uncover, although in quite an imaginative and dramatic fashion.[8]

(4) The actual juristic act of Jesus' "trial" is clouded in mist, in a manner that does not allow a proper comparison to Roman legal procedures.[9]

As already mentioned, many have regarded the messianic charge as a result of Jesus' eschatological message of the coming of the Kingdom of God and his call for repentance. Indeed, it has become common to perceive the historical Jesus as an eschatological prophet. However, the common assumption that Jesus' eschatological teachings led to his identification as a false messiah is problematic. There is a significant difference between a prophet and a messiah. Eschatological expectations were extremely prevalent in Second Temple Judaism.[10] There was nothing innovative or revolutionary in repeating the call to repent. Moreover, the coming of the Day of Judgment was announced by biblical prophets and repeated many times in Daniel, 1 Enoch, Jubilees, Psalms of Solomon, Assumption of Moses, and so forth. Yet, there is no other *explicit* self-claim of a person to be a messiah apart from the one attributed to Jesus in the Passion Narrative. Nor is there a specific figure identified as a messiah by other Jews, besides the early Christian phenomenon. Thus, eschatological expectations should not be equated with actual and concrete messianic claims.[11]

We should also question the argument that Jesus' eschatological teachings led the Jewish establishment to see him as a false messiah since Jesus' disciples did not designate him as a messiah. The evangelists did not present his teachings as the words of the Messiah, but as a sage/teacher[12] or a prophet,[13] and perhaps, as Jesus said about the Baptist, "more than a prophet."[14] When Jesus was asked at the temple, "By what authority do you so act," he refused to answer (Mark 11:28-33). If the evangelists, who passionately believed that Jesus was the Messiah, did not think that Jesus' disciples inferred from his eschatology that he was the Messiah himself, why did the high priest and Pilate reach a different conclusion? Why did they, perhaps for the first time ever, confuse the prophet with the Messiah?[15]

There were so-called (eschatological) prophets who were killed by the Romans, but these were activists who *organized* riots with many followers, not religious teachers.[16] Despite previous attempts to argue for Jesus' resemblance to such anti-Roman leaders,[17] evidence of Jesus' political or military preaching is meager.[18]

It is worth noting that the place of eschatology in the teachings of Jesus has been challenged by scholars who have argued for a non-eschatological Jesus, concluding that he was merely a sage.[19] Hence, Jesus could not have been arrested and executed as a false messiah. This trend has been opposed by many scholars[20] and cannot be discussed here.[21]

In any event, the reason for Jesus' arrest, trial and crucifixion, I suggest, lies elsewhere.

Jesus' Attack on the Temple: Authenticity and Intention

Several scholars have regarded Jesus' words concerning the destruction of the temple and his famous turning of the tables at the temple mount as the main reason for his arrest and execution.[22] I would like to support this view in two

different ways. First, I will show that these traditions have strong grounds in
the gospel tradition. Second, I will try to demonstrate that it is reasonable
to assume that Joseph Caiaphas, the Sadducean high priest, and the high
priestly circles were particularly sensitive to such attacks on the temple.

Mark mentioned twice a grave accusation against Jesus as one who
threatened to destroy the temple. During Jesus' hearing before the high priest
and his *sunedrion*, Jesus was accused of saying "I will destroy this temple (*ton
naon*, namely, the *hiekahl* and not the whole complex of the temple courts)
that is made with hands, and in three days I build another, not made with
hands" (Mark 14:58 NRSV). Although Mark presented it as an accusation
made by false witnesses (Mark 14:57, 59), it reappears in Mark's narrative
when certain Jews mocked the crucified Jesus: "Aha! You who would destroy
the temple and build it in three days; save yourself and come down from the
cross!" (Mark 15:29-30). Jesus' intention to destroy the temple is attested to
for the third time in the accusation against Stephen, again, made by false
witnesses (Acts 6:14). Most surprisingly, it also appears in the Gospel of
Thomas, when Jesus blatantly declared: "I will [destroy this] house, and no
one will be able to build it [again]."[23]

There are several reasons for regarding this saying as resulting from an
early and authentic tradition and by no means the creation of Mark. (1) There
are "multiple attestations" to the saying (Thomas, Acts, and twice in Mark).
(2) The saying is extremely exceptional and provocative. While the anticipa-
tion for a utopian temple that would come down from heaven (namely, not
made by human hands) is already attested to in the Temple Scroll (29:9-10),
there was no other Jew who had threatened to destroy the temple, and certainly not to rebuild it by himself.[24] It seems improbable that a later source
would create such a claim *ex nihilo*. In addition, the threat may cohere with
a violent demonstration concerning the "cleansing" of the temple (discussed
below). (3) The saying "I will destroy this Temple . . . and in three days I build
another" is unique in the gospel tradition, for there is no sign elsewhere in
Jesus' sayings that Jesus rejected the current temple or dreamt of a better one.
Nowhere in the gospels is there an actual attack on the temple or endorse-
ment of its destruction by the Romans.[25]

(4) All four evangelists have made considerable efforts to deny that Jesus
actually threatened the temple. Mark claimed the charge that Jesus had said
it was false.[26] Matthew (26:61) even toned down the charge, saying that
the false witness only claimed that Jesus had said "I am *able* to destroy the
Temple of God and to build it in three days." Luke omitted it altogether
from the trial, and later denied it when it reappeared in the charges against
Stephen. John (2:19-21) omitted it from the trial and placed it in the context
of the "cleansing" of the Temple, transforming its meaning to a positive one
and interpreting it as an analogy: "Jesus answered them: destroy this Temple,

and in three days I will raise it up . . . But he was speaking of the Temple of his body."[27] Clearly, none of the evangelists could identify with the straightforward assault on the temple, even when it had already been destroyed! This recognition reinforces the authenticity of the saying, or to be more precise, the authenticity of the *charge* against Jesus.

Even if Jesus did not actually say it (note that even Thomas believed the accusation), for the present purpose what matters is that others, including the Jewish leaders, believed he did! The reason that they supposed that Jesus announced that he will destroy the temple may lie in the manner in which contemporary Jews understood his "cleansing" of the temple.

Shortly after arriving in Jerusalem, Jesus caused a commotion at the temple: "He entered the temple (*to hieron*) and began to drive out those who were selling and those who were buying in the temple, and he overturned the tables of the money-changers and the seats of those who sold doves; and he would not allow anyone carry anything through the temple."[28]

Most scholars accept the authenticity of the passage,[29] and rightly so. Mark did not allude to this act or try to interpret it elsewhere, thus it is probable that he did not create this scene but merely used an existing tradition. The incident is so extraordinary and puzzling that it is not likely to be fiction.

But what did Jesus mean by interfering in the buying and selling of sacrifices and turning the tables of those who changed regular coins into the annual half-shekel dues? Numerous interpretations have been suggested: a protest against commerce at the temple,[30] against the politicization of the temple by the Herodian dynasty or the Romans,[31] or the corruption of the high priesthood;[32] professing or demonstrating the coming destruction unless the Jews repent their sins.[33]

In a previous study I have suggested that Jesus was protesting not against the temple but against the donation or transmission of morally impure money—corrupted by the people's sins—to the temple and that such a protest is grounded in Jesus' message in both Mark and Q.[34] Jesus' act was directed against the financial aspect of the temple cult. Awareness of the connection between wealth, piety, and the temple money is also attested to when commenting about the donation of the poor widow to the temple's treasury. Jesus praised her for contributing a penny because "she put in everything she had, all she had to live on" (Mark 12:41-44, Luke 21:1-4, which also attests to Jesus' supportive attitude towards the temple). The turning of the tables was directed not just against trading outside the temple, but specifically against money that was related to injustice and corruption. The corrupted wealth was morally impure, in a metaphorical sense, and blemished the sacrificial rite. It therefore violated the sanctity of sacrifices and rituals that were financed by this money. The problem was the money itself, before it was used for financing the sacrifices and offerings, before it was delivered to priestly officials. Jesus' actions were directed towards the lay people who were selling and *buying*, the money-changers and the dove sellers, without any hint of anti-priestly polemic.[35]

Jesus protested not against the temple itself or the priests, but against the more abstract unrighteousness that was transformed into the related corrupted money. Indeed this seems to be the same abstract immorality against which Jesus preached over and over again without pointing to a specific group or class. The reason for his protest in the temple court was that when this money was used for buying sacrifices, it threatened the moral (not ritual!) impurity of the temple cult.[36] As Mark 11:15 testifies, Jesus' action pertained to both the sellers/money changers and the buyers.

My interpretation is grounded in Jesus' teachings of the corruption of wealth and of moral impurity. Throughout the traditions about Jesus, and especially in Q, the Sermon on the Mount and the parables, two substantial problems are introduced: immorality and money. In these traditions, Jesus preached about moral behavior,[37] emphasizing that immorality produces impurity. He also spoke of the destitute as potentially more righteous than the rich and treats wealth unfavorably.[38] These two teachings lead to an obvious conclusion: wealth and materialism lead one astray from the true worship of God and from moral behavior; "No one can serve two masters . . . You cannot serve God and *Mammon*" (Matt. 6:24; Luke 16:13).[39]

I propose that in the "cleansing" of the Temple, this concept of corrupting wealth was interwoven with the other idea of the defiling force of sin. Although there is no direct attestation to the combination of the two, namely, that the money of the wicked is metaphorically defiled with their moral impurity, I maintain that such a perception is quite apparent. If wickedness is defiling, then its subject or "product," namely the money, may be contaminated.

The idea that wealth is not only corrupting but can also be defiled by wicked deeds is supported by several texts from Qumran (although in Qumran money bears substantive pollution—not just metaphorical—and is ritually defiling). In these texts, wealth (*hon*) is contaminated by the evil deeds of its possessor, as emphasized in the Community Rule (1QS), in two passages in *Pesher Hahbbkuk* (1QpHab), and in the Thanksgiving Hymns Scroll (1QH^a).[40] However, the most detailed text is the Damascus Document 6:13-17, which concerns temple impurity. Here the explicit cause of the temple's impurity is the fact that the money that was donated to the temple was "money of wickedness."[41]

In any event, common to all of the interpretations of Jesus' "cleansing" mentioned above is the supposition that the cleansing was an act of social criticism in order to reestablish the credibility of the temple cult, not a sweeping opposition to the temple. Still, the question arises: why not see the overturning of the tables as a symbolic destruction of the temple which reflects its rejection?

Some scholars have assumed that the historical Jesus had an anti-temple stance and aimed to replace the sacrificial cult.[42] I think that the evidence shows otherwise. Several passages point to Jesus' care and general commitment to the temple and the priestly system:[43] Jesus' order to the healed skin-diseased person "show yourself to the priest" (Mark 1:40-44), the poor widow's offering to the temple (Mark 12:41-44 discussed above), Jesus' visits in the temple.[44]

Jesus' Eucharistic words (Mark 14:22-24, assuming that they are authentic) in which he equated the bread to his body and the wine to his blood are usually viewed by his disciples as Jesus' self-portrayal as a sacrifice. The saying, however, does not necessarily mean that Jesus rejected animal sacrifice and replaced Jewish traditional cult with symbols related to his own body, transforming himself into an actual sacrifice of atonement. In fact, according to Mark, Jesus said it while he was eating the Passover sacrifice, namely, when he practiced one of the sacrificial rites himself. Furthermore, as Klawans has shown, Jesus' saying is a ritual metaphor that should not be taken literally. Jesus created an analogy between wine and blood or between bread and (human) flesh, without expressing any reservations whatsoever concerning real sacrifices. Rather, the use of sacrificial language aimed to *appropriate meaning to Jesus' Last Supper*, thus demonstrating that sacrifice was meaningful and symbolic.[45]

In fact, recent studies on the attitudes of the early Christians towards the temple conclude that even when they were at times somewhat critical of certain aspects, they were devoted to the idea of the sacrificial cult and the temple's sacredness.[46]

However, Jesus' audience at the temple mount, his adversaries, and the Jewish leaders who heard about it probably got a totally different impression. Given the ambiguity of the act, its violent character, and the sacred place in which the cleansing occurred, Jesus' contemporaries probably viewed it as an extremely offensive. Those who witnessed it were unaware of Jesus' intentions. What mattered is that a Jew violently interfered with ordinary worship and probably also said something critical of those who ruled the temple or the people who participated in the cult.[47]

Why Did the Sadducean High Priests React Harshly?

Jesus' words and act against the temple seem to be the most apparent reasons for the arrest because he was arrested by the temple authorities. Jesus was arrested by the "chief priests" (Mark 14:43) or "the officers of the temple police" (NSRV for *stratēgous tou hierou* Luke 22:52) and brought before the high priest (Mark 14:53; Luke 22:54; John 18:15), who was in charge of the temple and the cult. Joseph Caiaphas, the high priest who "sentenced" Jesus,[48] was probably a Sadducee.[49] In fact, most of the members of the high priestly elite were Sadducees.[50] The Pharisees, on the other hand, are not mentioned at all in the synoptic versions of Jesus' "trial."[51]

The Sadducees, and the Sadducean high priests in particular, were more sensitive to any violation of the temple's sacredness. In comparison to the Pharisees, the Sadducees held a stricter approach to the temple's ritual purity,[52] and a greater significance to the priestly cult. They regarded the temple and the sacrificial cult as more sensitive and vulnerable, and in a certain sense, more sacred, then the Pharisees. Any possible violation of the cultic order or any potential desecration of the temple was regarded as dangerous.[53] The Sadducees held that the masses should be restricted from approaching the sacred. Thus, for example, the Sadducees complained against the Pharisees' purification of the temple candelabrum. The need to purify it resulted from the Pharisees' permitting the laity to approach it within the temple's sacred precinct, thus defiling it by contact.[54]

Sadduceean high priests were involved in intense political attempts to prevent what a non-Sadducee would regard as a minor violation of the temple cult. Thus, Ishmael son of Phiabi led a delegation to Nero, applying to keep a screening wall which the priests had built to prevent Agrippa II from watching the sacrificial cult from his palace. Agrippa's staring at the priestly ritual was regarded as sacrilegious since it invaded the sancta.[55]

It therefore seems that a high priest who is in charge of the temple, and especially a Sadducean high priest, would feel extremely offended and threatened by Jesus' cleansing of the temple and his supposed saying about demolishing it. The reactions to the prophecy of Jesus son of Ananias about the temple's destruction (discussed below) also attest to this sensitivity.

Pilate, the Temple, and Cultic Uprisings in the Roman Empire

The fact that Jesus was sentenced to crucifixion by Pilate is attested to not only by all four gospels but also by Tacitus.[56] What did Pontius Pilate care about the temple charge?[57] Why did he interfere?[58] If Jesus' offense was indeed related to the temple, why was he crucified, a penalty which seems to indicate that Jesus was convicted in sedition against Roman rule?[59] Before suggesting an explanation, one should recall an additional case which indicates that the Romans minded such prophecies about the temple's destruction. In 62 CE, Jesus son of Ananias cried out in the temple (*naos*) foreseeing the destruction of Jerusalem and the temple time and again. He was arrested by the Jewish *archontes* (authorities) and brought before Albinus, the Roman procurator. Jesus son of Ananias was beaten but continued his predictions until Albinus pronounced him insane and released him.[60]

Scholars usually consider the temple as restricted to Jewish internal affairs.[61] Viewed from a Roman imperial perspective, however, the Jewish temple concerned Roman authorities as much as any major provincial cult. Threats on the cult or the violation of its solemn performance were considered anti-Roman acts that required a firm reaction by Roman authorities.

From a political perspective, the Jerusalem Temple was a Roman temple. The high priest was nominated by the Roman authorities (in 6–41 CE); the high priestly vestments of the Day of Atonement ritual were held by the Roman governor;[62] a daily sacrifice was dedicated for the sake of the Emperor (instead of the conventional pagan imperial cult);[63] and Roman army was stationed in the Antonia watching the temple (Acts 21:30-37). Indeed, the Romans regarded the temple as the symbolic center for their dominion in Judaea,[64] quite like their use in the imperial cult in other provinces,[65] but even more so due to the central role of the temple in ancient Judaism (and in the diaspora). Proclamations about its coming destruction or an act against its status quo were taken as attempting to disturb Roman patronage.

Pilate may have been especially sensitive to a threat on this grand symbol of the Jewish acceptance of the Emperor's rule. More than his predecessors, Pilate promoted Roman religion and the imperial cult in Judaea. In his coinage he used items related with Roman religious ritual, perhaps celebrating the religious roles of Tiberius. The Tiberium he dedicated to the emperor in Caesarea Maritima and the shields he set up honoring Tiberius in Jerusalem may be both interpreted as related to the imperial cult.[66]

Roman rulers and governors had good reasons to be watchful concerning violation of the public order in imperial temples. Several uprisings against Rome were first directed against the Roman imperial cults or a local cult that enjoyed a Roman patronage. These cults symbolized the imperialism to which the rebels resisted.[67] Comparing Jesus' subversive cleansing of the temple and the saying that was attributed to him about destroying the temple (and building a better one) to these other incidents demonstrated how Pilate might have understood Jesus' symbolic attack on the temple.

In a revolt in Germania, a priest called Segimundus who served at the altar of the Ubii (the Ara Ubiorum cult) tore his wreaths that symbolized his office and joined the rebels;[68] in Britain the revolutionaries burned the Temple of Claudius;[69] the Druid revolt in Gaul was accompanied by a prophecy that the (accidental) burning of the Capitoline Temple in Rome signified the end of Roman Rule over the Gauls;[70] last but not least, the Zealots began the Jewish revolt by the cessation of the daily sacrifice for the sake of the Emperor.[71]

Jesus' act and words may also have been regarded by the Romans as a resistance to the present state of affairs at the temple, an uprising not against the temple but rather for the sake of the temple. As we already saw, the cleansing may have been a call for a reform in addition to Jesus' verbal statement about the necessity to rebuild the temple. Indeed, many revolts in the Roman Empire emerged from the native cults.[72]

The rebellion of the Bessi in Macedonia, 11 BCE, was led by a priest of Dionysus who practiced divinations;[73] the revolt in Britain in 60 CE emanated from the sacred groves of the Druid priests, as a reaction to the dedication of a temple for Claudius, the conqueror of Britain;[74] in 69 CE, Julius Civilis gathered his Batavian followers to feast in a sacred grove and signified a religious vow by neglecting to cut his hair;[75] and Isidorus the priest led the revolt of the Bucoli near Alexandria in 172–173, which included a ritual killing and an oath.[76]

Prophecies and oracles of holy men—especially ones related to future destruction such as those of Jesus of Nazareth and Jesus son of Ananias—were taken very seriously by Roman rulers, specifically the emperors. When directed against Rome, they were considered a potential threat for Roman rule.[77] The Romans paid attention to the words and deeds of those who spoke in the name of the gods, especially when their message was far from flattering.[78] This is another reason why Jesus' temple saying could not go unnoticed by Pilate.

Conclusion

The temple charge in its Roman context is significant for understanding the Passion Narrative. The evidence from the Roman Empire provides an adequate setting for Pilate's stark response to Jesus' ostensible attack on the temple. One need not take into account Jesus' teachings, his call to repentance, and his eschatological pronouncements in order to explain why he was considered a potential threat to Caiaphas and Pilate. The "cleansing" of the temple and the words attributed to Jesus about his plan to destroy the temple (and perhaps rebuild a better one) were more troublesome and upsetting than the general and quite common eschatological theme used by so many before him. The Sadducean high priests were extremely sensitive to any symbolic violation of the sacredness of the sacrificial cult. The temple was also the last place the Romans would have tolerated a rebel's yell. Under such circumstances, even a non-eschatological Jesus, a Galilean sage, would be doomed as an anti-Roman dissenter, perhaps even "King of the Jews." In fact, I believe that similar anti-temple accusations led to the flogging of Peter and the apostles, the trial of Stephen, the arrest of Paul, and the execution of James.[79]

It is quite probable that this was not at all Jesus' intention. Put crudely, both the temple and Rome are hardly mentioned in his sayings. He was not a politician or even a citizen of Jerusalem and could not foresee the results of his deeds or how he would be understood by the Jewish and Roman authorities. Accidents happen. But their results are devastating.

We have seen that Jesus used the temple to transmit a certain message. His message was misunderstood by the Jewish leaders, and consequently both the high priests and Pilate regarded him as a major threat to the temple. However, he actually was not. The lesson for contemporary inter-religious relations is, in my mind, that misunderstanding and overreacting can have disastrous results. People's reactions become intense and extreme when key symbols and identity markers are at stake. Instead of inflating the differences they should pay attention to the similarities of their fundamental values before taking far-reaching and offensive steps.

Part Three

Jesus Research before and after German National Socialism

Remapping Schweitzer's Quest through Jewish-Christian Polemic, Apology, and Dialogue

Anthony Le Donne

In many ways, Albert Schweitzer's map still charts the topography for Jesus research. Not only was his (re)construction of Jesus inimitably compelling, his charting of the intellectual history of Jesus research provided a guide for almost all future research. It is as if the same architect who designed the landmark also plotted the contours upon which it rests. But while Schweitzer's landmark work still represents an important advance for the discipline, I will argue that his "Quest" paradigm—the basis for his intellectual history—is ultimately misleading.[1]

Following the lead of Schweitzer, most scholars who survey the various "Quests for the historical Jesus" begin with the so-called "Old Quest." In so doing, most surveys begin with Reimarus or Lessing. Stephen Neill was quite right to say that "Schweitzer had undertaken nothing less than a survey of the whole of the critical research on the life of Christ carried out in Germany (with a few glances outside) in the course of more than a century."[2] To the detriment of Jesus studies, most New Testament scholars have been less attentive than Neill. Far too many have construed Schweitzer's attempt to be comprehensive with a comprehensive achievement. Most surveys begin with post-Enlightenment German thought and follow Schweitzer's contours. It is quite common to discuss the impacts of Kähler and Bultmann (the so-called "No Quest" years), and Käsemann (the so-called "New Quest"), and end with the so-called "Third Quest."[3] But when seen through the lens of Jewish-Christian dialogue, this so-called "Old Quest" was by no means the first quest.[4]

This chapter will suggest that critical interest in the Jesus of history began, not in the Enlightenment, nor in German intelligentsia. While these phases represent important developments, the intellectual history of Jesus research must begin with an eye toward Jewish-Christian dialogue and debate. I will follow a particular pre-modern thread of Jewish-Christian dialogue and debate that evinces historical interest in Jesus before, within, and leading through the Enlightenment.

Schweitzer's Ethnocentric Romanticism

Building from eighteenth-century philosophers in Germany, European proponents of (neo)Romanticism were keenly interested in great "heroes" and "geniuses" who moved epochs forward.[5] For example, Scottish author/historian Thomas Carlyle (1795–1881) measured the major epochs of history by the (types of) heroes who moved history forward.[6] Dagmar Winter's chapter in this book explores the impact of this view of history on German Jesus scholarship before and after Schweitzer's contributions. Albert Schweitzer (1875–1965), alongside many others of like mind, was intently focused on the "discovery" of great or original thinkers. To his mind, Hermann Samuel Reimarus (1694–1768) represented epoch-setting heroism.

According to Schweitzer, "Before Reimarus, no one had attempted to form a historical conception of the life of Jesus."[7] Schweitzer immediately offers the possible exceptions of Hieronymus Xavier and Johann Jakob Hess. Neither is given more than a passing comment. His praise for Reimarus's "Aims of Jesus and His Disciples"[8] eclipses all previous voices. This work is "not only one of the greatest events in the history of criticism, it is also a masterpiece of general literature."[9] It is apparent that Schweitzer's admiration of Reimarus was part and parcel with his belief in German spiritual and mental superiority.

> When, at some future day, our period of civilisation shall lie, closed and completed, before the eyes of later generations, German theology will stand out as a great, a unique phenomenon in the mental and spiritual life of our time. For nowhere save in the German temperament can there be found in the same perfection the living complex of conditions and factors—of philosophic thought, critical acumen, historical insight, and religious feeling—without which no deep theology is possible.[10]

This "perfection" in temperaments culminates in Reimarus' "master-stroke"[11] but also sets the stage for an era of Jesus research. Indeed, within this romanticized elevation of Reimarus, Schweitzer was aggrandizing his own place in the history of human spirituality and intelligentsia.

I learned an amusing (but not quite true) aphorism in the Protestant seminary I attended: *most theologians are dead Germans.* The intended effect of this quip is to emphasize the enormous impact that German theology has had on western Christianity. Both intellectually and spiritually, Germany has produced a vast constellation of stars. Among the very brightest is Schweitzer himself. But we must not be blind to ethnocentric bias when we see it.[12] Perhaps we ought not judge Schweitzer too harshly for the prejudices of his time and place, but we do have an obligation to judge ourselves by our own values. It runs contrary to our (the Academy's) recent critiques of almost all forms of nationalism to blindly follow Schweitzer's lead.

Moreover, even in his own time Reimarus was less of an innovator than Schweitzer supposed. Much of his portrait of Jesus was taken from deists like Thomas Chubb (1679–1746) and Matthew Tindal (1657–1733). It is safe to say that Schweitzer was looking for a genius to mark and make sense of the thought-world that he inherited. That this genius happened to be a German only confirmed the preconceived notions of his cultural and national milieu. But contrary to his mapping of the terrain of Jesus scholarship, critical assessment of the Jesus tradition began long before this milieu.

Pre-modern Critical Evaluations

Where to begin? Should we begin with the Jewish historian Josephus (about 37–100 CE)? While attempts to reconstruct his words about Jesus have proved inconclusive, I am reluctant to ignore them altogether. It is likely that this tradition includes the insertion of christological claims.[13] But it is also likely that the core of Josephus's statement about Jesus provides an early historical synopsis. John Meier reconstructs the text in this way:

> At this time there appeared Jesus, a wise man. For he was a doer of startling deeds, a teacher of people who receive the truth with pleasure. And he gained a following among many Jews and among many of Gentile origin.[14]

Graham Stanton suggests: "Jesus was a doer of strange deeds, and a deluder of the simple-minded. He led astray many Jews and Greeks."[15]

As I will discuss below, Josephus's "testimony" to Jesus became useful in Jewish-Christian debate much later, but not in a way that was favorable to Jews. But does Josephus represent an early critical evaluation of the Jesus of history? I am inclined to answer positively, but many historians will doubt Josephus as a starting point due to our inability to arrive at a pre-Christian core. As such, we will need to find a less dubious starting point.

Should the story of critical evaluation of the Jesus tradition begin with Origen (185–254 CE)? As a Christian theologian, Origen doubted the literal interpretation of the temptation narratives as early as the third century (*De Principiis* 4.16). Or should we begin with the rabbis who offered a demy-thologized account of Jesus' miraculous conception (*Shab* 104b; compare *Sanh* 67a)? Origen's doubt of the historicity of the temptation narratives is hermeneutically relevant because he opens the possibility that many epi-sodes in the canonical Gospels should not be admitted to the historical record. However, Origen's comments have less to do with his aim to define history and more to do with his affinity for allegorical interpretation. Origen is not trying to set the record straight (if I may use this modern phrase); rather, he is arguing that the significance of Scripture must be found on a deeper, spiritual level.

The rabbis, on the other hand, were indeed interested in setting the record straight, even if they were polemically motivated. In contrast to the portraits of Jesus in Christian commemorative veneration, some rabbis argued that Jesus was either a fool or a false teacher who studied magic in Egypt.[16] But it is notoriously difficult to construct a coherent mnemonic trajectory from this literature. Various statements from various rabbis from various genera-tions give us little more than disparate puzzle pieces associated with several different names.[17] And to further complicate matters, "some passages that were not originally about Jesus became misconstrued as such, leading rabbis further astray. Above all, the Jesus to whom the rabbis reacted was not the historical man but the Gospels' reconfiguration of him."[18]

In this literature, Jesus' supernatural deeds are explained as foreign sor-cery. From this a mythology developed. It was purported that Jesus embed-ded (tattooed?) what he learned in Egypt into his flesh. The Talmud also creates confusion about whether Jesus was the son of Stada or Pandera. Mary's identity is also confused. Was her name Stada? Was she Mary Mag-dalene? Peter Schäfer's recent study concludes that despite this confusion, the varying Talmudic traditions presuppose that the mother of Jesus had both a husband and a lover.[19]

More will be said about these traditions below, but the trouble with the Talmudic passages as a starting point for critical assessment is twofold: (1) when do we date the tradition that this text represents, and (2) is Jesus of Nazareth really the object of this polemic? I am inclined to see this tradition akin to (but not dependent upon) the second-century indictment of Celsus against Jesus (Origen, *Cels.* 1.28).[20] If this is so, the critical evaluation of Jesus over and against the biblical witnesses begins with polemic, perhaps with Jewish-Christian debate. But before moving on, it should be pointed out that while we may doubt the methods and conclusions of such early "quests," they are undoubtedly attempts at historical reconstruction.

Overlooked by Quest surveys is the seminal contribution of Augus-tine of Hippo (354–430 CE). Augustine's *Against Faustus* provides a very early critical evaluation of the Jesus tradition. Recently Paula Fredriksen has shown that Augustine discusses Jesus' Jewishness with an eye toward Jewish-Christian relations.[21] Augustine conveys a debate between himself and Faustus on the subject of Manichaeism. Whether or not *Against Faustus* is an account from memory or wholesale invention or a combination of both is not quite as relevant as the fact that it represents a critical evaluation of both Jesus and Judaism from a Christian perspective.[22] What Fredriksen points out that warrants repeating is that the violently anti-Jewish argument of Faustus and the "less" anti-Jewish argument of Augustine are *both* Christian perspectives. While the Church commemorates one as orthodox/heterodox and the other as heresy, both represented segments of Christianity in the fourth century (and early fifth).

The guiding hermeneutic of Faustus was the filter on the New Testament left behind by the Gnostic founder of Manichaeism: Mani (216–276 CE). Mani's wholesale condemnation of Judaism (à la Marcion) resulted in the subtraction of Jewish Scripture from the Christian canon. When this lens of anti-Judaism was focused on the New Testament, certain portions of it had to go too. What could easily be construed as anti-Jewish statements by Matthew, John, Paul, and so on were deemed authentic; that is, the anti-Jewish portions were deemed historical. Conversely, Faustus attempted to diagnose textual corruptions by sifting out the many passages that sounded far too Jewish.

According to Mani and then Faustus, these must have been added to the New Testament by the "Judaizers," purportedly scribes with Jewish agendas and enemies to the truth of Christianity, that is, the truth perfected in the prophecies of Mani. Thus anti-Judaism was among the very first hermeneutics used to evaluate the Jesus of history.

Augustine, on the other hand, maintained the value of Jewish Scripture, most often through christological allegory. He was also unwilling to sift out "Jewish sounding" portions of the New Testament. No doubt, Augustine propelled Paul's supersessionism (if we may call it that) toward Christian anti-Judaism, to damaging effect.[23] Jews were, in his estimation, "unwilling witnesses" to Christology.[24] In light of his hermeneutical agenda, one could argue that Augustine's anti-Judaism was more subtle and thus ultimately more insidious.

But given the alternative versions of anti-Judaism during his time, his small steps toward religious tolerance should not be belittled. More than once, Augustine's condemnation of violence against Jews was remembered and likely saved synagogues, Scriptures, and Jewish lives.[25]

Given Augustine's complicated and unique place in the history of Jewish-Christian relations, his representation of Faustus provides an important touchstone for Jesus historians. In reaction to Faustus's hermeneutic

of anti-Judaism, Augustine became something of an apologist for the nec-
essarily Jewish heritage of Christianity. Jesus' Jewish heritage was not only
historically factual; it was foundational for his vision of salvation history.
Jesus was not a spiritual phantom who left no footprints when he walked.
For Augustine, Jesus Christ was the Jewish messiah, *which made him Jewish*.
Thus the move to situate Jesus within Judaism (however nominally) resulted
in a move toward religious tolerance. In retrospect, neither move eclipses
Augustine's anti-Jewish supersessionism. But against the backdrop of Manichaeism, these steps might reflect the seeds of both historical Jesus research
and Jewish-Christian dialogue.

Even if the other early examples of critical evaluation of Jesus mentioned in this section are deemed dubious, there should be little doubt that
Augustine's apologetic for the Jesus of history is a worthy place to begin a
survey of Jesus research.

Further Examples of Pre-modern Critical Evaluation

While important, Augustine should not be seen as a solitary genius who
foreshadowed any particular epoch. *Against Faustus* most likely represents
a climate of dialogue and debate that sometimes included the topic of
Jesus and his relationship to Judaism. Augustine's apology for Jesus as an
historical figure is situated amidst a dark history of religious misgivings
and polemics punctuated by violence, forced displacement, pogroms, and
attempts at genocide. At the risk of oversimplification, it must be said that
the vast majority of this violence was anti-Jewish in nature and perpetrated
with ecclesial support and theological impetus.[26] While it is possible to
overstate the ecclesial nature of this history, there is a much larger danger of secularizing this history. Most of political history is religious history. Little is gained by blaming cultural prejudice or political motivation
as if these were not married to Christianity over the course of European
history. We must also recall episodes where political officials spoke more
humanely than the clergy. Charlemagne (768–814), for example, created
the office *magister Iudaeorum* (or "Master of the Jews") to function as an
advocate for otherwise disenfranchised Jews in the Roman Empire. This
was meant to provide a state-appointed stalwart against Christian persecution (including violence) of Jews.[27] In short, during the medieval period,
violence against Jews was most often perpetrated by Christians and supported by the Church.

Surviving from the first centuries of Christianity and medieval Chris-
tendom is a genre referred to as the *contra Iudaeos* writings (Christian polemics against Jews). These writings generally include idealized portraits of

Christian apologists deconstructing Jewish straw men. These debates usually appeal to Jewish Scripture as proof-texts to support christological claims, and they often conclude with accounts of defeated Jews submitting to baptism. In this way, some of this literature gives us a window into the hopes of many medieval Christians concerning Jewish conversion to Christianity. While they rely on caricature, the *contra Iudaeos* writings give us a general picture of talking points of Jewish-Christian debate from an idealized Christian perspective. Perhaps, then, they reflect historical memories of such debates.

It is uncertain whether these writings were used to train Christians for debates, for catechism, or whether they were written with Jewish audiences in mind. Perhaps it was a combination of all of these.[28] Many modern Christians and Jews will recognize right away the problems that such caricatures create for authentic and constructive dialogue, not to mention the overt agenda to deconstruct Judaism!

These debates generally discuss Jesus' virgin birth and/or preexistence. They are generally *not* interested in Jesus' historical teachings, his vocation as a healer/exorcist, his travels, conflicts, relationships, and so on. It seems that Jesus' historical context, including his Jewishness, is rarely a topic of conversation. However, one such text suggests that on some occasions these debates included conversations about the Jesus of history.

Claiming to recount late fifth-century events, there is a story preserved in Old Slavonic and Greek[29] about a Persian king[30] who called for a debate among Christian bishops, Jewish rabbis, and "pagans" represented by a philosopher named "Aphroditianus."[31] In this story, the three sides (Christians, Jews, and pagans) take turns debating. The first three parts of this story purport arguments between the bishops and Aphroditianus while the rabbis moderate. In the fourth part, the pagan philosopher moderates a debate between two rabbis named "Jacob and Pharas" and the bishops. These exchanges are, for the most part, mutually respectful. When the arguments become too heated, the king reminds all parties to conduct themselves appropriately.[32]

In this context, the bishops appeal to the brief account of the life of Jesus by the first-century Jewish historian Josephus (mentioned above). The bishops are most likely using a Christian version of this passage, one that inserts Christian faith affirmations into the original account. But what is most interesting is *why* the bishops appeal to Josephus at all. The most likely motive for doing so was to appeal to a decidedly Jewish source for the life of Jesus outside the New Testament. In the same way that the Jewish prophets of the Old Testament were valued by Christian apologists, Josephus's Jewishness was useful for their agenda. Josephus, as a Jewish witness to Jesus, provided something that Christian historians could not: a credible voice for a fifth-century Jewish audience.

Notice, again, that the topic of the "historical Jesus" emerges in Jewish-Christian dialogue. Even if we were to conclude that this story of the events in Persia is fiction representing Christian indoctrination,[33] the story itself suggests that the Jesus of history became topical among Christians when the topic of Judaism was in view.

As one would expect in such a climate, medieval Jews reacted against such proselytizing and overt acts of hostility by Christians. With their culture and general welfare at stake, rabbis had need for a counter-narrative—one that could combat the narratives presented to Jews by Christians. Thus emerged a tract called *(Sefer) Toledot Yeshu* ([*The Book of*] *the History of Jesus*). This tract was first mentioned by two ninth-century French archbishops, but it was most likely in circulation long before it came to their attention.[34] Cook calls this tract a "parody" of the life of Jesus found in the Gospels by incorporating elements from earlier Jewish polemics:

(1) Mary (Miriam of Bethlehem) was the victim of rape by Joseph Pandera.
(2) Jesus fled to Galilee in shame but later returned to Judea.
(3) Jesus managed to write down the divine name engraved upon the foundation stone of the Jerusalem temple and this allowed him to perform "magic."
(4) He was arrested and indicted on the charge of foreign "magic."
(5) The body of Jesus was stolen by his disciples to purport his resurrection.

Cook rightly observes that this counter-narrative was constructed of polemic and further propels historical anachronisms and inconsistencies. But there can be no doubt that it was an attempt to reframe the discussion of the "Jesus of history." Moreover, and importantly for the thesis of this chapter, Jewish-Christian debate was the motive for doing so.

At this point in my survey, I face two dangers. First, if I move forward too quickly, I risk understating centuries of bloody persecution. Forgetting this history has had dire consequences for Jewish-Christian relations and for the telling of our histories together. The second risk I face is skipping over exceptional relationships between Jews and Christians like that of Rabbi Ephraim of Bonn and Abbot Bernard of Clairvaux.[35] Authentic dialogue is not helped by simplistic sketches of heroes and villains in history.[36] However, for the sake of space and focus, I will leave much unsaid, but regrettably so.

Martin Luther and Rabbi Emden

I began this chapter by exposing Schweitzer's Romanticism-guided predisposal to the discovery of an epoch-creating genius. While we should be cautious to aggrandize any representative of an epoch, it is difficult to overstate the impact of Martin Luther on both Christianity and Judaism. Besides Jesus there is perhaps no figure who is remembered so differently by Jews and Christians. The long shadow of Luther is cast over all subsequent Jewish-Christian dialogues.

Without exception, when I lecture to fellow Christians about Martin Luther (1483–1546), there is a common refrain of horror and embarrassment. Ignorance of Luther's anti-Judaism among most Christians (even Lutherans) makes this topic a sickening experience. When his advice to burn Jewish holy books and synagogues, to prohibit rabbis from teaching or face execution, and to round Jews up for forced labor is brought to light, most Christians are shocked. When this advice to German political officials is compared with the events of *Kristallnacht* (November 10, 1938—in celebration of Luther's birthday), most Christians are horrified.[37] Most readily see the connection between Luther's venom and historical events of a largely Lutheran Germany culminating in the Holocaust/Shoah.[38]

Luther's relationship with Judaism, of course, is well-trodden ground for academics. Earlier in his life (1523), Luther wrote:

> When we are inclined to boast of our position, we should remember that we are but Gentiles, while the Jews are of the lineage of Christ. We are aliens and in-laws; they are blood relatives, cousins, and brothers of our Lord. Therefore, if one is to boast of flesh and blood the Jews are actually nearer to Christ than we are. . . . If we really want to help them, we must be guided in our dealings with them not by papal law but by the law of Christian love.[39]

Here the "early" Luther uses this essay to condemn the abuse of Jews by Roman Catholics. He also offers advice for proselytizing (as opposed to forced baptism). Luther even calls the Jews the first elect of God with the particular privileges associated with that status. Given Luther's emphasis on concepts related to election, this is no small concession! While Luther intends to combat Christian motives for religious persecution against Jews (here we probably see Augustine's influence), I would argue that we witness the seeds of Luther's eventual venom against the Jews.

Luther believed that earnest Christian kindness (informed by correct Christian doctrine) would bring about the conversion of many Jews. Luther never saw his hope realized. His exhortation to show respect and kindness was linked with his motive to proselytize. Later in life, when this ulterior motive proved unfulfilled, his superficial respect and kindness soured. Christians have a long history of failing to realize that motives to proselytize are most offensive to Jewish sensibilities. Luther is the chief example.

What often goes unnoticed here is that this early essay is the nearest Luther comes to showing an interest in the Jesus of history. Reminiscent of Augustine's apologetic for Jesus' Jewish heritage, Luther finds in this discussion an occasion to become an advocate for Jews. Tragically, both his interest in Jesus' Jewishness and his sympathy for Judaism disappear in his later works. As we will see shortly, this shift sets the stage for the so-called "No Quest" years of Jesus research in Lutheran Germany. Of course, Luther was a product of his context in this respect. One could point to numerous parallel episodes of anti-Judaism. I will highlight only one.

In sixteenth-century Poland, a group of Shabbateans led by Jacob Frank were excommunicated by the Polish rabbinate. Out of spite, the "Frankists" complained to multiple Catholic bishops that they were being persecuted because they had "confessed the Trinity." Knowing that the Catholic hostility against Jews was easily stirred, the Frankists provoked the Church toward a predictable end. The result was a command from the bishop to burn all copies of the Talmud in the bishopric of Podolias. As a show of solidarity, the Frankists agreed to be baptized.[40]

Rabbi Jacob Emden (1697–1776) was called upon for advice. Optimistic that Polish clergy would be reasonable, Emden advised a direct appeal to them for help. Emden believed that the religion instituted by Jesus and Paul was a moral institution at its roots. Moreover, Emden suggested that the local Catholic community might be reasonable and willing to dialogue. After all, the Frankists were thought to be "sexual deviants" (they had incorporated sexually ecstatic rituals into their worship), and thus could not possibly be good Catholics.

This occasioned an alternate interpretation of Christian origins. In Emden's estimation, both Jesus and Paul were well within the bounds of Halakha, establishing a religion for Gentiles based on the Noahide commandments.[41] Emden navigates several New Testament passages arguing that Jesus and Paul sought to uphold the Torah for Jews and observed it fully. Emden suggested that their gentile followers found the yoke too burdensome and eventually departed from the Noahide commandments.

Emden's short letter should be seen as a forerunner to modern Jewish-Christian dialogue and historical Jesus research. At about the time Gotthold Ephraim Lessing (1729–1781) was experiencing a crisis of Christian faith because historical truth could never provide certainty about Jesus, Jacob Emden's optimistic reconstruction of a Jewish Jesus provides a fascinating contrast. Although every Jesus historian is familiar with Lessing's short essay, very few are familiar with Emden's. Again, we see Jewish-Christian relations provide a platform for a critical appraisal of the Jesus of history.

Enlightenment Forerunners and Representatives

Most Jesus "Quest" surveys begin with the philosophical frameworks of the Enlightenment, particularly with Reimarus. Reimarus remains an important figure for historical Jesus research, but I see little reason to call him the "father" of the discipline in echo of Schweitzer. When the Talmud, Augustine, Emden, among others are taken seriously, we already see critical evaluation of the Jesus of history in Jewish-Christian polemic, apology, and sometimes genuine dialogue. Unless this half of the story is told first, we risk misconstruing the impact of modern Jesus studies.

When "Quest" surveys begin with the Enlightenment, historical Jesus research is described in terms of skepticism, ecclesial pressure, and the eventual victory of honest intellectual secularism. I contend that this is only half the story and thus ultimately misleading.

Preceding both Lessing and Reimarus stands the forerunner to modern historical Jesus research: Benedict (Baruch) Spinoza (1632–1677). Not only does Spinoza set "modern" historical Jesus research in motion, but his relationship with Judaism is a window into the perception of Jewish excommunication (*ḥrm*) at that time. Years after his parting with the "Nation of Israel," he anonymously published *Tractatus Theologico-Politicus* (1670). Therein Spinoza contested the abuse of Scripture by the Catholic Church. He argued that Christian Scripture should be divided into two genres: revelation and history. "Revelation" was projected through the temperaments, dispositions, and beliefs of the prophets, while history has much more of a plain sense. History, according to Spinoza, could be studied objectively and without prejudice. The notable caveat to this latter category was the supernatural. In Spinoza's words:

> We have now more than sufficiently proved our point, that God adapted revelations to the understanding and opinions of the prophets (2:125). . . . We can come to no different conclusion with respect to the reasonings of Christ, by which He convicted the Pharisees of pride and ignorance, and exhorted His disciples to lead the true life. He adapted them to each man's opinions and principles. (2:133–34)

In a similar vein, Spinoza held that Christ did not himself believe in angels and demons, but spoke of these in order to be intelligible to his ancient audience (2:135–37). Concerning the Gospels (which he considered history), he wrote:

[T]he narratives generally contain miracles—that is, as we have shown in the last chapter, relations of extraordinary natural occurrences adapted to the opinions and judgment of the historians who recorded them. (7:12)

So, in Spinoza's view, the Gospels were processed through at least two filters: the human minds of the disciples as they witnessed Jesus and the human minds of the evangelists as they recounted Jesus. I have argued elsewhere that we see here the very birth of the modern historical critical method.[42] If so, it is noteworthy that Spinoza must do so in safe distance from both Judaism and Christianity; yet he remains conversant with both religions occupying something of a liminal ground between the two.

Spinoza's legacy is often (and correctly) described in secular terms. There is much in his program that prefigures the naturalist Bible offered by Thomas Jefferson (1743–1826)[43] and the skepticism of the supernatural by Lessing. Therefore I would argue that Spinoza provides a bridge between medieval Jewish-Christian debate and the Enlightenment's belief in a closed universe. Standing at this threshold, his description of an enlightened Jesus (however anachronistic) marks the emergence of modern historical Jesus research.[44] But Spinoza was so far ahead of his time, we must say that he "prefigures" modern research.

My survey finally moves toward the Quest topography plotted by Schweitzer.[45] What I hope has been clear in this chapter is the context of Jewish-Christian relationship in which Reimarus was situated. Reimarus's anti-Judaism is well known, but what is less acknowledged is the opposite stance of Lessing.

Before Lessing published what Schweitzer called the "master-stroke" of Reimarus's genius, Lessing agonized over this decision. Lessing was worried about the impact that Reimarus's portrait might have. With this weighing on him, he sought the advice of his great friend, the most influential Jewish thinker of the day, Moses Mendelssohn (1729–1786).[46] Hand in glove with his respect for Mendelssohn, Lessing was opposed to all forms of anti-Judaism. Lessing debated publicly and published against fellow Christian (Lutheran theologian) Johann Melchior Goeze on the topic.[47]

In these debates, it became clear that the impetus of Lessing's questions about revelation and reason grew from his comparison of the Abrahamic religions. Vexed by his heterodox interlocutor, Goeze complained to the Duke of Brunswick. The duke stepped in and Lessing lost his academic freedom concerning matters of theology. Many consider Lessing the man who provided the impetus to launch the "First Quest" (a misnomer) in 1774. But his career as an overt theologian was over in 1778. Having been muted, Lessing found an outlet for his theological leanings by writing the play *Nathan der Weise* (subsequently, *Nathan the Wise*) in 1779. Lessing's "Nathan" was modelled after his friend Mendelssohn, and many consider the play to be a plea for religious tolerance. It is worth asking whether Lessing might have published the "Fragments" during this period because he hoped to find in Jesus a way past the differences among Christians, Muslims, and Jews.[48] I am inclined to think that Lessing's challenge to traditional understandings of Jesus was (at least in part) motivated by his interest in interfaith dialogue.

The Modern European Jesus

In the mid-nineteenth century, European Christian philologists began to revisit non-Christian biblical and post-biblical literature. These scholars recognized their need for Semitic language specialists and enlisted the help of Jewish scholarship.[49] Shortly after the so-called "First [Old] Quest" began, this Jewish-Christian collaboration spurred publications from Jewish scholars on the topic of Christian origins.[50] Abraham Geiger (1810–1874), best known for his impact on Reform Judaism, emerged as a Jewish theologian and historian of the Second Temple period.[51] Geiger was keenly interested in both historical Jesus study and modern tensions between Jews and Christians in Europe. Geiger (reminiscent of Emden) argued that Jesus was a Pharisee who emphasized Jewish liberty over and against the draconian postures of the temple-based Sadducees. Eventually, argued Geiger, Jesus' disciples were influenced by Sadducees and gentiles and so departed from Jesus' original aims. Susannah Heschel writes,

> Geiger's counterhistory constituted a transvaluation of Christian arguments against Judaism and functioned as a passionate defense of Judaism. His scholarship was not an effort to Christianize Judaism; it was an effort to Judaize Christianity. It is not surprising that Christian reactions were marked by outrage.[52]

According to Heschel's compelling argument, Geiger's interest in Jesus' Jewishness stemmed from his interest in Jewish-Christian relations. She argues that Geiger specifically aimed to undermine the traditional Christian narratives of Western Europe. In this way, we might see a parallel to Lessing's agenda from the Jewish side. Geiger's agenda to "Judaize Christianity" was met with hostility by both Christians and Jews.

My survey is now firmly within the modern period of Western Europe. One of the most influential effects of the Enlightenment on this period was the (pseudo)science of race.[53] Joseph Arthur Comte de Gobineau (1816–1882) was a French aristocrat and amateur scientist. Gobineau claimed to be able to accurately predict the characteristics of people groups by measuring the various sizes and shapes of their skulls.[54] The popular acceptance of the pseudoscience of race evinces the marriage of two social currents in Europe: (1) scientific optimism—children of the Enlightenment were anxious to believe that scientific rigor was the silver bullet for social problems, and (2) anti-Judaism—the common European caricatures of Jews were so firmly entrenched that the emerging field of racial science simply reinforced them. The result of this marriage was scientifically sanctioned anti-Semitism. This, of course, was one of the chief interests of National Socialism in Germany.

French Catholic scholar Ernest Renan (1823–1892) was keenly interested in this emerging approach to racial theory.[55] Renan believed that racial identity was crucial to understanding collective identities.[56] This agenda would eventually have dire consequences for his portrait of Jesus. Renan would eventually become an important figure in what previous studies have called the "First [Old] Quest." While Renan did not deny that Jesus was from Jewish lineage, he claimed that Jesus was able to cleanse himself of Judaism[57] and eventually became not a Jew but rather the "destroyer of Judaism."[58] This line of thought became a guiding hermeneutic for the "Institute for the study of Jewish influence on the life of the German churches and the removal of this influence" as antisemitism reached a tipping point in Nazi Germany.[59]

Students of Jewish-Christian relations know well that theological anti-Judaism runs in conjoining parallel to secular antisemitism in this context. Indeed, many argue that making a significant distinction between these two threads is dangerous. In contrast, very few historical Jesus scholars acknowledge the influence of anti-Semitism on the so-called "No Quest" years in German scholarship.[60]

The Supra-historical Jesus

Martin Luther's shadow perhaps looms largest over twentieth-century Lutheran Germany. Martin Kähler (1835–1912) appealed to Martin Luther's disinterest in the Jesus of history in order to undermine biographies of Jesus. Instead of offering a life of Jesus, Kähler moves the discussion toward a "supra-historical Savior."[61] By supra-historical, he meant that Christ's real significance transcends his historical context, making him a universal reality connected with every historical context. Kähler's Christ was thus untethered from his first-century context. Whether intended or not, Jesus' connection to Judaism was made altogether incidental in a climate where the topic of Judaism was most controversial.

Previous surveys have (perhaps misleadingly) called this period the "No Quest" years in Germany. This brings us to one of the brightest stars on the stage of Jesus research, Rudolf Bultmann (1884–1976). There may not be a theologian as influential and at the same time so caricatured. It has become commonplace to reduce Bultmann to a selection of sound bites. His most famous statement has made him the poster-child for the so-called No Quest years:

> I do indeed think that we can now know almost nothing concerning the life and personality of Jesus, since the early Christian sources show no interest in either, are moreover fragmentary and often legendary; and other sources about Jesus do not exist.[62]

The extent to which this statement is misconstrued is unfortunate. When read in context, Bultmann is reacting against the attempts to conjecture Jesus' personality, which he later contrasts with a person's works. He argues that the latter is available for historical reconstruction while the former is not.

Moreover, with this statement, Bultmann was offering delimitation for a book he had written on the topic of the historical Jesus![63] The truth is that Bultmann was a much more complicated thinker and influence than is normally credited. For my present interests, it is noteworthy that Bultmann was a critic of the Nazi Party in a time when this was hazardous. Bultmann's emphasis on Jesus' Jewishness was contrary to the tendencies of that time. Moreover, Bultmann was outspoken against all forms of anti-Semitism and against the specific program of "dejudaization."[64]

However, it is of crucial importance to recognize that Bultmann's Christ of existential encounter all but eclipsed his portrait of Jesus as a Jew. For Bultmann, the historical Jesus was an important precursor to Christian theology. But it cannot be denied that the supra-historical Jesus was the *telos* of his program. Whether or not the supra-historical Jesus was propelled forward with good intentions, this program diminished Jesus' historical value in a context that wielded the name of Christ as a bludgeon against Judaism. As seen with Renan above, Bultmann's statements against political aggression should not go unnoticed. But both Renan and Bultmann (perhaps, to an extent, unwittingly) contributed to a series of historiographical missteps that made the Jewishness of Jesus irrelevant.

The shadow of the Holocaust/Shoah makes it almost impossible not to wonder about the implications of the moves toward a supra-historical Jesus in this context. This, of course, extends the already large shadow of Luther. Such a topic cannot be explored in any thorough way in a single chapter. But what can be said is that if any context needed a historically rooted—*and particularly Jewish*—Jesus, it was twentieth-century Germany. Only recently have Jews and Christians been able to begin to make sense of the incomprehensible events of World War II Europe. As the field of biblical studies catches up with other fields in the humanities, it will be necessary to reassess the so-called No Quest years in Germany more thoroughly. I suggest, that is, that we are obligated to take seriously the social and political climate of these few years—and not only these, but the decades framing these years.

Famously, Bultmann's pupil Ernst Käsemann (1906–1998) publicly challenged the place (or lack thereof) that the historical Jesus played in Bultmann's program.[65] As Käsemann's launch of the so-called "New Quest" is discussed extensively elsewhere, I will leave much unsaid here. However, I should point out that the paradigm of No Quest (or "no biography") and New Quest is perhaps only helpful when thinking about the phases of German scholarship. While Bultmann's program was eventually global in impact, Jesus studies did not come to a halt globally. It should also be pointed out that Käsemann's suggested way forward for historical Jesus research served to emphasize that in Jesus that was "dissimilar" to both Judaism and Christianity. Käsemann's program, however, seemed to push Jesus closer to Christianity and further away from Judaism.[66]

Characterizing the past few decades of Jesus research (what has been commonly called the "Third Quest") under a single umbrella is impossible.[67] The period from 1980 to the present has seen more publications on the historical Jesus than any other. Perhaps the framework of this era is represented by the standardization of "authenticity criteria,"[68] or the reconsideration of the relationship between Jesus and imperial politics.[69] Both of these developments are enormously important for any survey of historical Jesus research. But by all accounts, Jesus' relationship to the varied particularities of Second Temple Judaism has been the dominant impetus of Jesus research since the mid-1970s. I would refer the reader to my consideration of Geza Vermes's important contribution in the introduction of this book. The topic of "Jesus the Jew" has won the day. The nuance and sophistication of this discussion have proved enormously beneficial for historical Jesus research.[70] Moreover, it has invited prominent voices from both Jewish and Christian perspectives. As I round out this chapter, I will only quote this description by James Dunn:

> In the closing decades of the twentieth century the most helpful advance in life of Jesus research was the recognition that the quest must primarily have in view *Jesus the Jew* and a clearer and firmer grasp of the consequences. What distinguishes this "third quest of the historical Jesus" is the conviction that any attempt to build up a historical picture of Jesus of Nazareth should and must begin from the fact that he was a first-century Jew operating in a first-century milieu. . . . What more natural, one might think, what more inevitable than to pursue a quest of the historical Jesus the Jew?[71]

Dunn goes on to demonstrate that while such a premise seems "natural" and "inevitable" to contemporary historians, the extent to which previous eras were either disinterested or adversarial to this premise is remarkable.[72]

What this survey has attempted to show is that amidst a vast sea of indifference and hostility to Jesus' Jewishness, there have been remarkable exceptions to this rule. Moreover, it seems that the common thread running throughout these exceptions is that they generally occur as Jews and Christians interfaced in polemic, apologetic, and sometimes genuine dialogue. By tracing this thread, I have suggested that the intellectual heritage of Jesus research begins long before the Enlightenment and (alongside other threads) guides several important intellectual developments during the modern period. Jesus historians would do well to acknowledge this heritage and perhaps we will do better if it becomes our *telos* as well.

In light of this survey, here are a few questions that come to mind:

1. Faustus's hermeneutic was that of anti-Judaism. In his view, Jesus was historical in as much as he was anti-Jewish. Have we taken our hermeneutic from the opposite extreme? Do we deem ahistorical anything that smacks of anti-Judaism?

2. Augustine, Luther, Emden, Geiger, and others engage the historical Jesus question when confronted with Jewish-Christian tension. What is gained and lost when Jewish-Christian dialogue becomes the occasion for historiographical rigor?

3. What do we make of the close proximity of the so-called No Quest years to the Holocaust/Shoah? What was the relationship between the supra-historical Jesus and the non-Jewish Jesus?

The Dissimilar Jesus: Anti-Semitism, Protestantism, Hero-Worship, and Dialectical Theology

Dagmar Winter

I s Christian theology that is Christo-centric and Jesus-centered institutionally anti-Judaist? The theological dilemma for Christians is arguably as old as the New Testament itself: how to understand and positively appreciate Jesus in his distinctiveness without being negative about Judaism. The tragedy is that this dilemma has not always been seen as a problem! A number of cultural, philosophical, and theological concepts have coalesced in various ways over two thousand years to remove Jesus from his Jewishness and to paint an ever darker image of Judaism.

This essay will not discuss the issue of anti-Judaism in the New Testament itself. Rather, we shall look at the concepts and motives that have led to descriptions and images of Jesus which are implicitly or explicitly dissimilar from Judaism.

Stages of Jesus Research[1]

Jesus research has undergone different stages through the centuries, particularly in the last few decades. Anthony Le Donne has written about the early beginnings of critical research in his chapter of this book.

Deism

With the period of Enlightenment, Jesus research in that sense of the term really began. It was the English Deists who in the eighteenth century developed an interest in what Jesus was *really* about and proposed a critical reading

of sacred history just as of any other history: the programmatic beginning
of biblical criticism. For understanding Jesus, this meant that Christian
Deists sought to recover the true Gospel of Jesus from the religious notions
of his followers. The fact that the Christian Deists viewed Jesus as a "proto-
Christian Deist" set them up to draw a contrast between Jesus as he was
traditionally understood and his background. A particular driver for Deism
was an anti-dogmatic, and in that sense anti-Christian, stance. However,
interestingly, Thomas Morgan (d. 1743) thought that the New Testament,
due to its corrupted nature, did not make the necessary distinction between
Judaism and Christianity. Morgan identified Judaism with "national Prejudices." Moreover, argued Morgan, since "no two Religions in the world can
be more inconsistent and irreconcilable than Judaism and Christianity," Jesus
was clearly distanced from the Jewish faith.[2]

Reimarus and Strauss

Hermann Samuel Reimarus (1694–1768) is generally heralded as standing at
the beginning of the quest for the historical Jesus in our modern understanding. While Reimarus certainly echoed the Deists' approach of distinguishing
Jesus from his disciples, he understood Jesus as an entirely Jewish prophet,
whereas he saw Jesus' followers as being the deceiving source for Christianity. Hereby the methodological foundation for the theme of dissimilarity was
laid, albeit with Jesus being dissimilar to what the early Christians made of
him rather than dissimilar to Judaism. In his *Life of Jesus*, David Friedrich
Strauss (1808–1874) introduced the concept of myth—replacing Reimarus's
idea of deception—into understanding how the Jesus tradition was formed.[3]

The Old Quest

The classic old or "first quest" of the historical Jesus flourished in Germany
in the nineteenth century. The chief motivation for finding out about the
historical Jesus lay in the dominant liberal theology of its time. The "real" life
and message of Jesus was seen as a helpful critical antidote to a dogmatic
and christological understanding, focusing instead particularly on Jesus' ethics. The goal of the quest was the historical figure of Jesus emerging as an
authoritative personality from the pages of the New Testament which had
been painted over by the early Christians. While, as with Reimarus, the
attempt to separate Jesus from early Christian interpretation and Christology might have led to placing him more firmly into a Jewish context, this
did not happen. There were some notable exceptions among Talmud and
Aramaic scholars, but in general anti-Jewish sentiments and the idea of a
personality towering above his contemporaries resulted in emphasizing Jesus'
dissimilarity to Judaism.[4]

The Collapse of the Old Quest

The collapse of the Old Quest came about by the writing of yet another book on Jesus, however, with devastating conclusions for the quest. Albert Schweitzer's (1875–1965) history of the life-of-Jesus research in the nineteenth century included an outline of the life of Jesus, and both elements caused the collapse of the quest: Schweitzer showed that the historical Jesus as presented was a mere projection, in fact a reflection of the face of the writers. And he understood Jesus as so entirely caught up in apocalyptic ideas of his time that it was not possible to fulfill the liberal theologians' dream of a truly relevant presentation of the historical Jesus.[5]

This historical judgment of the futility of the quest was further strengthened when Rudolf Bultmann (1884–1976), a proponent of dialectical theology, pointed out the theological irrelevance of the historical Jesus, apart from the mere fact of his having come to earth at all. Both Schweitzer and Bultmann place Jesus firmly within Judaism but cannot make this fact theologically fruitful. For Bultmann, the historical Jewish Jesus was not part of New Testament theology (this begins with the proclamation of Easter) but part of its "pre-history" or presupposition. This was an insight gained from the study into the history of religions. It was Wellhausen (1844–1918), mainly an Old Testament scholar, who had famously declared that Jesus was a Jew rather than a Christian.[6]

So from a variety of angles, in the old quest and at its collapse, the historical Jesus was seen as dissimilar primarily to the early church and Christian doctrine.

The New Quest

The end of the old quest and waning interest in the historical Jesus was a particular German phenomenon which was not nearly as marked in the Anglo-Saxon world. German interest was reawakened in the Bultmann school in the 1950s. For reasons that are elaborated later in this chapter, here Jesus was seen as dissimilar primarily to Judaism—for it was the continuity between Jesus and the early church which justified and motivated the renewed interest in the historical Jesus.[7]

The birth of the new New Quest was brought forth by Ernst Käsemann (1906–1998). In a lecture in 1953 to a group of Bultmann's pupils, Käsemann appealed to what Bultmann had conceded as the *implicit* presence of the Easter Kerygma in the pre-Easter Jesus. Important for us here, Käsemann also formulated criteria for unearthing the historical Jesus, in particular the criterion of dissimilarity which was clearly weighted to stress Jesus' dissimilarity to Judaism. This became largely the framework for the New Quest.[8]

The Third Quest

While there were individual Jewish scholars contributing to the study of the historical Jesus during the Old Quest,[9] the field opened up in the early 1980s with the Third Quest. Following a geographical shift from Germany to the Anglo-Saxon world, British and U.S. American scholars were and are the leading proponents of the Third Quest.[10] The clear focus of this stage of Jesus research is historical, and in that sense it shares the non-apologetic stance of the Old Quest. However, in a clear departure from anti-Judaistic tendencies of previous eras, the Third Quest is well informed by Jewish scholars and by a thorough understanding of Second Temple Judaism (rather than a Judaism defined by Jesus' life). Thus the Third Quest is an interdisciplinary approach, embracing sociology and archaeology. Consequently, dissimilarity to Judaism is no longer seen as a virtue. The approach of the Third Quest is backed up with methodological reflection on criteria in Jesus research, replacing the criterion of dissimilarity with the criterion of plausibility.[11]

Next Stage?

Given the historical focus of the Third Quest, a possible next stage will study what it means that Jesus was a historical figure. Human perception, memory, and history are explored by Anthony Le Donne some thirty years after the beginning of the Third Quest.[12] It remains to be seen how this will be made fruitful for our understanding of Jesus the Jew.

Motives for the "Dissimilar" Jesus

Motives for the "dissimilar" Jesus can be grouped into four types:

A. The Anti-Semitic or Anti-Judaist Approach to Judaism

We are looking at the understanding of Jesus in a Christian context, which implies a principally positive view of Jesus. Therefore, any negative view of Judaism theologically or indeed racially of the Jewish people necessarily motivates removing any Jewishness from Jesus as far as possible and emphasizing his dissimilarity to Judaism.

B. Theological Conflicts Projected Vicariously onto Jesus and His Contemporaries

While the motivation under A is mainly anti-Semitic, mixed with theological anti-Judaism, the chief motivation under B is based on the adversarial stance of Protestantism. Protestant scholars would seek to see themselves and their theology represented by Jesus who is cast into the mold of a Protestant Reformer. In this setting, the Jews take on the role of the Roman

FIGURE 8.1: MOTIVES FOR THE "DISSIMILAR" JESUS

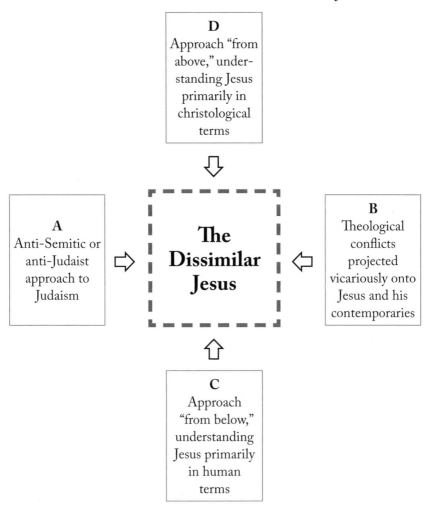

Catholic counterparts to Protestants. Thus, by implication Jesus is described as dissimilar to Judaism.

Another important theological motif is the apologetic interest of critical New Testament scholarship: in order to prove its value and fruitfulness for ministry, it does well to concentrate on aspects which serve to identify Jesus with Christianity rather than Judaism.

C. Approach "from Below," Understanding Jesus Primarily in Human Terms

Interest in the human side of Jesus, his consciousness and personality, necessitate emphasizing his distinctiveness and uniqueness in human and historical terms. If Jesus were just a normal person, there would be little point in spending time on him. Understanding him as a special person easily leads to the attempt of contrasting Jesus with his contemporaries who are Jewish and showing them in less than favorable light.

D. Approach "from Above," Understanding Jesus Primarily in Christological Terms

Finally, there is the approach which is guided by a theological reflection on the person of Jesus, akin to a Christology from above. In the case of Bultmann, his theological non-interest in the historical Jesus (despite writing a Jesus book) throws the relevance of Jesus' Jewishness into question. At the same time, dialectical theology's emphasis on God's transcendence influenced the way the post-Bultmann period (the so-called "Second Quest") described the historical Jesus: the resurgence of interest in the historical Jesus remained largely focused on his message and the essentials of his teaching, emphasizing the continuation between this and the post-Easter kerygma and early Christian proclamation of faith.

All these varied interests in a "Dissimilar Jesus,"—dissimilar, that is, to Judaism and occasioned by particular cultural, theological, and political situations—are methodologically underpinned by the Criterion of Dissimilarity.[13] In its effort to appraise the historical value of its source material on Jesus, Jesus research developed criteria, applied mainly to the New Testament as the prime source for Jesus. The goal in this undertaking was to identify historically authentic material and to distinguish between this and inauthentic Jesus tradition assumed to be either of Jewish-Christian or later Christian origin. The Criterion of Dissimilarity sought to secure an assured minimum of authentic Jesus tradition by including in this everything that was dissimilar either to Jesus' Jewish contemporaries or to his later followers.

There were two particular uses of this criterion of dissimilarity which made this all the more problematic. First, some scholars saw this critically assured minimum as a criterion or filter for any further material. Secondly, the dissimilar pieces of tradition were understood as the characteristic and essentially Jesus-like pieces. In both cases, a huge bias appears which makes it increasingly likely for Jesus to be isolated from his context. The most important trait that emerges from this kind of Jesus research, methodologically determined by the criterion of dissimilarity, is that Jesus was very unlike his Jewish context.

The classic formulation of the Criterion of Dissimilarity can be found in a lecture which Bultmann's student, Ernst Käsemann, gave at the reunion of the "Old Marburgers" in 1953:

> In only one case do we have more or less safe ground under our feet: when there are no grounds either for deriving a tradition from Judaism or for ascribing it to primitive Christianity; and especially when Jewish Christianity has mitigated or modified the received tradition, as having found it too bold for its taste.[14]

It is worth noting that Jesus' dissimilarity towards Judaism became on the whole much more important in the post-Bultmann school of Jesus researchers than Jesus' dissimilarity towards early Christianity. This is the case because following the period of intentional non-interest in the historical Jesus, Bultmann students were keen to show the significance of the historical Jesus for the Christian faith, thus leading them to be far more favorably disposed towards continuity between Jesus and early Christianity than between Jesus' Jewish contemporaries and Jesus. The reason for this was in part also the attempt to defend historical-critical scholarship against the critique of biblically conservative voices in the church at the time: if, by focusing on continuity, historical-critical scholarship could be seen to demonstrate the reliability and faithfulness of early Christian witness to Jesus, then the case for such scholarship in the service of the church was well made.

A. Jesus, the Non-Jew: Anti-Judaism and Anti-Semitism

This essay is not the place to study the interrelationship between, and overlapping of, anti-Semitism and anti-Judaism. What is clear, however, is that during the Nazi period, some German scholars sought to eradicate all traces of Jewishness in Jesus in order to restore the "original and authentic" teachings of Christianity, complete with an Aryan Jesus who was as dissimilar to Judaism as possible.[15]

However, the idea of an Aryan Jesus predates the Nazi Christians and was supported by a long-standing anti-Judaism and anti-Semitism in Christianity, indeed in pagan antiquity.[16] The anti-Semitism of the Greco-Roman world, in which the budding movement of Christianity tried to find a foothold, increasingly led to Jesus' crucifixion being presented as the fault of "the Jews"; this is particularly obvious in John's Gospel. In this context, any debates or discussions Jesus may have had with his Jewish contemporaries were interpreted not as internal Jewish arguments but as indicators of a fundamental and essential parting of the ways. Thus, as the young identity of Christianity was defined, it was increasingly defined over and against Judaism. This non-Jewish identity became politically expedient in an anti-Semitic Roman Empire. The myth of Jews as Christ killers and subsequently in medieval times as ritual murderers of Christian children and so on grew an unholy alliance of anti-Semitism and anti-Judaism.

Luther's attitude to Jews was complex. On the one hand, he wrote in 1523 "That Jesus Christ was born a Jew" and argued for kind and caring behavior towards Jewish people, albeit in order to facilitate their conversion to the Christian faith. However, twenty years later Luther's "On the Jews and their Lies"[17] was seen by many to be the archetypical document to justify persecution and pogroms from the sixteenth to the twentieth century. While scholars argue over the extent to which Luther was driven by theological or racial concerns, a very important fusion occurred in Luther's thought which served to bolster Jesus' dissimilarity to Judaism: while Luther was clearly influenced by anti-Semitic writings, his chief theological accusation, justification by works—versus his own justification by grace—was directed against both Jews and Roman Catholics. This was to become formative for the burgeoning field of biblical study which flourished primarily in Protestantism. This will be developed further in the next section.

A number of factors in the nineteenth century led to a further weakening of any positive linking between Jesus and Judaism. Firstly, the German romantics "went East." Sanskrit studies made Buddhist texts available, and the subsequent fascination with Eastern religion meant a further loss of focus on the Hebrew roots of the Judaeo-Christian faith. In fact, in search for originating myths, attempts were made to locate the roots for the Christian faith in Indian mythology, including speculation that Jesus might have spent some of his formative early adult years among Buddhists. Rudolf Seydel (1835–1892) pointed out many parallels in the teachings of Jesus and Buddha,[18] and scholars variously attributed the inspiration for Jesus' message to the Greek world, Hinduism, or Buddhism in India or Iranian culture.

The second factor concerned Galilee. Ernest Renan's book on Jesus was one of the earliest prominent and popular attempts of perceiving Galilee as the specifically non-Jewish inspiration for Jesus.[19] In a highly romanticized way he describes the delights of Galilee which, according to Renan (1823–1892), inspired in Jesus "a lively antipathy to the faults of the official representatives of Judaism."[20]

Using his Galilean background in order to distinguish Jesus from Judaism became a very fruitful topic of scholarship. The Assyrian invasion of the eighth century BCE was the historical argument for explaining why Galileans were racially not Jews. Emil Schürer (1844–1910) and Houston Stewart Chamberlain (1855–1927) were among the best known writers to champion this view.[21] Thus Galilee as the main place of Jesus' ministry—apart from Jerusalem, where he was of course executed—was dissociated from Judaism and associated with true Christian if not Aryan faith.

Schürer's work was foundational for Christian scholars' study of Judaism. While a reliable account of Judaism is intended, the real focus of the work is the development of the Christian faith, and it is with this lens that Judaism is viewed. The most obvious linguistic indication of the problem which implies the withering of Judaism in the face of the Christian faith is the common term used for Judaism in the time of Jesus: *Spätjudentum*— late Judaism. Schürer was keen to highlight the theological issues he saw between Judaism and the Christian faith (more on this in the next section), whereas Chamberlain's views are much more clearly racially motivated, and he claimed unequivocally that Jesus was an Aryan.

And finally, a third factor was nineteenth-century New Testament scholarship's discovery of various strands within early Christianity, especially a closer understanding of the distinctiveness of Jewish and gentile Christians. Ferdinand Christian Baur's (1792–1860) tendency criticism meant that rather than perceiving early Christianity as a monolithic block, conflicts and differing traditions became apparent. Baur sought to demonstrate that there were competing factions ("tendencies") behind the New Testament text that he understood in the Hegelian framework as the Petrine group (thesis) and the Pauline group (antithesis). While such tendency criticism in itself does not necessarily lead to anti-Judaism, it does provide the necessary tool for a critical evaluation of early Christianity and a differentiation of Jewish or Hellenistic elements within it.

These three factors taken together—the alternative offer of Eastern originating myths and religions, the possibility of a racially and theologically non-Jewish Galilee, and the historical-critical tool to differentiate and peel away different layers in early Christianity—enable the more disastrous and crass purging of Jewishness from Jesus, so as to present a Jesus who is primarily dissimilar to Judaism.

In Germany this was all happening in the general political context of the Berlin anti-Semitism row and the Dreyfus Affair. The term *semite* became a useful negative foil for Indo-Europeans and Aryans. With the growing anthropological rather than doctrinal perception of Christianity in the nineteenth century, the term *Judaism* became more detached from its religious meaning and could therefore gain a much stronger racial connotation.

At its worst culmination, all this led in Nazi Germany to the "Institut zur Erforschung und Beseitigung des jüdischen Einflusses auf das deutsche kirchliche Leben" in Jena—the Institute for the Study and Eradication of Jewish Influence on German Religious Life.[22] Through the work of this Institute, ". . . Jesus was transformed from a Jew prefigured by the Old Testament into an anti-Semite and proto-Nazi."[23]

B. Jesus, the Adversarial Protestant

Law and grace are the key poles which define Protestant thinking, especially in the Lutheran school of thought. By nature—*nomen est omen*—Protestant theology has a history of being adversarial and arguing against what it understands to be a misguided theological understanding. Luther's great reformation insight is drawn from the Apostle Paul's writing in Romans 3. Paul himself deals robustly with his "judaizing" opponents, and this verve is picked up by Protestant theologians and applied to Roman Catholicism.

Luther saw the Jews as representatives of the chief theological theme inimical to Protestant theology, namely salvation by works, through the law, whereas he identified Jesus' chief mission with his own, preaching salvation by grace alone. Consequently, there was a systemic drive within the minds of most Protestant biblical scholars to separate Jesus (that is, grace) from Judaism (that is, law).

The influential New Testament scholar Julius Wellhausen (1844–1918) saw the law as the main point of difference between Israel and Judaism. Wellhausen positioned Jesus in close proximity to the Prophets of Israel (this is the "prophet-connection-theory") after which Judaism was said to have become more and more legalistic, reaching its high point in the Pharisees, seen as the "super Jews." In contrast, according to Wellhausen, Jesus continued the earlier natural time of Israel and brings it to blossom in the gospel.[24] This effectively removes the possibility of any dependency on his Jewish contemporaries which Jesus' teaching might have had.

Ferdinand Weber (1836–1879) linked Jewish law with legalism in that Protestant sense and described the essence of Jewish religion as legalistic. Tellingly, one of his publications is called "The System of Jewish Pharisaism and Roman Catholicism."[25] A doctrinal issue from within Christianity is projected into Judaism.

This theme is further developed in Schürer's *History of the Jewish People* with its infamous §28, "Life under the Law" which further popularized Weber's perspective on Judaism. Wilhelm Bousset (1865–1920) articulates quite clearly the parallels he sees between legalistic Judaism and Greek Orthodox and Roman Catholic churches with their emphasis on legalistic, ceremonial, and particularistic tendencies.[26]

The issue is superbly summarized by Bousset's opponent Albert Kalthoff (1850–1906):

> Previous scholarship, often enough without any awareness of doing so, is guided by a particular theological interest, namely opposition to the theology of the Roman Catholic Church. A source is sought that presents the historical personality Jesus, in order to prove on the basis of this source that only the Protestant understanding of Christianity is correct, and that

therefore the Catholic understanding represents a distortion and degeneration of Christianity. Authentic sayings of Jesus were sought, and are still sought, or their original and authentic meaning that Jesus himself intended, with the intention of providing an argument for one's own church and theology and against the church and theology of others.[27]

Significantly, this thrust of locating Protestant identity in Jesus was continued in the post-Bultmann New Quest of Historical Jesus research. Günther Bornkamm (1905–1990) is a prime example for this. *Jesus von Nazareth*, which was published in 1956, was the standard work of its time and highly influential among theologians and the general public alike. It is worth noting that from the start Bornkamm is at pains to put great distance between himself and anti-Semitic and anti-Judaist scholars on Jesus and Judaism. In subsequent editions of his 1956 book he also improves his references to and description of Judaism.[28]

Bornkamm's passion is to show the relevance of the historical Jesus for the Christian faith. He seeks convergence between the story of Jesus and the message of Christ. That he does so as a Protestant theologian is very apparent in his description of the new righteousness which Jesus proclaims. And correspondingly, for Bornkamm law, works and achievement characterize Judaism and its teaching.[29] He is particularly critical of what he describes as its casuistry. Bornkamm describes Jesus as a good protestant Reformer versus excesses of medieval Roman Catholicism when he has Jesus remove the idea of divine reward from the hopeless web of Jewish doctrine in favor of revealing divine justice and grace.[30] Similarly, while Bornkamm is keen to avoid caricaturizing of Pharisees, Jesus is characterized by a strong adversarial stance towards them with their legalism and atomizing piety.[31]

Therefore, against a backdrop of anti-Judaism and anti-Semitism, adversarial Protestant identity contributes to the presentation of a Jesus who is profoundly dissimilar to Judaism.

C. Jesus, Hero and Genius

As romantic interest in Jesus grew and doctrinal interest waned during the nineteenth century, the admiration of the hero and genius in Jesus began to play an increasingly important role. Jesus, the individual, with his role in history, was thereby set up to be dissimilar to his contemporaries and context.

The classic formulation of the role of the individual in history by Jacob Burckhardt (1818–1897) states how history is from time to time carried forward by one great individual.[32] The ideal of the great history-making personality was most fully developed in the thought of Thomas Carlyle (1795–1881). As outlined in his most famous work, *On Heroes, Hero-Worship, and the Heroic in History*, he saw progress in history brought about by the work of brilliant individual men.[33] Distinct from this is the idea of the genius which equally fascinated the nineteenth century. There is a strong religious connotation as the superhuman genius carries divine characteristics.

As scholars began to examine the historical figure of Jesus, both concepts of genius and hero were easily applied to him.[34] And both the concept of hero and genius bear not only a special relation to the divine, they also indicate a fundamental difference to the milieu whence their protagonist emerges. What had hitherto been a doctrinal appreciation of the uniqueness of Jesus was replaced with Jesus as the unique hero and genius.

Many scholars, such as Keim, Baumgarten, Bousset, Wellhausen, Wrede, Holtzmann, and others, saw in Jesus the great personality and the religious-moral genius who had it in him to transcend Judaism—for Judaism was the most obvious dark background against which this historical figure could shine. In earlier times, of course, there had been great men, the Old Testament prophets, and they had founded the religion of Israel. The concept of the demise of Judaism thereafter meant that, with the theory of prophetic connection, Jesus can be seen to pick up the threads again and be an even greater hero and genius by founding universal Christianity. It now becomes clear that it is actually the idea of the great hero and genius which underpins the theory of Jesus' prophetic connection.

While Jesus, the hero and genius, undoubtedly carries religious overtones, the basic approach is a human, "from below" one. This necessitates some acknowledgment of his background and context. The theory of accommodation provided the perfect solution: clearly, in order to communicate, Jesus would have had to accommodate his contemporary listeners by speaking their language and culture.[35] This, however, is "just" an accommodation: with the theory of accommodation, even obvious parallels and convergence between Jesus' and Jewish teaching of the time are rendered meaningless.

Therefore, the real Jesus, the great hero and genius, is necessarily and implicitly quite dissimilar from his context.

D. Christ Rather than Jesus

In this section we shall touch upon the effect dialectical theology had on the perception of Jesus within Judaism. Dialectical theology was a reaction against the liberal theology of the nineteenth century. It stressed the otherness of God and denied that it was a mere quantitative rather than qualitative leap to draw inferences from humanity to God. Therefore, dialectical theology did not look to the person of the historical Jesus as the source of its theology but rather to the post-Resurrection kerygma of the New Testament. Reconstructing the historical Jesus was no longer a priority. Indeed, it is arguable that taking the weight of theological-apologetic expectation away from New Testament study liberated it and secured it some space within to operate freely.

The effect of dialectical theology for us here is twofold.

Firstly, there is the devaluing of any historical details about Jesus beyond Bultmann's famous "bloßes Dass seines Gekommenseins" (that is, the mere fact of Jesus having come). In his *Jesus*, Bultmann locates Jesus almost entirely within Judaism.[36] While not suggesting that Bultmann was anti-Semitic, there is an unfortunate connection between the much reduced theological evaluation of the historical Jesus and his classification within Judaism. Implicit in this judgment is the clear separation between Judaism and Christianity. While the nineteenth-century quest for the historical Jesus sought to locate Christian identity in him and therefore tended to remove him from his Jewish background, the opposite is the case here: The Christian kerygma is based on the risen Christ and the historical Jesus can remain safely within Judaism. Incidentally, in this separation Bultmann also expresses the Lutheran distinction between law and gospel.

Nevertheless, where Bultmann does see in Jesus seeds of Christian theology, these seeds take the form of Bultmann's own theology: "according to Jesus' thought the Kingdom is the marvelous, new, wholly other."[37] Due to the particular thrust of Bultmann's dialectic and existentialist[38] theology, even when he sees seeds of Christian theology in Jesus' teaching, for example in its immediacy, they are implicitly, but clearly distinguished from any Jewish teaching and thus fundamentally dissimilar to it.

Secondly, dialectical theology's emphasis on God's complete otherness subsequently influenced renewed Jesus research of the New Quest, leading to a subtle historicizing of Jesus' otherness and dissimilarity. The latter could be seen as dialectical theology's version of the tendency to historicize dogma regarding Jesus. This is best seen in Bornkamm's remark: "Jesus belongs to this world. Yet in the midst of it he is of unmistakable otherness."[39]

Again, as with Bultmann, it would be simplistic to accuse Bornkamm of having set out primarily to diminish the importance of Judaism for Jesus. Rather, as Käsemann says, the critique of first-century Judaism embodied in Jesus would strike at every ancient religion.[40] Judaism, of course, is simply there, it is where Jesus comes from. As such, it becomes the obvious target for projections of issues, conflicts, and theologies which historically are not necessarily related at all—but to which *we* wish Jesus to be dissimilar.

However, for us today, the inability of scholars in the mid-twentieth century to see any connection between a non-Jewish Jesus, based on a theological anti-Judaism, and the horrors resulting from anti-Semitism, is staggering and barely comprehensible. This inability bears witness to the human condition for which nothing is more powerful than denial, and, when biological racist anti-Semitism is completely separated from the theological effort of demonstrating the supremacy of Christianity over Judaism, it also shows a remarkable failure to recognize that (theological) scholarship cannot occupy a neutral place in this world.

Conclusion

I remember an occasion when I was asked to speak to a group of young people on the given theme "Different but just as good." It was the organizers' thinly veiled attempt to accept the unacceptable, diversity rather than uniformity. However, the title already gave away their problem: because they couldn't say "different" with sufficient cheer, the hasty qualification "*but* just as good" was supposed to salvage the statement.

I have attempted to sketch out some contributory factors that made it appear so compelling to Christians involved in New Testament studies that Jesus must have been fundamentally dissimilar to the Judaism of his time. My opening question asked whether Jesus can be positively appreciated in his distinctiveness without being negative about Judaism.

Mercifully, our knowledge of Second Temple Judaism is much enhanced and no longer relies on works which are fundamentally Christian apologetics. The chief reason for this is the Third Quest[41] in Jesus research. The (re-)emancipation of the historical quest for Jesus from the field of theology and Christology removed the need for a Christian apologetics which sought convergence with early Christianity rather than with Jewish teaching. A better understanding of sociology and social history embeds any historical figure in its time and so the "individual" Jesus loses some of his importance. And finally, already pre-dating the Third Quest, Jewish scholars (re-)discovered Jesus and contributed to the discussion and our knowledge of intertestamental literature increased. All this was further enforced by a growing recognition by New Testament scholars themselves that anti-Judaism was a problem.

As a result, our rigid image of Judaism at this time has been overcome, and we can see Jesus as a distinctive yet truly historical figure in and among a very colorful tapestry made up of Jewish thinkers and teachers, each contributing distinctive threads. This is a much more organic image in which being different, being at variance, is not necessarily a negative thing at all. From whichever side you look at it neither Jesus nor "Judaism" is "different *but* just as good."

The saga of Jesus' proposed dissimilarity to Judaism is a long and sorry one for New Testament studies. There is no need for Christocentric or Jesus-centered Christian theology to be anti-Judaist, and we need to be alert to the temptation of functionalizing another religion, group, or culture in order for them to become the dark foil against which to present a rather glaring light of Christian faith.

Christian theologians need to learn to say "mother Judaism"[42] and take seriously the fifth commandment.

Jesus within Judaism: The Political and Moral Context of Jesus Research and Its Methodology

Gerd Theissen

Whether Jesus was situated within Judaism was not at all an academic question. During the National Socialist Regime of 1933–1945, it was a political and moral issue in Germany. Anti-Semitic prejudices and politics exercised a disastrous influence on scholarship. Already before the Third Reich some writers denied that Jesus was a Jew.[1] During the Third Reich it was a popular thesis among the so-called "German Christians." After 1945, the question for the Jewishness of Jesus seemed to become again a purely academic question in New Testament scholarship. But there remained a suspicion of biased traditions in society, church, and academic theology—even in spite of the wish to revise dark anti-Jewish traditions.

Born in 1943, when the holocaust reached its peak, I grew up in a country that became more and more aware of the inconceivable genocide committed by our own people during the war. I learned that how I thought about Judaism and how well I was able to resist anti-Semitic tendencies were crucial criteria of my humanity. I encountered this basic conviction both at school and at the university, where I studied theology (1962–1968). All my teachers on the theological faculty of the University of Bonn had been members of the Confessing Church, opposing National Socialism. For them it was a matter of course that Jesus was a Jew, but they emphasized at the same time that he started a movement that transcended Judaism. They interpreted his conflicts with Law, Temple, and the Jewish elites as the beginning of a break with Judaism. Jesus seemed to be the first Christian theologian. Theological interests dominated Jesus research during those years. But the next generation of scholars (c. 1970) inaugurated a turn to real and social history in all the humanities, including biblical and New Testament studies. We developed a new sensitivity for the origin of Christianity within a Jewish society and religion.

In 1977, I published a small book titled *Sociology of Early Palestinian Christianity*. This book began with the statement: "Early Christianity began as a renewal movement within Judaism brought into being through Jesus."[2] In those days such a statement was criticized. But now nearly all contemporary New Testament scholars would agree. Today we have a contrary suspicion: that the shock of the holocaust did not allow us to evaluate the conflicts of Jesus with his contemporaries in a balanced way. The Jewish historian Joseph Klausner once stated in his book on Jesus before the era of National Socialism: "In spite of all of this, something was in [Jesus], out of which something that was not Jewish developed (Trotz alledem aber war etwas in [Jesus], aus dem sich 'Un-Judentum' entwickelte)."[3] Are we New Testament scholars, with post-holocaust sensibilities, inhibited to discover such non-Jewish aspects in our Jesus research? The basic question is therefore: is academic methodology able to correct our biases and prejudices? We may not be able to answer this question definitively, but perhaps we can avoid some errors. Perhaps a first methodological step is to acknowledge the biases of our own historical context. Therefore this essay has two parts. The first part deals with German New Testament scholarship on Jesus in the context of German history before and after 1945. I can only give a short sketch how anti-Semitism and the opposition of anti-Semitism influenced Jesus research in Germany. The second part of this essay sketches a methodology for how to deal with the question of placing Jesus within Judaism—not in order to overcome all prejudices but in order to achieve plausible and responsible statements on Jesus' position within Judaism and to correct some errors.

1. Jesus Research in Its Political Context: German Politics and the Historical Jesus

a) *Jesus Research and Politics before 1945*

National Socialism claimed that Christianity was a branch of Judaism. Christianity was in their view a tool of Judaism that paralyzed the vitality of other peoples by religious scrupulosity, that is by an overbearing system of morality and by an authoritarian God.[4] According to National Socialism both Judaism and Christianity had poisoned the mentality of the German people. Therefore many of them left the church.

Other patriotic Protestants formed the movement of the "the German Christians" (die "Deutschen Christen") and called for a nationalistic transformation of the Christian Faith. The radical wing of these "Deutschen Christen" advocated the following: (1) The Old Testament should be abolished because it was a Jewish book. (2) The New Testament should be interpreted in an anti-Jewish way: Jesus should be seen as liberator from Judaism, and Pauline theology should be dismissed as a Jewish distortion of the true Gospel of Jesus. According to their view, Paul's teaching on sin, atoning death, and judgment was poison for a healthy vitality of the German people. (3) All protestant churches should be united in one national church while (4) all Jewish Christians should be excluded from this church.

It is true, the German Christians failed in the beginning. They did not assimilate all Protestant churches, they did not establish a unified national church, and they could not introduce the "Arierparagraph" within all churches. Many moderate German Christians, moreover many of the academic theologians among them, resigned from the movement in November 1933, protesting against the abolishment of the Old Testament and the refusal of Pauline theology; however, many of them continued to support National Socialism and were often infected by anti-Semitism.

In contrast, other Christians formed the Confessing Church opposing both the radical and moderate national socialistic Christians. The Confessing Church was a minority. This minority was not free of traditional theological anti-Judaism, even if they refused anti-Semitism as a racist construct. Only three churches in Germany resisted the German Christians as whole churches: Württemberg, Bayern, and Hannover. All other German protestant churches were split. In general, the church leadership was dominated by German Christians, whereas many parishioners who belonged to the Confessing Church opposed this leadership and established separate congregations.

In 1939, the majority of the official churches founded the "Institute for the study of Jewish influence on the life of the German churches and the removal of this influence" ("Institut zur Erforschung und Beseitigung des jüdischen Einflusses auf das deutsche kirchliche Leben") in Eisenach.[5] The institute sought to demonstrate that Christianity was not a Jewish movement, but from the outset a departure from and replacement of Judaism. The church leaders hoped to convince the Germans that it was not necessary to leave the church in order to get rid of Jewish influence. After all Jesus had already began the abolishment of Jewish traditions and piety. According to the institute, Jesus had established himself as a liberator from Judaism.

The academic director of the institute was the New Testament scholar Walter Grundmann (1906–1976). He cooperated with other New Testament scholars such as Johannes Leipoldt, Georg Bertram, and Carl Schneider. Schneider (1900–1977)[6] wrote the small book "Early Christianity as anti-Semitic movement" (*Das Frühchristentum als antisemitische Bewegung*) (1940) with the thesis that Jesus originated in the Galilean lower classes, opposed the upper classes and their Jewishness, and was influenced by the surrounding Hellenistic culture. Jesus fought against Judaism. He liberated his followers from Judaism. This kind of anti-Semitism we may call a "redemptive anti-Semitism" (*Erlösungsantisemitismus*—a word coined by S. Friedländer). Judaism was for these national socialist theologians the embodiment of all evil. Dejudaization was therefore salvation from all possible evil and the center of their modernizing program for Christianity. The most intelligent of these "German Christians" was Emanuel Hirsch, professor of theology at the University of Göttingen. According to him, historical-critical research on Jesus had succeeded to discover the anti-Jewish Jesus behind the legendary traditions that often mitigated Jesus' opposition to Judaism. Emanuel Hirsch combined a historical-critical theology with an authoritarian political ethics. He interpreted John 10 in the following way: Jesus is the good shepherd who leads his sheep out of the sheep shelter, that is, out of the slavery of the Jewish law.

The great New Testament scholar at Marburg, Rudolf Bultmann (1884–1976), mocked Emanuel Hirsch's interpretation of John 10 saying: What nonsense, in the evening the shepherd will lead his sheep back into the sheep shelter![7] Bultmann joined from the outset the Confessing Church[8] and protested against the discrimination of Jews in the German society in a public lecture at the university.[9] Together with his colleague Hans von Soden he organized a protest against the discrimination of Jews within the church in 1933. At the peak of Hitler's power (1941) he published *New Testament and Mythology* together with a polemical article against the German Christians and their nationalistic interpretation of history. He developed his modernizing program for Christianity as an alternative to the program of the German Christians. His message was: we need not overcome Judaism, but mythology. He argued that modernized Christianity must not require dejudaization, but demythologization.[10] The mythical elements in the Christian faith must not be eliminated, but must be interpreted because they contain an existential truth about the human situation in the world.

Already in 1926, in a small book titled *Jesus*, Bultmann claimed that Jesus stayed within Judaism all his life.[11] He adhered to this position in all his later publications. Jesus was no liberator from Judaism. But Bultmann minimized the theological relevance of the historical Jesus: what is relevant for Christian faith is only *that* Jesus lived, not *how* he lived. The Jewishness of Jesus was therefore for him a historical fact but was not crucial for Christian faith. But historically he considered the conflicts of Jesus with his opponents as conflicts within Judaism, not as conflicts with Judaism as such. Bultmann distinguished between the Jewish Law as God's will and "Jewish legalism" as a way of interpreting the law. Therefore, he could on the one hand state that Jesus represented the Jewish Law ("Gesetz") as a demand for radical obedience, and on the other hand he could underscore Jesus' protest against "Jewish legalism (Gesetzlichkeit)" as an attempt to transform radical obedience into a casuistic network of merits. His distinction between legalism and law may be criticized, but Bultmann insisted indeed that Jesus acted and lived as a Jew.

Even more important is that Bultmann's existentialism denied a timeless essence of Judaism. Jews and Christians are what they decide to be. No person is fixed on his or her religion or his or her people. Christian faith started, according to Bultmann, with the cross and resurrection. Consequently it was possible for human beings to seize a new self-understanding that is the Christian way of living *sola gratia, sola fide,* and *sine lege.* This Christian faith was interpreted as a path to human authenticity by Paul and John. It was Paul who criticized not only legalism but the law as such. Due to Paul's criticism, early Christianity developed to be an independent religion outside of Judaism (whereas the Nazi-theologians criticized Paul for having re-judaicized the Christian faith).

b) Jesus Research after 1945

After the war Bultmann's pupils renewed Jesus research, starting the "new quest" for the historical Jesus with a seminal article of Ernst Käsemann (1906–1998) on "The Problem of the Historical Jesus" (1953).[12] He and other pupils of Bultmann argued that the Easter faith and its interpretation in Pauline and Johannine theology were not the starting point for Christian faith, but the historical Jesus and his preaching. Stressing this continuity between the historical Jesus and Paul, Käsemann and others refused one of the main concerns of the German Christians in New Testament interpretation: the devaluation of Pauline theology by contrasting Paul with Jesus. They opposed the German Christians by stating that there was a historical continuity and a theological accordance between Jesus and Paul.[13] Paul was no longer the theologian who had distorted the message of Jesus with Jewish categories. But their hero Paul represented a "high Christology." Jesus was for him much more than a common human man; he was a divine being. Therefore, if there was continuity from Jesus to Paul, Jesus himself must have had something like a high Christology during his lifetime; Jesus' preaching, they argued, must have revealed an adumbration of his divine authority after Easter. This divine authority of the historical Jesus transcends a monotheistic faith that worships God as the one and only God. It transcends Judaism. Looking for continuity between Jesus and Paul, the pupils of Bultmann had therefore to contrast the historical Jesus with Judaism. This is why we encounter in their writings a non-Jewish Jesus.

We should never forget that this was a consequence of a rehabilitation of the Jewish Paul against the national socialist Christians, who opposed this Jewish Paul to a non-Jewish Jesus. According to them Jesus was influenced by gentile mentality in Galilee. Some of them even claimed that Jesus was an Aryan, the offspring of a Roman soldier.

With regard to Paul, the pupils of Bultmann opposed the German Christians; concerning the relationship between Jesus and Judaism, they seemed at first glance to be in line with the idea that Jesus lived in opposition to his Jewish environment. But did the pupils of Bultmann really show affinity to the German Christians in this regard? I am sure all my teachers would be upset by such a reproach. Most of them were opposed to National Socialism. Let us therefore try to understand why they contrasted Jesus with Judaism, even if we do not share their point of view.

They were driven by an internal logic: they had learned by their teacher Rudolf Bultmann that Christian faith started with the cross and resurrection and that the criticism of the Law in Pauline theology was due to this faith. When they established the thesis that Christianity started with the historical Jesus, they necessarily had to look for all hints that Jesus claimed a role that transcended his Jewish environment. Therefore, they interpreted his conflicts *within* Judaism as conflicts *with* Judaism. The Sabbath conflicts were seen as conflict with the Law as such, not with a certain interpretation of some limited laws. If Jesus really was the beginning of Christianity he had to start an exodus out of Judaism.

In my opinion, what they represented was an existential allo-Judaism (a projection of otherness onto the Jews) that sometimes could change into an existential anti-Judaism but could also become a Philo-Semitism (recognition of the positive impact of Jews in history).[14] The existential anti-Judaism in the so-called "new quest" was a heritage of traditional protestant anti-Judaism—a modernized version of the contrast between law and Gospel (or between *lex* and *evangelium*). Judaism represented the Law; the Gospel liberated from the Law. For many Protestants the Jewish contemporaries of Jesus and Paul had affinity to the "legalism" of the Catholics. Both Jews and Catholics represented a cross-cultural attitude to God. The existentialism of the Bultmann-school denied all essentialism. There exists no Jewish or Christian essence. Jews and Christians are what they decide to be—even if their decision reacts to a kerygma that comes from beyond all that human beings can decide.

I should therefore stress that the existential theologians of the Bultmann-school never advocated the traditional Christian anti-Judaism that criticized Jews because they allegedly had killed Jesus and suffered therefore by a curse. According to this traditional anti-Judaism, Jews could escape such a curse by conversion and baptism. We never met such ideas in the writing of the Bultmann-school. It should also be stressed: all pupils of Bultmann refused racial anti-Semitism that excluded even the possibility of such a conversion. The attitude of these protestant existential theologians was rather an allo-Judaism, defining Judaism as an alternative possibility to Christianity comparable to catholic faith. Both Jews and Catholics were deemed to be representatives of a legalism of works (of "Werkgerechtigkeit"). Both had within their traditions the possibility to behave in an alternative way. G. Bornkamm, one of the pupils of Bultmann, stressed for example that Jewish piety was not at all merely casuistic Torah-observance but also a sapiental Torah-piety without casuistic.[15] But it is true: allo-Judaism can change either to anti-Judaism or to Philo-Semitism. If Jews were "the other ones," and if they were the most relevant "alterity" to one's own "identity," they may be admired as the bearer of God's revelation but may also be refused if other people claim the revelation exclusively for themselves.

Therefore we have to ask: was this existential allo-Judaism of Bultmann's pupils a hidden heritage of the era of National Socialism? Did they sometimes follow unconsciously some anti-Jewish traditions? It is indeed possible that scholars sometimes follow unconsciously a dark tradition in spite of the fact that they consciously refuse this tradition. We must take into regard that Ernst Käsemann, the founder of the new quest for the historical Jesus, was an enthusiastic German Christian in 1933, before he became aware of his error and went along with the Confessing Church in the spring of 1934.[16] He was imprisoned for some months because of his opposition against National Socialism. But was he really free of anti-Jewish theological traditions?[17] The historical methodology of E. Käsemann, the so-called "criterion of double dissimilarity," guarantees as a result a Jesus who lived much more in contrast to Judaism than to Early Christianity. The theological presupposition of his methodology appeared once in a discussion between Bultmann and his pupils in the 1970s. When Bultmann argued against the contrast between Jesus and Judaism saying that Jesus' call to decision was an expression of the Jewish law, Käsemann answered emphatically: if this is true, "the resurrected Jesus has the task to redeem us from the earthly Jesus."[18] Here appears the pattern of a "redemptive anti-Judaism" that reminds the redemptive anti-Semitism of German Christians. Jesus is seen as the liberator from the (Jewish) Law. Here it is the kerygmatic Christ who liberates from the historical Jesus as representative of the Law. Here it is not alone legalism but the law itself that should be overcome.

But existential allo-Judaism may also be transformed into Philo-Semitism. When Judaism represents an alternative way of living, why should this alternative way not be more attractive than the Christian way of life? And when the pupils of Bultmann thought that Jesus' preaching "implicitly" embraced Christian faith that became first "explicitly" after cross and resurrection, why should we not conclude from such continuity that Christianity is an implicit possibility of Judaism—originating with Jesus who lived and preached as a Jew? I have concluded from the Jesus research of my teachers that it is impossible to construct Christianity without Judaism. I am convinced: it is impossible to love the New Testament without the Old Testament. It is impossible to love Jesus without loving his people.

I think, therefore, it is unfair to say that the "new quest for the historical Jesus" is a continuation of the anti-Semitism of the German Christians. The representatives of the new quest sharply opposed the contrast between Jesus and Paul that is one of the two ideas of German Christians in Jesus research, but they enhanced—compared with their teacher Bultmann—the contrast between Jesus and Judaism. They lacked a sensitivity that their ideas converged with the second idea of the German Christians that the historical Jesus was the liberator from Jewish law. Therefore Walter Grundmann, the academic director of the *Eisenacher Institut,* could continue his career after the war, mitigating his anti-Jewish tendencies in Jesus research, but without remarkable differences in his statements on Jesus compared with those of the Bultmann-school. The crucial difference has always been that the existential theologians of the Bultmann-school refused all essentialism. They argued that Judaism cannot be determined to behave in this or that way. An existential anthropology refuses such essentialism—whether it be a cultural, racial, or theological essentialism.

Today the intellectual situation has changed. We have a broad discourse on alterity and identity in the whole society. Moves toward tolerance and integration of minorities mark the agendas of all modern societies. There can be no doubt that popular movements with ethnic prejudices have revitalized. Anti-Semitism has not disappeared and is on the rise again. Our political context has changed. This has an impact on Jesus research. Judaism has discovered Jesus as a Jew. Muslims discover Jesus as a predecessor of Muhammad. Jewish, Christian, and agnostic scholars participate in Jesus research. That is the historical and political context of the so-called "third quest for the historical Jesus." Since the 1980s, within this third quest, originated a new consensus that Jesus was embedded in Judaism. All agree today that Jesus was a Jew—not only by birth but by his theological convictions. But what was his place within Judaism? Was he a marginal Jew? Was he a Jewish Cynic representing also Hellenistic influences? Or was he a Jewish prophet?

But how can we today, by a controlled methodology, investigate the question of Jesus' relationship to Judaism? Is not such a question always endangered by ideologies? If we today would, for example, discuss whether a citizen of the USA or Germany is a true American or a typical German—we find that it is nearly impossible to avoid ideologies concerning the "essential features" of an American or a German. In such discussion embarrassing prejudices are always at work. And the same is true for any discussion about whether Jesus was a Jew.

2. A Methodology: Jesus' Place within Judaism[19]

As far as I see there are three methodological ways to explore Jesus' place within Judaism. I label them (a) comparison by structure (b) comparison by groups, and (c) comparison by forms of expression. What do I mean by "comparison by structure"? We have to ask: What are the basic features of Judaism in the time of Jesus? What was the structure of its religion in those days? And can we recognize these basic features in Jesus' life and work? Do we recognize the structure of Judaism in his work and proclamation?

What is a "comparison by groups"? There were many groups within Judaism in those days. They resemble Jesus and his movement in some respects, and they differ in other respects. We must look for similarities and dissimilarities from group to group so that we may place Jesus within the framework of these groups. The advantage of this methodological approach is that we may work without a definition of Judaism as a whole. Such a definition is often one-sided and ideological.

And what is a "comparison by forms"? All religions have comparable forms of expression; narrative myths, ritual signs, and ethical norms are among the most prominent. The most important for our interests are rites and rituals. These expressions signify togetherness and boundary markers. In short, such expressions form collective identity. We have to compare the attitude of Jesus and his movement to the ritual forms of Judaism, for example, his attitude toward holy places and holy ceremonies.

a) Comparison of Structures

Comparing the structure of a religion seems at first glance very promising. We must give definition to what Judaism was in those days by exploring its basic structure as a whole. But an initial problem emerges: if we come across some characteristics of Jesus' life and work that do not fit this definition of Judaism, it may be that our definition is wrong or one-sided. Perhaps the definition does not cover everything that was essential for the structure of the Judaism of Jesus' day. Let me illustrate this by an attempt at a structural definition. We may say that Judaism is marked by (1) monotheism, that is the faith in the one and only God, and (2) by covenantal nomism, that is the conviction that the one and only God has a special link only to one people, whom he had elected by his covenant, and to whom he had given the Torah which helps them stay within this covenant.[20]

Does the Jesus tradition fit these two characteristics of Judaism? There is no doubt Jesus was a monotheist. His proclamation of the Kingdom of God is radical monotheism. It is the message that the one God would and should reign on Earth, setting an end to all evil powers. But what about covenantal nomism? It is true, Jesus represents restoration eschatology.[21] The link with

God and his people should be renewed, the temple should be renewed, and the twelve tribes of Israel should be gathered again. Israel should be restored. But we find also some characteristics in his preaching that seem to go beyond covenantal nomism, which contains two elements: the election (as the basis of the covenant) and the Torah (as the basis of nomism).

Already with John the Baptist we sense a shaking of the consciousness of election; Jews should not rely on their being Abraham's children. God is able from stones to raise up children to Abraham (Luke 3:7-9; Matt. 3:7-10). One could say that it was only John the Baptist who said this, not Jesus. But nobody doubts that John the Baptist belonged to Judaism. If one frames the question of election in this way, such a redefinition of Jewish election by no means forces us outside the general boundary markers of first-century Judaism.

In the Jesus tradition we find (in Q) a very dark word in the Torah which may be reconstructed in the following way: "The law and the prophets were until John; since then until now the kingdom of heaven has suffered violence and men of violence take it by force" (Luke 16:16; Matt. 11:12). It is possible that we find here a question mark behind the validity of the Torah—though other interpretations are possible.[22]

Let us suppose that these two traditions do not fit covenantal nomism (though we may interpret them in a way which makes them fit better within the structure of covenantal nomism). But what would be the consequence? Both traditions are prophetic elements. Prophecy expects that God will act in a new way. Prophecy announces God's judgment. Prophetic pronouncements were abundant in the days of Jesus and are represented by John the Baptist and also by other prophets. Perhaps we must therefore complete our list of Jewish essentials. We should add to monotheism and covenantal nomism perhaps a third element: prophetism. While the Torah provides stability to Judaism, prophetism (and the interpretation of the Torah) provides flexibility.

But how can we avoid begging the question? Expanding our definitions to accommodate exceptions makes whether Jesus was a Jew or not (whether he stayed within Judaism or whether he started an exodus from Judaism, which perhaps his followers completed) an arbitrary choice of definitions. In other words, with this method alone, Jesus' Jewishness becomes a matter of arbitrary definition. The question of the Jewishness of Jesus is too important to be left as such. Therefore the next two comparisons are crucial.

b) Comparison by Groups

There were many groups in the Judaism of Jesus' days.[23] Since the days of the Maccabees there was great vitality in Judaism to develop new ideas concerning Jewish identity and ways of life within Judaism. All these groups have some elements in common; other elements are different. We can discover a network of resemblances and differences beyond those elements which

necessarily are common to all. These groups belong together by family simi-
larity (in the sense of L. Wittgenstein).[24]

There are remarkable differences between the elder groups dating from
the times of the Maccabees—the Sadducees, Essenes, and Pharisees—and the
younger groups dating from the time of the Herodians; the followers of Judas
Galilaios (which are often called Zealots by mistake), the followers of John the
Baptist, and the sign prophets. Firstly, the elder groups reacted against Helle-
nization, while the younger reacted against Romanization. Secondly, the new
groups originated around well-known charismatic figures, which we know by
name, whereas the founders of elder groups are anonymous (for example, the
teacher of righteousness, the founder or re-founder of the Essenes). Thirdly,
the new groups are a radicalization of Judaism. Judas Galilaios represents a
political radicalization: the law obliges to resist the Romans. John the Baptist
represents a ritual radicalization: conversion and baptism are necessary due to
the impurity of the whole person. The sign prophets represent a soteriological
radicalization: salvation and liberation from the Pagans are immediately near.
There is only one non-Jewish group which can be compared with Jesus and
his movement: the Cynics, because they were itinerant philosophers, resem-
bling the itinerant charismatics of the Jesus movement.

Concerning the comparison with the Sadducees, it is possible that Jesus
(or the Jesus tradition) uses Sadducean arguments against the oral tradition
of the fathers (Mark 7:5ff), but Jesus opposes at the same time their denial
of the resurrection (Mark 12:18ff).[25] On the other hand, he shares the belief
in resurrection with the Pharisees but opposes at least some of their traditions of the fathers. We may say that he is situated in the middle between
Sadducees and Pharisees. Is he really a marginal Jew?[26] He seems to be a
Jew in the very center of Judaism. Concerning the comparison with the Essenes, he shares their opposition against the Jerusalem Temple establishment.
Inasmuch, he also stands against the Sadducees, who had support among
the priests and high priests at the temple. However, Jesus does not live in a
counter-cultural community with a special calendar of feasts as the Essenes
did. He shared the calendar and feasts with all other Jews—even with the
priests and high priests. Again we may say Jesus is situated in the middle
between Essenes and Sadducees.

Now let us have a look at the younger groups. Concerning the followers
of Judas Galilaios, the "fourth philosophy" of the Jews according to Josephus, he shares a radical theocratic axiom with Jesus: the one and only God
should reign alone, and no other. But Jesus makes this axiom concrete not
with help of the alternative "God or Caesar" (that is, not within the political
field), but with help of two other oppositions: firstly, the opposition between
"God and Mammon" (Matt. 6:19) that is within the economical or the social
field, and secondly, the opposition between "God and Satan." As such, Jesus

proclaimed the kingdom of God as liberation from the reign of Satan and his demons. (In this regard he is far away from the Sadducees, who denied the belief in demons.)

Concerning the comparison with John the Baptist, Jesus shares John's call to repentance in view of a near eschatology. Jesus shares also the Baptist's ethical radicalism: if one does not produce fruits of repentance one cannot be saved. But the historical Jesus did not connect repentance with baptism as a new ritual. John's baptism (as it was invented anew in John's ministry) says implicitly that all other purity rituals are not sufficient to establish purity. Therefore the baptism of John was implicitly a criticism of the many other forms of ritual baths in contemporary Judaism. This is why the Baptist's movement is a ritual radicalization of Judaism. Jesus shares its distance towards many purity rites, but he also shows a certain distance towards the new baptism. Jesus did not baptize (in spite of John 3:21). And that fits his convictions. Baptism cannot be very important for Jesus, since he is convinced that only things, which come out of man, defile (Mark 7:15).[27] Jesus shared the ethical radicalism of the Baptist but not his ritual radicalization; he did not practice a new ritual which would have separated him and his followers from other Jews.

Concerning the sign prophets, Jesus shares their expectation of an eschatological salvation in correspondence with the salvation history of Israel. He shares their soteriological radicalism saying that salvation is near. Salvation is not only near, but even present in his words and deeds (Luke 11:20). Jesus announces, like the sign prophets, a future event—a new temple. Like the sign prophets he leads his adherents to the place where this miraculous new temple will be erected. But all other sign prophets had a nativistic tendency; they show this by their symbolism and aggression toward the stranger. For example, many announce a new exodus or a new conquest of the holy land. Jesus, on the contrary, expects that the gentiles and aliens will come to the kingdom from all directions and that they will eat together with Abraham, Isaac, and Jacob (Matt. 8:11ff.). Jesus shares the soteriological radicalism of the sign prophets without their nativistic hostility against aliens and strangers.

What is the preliminary result? In comparison with the elder groups, the Sadducees, the Pharisees, and the Essenes, Jesus is situated in the middle of them. He represents a common Judaism.[28] We may say he represents the "golden mean" between extremes, but in comparison with the younger movements we must say he shares their radicalism but gives this radicalism a new form. His is much more of a theocratic, ethical, and soteriological radicalism than a political, ritualistic, and nativistic radicalism. How should we interpret this mixed result—the "golden mean" on the one hand, radicalism on the other? On the one hand, Jesus seems to be deeply rooted in the midst of common Judaism between different wings. On the other side, he seems to be a radical Jew like other radical Jews in those times. But we have not yet compared Jesus with the Cynics. Perhaps we will find here a solution for our problem or a model for a solution. But let us first try a comparison of forms.

c) The Comparison of Forms of Expressions

Myths, rituals, and ethics are different religious forms of expression. We should separately compare Jesus' attitude to the myth, the rites, and the ethics of Judaism.

Concerning the "mythology" of Judaism we may say that central in the pronouncement of Jesus is the kingdom of God. This is an eschatological myth. Jesus never explains what the kingdom of God is. His audience seems to be familiar with this concept. It is an expression of the basic axiom of Judaism, of monotheism. Of course we find some distinctive elements in the preaching of Jesus. Above all Jesus emphasizes the imminence of the kingdom alongside its future reality. Furthermore, Jesus emphasizes its inclusiveness instead of its exclusiveness: the gentiles (like other less reputed groups) have a chance to enter the kingdom. But these distinctive features are only variants within the basic belief in the one and only God. Jesus is embedded in Jewish monotheism. His "myth" is an eschatological dramatization of Jewish monotheism. The one and only God shall soon prevail over Satan and all dark forces.

This is corroborated by our comparison of the ritual "sign" language within the Jesus movement and Judaism. There are three holy places in contemporary Judaism: the temple, the synagogue, and beside these public places, the house—which some Jews would like to treat as a sanctuary, extending the holiness of the temple to their home. What is Jesus' attitude to these three places? Jesus shows an opposition to the temple but dreams of a new temple. His dream presupposes identification with the temple, though not in its present shape but as a new temple in a time to come. If the Sadducees and the priests are those who supported the present temple, his prophecy of a future temple symbolizes a deep conflict with the religious elite. Jesus also occasionally shows a very critical attitude to the house and the family, for example, when he says to let the dead bury their own dead (Matt. 8:22). Here he in no way treats house and family as sanctuary. If the Pharisees tried to transfer the holiness of the temple to the house, Jesus differs in this regard remarkably from such a Pharisaism. Last but not least, Jesus visits synagogues. He preaches there. But these synagogues are not the only places where he gathers his audience. He also taught in open air. In contrast to his opposition towards temple and house, we find a more balanced attitude towards the synagogue. The synagogue is the place of hearing God's Word. But wherever God's Word is heard in other places, that place is also holy.

The transmitters of his words have embedded a collection of his most famous words, not in a synagogue preaching, but in the Sermon on the Mount corresponding to Mount Sinai. We may therefore say that Jesus represents a Judaism of laymen, not of priests or scribes, a Judaism that has its role in life ("Sitz im Leben") in the synagogue and in everyday life. Jesus is not at all an exotic Jew but in many regards the representative of lay-piety. We must further underline: Jesus never criticizes circumcision, and we do not hear that he ate forbidden food. These ritual norms (circumcision and the food laws) are Jewish boundaries and identity markers. Even more important is that he did not baptize. John the Baptist and the Essenes both separated their adherents or members from other Jews by rituals—the Essenes by repeated washings, the Baptist by a unique baptism. The creation of new rituals is often the beginning of a schism in the history of religions. But Jesus did not continue this line. Only with his last supper he founded the basis for a new ritual. That he is quite integrated into Judaism (especially with ritual boundary markers) is a very important fact; the followers of the Baptist and the members of the Essenes are more distant from common Judaism than Jesus and his followers. But no scholar of Second Temple Judaism doubts that the Essenes and the adherents of John are representatives of Jewish life and theology. If Jesus is more integrated in common Judaism than these groups, he must be situated in the midst of Judaism.

Let us now deal with Jesus' ethics. There is no doubt that Jesus' ethical teaching is based on Judaism, on the Torah, on wisdom traditions, and on Jewish eschatology. But there is a distinct radicalism in his ethic which is quite unusual. It is his itinerant radicalism, being without home, without labor, without family. The instruction to sell all that you have is striking. We find no comparable demanding ethos in Judaism. The lifestyle of this itinerant radicalism makes Jesus and his followers outsiders. In this regard he and his followers were indeed "marginal Jews." Here we find analogies only outside Judaism with the Cynics. Although I do not think that Jesus was deeply influenced by Cynic philosophy,[29] Cynic itinerant philosophers may have been known in Galilee and Palestine. When Jesus says in his mission speech to the disciples: don't take a bag, don't take a staff with you (Luke 10:4; Matt. 10:9), he forbids two "identity markers" of Cynic itinerant philosophers. The disciples should be distinct from Cynics in their visible outfit. In the Jesus tradition there is more of a tendency to stress the dissimilarity with Cynism than the similarities. But this tendency to stress the difference is indirectly a testimony for similarities: the basic phenomenon—itinerant preachers and philosophers—is very similar. And their ethos of a distance from house, family, and wealth is comparable.

Again we have a mixed result. On the one side Jesus is deeply rooted in Judaism. He shares its basic convictions. His central idea of the coming of the kingdom of God is eschatological monotheism and a restoration of pure Judaism. With regard to rituals Jesus is more integrated within Judaism than the Essenes or the Baptist. But his itinerant ethical radicalism is a little bit strange. In this regard he is a marginal Jew. Of course it would be a valuable result already if we could say it is too simple to say that Jesus is a marginal or a radical Jew; or to state that he in many regards is a representative of common Judaism; or that he is very akin to Pharisaism in spite of his conflicts with Pharisees; or to state that in some regards he is at the center of Judaism while in other regards at the edge of Judaism. At this point it will be advantageous to fill out this result by interpreting our data in juxtaposition with the Cynics.

With regard to their lifestyle, Cynics were outsiders or marginal inhabitants of Hellenistic culture and society. But at the same time they represent in pure form some of the basic ethical axioms of Hellenistic philosophy. They taught by their words and life that human beings are autonomous beings. They have *atarkeía*, or "independency." They saw virtue in the control of their emotions and passions. They differentiated between those things that nature demands and those things that only human convention demands. Because they lived at the border of their society they had the liberty to mirror to this society in its most basic convictions without feeling the practical pressures of everyday life.

Jesus and his followers were neither Cynics nor Jewish variants of Cynics; however, their radicalism may be explained as analogous to the Cynics' place within Hellenistic culture.[30] The lifestyle of itinerant radicalism places Jesus and his followers at the margin of Jewish society. But this marginal lifestyle gave them the liberty to represent the conviction of the whole society and culture in a very radical and clear form—not compromised by the constraints of everyday life. Therefore, our mixed result is no contradiction: on the one side Jesus represents common Judaism, often in a position between two other groups which are much more extreme, and on the other side Jesus and his followers exercise a marginal lifestyle. And it is their lifestyle which gives them the chance to mirror the basic convictions of their society to its inhabitants. Jesus and his followers have the same function with regard to the Jewish culture of their days as the Cynics had with regard to the Hellenistic culture of their time. This functional analogy is much more important than any possible influence from Cynic philosophy on Jesus.

We have seen the question of the Jewishness of Jesus has never been a pure academic question. There has always been a social, moral, and religious context that has had an impact on this question and possible answers. But academic research is not determined to be totally dependent of moral agendas. We have a chance in a reflective and argumentative way to discuss this issue. We can refuse and correct an erroneous and biased picture of Jesus: he was no liberator from Judaism; he was a son of his Jewish people, deeply rooted in Jewish faith and traditions. That Jesus became the posthumous founder of a new religion is a different problem that cannot be dealt with in this article.

What is significant here for Jewish-Christian dialogue? The theologians opposing National Socialism, like my Bonner professors, and those who supported National Socialism, like the ambiguous figure Emanuel Hirsch, have this in common: all claimed a superiority of Christianity vis-à-vis Judaism. Jesus, it was argued, should be the figure to legitimize this superiority. There is no doubt there is something new in the message of Jesus. There is no doubt that after his death a new religion developed in his name. But should Christianity therefore claim superiority? I have tried to summarize my personal answer in a short meditative text (figure 9.1).[31]

FIGURE 9.1: SHORT MEDITATIVE TEXT

Eine moderne Diagnose sagt über Menschen,	A modern diagnosis of people:
Die an Religion erkrankt sind:	They fell ill with religion;
Ein aufklärungsresistenter Bazillus habe sie befallen.	A clarity resistant bacteria has stricken them.
Sie seien die Fußkranken der modernen Gesellschaft.	They are the footsore wanderers of modern society.
Die Diagnose folgt alten Mustern.	The diagnosis follows old patterns.
Die Christen waren Kinder des Judentums,	The Christians were Judaism's children,
Aber kritisierten die Juden,	However, they criticized the Jews,
Weil sie ihrer Wahrheit nicht folgen wollten.	Because they did not want to follow their truth.
Das Christentum brachte aufgeklärte Kinder hervor.	Christianity produced enlightened children.
Sie kritisierten die Christen,	They criticized the Christians,
Weil sie mit ihrem „Fortschritt" nicht Schritt hielten.	Because they did not keep up with their "progress."
Die Aufklärung wurde durch ihre postmodernen Kinder überholt.	Their postmodern children moved beyond the Enlightenment.
Sie kritisierten Relikte vormoderner Wahrheitsansprüche in ihr,	They criticized their entrenched premodern truths,
Etwas Unbedingtheit vom Sinai,	Some absoluteness of Sinai,
Etwas Metaphysik aus Griechenland,	Some metaphysics from Greece,
Die Seligpreisungen aus Galiläa.	Some beatitudes from Galilee,
Soll man diese Relikte der Wahrheit austilgen?	Should one efface these relics of truth?
Oder soll man sich die Juden zum Vorbild nehmen,	Or should one see the Jews as a model of those,
Die an ihrer Tradition festhielten,	Stuck to their tradition,
Als andere sie für überholt erklärten?	When others explained them away as outdated.
Sie sind vorbildlich	They are exemplary
Für das Christentum.	For Christianity.
Für die Aufklärung	For Enlightenment Clarity
Und ihre postmodernen Kinder,	And their postmodern children,
Wenn sie einst selbst überholt sein werden.	If they are overtaken themselves.
Auf dem Weg zu Gott	On the way to God
Waren Juden immer voraus.	The Jews were always in front.

Part Four

Jesus in
Jewish-Christian Dialogue

CHAPTER TEN

The Importance of Jewish-Christian Dialogue on Jesus

James D. G. Dunn

To respond adequately (I hope) to the chapters in this volume has been a fascinating and sometimes frustrating challenge. It proved simplest to respond to each essay/chapter in turn.

Leonard Greenspoon's chapter takes us into the intriguing issue of what constitutes a legitimate or appropriate translation. And the central issue he elaborates is very important, for it is certainly the case that the rendering of Jewish names by later equivalents has tended to obscure their Jewishness. But while empathizing with this concern, we must remember the "what" and "why" of translation.

It is a basic fact that the same name is regularly rendered differently in a different language. For example, as the entry "James (name)" in Wikipedia clearly indicates, my own first name, "James," is rendered in a bewildering variety of forms in different languages—for example, Jacobus, Jakob, Iago, Diego, Jacques, Seamus, Hamish. And the equivalent of the English "Jesus" includes Isa, Josue, Yeshua, and Gesu. In such circumstances, translation which retains the original language form is not actually translation. It may help jolt a reader with a reminder of the original language form, and such a jolt will often be valuable, especially when original identity, in this case the Jewish identity of Jesus and his first followers, is concerned. But we should not forget the purpose of translation—to translate foreign terms and idioms into the common language and idiom of the readers, that is, to show that what the terms and idioms communicate can be communicated in their own language, can be part of their own language world. To translate *Yeshua* as

"Jesus" is a way of saying, "This person is not hidden from you by language but is accessible to you through your own language." If the original Aramaic is translated into Greek, and the Greek into English, then there is no reason why *Yeshua* should not be translated into "Jesus."

To claim that such and similar rendering presents all those named in effect as Christians over against (evil) Jews is rather facile, since the New Testament itself makes clear that the title "Christian" did not emerge for some time after Jesus' execution (Acts 11:26). Most Christians may have forgotten that the first followers of Jesus were all Jews, or may never have had it pointed out to them, but it is obvious to any inquiry on the point and is usually accepted without question when pointed out. And to render "scribes and Pharisees" as "Scripture scholars and religious experts" is no solution, obscuring as it does why scribes were called "scribes" (a learned minority who could write!), and that there was a significant body called "Pharisees" (an appropriate English rendering of *perushim*) who were not the only "religious experts."

A more serious critique highlights the unwillingness of translators to render Luke 3:29 appropriately—though one might well ask whether the KJV's rendering of Joshua as "Jesus" in Acts 7:45 and Heb. 4:8 was more responsible. But Greenspoon goes on to the more challenging case of the appropriate rendering of *hoi Ioudaioi* particularly in John's Gospel. Here again we have to accept that the translation "the Jews" has contributed to Christian anti-Judaism and anti-Semitism over the centuries (particularly John 8:31-44). But is the answer to translate other than "the Jews"? It is a question over which I have agonized in the past, in dialogue with Irvin Borowsky and Howard Kee. And, somewhat regretfully, I have had to conclude with Joseph Blenkinsopp that the primary task of a translation is to translate what the original text actually says. We may well wish that the text had expressed itself differently, or with greater precision. And any translation carries with it a degree of interpretation (sense equivalence and not just simple word equivalence). But the fact that "the Jews" in at least many cases in John refers to Jewish leaders (individual Jews fear "the Jews") is a matter for exposition and not translation.

The real responsibility (and guilt) lies with those who have failed to point out such features, that "the Jews" are as often used in John's Gospel of the crowd who have still to make up their minds regarding Jesus, and that various Gospel passages should not be read in church or preached on without the historical circumstances which occasioned such wording being explained. The fault lies not with the translation so much as the way the translation has been used. In such cases explanatory footnotes would be appropriate— as indeed an appendix glossary of proper names (Hebrew/Aramaic, Greek, and English)—but a translation which translates what we think the author ought to have said is not the answer. It is the bareness, the baldness, of the translation which reminds us that this is an ancient document that reflects the conditions in which it was written, and that should remind us that it has to be explained and not just transposed from first to twenty-first context without clarification.

Joel Lohr's chapter justifiably focuses on the parable (or as he prefers, the story) of the Sheep and the Goats (Matt. 25:31-46). He makes an impressive case for reading the story within a Jewish context of understanding, as a story about the judgment of (the) gentiles. In the story, in Lohr's view, the *ethnê* are not the nations as a whole (including Israel); rather, the term has its usual reference in the literature (and in Matthew) as referring to the nations other than Israel (although I cannot help wondering whether he gives sufficient weight to "*all* the nations"). Similarly the needy to whom some of the gentiles ministered are not to be limited to Christians in general or to Christian missionaries in particular. Following Ulrich Luz, Lohr proceeds to set the passage persuasively within the unfolding intention of Matthew, of his condemnation of Jewish leadership and his openness to gentiles. His paper includes reflections on whether the story can be traced back to Jesus and on its relevance to contemporary Jewish-Christian dialogue.

On the question of the source of the story, it is indeed most likely that its Matthean form (the only form we have!) reflects a late first century context (like so much of Matthew's material). The picture of the Son of Man "seated/ sitting on the throne of his glory" in judgment (Matt. 19:28; 25:31) probably reflects influence from the *Similitudes* of Enoch, where the Elect One is repeatedly said to sit down "on the throne of his glory" to judge (particularly 1 Enoch 55:4; 61:8; 62:3; 69:27). These two passages in Matthew, indeed, are the only Son of Man passages in the Synoptic tradition in which influence from the *Similitudes* is traceable—one of the factors that suggests that the *Similitudes* were too late in composition to influence the Jesus tradition at an earlier stage.

Whether that is enough to warrant the conclusion that the whole story/ parable is a late (Christian) composition is not as clear as might be hoped. Jesus was remembered as telling various stories about judgment—the Wheat and the Tares (Matt. 13:24-30; GThom 57), the Fishnet (Matt. 13:47-48), and the Rich Fool (Luke 12:16-20; GThom 20). Elsewhere he speaks of positive response to his emissaries as positive response to Jesus himself (Matt. 10:40// Luke 10:16). And Matthew, although restricting Jesus' mission to "the lost sheep of the house of Israel" (10:6; 15:24), had already indicated what we might describe as Jesus' eschatological openness to gentiles (8:11-12). Moreover, the Jesus who pulled Lev. 19:18b out of the sequence of various commandments (Leviticus 19), to give it an unprecedented priority (Mark 12:28-31 pars.), would no doubt have been aware that Lev. 19:34 extended the commandment ("love your neighbor as yourself") to include the resident alien. Not only so, but a Jesus who illustrated this commandment with the story of a Samaritan acting as good neighbor to a Jew fallen among thieves (Luke 10:29-37), could well have told a story of non-Jews acting with compassion towards the needy. So such a story could well have been part of Jesus' repertoire.

That this raises, as Lohr notes, problems for those who fear that such a story would undermine the gospel of grace through faith should not allow the principal message of the story to be undermined. The issue, it should not be forgotten, has been central to the Christianity/Judaism confrontation— as though any emphasis on the importance of doing good (being a good neighbor) is expressive of a Jewish "works righteousness" and undermines the Christian gospel. But a passage like Rom. 2:6-11 should remind us that for Jesus and the first Christians, including Paul, final judgment could be expressed as dependent on whether individuals have done good or evil. The Paul who was open to gentiles, not having the law but doing what the law requires (Rom. 2:12-16, 26), would presumably find no reason to object to Matthew's story of the Sheep and the Goats. There is a preciousness in some Christian "embarrassment" over such passages, which results in the message of these passages being dismissed, and "doing good," as something for which God looks and God commends, being devalued.

As for the relevance of this story to continuing Jewish-Christian dialogue, its positive value should be given more attention, as Lohr observes. For even if Matthew's Gospel reflects a deepening rift between the embryonic Christian assemblies and the Jewish leadership of the period, this story shows how Jewish is the message which Matthew sought to commend—its openness to the righteous gentile and its commendation of being a good neighbor. The awkwardness that the passage poses to the traditionally defined Christian gospel is precisely the point of contact and continuity between Christianity and Judaism.

Anne Lerner's analysis of the story of Jesus' encounter with the Syrophoenician woman (Mark 7:24-30; Matt. 15:21-28) brings out the distinctive features of each version in a very helpful way. I query her judgment at only one point: that the *logos* of Mark 7:29 should be rendered "word" and referred to only one word used by the woman (*kyrie*). But *logos* can mean also "statement, what you say," as well as an "assertion" or "subject matter" (BDAG). Lerner recognizes that *logos* has a wider semantic range, but she settles on only a single word within the larger statement. However, it is more natural to take Jesus' commendation as a reference to the woman's whole, bold statement (7:28). Beyond that one point, it would have been helpful had Lerner added some reflection on Mark's positioning of the episode immediately after Mark 7:1-23, and on Luke's omission of the story and the preceding discussion of purity. There is probably some undisclosed strategy in both cases that needs to be brought to the surface.

On Mark's and Matthew's telling of the story itself, I wonder if more attention should be given to the rhetorical effect presumably intended by the construction of the story. Is Jesus presented as being (unexpectedly) obdurate and as using offensive imagery ("dogs") as a narrative strategy, that is, simply or primarily to highlight and emphasize by way of contrast the woman's persistent and insistent faith? The complaint is rightly made in Jewish-Christian dialogue that the Judaism of Jesus' time has so often been presented in highly negative and disparaging terms in order to make Jesus stand out by way of contrast. But here it is Jesus who is presented in an untypically negative light, and it is the woman who takes him on in the terms he has set and wins his approval and commendation. The sharpness of her response ("Because of what you have said") and the insistent faith thereby expressed wins a response from Jesus whose only precedent in Mark is the woman with the hemorrhage (Mark 5:25-34), and in Matthew is the centurion of Capernaum (Matt. 8:5-13).

Finally, I gladly add that I warm to Lerner's final words "when we find a text in our tradition that troubles us—and every tradition has them—we need to confront that text and honestly face its flaws, rather than hiding the text or explicating the flaws away. When we willingly hear the perspectives of those outside our faith traditions as well as those within, we better understand each other and the multifaceted nature of our traditions."

I find Michael Cook's essay rather frustrating. It asserts the presence of ten "anomalies" in Mark's presentation of Jewish groups. It assumes a post-70 date for the writing of Mark's Gospel and a basic ignorance of pre-70 conditions in Judean and Galilean society on the part of Mark so that he had to depend for his information on various "sources." Furthermore, Cook is confident that he can sufficiently identify these sources and therefore discern Mark's use and editing of them. The result is a document (Mark's Gospel) which has little historical value and on which can be placed much of the blame for the negative Christian assessment of Israel's leadership.

However, several (at least) of the "anomalies" seem to be in the eye of the beholder rather than in the text or in the historical situations being envisaged. "Herodians (*Hērōdianoi*)" are certainly a somewhat obscure group, but the term presumably refers to "partisans of Herod," as the name implies, referred to by Josephus as *Hērōdeioi* (*War* 1.319) or as *hoi ta Hērōdou phronountes* (*Ant.* 14.450). "Chief/high priests (*archiereis*)" most obviously refers to the former high priests as well as the one currently in office, as again in Josephus (*War* 1.31; 2.243, 301, 316, 318, 320, 322, 331, 336, 342, 410–11, 422, 428, 566; etc.). That Pharisees (also well known from Josephus) were normally located in Jerusalem but may have travelled to Galilee (to take stock of the prophet from Galilee) is suggested by Mark 7:1. That the determinative move against Jesus was made by the high priestly faction (probably in reaction to Jesus' action in and words about the Temple—Mark 14:58 and so on), and that the Pharisees were not particularly involved, is indicated also by John, as well as the Synoptists. That "scribes," so named because they belonged to the small learned minority who could write (and read), were variously attached to prominent groups like Sadducees and Pharisees is highly likely.

Cook seems to be eager to attribute Mark's accounts to post-70 ignorance of pre-70 conditions in Israel. He can confidently assert that "in Mark's day the Pharisees were the new native personnel whom Rome had installed over the holy land." Mark, he thinks, was written circa 71, though he will be aware that opinion on Mark's date of writing varies from closely pre-70 (c. 68) to a little after 70. But from where did he write? How well did he know the post-70 situation in Israel? And were the "Pharisees" already so well established "over the holy land" by roughly 71?

Cook's dependency on source criticism is rather dated (1921, 1928, 1961), and his presumed sources all seem to be literary or quasi-literary in character, with apparently no thought given as to whether what might properly be called historical (oral) sources are a possibility worth some discussion. But, to take one instance, in the issue whether individuals should wash their hands before partaking of a meal (Mark 7:1-8), Mark was obviously drawing on earlier material since he has to explain the concerns being expressed, including the uniquely Jewish sense of the word *common*, that is, not set apart to be holy, and therefore "unclean, defiled" (7:2, 5). It is, of course, true, as Ed Sanders has noted, that it cannot be ascertained from rabbinic sources whether the related halakha was already being observed at the time of Jesus (or pre-70?). But the fact that a whole Mishnah tractate is devoted to the subject, *Yadaim* ("Hands"), indicates a long tradition history of halakhic concern. So the representation of a tradition ("the tradition of the elders") that was already well established in Pharisaic table-fellowship is entirely plausible, even if Mark exaggerates in attributing the practice to "all the Jews" (7:3).

I find, then, Cook's argument unpersuasive. The "anomalies" on which his whole thesis is based are readily explainable by a combination of historical irregularities, of oral tradition being variantly performed and transmitted, and by a degree of editorial freedom in fitting particular traditions/episodes into a developing plot. The artificiality of an editing process predicated on a somewhat arbitrary manipulation of jigsaw pieces is too remote from the much more plausible historical likelihood of living traditions passed from earlier disciples to Mark's generation to be very convincing or more than of interest to idle curiosity. Consequently, I also find Cook's parting shot—"that we must deem Mark *the* pivotal Gospel if we are most fundamentally to comprehend the generative process of Christian anti-Judaism"—to be overstated, exaggerated, and unjustified.

Donald Senior traverses the much traversed issue of how to read Matthew's Gospel on the Jew/Gentile issue of earliest Christianity, and in the Judaism/Christianity debate of today. He rightly stresses the Jewish character of the Gospel and how much it illuminates the Jewish context of Jesus' mission. He justifiably highlights that Jesus saw his mission as a mission to Israel. He draws out helpfully the distinctiveness of Jesus' interpretation of the law. And he ruminates on the difference that Matthew's high Christology makes, even if its roots in Jesus' own teaching and actions are clearly discernible. I resonate with the essay as a whole.

I would like to see more thought given to the issue of Jesus' aim as "the restoration of Israel." If that is indeed a fair way of describing his aim, it certainly sets Jesus firmly within a Jewish context, which can and should resonate with most Jews today. But do Christians take it with sufficient seriousness? Or do they quickly pass over the fact that the kingdom of God, as Jesus seems to have envisioned it, did not come within the lifetime of his own generation, or that the Son of Man has not come on clouds of heaven? As the Jesus of history/Christ of faith controversy has always realized, the more the "fundamental Jewish character of Jesus" is stressed, the greater the gulf between the (Jewish) Jesus of history and the Christ of (principally gentile) faith. How can we ensure that Jesus is fully located within Second Temple Judaism, and is a genuinely Jewish voice within Second Temple Judaism to which Jews (as well as others) should listen today, unless we address the uncomfortable features of Jesus' mission and (unfulfilled) hopes? Does the resurrection of Jesus actually block off the continued reassertion of the Jewishness of Jesus and of his mission as indicated by Matthew? I am very sympathetic with the view that Christianity as theologized by the Jew Paul should be seen as fulfilling Israel's mission to be a light to the nations. And to that degree I agree with Joseph Ratzinger that the Jesus of Christianity, of Matthew's Christianity, should be seen in the same light. But I would like it to become a topic within Jewish/Christian dialogue, including its problematic features, more seriously and more extensively than it is.

As to Jesus and the law, I agree with most of what Senior (and Meier) say, though I am puzzled by the opinion that 19:9 is "a Matthean reference to marriage within forbidden bloodlines which rendered the marriage invalid in the first place." And the treatment of Lev. 19:18 and love of enemies as highly distinctive features of Jesus' teaching is very impressive. But I would like more to have been made of what seems to be a characteristic feature of more or less of all Jesus' teaching on law issues: that time and again he presses beyond the surface level of the issue to the deeper heart of God's intention in giving the law. That included a pushing behind various halakhoth and traditions to what the law actually said, but also pushing through the individual commandment to the inner spirit. Such teaching evidently did bring Jesus into controversy with various Pharisees, and we should not play that down. But at the same time, they were very Jewish controversies. If the challenge for Christians with regard to Jesus and the law is to give proper recognition of Jesus' devotion to the law, the challenge for Jews is to hear Jesus' teaching on the law and Halakha as a genuinely Jewish voice. Should Jesus not have been included, with Hillel, Shammai, Akiba, and so on in the Mishnah, as rendering opinions and judgments which are still of value for subsequent generations of Jews? If we cannot go that far in discussion, then the issues of Jesus' resurrection and of his status as Son of God will never reach the table for serious discussion.

Eyal Regev's attempt to dismiss the accusation of being a false Messiah as the reason for Jesus' execution is all too cavalier to be given serious attention. His questioning is brief, so it would be unfair to respond in detail, but its inadequacy cannot escape mention.

In *Jesus Remembered* I indicated the evidence which led me to conclude that the question of messiahship was an issue during Jesus' mission, most of which Regev ignores. The basic datum is that Jesus was crucified (a Roman punishment of those regarded as rebels) and that the titulus on the cross gave as the reason for the execution that Jesus was "the king of the Jews"—not a Christian title. I remain persuaded by the argument of Nils Dahl that it is highly implausible to claim that the report of such a titulus is a (subsequent Christian) attempt to historicize a dogmatic motif. There are also other episodes during Jesus' mission in which it is indicated or suggested that the question whether Jesus was Messiah was raised—including the episodes entitled "the feeding of the 5,000" (Mark 6:32-44 pars.), "Peter's confession" (Mark 8:27-30 pars.), and "the entry into Jerusalem" (Mark 11:1-11 pars.). I believe that the evidence also indicates that Jesus declined the messianic role apparently envisaged, and the argument that Jesus himself was a revolutionary has never cut much ice. But that the charge of Jesus as "Messiah" was the grounds/ excuse for handing Jesus over to Roman authority and for the Romans to regard his execution by them as justified still remains the most obvious reading of the available data, whatever we make of the actual exchanges recorded between high priest and Jesus or between Roman procurator and Jesus.

Regev also ignores the implications that the hope of a royal Messiah was still flourishing at the time of Jesus, as suggested by *Ps. Sol.* 17:21-24, the messianic expectations at Qumran, and the prayer of *Shemoneh 'Esreh* 14. It is true that the later troublemakers, Theudas and the Egyptian, were regarded as prophetic figures and not as messianic pretenders (Josephus, *War* 2.258-63; *Ant.* 20.97-8, 167-72). But Regev also ignores the royal/messianic pretenders, Simon and Athronges (*War* 2.57-65; *Ant.* 17.273-84), in the period immediately following the death of Herod the Great in 4 BCE. Such selectivity, even in a brief presentation, hardly begins to do justice to the full range of evidence.

The major thesis of Regev's chapter has much more going for it. I entirely agree with him on the high historical probability that Jesus was remembered as saying something about the destruction of the Temple, and quite possibly also about the (re)building of the eschatological Temple. I also agree that there is much more to be said for a positive assessment of Jesus' attitude to and teaching on the Temple. After all, when in Jerusalem Jesus is remembered as regularly in the Temple, and thus presumably observant of the purity rituals required. The teaching attributed to him in Matt. 5:23-24 assumes continued observance of the sacrificial cult. And had Jesus been known as a severe critic of the Temple, it is hardly likely that the earliest Jerusalem body of his disciples would have been so observant of Temple and Torah as Acts 3:1 and 21:20 imply.

On the other hand, Regev's argument that "the cleansing of the Temple" was not critical of the Temple authorities but was a protest about the use of "impure money," motivated by a concern for the dangers of wealth and materialism, has a very thin basis. Not that I question that such a concern is evident earlier in Jesus' mission. It is just that there are no hints of such a motivation in the accounts of the Temple "cleansing." And the clearly attested reference to Isa. 11:17 and allusion to Jer. 7:11 (Mark 11:17 pars.) are dismissed far too casually by Regev. So too, if Jesus was known as one who pronounced sins forgiven (Mark 2:5 and so on), without reference to the cult, or as having asked serious questions about the importance of ritual purity (Mark 7:14-23 par.), then he would certainly have been regarded as some kind of threat to priestly and Sadducean prerogatives and authority. The "cleansing of the Temple" fits well in that context; a critique of Sadducean control and administration of the Temple can readily be distinguished from a critique of the Temple per se. Regev is fully ready to recognize Sadducean hostility to Jesus but bases it on a misunderstanding of Jesus' motivation and action—although that never seems to have been a factor in the telling of the episode and its consequences.

Regev rightly acknowledges the difficulty of fitting his reconstruction to the outcome, of Jesus handed over to Pilate and executed by crucifixion. The possible parallels and precedents which he cites hardly fit the situation envisaged for Jesus (Regev even tries to reintroduce the "king of the Jews" charge). It is at such stages in an argument that I begin to become a bit impatient. When an argument has to sweep the bottom of the barrel for support, while blithely ignoring or putting down the more immediate and obvious evidence (because it doesn't "fit"), I have to wonder whether there is very much to be said for the argument itself.

Anthony Le Donne justifiably sets the quest of the historical Jesus in the context of Jewish-Christian dialogue. The reminder that during the dark days of Christian anti-Judaism and anti-Semitism, there were those, all too few it would appear, who looked for positive interaction and overlap between Christianity and Judaism in their respective views of Jesus is salutary. As depressed as we can hardly avoid being by that doleful and horrendous Christian heritage (so clearly indicated by Susannah Heschel), Le Donne reminds us that we should at least take good cheer from the memory of the friendship of Lessing and Moses Mendelssohn, and from the memory of Rabbi Jacob Emden and Abraham Geiger. On a broader framework we could also mention, for example, George Foot Moore and James Parkes, Samuel Sandmel, and today such as Alan Segal and Daniel Boyarin, as well as Geza Vermes.

There were, however, two points in the history of Jewish-Christian dialogue whose significance should not be lost to sight. One is the beginning of historical criticism as the outcome of the Enlightenment. There is a before-and-after at this point which should not be neglected, and which can be obscured by ranking Origen, or the Talmud, or Augustine in the same category of interest as the "historical Jesus." The application of the newly emerged scientific method to the study of history brought with it a willingness to question traditional views of historical data and accounts as never before. It brought with it a readiness for self-criticism, a willingness to examine afresh even sacred tradition which had determined cultural attitudes and values for generations. A Western Christianity which has criticized Luther's tract against the Jews is yet to be paralleled by an equal willingness on the part of Orthodox Christianity to criticize Chrysostom's equally anti-Jewish tract.

The second point worth mentioning is the post-1945 awakening within Christianity and Christian scholarship to the horrific outworking of European Christian anti-Semitism in the Holocaust/Shoah. The Second Vatican Council's "Nostra Aetate" marked a new openness in traditional Christianity to the Jews as a people and to Judaism as a religion, and opened the door to cooperation between Jewish and Christian scholarship which before that usually had to be confined to the study or to off the record communication. Le Donne reminds us that "the common European caricatures of Jews were so firmly entrenched that the emerging field of racial science simply reinforced them." The same deeply entrenched attitudes to Judaism in the post-1945 situation are indicated by the continued use, in German textbooks into the late decades of the twentieth century, of the term *Spätjudentum* ("late Judaism") to refer to the Judaism of Jesus' time—the underlying (usually unrecognized) theology being that from a Christian perspective the only function of "Judaism" was to prepare for the coming of Jesus and of Christianity (so "late Judaism" = the last positive function for Judaism).

On Le Donne's parting questions I will limit myself to observing that historical method, historical-critical method, ceases to be truly historical when it ceases to be self-critical. I don't see how anti-Judaism can be regarded as ahistorical when it has been such a prominent historical feature of nearly two millennia of European history. Historical method should face up to the reality of anti-Judaism wherever it appears, in the past or still today. I would hope that "historiographical rigor" would advance any dialogue between partners willing to face up to even discomfiting truth. Certainly the "No Quest" period, insofar as it attempted to remove faith in Jesus from historical scrutiny, does not provide a model for Jewish-Christian dialogue.

Since Dagmar Winter's and Gerd Theissen's chapters cover so much of the same ground, I will respond to them together. Theissen's is a fascinating account of the pre-1945 and post-1945 Jesus research in Germany, and Winter's of the different ways in which and degrees to which "the dissimilar Jesus" has been the real goal of "historical Jesus" research. I am grateful for the many insights and illustrations of how pervasive, sometimes subtle, sometimes blunt, was the anti-Jewish motivation in the various stages of the "Quest."

Winter reminded me of the persistent assumption which has driven so much of the Quest: that the "real" Jesus must have been different from traditional views of Jesus, and that this "real" Jesus is extractable from the sources, rightly evaluated and read. So the "real" Jesus cannot have been too close not only to the dogmatic Christ of later centuries but also to the Christ of faith of post-Easter Christianity. The same suspicion that the traditional reading of the sources hides the "real" Jesus (and the "true" beginnings of Christianity) motivates current attempts to read these beginnings through the apocryphal Gospels and reaches its end-point in the fantasies of novels such as *The Da Vinci Code*. But how much more convincing is Jesus, "hero and genius," as the objective to be sought by Questers?

Theissen brought home to me something I had not fully appreciated: that Bultmann's demythologizing program was in effect his alternative to and way of dealing with the German Christian attempt to dejudaize Jesus. Theissen's question as to whether Käsemann really escaped the anti-Jewish theological traditions of the German Christians gives a considerable cause for pause (I recall being unnerved by Käsemann's assertion that it was "the Jew as a representative of the pious person"[1] who was the real opponent of Paul's discussion in Romans 2–3). And Theissen's observation that Grundmann was able to continue his career after the war (something which always puzzled me), because the moderated anti-Jewish tendencies of his Jesus research were not inimical to the views of the Bultmann school, is very sobering.

Certainly the degree to which German New Testament and Jesus scholarship have been influenced, as a kind of default reaction, by Luther's antithesis between gospel and law, and its transposition to an antithesis between Christianity and Judaism, continues to be a disturbing factor in our appreciation of German scholarship—not least given its dominant influence in biblical scholarship for most of the last two hundred years. Also a disturbing factor is the degree to which Christian reaction to Second Temple Judaism was so often influenced by and a mirror of Protestant reaction to Catholicism, so evident already in the theses of F. C. Baur which continue to influence historical methodology. The attempt to maintain that Jesus critiqued only the Halakha, and not the Torah itself, was not enough for too many scholars: Paul's rejection of the law must have been foreshadowed by Jesus. Theissen recalls that for his teachers in the 1960s, "Jesus seemed to be the first Christian theologian." Winter notes that "the dissimilar pieces of tradition were understood as the characteristic and essentially Jesus-like pieces," missing the point that the Jesus "characteristic" of the Jesus tradition could certainly not be identified with "the dissimilar Jesus." Winter also refers critically to Schürer's use of Spätjudentum, complementing the point I have already made regarding the theological presupposition of the term, but also not mentioning the continued use of the term in German textbooks to refer to Second Temple Judaism into the late decades of the twentieth century—a usage apparently unquestioned as to its suitability, despite the fact that Judaism has continued to flourish for another two millennia! How could historical scholarship have allowed such a usage to continue unchallenged?

Theissen's own brief analysis of Jesus' Jewishness is helpful and shows quite clearly that in a historical appreciation of the rich diversity of Second Temple Judaism there is plenty of room for Jesus—closer to the beating heart of Israel's religion than other Jews and Jewish groups of the time, some more marginal than others. (I like Theissen's suggestion that "Jesus represents a Judaism of laymen, not of priests or scribes"; but do we really want to assert that Jesus sought "a restoration of pure Judaism"?). This attempt to locate Jesus within the diversity of Second Temple Judaism remains the challenge for Jewish-Christian dialogue, as also in regard to Paul: can both Jesus and Paul be recognized/heard as authentically Jewish voices from within Second Temple Judaism? If only one or two strands from within Second Temple Judaism are acknowledged by Judaism and Christianity as their authentic predecessors (different strands in each case), then it remains a challenge to both Jew and Christian as to how to assess the authenticity and continued relevance of the other strands—an appropriate agenda for Jewish/Christian dialogue.

As Winter points out, the degree to which Christian scholarship has made its objective to find a Jesus of history who is recognizably the same person as or is manifestly continuous with the Christ of faith continues to be a major factor in the swings and roundabouts of the Quest. Also, it is almost an unavoidable corollary to such a concern that the "historical Jesus" to be found must be somehow "other" than (simply) a Jewish prophet. In fact, the history of Jesus research reviewed by Winter and Theissen leaves Christians (and Jesus scholarship generally) posed with the same two-sided issue, an issue which has ever lurked on or below the surface, implicit or explicit, and which retains a Gorgon-like influence on the whole discussion: must it follow that the more Jesus is linked in to the Judaism of his time, the wider becomes the gulf to be bridged between Jesus and Paul (the Jesus of history and the Christ of faith); and the more Jesus is linked in to the Christianity which followed, the wider becomes the gulf between Jesus and his native Judaism (Jesus the Jew and the Christ soon to be of dogma)? As Winter and Theissen remind us, the weight of emphasis and interest on this issue has swung back and forth for most of the quest of the historical Jesus. Can it ever be satisfactorily resolved? Or does it simply provide an ever renewed agenda for successive generations?

This volume presents and contributes to a series of issues which can and should provide the agenda for continued Jewish-Christian dialogue. How should translations, especially for use in Christian lectionary and liturgy, deal with such terms as "the Jews," particularly in John's Gospel? Are the themes of continuity between Judaism and Christianity fully enough explored and expounded—not least so far as the value of doing good and final judgment "according to works" are concerned? How should we deal with "awkward" texts and challenging readings of our texts—preferably by including them early on in the discussion, rather than simply leaving them out of the overall picture as problem texts to be resolved at some indeterminate time in the future? Is the Jewishness of Jesus yet to be fully appreciated: have both Jew and Gentile really grasped what he was on about in his principal message about the kingdom of God, and can the issue of his unfulfilled hopes be resolved without taking more seriously the way in which failed prophecies were handled in the preceding generations? Is Jesus sufficiently recognized to be an authentic Jewish voice, speaking with challenge and authority to Jew as well as Christian? Can we distinguish historical criticism in regard to Jesus from the attitudes and values which have motivated such criticism for the last two centuries? And the old chestnut to which I keep returning: how can we recognize sufficiently both the Jewishness of Jesus and that the "Jesus of history" can hardly be cut off from the "Christ of faith" and maintain both insights in positive dialogue between Jew and Christian? For myself, as a Christian participant in the Quest and the ongoing dialogue, it is of essential importance that Christianity recognizes more fully its integral Jewishness and recognizes how important it is to the character of Christianity that the Jewishness of Jesus be fully acknowledged and accepted. Otherwise Jesus can be so quickly lost to sight in the mists of myth.

To take part in the above dialogue has been an honor and a pleasure. The very fact that such a volume could be attempted, drawing together a cross-section of Jewish and Christian scholars, and tackling some sensitive as well as fundamental issues, is itself an important sign of the times. That research into the historical figure of Jesus and attempts to assess his significance can be carried forward as a genuine and open dialogue is itself a major step beyond what was so much more typical of the twentieth century. My hope is that this volume foreshadows a developing dialogue between those operating from different perspectives (Jewish, Christian, Muslim? other?) on particular episodes and themes in which theses can be explored and debated in a continued spirit of mutual respect and truth-seeking scholarship—and further, that the larger issues brought to the fore in the last two contributions in particular, and indicated in the previous paragraph, can be pursued in an irenic and self-critical spirit. In short, my hope is that the dialogue will continue and prove to be increasingly fruitful and that this volume will contribute positively to the wider Jewish-Christian dialogue.

CHAPTER ELEVEN

Jesus in Jewish-Christian Dialogue

Amy-Jill Levine

My assignment for this volume is to produce an essay under the rubric of "Jesus in Jewish-Christian Dialogue." Since with the exception, perhaps, of the preposition "in," all the terms in the title require definition, I shall use each to frame my responses to the contributions on the previous pages.

Jesus

The idea *that* Jesus is located in early Judaism does not require defense within the academy, or in Jewish-Christian dialogue. The Christian Scholars' Group's 2002 statement "A Sacred Obligation" summarizes the consensus view in its second proposition, "Jesus of Nazareth lived and died as a faithful Jew"; it glosses the statement by explaining, "Christians worship the God of Israel in and through Jesus Christ. Supersessionism, however, prompted Christians over the centuries to speak of Jesus as an opponent of Judaism. This is historically incorrect. Jewish worship, ethics, and practice shaped Jesus' life and teachings. The scriptures of his people inspired and nurtured him. Christian preaching and teaching today must describe Jesus' earthly life as engaged in the ongoing Jewish quest to live out God's covenant in everyday life."[1] This is the starting place of much Jewish-Christian dialogue. Those who do not begin here typically do not enter the dialogue. Christians unsympathetic to the proposal are not often found sharing a bagel with members of Hadassah; Jews choosing to believe negative Talmudic comments about

Jesus,[2] or denying that Jesus never existed, will not be at the dialogue table either, and, if they were, would likely fuss about the hechsher on the bagel.

The Christian Scholars saw no need, in their statement, to distinguish the "historical Jesus" from the Gospel portrait. This is, for dialogue, an appropriate omission. Jewish-Christian dialogue is typically not interested in separating tradition from redaction, in drawing out some anterior Jesus who exists behind, and is distinct from, his contextualization in the Gospels. This may be a good thing: Christianity is not based on the "historical Jesus" but on the New Testament and its interpretation.

Nor is that anterior Jesus particularly usable in a dialogue setting, since there is no academic consensus, other than the vague "He fits into his Jewish context, more or less," of who he was. There are about as many Jesuses as there are people who have heard of him. The academic has produced its Jesus the anti-Roman agitator, Cynic-sage, Galilean Hasid, pedagogue of the oppressed, Marxist community organizer, Pharisee, itinerant radical, eschatological prophet, apocalyptic visionary, shamanic healer, mystic, homosexual, celibate, married father, sacerdotal ritualist. For the participants in the dialogue, the starting place on the topic of Jesus is, and should be, the Gospels of Matthew, Mark, Luke, and John, and not the *Gospel of Judas* and the *Gospel of Thomas*, let alone the gospels of Bart, Marcus, John Shelby, and John Dominic, no matter how interesting or historically grounded they are. The "Jesus" of "Jewish-Christian dialogue" is primarily the Jesus of the Gospels and the Church, not the Jesus of the academy.

The current Quest, which is more interested in contextualizing Jesus within early Judaism—although much of the work still highlights, for better or worse, where he is dissimilar (more on this below)—is also increasingly less interested in finding the anterior Jesus. Distinguishing tradition from redaction is a compromised if not doomed endeavor. The criteria of authenticity—already problematic, as Professor Theissen points out in his remarks about how "dissimilarity" served often apologetic aims of distinguishing Jesus from Judaism however broadly defined—are proving to be of increasingly less value since they cannot yield a consensus. Multiple attestation fails because we cannot determine what sources are independent: the tide is shifting on John and the Synoptics, with increasing arguments for interdependence; we cannot firmly distinguish Q from Matthean or Lukan redaction; we cannot prove a Q at all. Our construction of early Judaism has moved so far away from the idea of the "normative"—not just to the "formative," but to an "even this could fit" model, that anything Jesus does coheres with something in his context. Ironically, conservative Evangelical scholars who in the past found the very idea of using such criteria to distinguish between tradition and redaction anathema, are today using the criteria with the (not unexpected) result that *everything* the Gospels attribute to Jesus has an historical basis.[3]

The approach Professor Lohr offers, namely, "to show that this passage [in Matthew 25], even if it cannot be plausibly explained as an early memory of Jesus' own teaching, is one deeply grounded in a first century Jewish worldview," may offer more to the dialogue. Professor Senior takes a similar approach: "There is much to learn about the historical Jesus through the lens of Matthew's Gospel. Matthew's portrayal of Jesus in such emphatic Jewish tones, the subjects of the controversies over interpretation of the law between Jesus and his opponents, the passing descriptions of Jewish life and customs that are part of the Gospel narrative—all of these and more offer contact points with the historical circumstances of Jesus in his own context." For Jewish-Christian dialogue, the focus is less on whether Jesus did or did not say or do something—since we cannot reach any consensus on the answers— than on what might the Jesus tradition tell us about the relations between the followers of Jesus and those who chose to follow other streams of Judaism then, and perhaps, now. The memory of Jesus' own followers, a memory preserved in the New Testament, becomes the basis for discussion.

Indeed, perhaps the dialogical pendulum has swung away from Jesus and toward Judaism. Rather than use all the sources at our disposal to try to determine, using the criteria of authenticity, what Jesus said and did, today we use the Jesus tradition to reconstruct a more fulsome view of first-century Judaism. And whereas we cannot determine the anterior Jesus, we are in a better position today to determine that anterior Jewish context. As Professors Cook and Regev demonstrate, we can show how people who may have had memories of Jesus, but who had no firsthand knowledge of his immediate context, reconstructed his opponents.

Given this situation of a diverse Jewish context and a general acceptance of Jesus of the Gospels—both the Synoptics and John—as having increasing historical credibility, where can progress be made? Perhaps, as a suggestion, we might attempt greater precision in our language.

I propose a moratorium on the term *marginal* in Jesus research (I would also like to banish the term *radical*, but one excision per essay is sufficient). The problem with "marginal" is that it rarely articulates the presumed norm while at the same time implicitly critiquing that norm for creating the situation of marginalization. Thus Professor Lerner, echoing numerous other readers of Mark 7 and Matthew 15, speaks of the "quadruply marginalized Greek, Syrian, Phoenician woman." But Greeks are hardly "marginal" to the Roman Empire, or Syro-Phoenicians to the region of Tyre and Sidon. As for women being "marginal," missing is the question, "to what?" This clever woman may well be the single mother, impoverished and, because of her demon-possessed daughter, scorned by all; on the other hand she may be a well-educated, wealthy, savvy woman who, in the mold of the Great Woman of Shunem (see 2 Kings 4), gets what she wants from G-d's representative.[4]

Professor Senior also appeals to "marginality" in his citation of Dennis Duling's claim that Matthew's situation was one of marginality, given the experience of being "condemned to live in two different, antagonistic cultural worlds, but does not fully belong to either." "Condemned" is a strong term. The people in Matthew's community (if we can even speak of a "community"; since a text is not a community, we do not know what other texts shaped Matthew's initial readers, and we cannot find consensus either on the identity of the author or the composition of the church) were not "condemned" to be in two different cultural worlds: this is a position they chose. Moreover, there is no reason to presume that they felt marginal: they may well have felt fully at home in a robust, wealthy, established church or network of churches. Whether relations with the local synagogue (presuming there was a local synagogue) were antagonistic, or whether the writer of the Gospel sought to develop that antagonism, cannot be determined. Or again, they may have celebrated their marginality, as those who choose to be "in the world but not of it" often do.

Professor Senior also adduces the "marginal" moniker in his extended evocation of John Meier's study of Jesus as a "marginal Jew" who was "thoroughly within the broad range of first century Judaism yet whose prophetic teaching, intense healing activity and personal claims to unique moral authority placed him on the margins of the dominant perspectives of his contemporaries." A few points in this provocative sentence require elaboration. First is the intriguing choice of the term *marginal* to describe someone who claims moral authority and engages in prophetic teaching. Why is the term *marginal*, rather than, for example, *outstanding*? One who is "outstanding" is distinct from the crowd, but the term usually has positive rather than negative connotations. In turn, if we take more recent examples of people who claimed prophetic teaching, intense healing, and personal authority—Aimee Semple McPherson, or Oral Roberts, or Benny Hinn for that matter—the first term that comes to mind, at least to my mind, is hardly "marginal."

Not only is Jesus characterized as "marginal" in much New Testament studies, but so are the people to whom he ministers. Professor Senior continues: "In this array of characteristics should also be added what appears to have been the historical Jesus' association with those on the margins of society—the sick, the poor, the socially despised (for example, tax and toll collectors, what Matthew's Gospel calls 'the lost sheep of the house of Israel'; 10:6; 15:24), and even the occasional Gentile (for example, the Centurion of Capernaum; the Canaanite woman)." With all these people on the margins, one might wonder who is in the center. Romans are hardly marginal in the Roman world, and centurions are not easily pushed to the side. The "sick" do not appear on the margins but are typically embedded in family systems or with friends willing to dismantle roofs on their behalf. Tax and toll collectors are not marginal in the sense of being pushed out; rather, they have deliberately removed themselves from the welfare of their fellow Jews. Drug dealers, insider traders, arms purveyors, and agents of enemy foreign governments are not usually described as marginal. The tax collectors, at least in the Gospels, are found among the rich, not the poor. In Luke's Gospel they are sufficiently integrated into society that they too find reconciliation in the Jerusalem Temple (see Luke 18:9-14). If the "poor" are in the "margins of society" then what exactly is the society to which they are marginal, and how are they marginal? They are welcome in synagogues and the Jerusalem Temple; they are supported by tithes and charitable donations; they have a recognized social role.

My point is not to romanticize the poor or to deny the difficulties of life in a subsistence economy; it is to flag the impression the use of "marginal" conveys. For there to be marginals there have to be elites and centrists, and in the presentations made to church groups, the lasting impression is that "Jews" are elite folks who create marginal people by deliberately, systematically marginalizing them, and Jesus, (and so Christians are) the good people who have been marginalized. Worse, the standard view is the Judaism creates these marginals by its purity laws, despite the fact that purity, which impacts rich and poor, male and female, is a social leveler.

Thus to speak of Jesus as a marginal Jew who ministers to other marginals has a politicized import that I doubt is intended by most who use the terms. But the impression of Judaism as a "marginalizing" tradition remains nonetheless. Indeed, perhaps the new constructions of early Judaism, in all its diversity, are the most compelling arguments for the banishment of the term *marginal*. Margins, by definition, require a center, but the construction of Judaism, with the breakdown of the idea of a "normative" Judaism, is one that is remarkably decentered. Here Theissen's observation that Jesus, rather than being marginal, "seems to be a Jew in the very center of Judaism" may be more on the mark.

Jewish

The intractable question of "Who is a Jew" has been in place since Jews have been in place. Were those who "made themselves Jews" (*mityehudim*) according to Esther 8:17 "Jews"? Are proselytes "Jews"? At what point do followers of Jesus cease to be Jews, presuming that they were Jews initially? What of messianic Jews today? What of the child of a Jewish father and gentile mother, especially if that child is raised as a Jew? At least today, the consensus view is that Jesus was a Jew. The question then is, "what sort of Jew within what sort of Jewish matrix?"

On these questions, the academy and the lay participants in dialogue typically part company. In-depth discussions of the construction of early Judaism do not find much purchase in dialogue contexts. The reason for this lack is twofold. On the one hand, most approaches to locating Jesus within his Jewish matrix rely primarily on Second Temple sources rather than rabbinic texts. At this point, the lay dialogue participants are hampered by lack of access to, even knowledge of, sources. Anyone can obtain a New Testament and talk about it. Many can even read the Greek. But few among the general public have the skills to read *1 Enoch* in the Ethiopic, let alone figure out which of its 100+ chapters is relevant for discussion.

On the other hand, the literature used to locate Jesus within Judaism is of comparably little interest to those invested in Jewish-Christian dialogue. The focus on Second Temple texts actually puts the Jewish dialogue partner at a religious disadvantage. Whereas for Jesus, Christians rely on canonical materials (the *Gospel of the Ebionites* does not find much airtime in dialogue contexts), the Jews are given in this scenario a set of alien literature. Professor Lohr appeals, correctly, to Marius Reiser's *Jesus and Judgment* to conclude, "Judgment is a central idea of Judaism, and in fact it might be said that a final judgment is a defining characteristic of Jewish thought." The point might be nuanced: it is a central idea found in Second Temple literary sources. The index of Reiser's volume, double columns running from page 363 to page 390, is replete with citations from *1 Enoch*, *Jubilees*, various Maccabean books, *Psalms of Solomon*, *Sibylline Oracles*, Sirach, *Testament of Abraham*, *Testaments of the Twelve Patriarchs*, the Dead Sea Scrolls, Josephus, and Philo; but citations to rabbinic literature take at most a page and a half. The "Judaism" in which most scholars situate Jesus is not a Judaism that is part of what Jews today recognize as their tradition. Thus the question of historical value is skewed. Pseudepigraphical materials are, to most dialogue participants, not only foreign but also irrelevant for contemporary use. That many participants in this dialogue do not know their way around rabbinic literature makes the process even more complicated.

But complication should not prohibit progress. The articles in this collection suggest a few areas where the role of Jesus in his Jewish matrix might be developed for the benefit of Jewish-Christian dialogue. Here are six.

First, Professor Theissen observes that his 1978 statement, "Early Christianity began as a renewal movement within Judaism brought into being through Jesus,"[5] is accepted "nowadays [by] nearly all contemporary New Testament scholars." Here we might seek precision on what is being renewed or restored or revitalized, whether other groups are in the process, and even if the term remains helpful. The idea of a renewal movement suggests that the original situation suffered a gap or lack, that it had become ossified, or off-track. Thus the term itself, especially if it is not applied to other movements of the time, threatens rhetorically to recreate the negative impressions of terms like *Spätjudentum*, whose negative connotations Professor Winter accurately describes. Next, we do not typically use terms like *renewal* to describe the origins of the Unification Church or the Church of Latter-day Saints, or the Lutheran Church, although all new religious groups can be compared, to some extent, to Christian origins.

Second, the study of Jesus (and the Gospels) helps us fill in more details about first-century Judaism. Jesus is the first person in documented history to be called "rabbi" (and Paul is the only Pharisee from whom we have written records); the Gospels, tendentious though they may be, tell us about synagogues and the temple, pilgrimage and fishing, the public role of women and the general care given to the sick by friends and family, the strong paternal roles held by Jewish men who were expected to love and care for children, and so on. In earlier times, as several essays show, Jesus was yanked out of Judaism; today, not only can he be located within Judaism, but also his presentation can be used to flesh out what that Judaism looked like. Indeed, the "quest of the historical Jesus" has become the midwife to the "quest of the historical Pharisees" and the attempt to determine, as best as we can, the picture of Jesus' Jewish context.[6]

Third, my language in speaking about Jesus within first-century Judaism or a Jewish context is deliberate: I do not speak about him in his "Judean" context or within "Judean" culture. There is an increasing tendency among parts of the academy to translate the Gospels' *hoi Ioudaioi* not as "the Jews," but as Professor Greenspoon points out, to translate it as "the Judeans" (if not as "the leaders," and so avoiding anything that even sounds related to the term *Jew*). This translation, although usually offered with the good intention of preventing anti-Jewish readings, not only eliminates "Jews" from the New Testament, but also supports the Nazi view that Jesus was not a Jew (Judean) but a Galilean (a point Dr. Winter helpfully develops) and, by extension according to Nazi historiography, an Aryan;[7] it takes the focus off Jesus' orthopraxy and orthodoxy and accentuates a geographical identity; it strips Jesus of any connection to rabbinic Judaism, let alone to Jews today. To eliminate the "Jews" from the New Testament will not work: we cannot and should not attempt to erase problematic texts. Rather, we educate people on how to understand these texts.

Fourth, as Professor Greenspoon's helpful inclusion of David H. Sterns's work reminds us, today's messianic Judaism remains a generally unexplored area in Jewish-Christian dialogue; in the discussion of what "Jewish" means, the place of the messianist today remains, as does much else, complicated. Jews (that is, those who are recognized by the mainstream Jewish community as halahkically Jewish by descent) who accept belief in Jesus as the messiah, with varying christological views, are still Jews, and many of them wish to be known as Jews rather than as Christians. Although generally not counted in a minyan, generally refused burial in Jewish cemeteries, and not admitted to Israeli citizenship under the Law of Return, they are still Jews.[8] If there is to be greater Jewish recognition of Jesus as a first-century Jew, and not only of Jesus as a Jew, but also of all those initial Jews who claimed him messiah—and if we recognize that there is no clear marker for the first several centuries of when these Jews ceased to be Jews and became simply Christians—then we should consider how this appreciation relates to messianic Jews today.

Fifth, Professor Greenspoon comments on how, given translation choices, "only certain figures of the Christian Scriptures remain clearly identifiable as Jews—not John the Baptist, not Mary, not Jesus, nor James and Paul: even their names are not biblically Jewish." Yes, and (rather than "yes, but"), perhaps we might use these adapted names to talk about the broad basis of Jewish identity even in the first century. Philo is hardly a Jewish name if by "Jewish" we mean Semitic or biblical. Nor, for that matter, is Amy-Jill or Leonard. Jews then, as Jews now, adopted the languages of the land where they lived. And people then, as people now, adapted the names of foreigners to their own languages.

I share Professor Greenspoon's doubts that a more "Jewish" sounding New Testament, with *Yeshua* the son of *Maryam* and *Yosef*, would do much to enhance Jesus' connections to Judaism. Rather, I suspect the terms would be alienating to some Christians and create a romanticized notion of biblical Judaism for others. Translation, like language use, will always be an issue in Jewish-Christian relations. However, the broader issue is a cultural one: here we might look at children's Bibles, Christian sermons and Bible studies, artistic depictions, movies, music—areas often less impacted by academic biblical studies than Jewish-Christian dialogue groups. Biblical names do not necessarily signal "Judaism" or a "Jewish connection": culture does.

Sixth and finally, the study of the historical Jesus both in the New Testament and over time should strip Jews of the view that we have always been victims and that we have never uttered reciprocal negative statements about Jesus or Christianity. Professor Le Donne notes rabbinic and early medieval calumnies ("setting the record straight" is a polite way of describing some of these texts). While the problematic comments in the New Testament, especially those read liturgically to the faithful, are not directly comparable to obscure Talmudic statements, the fact that those latter statements exist should be acknowledged. Dialogue cannot take place if one participant claims a moral high ground, if histories produce feelings of either inherited guilt or inherited righteousness, and if the difficulties of the past are ignored.

Christian

Professor Senior states, "A key question—particularly for a Christian audience—is to what extent one can find continuity between the person and mission of the historical Jesus and the profound religious identity ascribed to him by Christian faith as in Matthew's Gospel." Dr. Winter asks, "Is Christian theology which is Christo-centric and Jesus-centered institutionally anti-Judaist? [Can Jesus] be positively appreciated in his distinctiveness without being negative about Judaism?" The interrelated questions raise the problem of supersessionism or replacement theology.

The question of continuity is always a question of discontinuity. For the (non-messianic) Jew, there is an inevitable discontinuity between the historical Jesus and the Christ of faith: one is or can be appreciated, and one is worshiped. For the Christian with any sense of Christology, these are not mutually exclusive options. The Christ is fully human and fully divine; there is full continuity between his historical person and his soteriological, Trinitarian Person. For the Christian, Jesus has to be more than a really interesting first-century Jew, but he also has to be that first-century Jew. Indeed, I suspect that for Christians, in general, the weaker the Christology, the greater the incentive to remove Jesus from his Jewish context. If he sounds pretty much like everyone else, why follow him? The high Christology emphasizes his distinction (which is not the same thing as his "marginalization") and his uniqueness, with "unique" being a theological, not historical, descriptor.

As for a Christo-centric theology being anti-Jewish: to some extent, this is inevitable. These days, in the context of Jewish-Christian conversation, a number of participants, especially Christians, do back-flips in the attempt to avoid supersessionism. I find such well-meaning gymnastics ultimately unhelpful. To say "Yes" to Jesus is necessarily to say "whatever Judaism was, and is, it is not right, or true, at least for me." One could use the spousal analogy: to fall in love with one person does not necessarily imply a denigration of everyone else. But this is hardly good news to the spurned suitor. Perhaps a helpful way of avoiding the guilt that sometimes accompanies Christian supersessionism—a guilt prompted by two thousand years of often-ugly domination—is to put the question in reverse: is Jewish theology which (by its very existence) denies Christian claims "institutionally anti-Christian"? The answer: not quite in the same way, since Christians and Christianity do not generally show up in Jewish liturgical texts, but still the answer is an affirmative one. Therefore, we might do well to acknowledge that we will agree to disagree, that our "yes" implies, inevitably, a "no" to the other, and we move on. Perhaps a category of "benign supersessionism" is in order. It may be a necessary part of the body of both Church and Synagogue; one keeps an eye on it lest it become malignant, and one lives with it, unpleasant though that may be. Once the acknowledgment is made, the key is turned and the door is open to explore Jesus' continuity with his Jewish context—as one part of Jewish-Christian dialogue.

But Jesus is not the only "key" to the dialogue. As noted above, Christianity is not a religion about the historical Jesus; it is about the Christ of faith. To stop at the historical Jesus, especially a Jesus constructed as anterior to the Gospels, is to abort (I use the term with all its contemporary connotations) the Church's proclamation. Therefore, Christians and their dialogue partners must attend to the Gospel portraits of Jesus. Here papers such as those by Professor Cook and Regev are helpful. Neither necessarily impinges on christological claims; the former looks at Mark's constructions of Jesus' opponents; the latter looks at what might have motivated Jesus' Temple incident. Both help to recover Jewish history; both provide a clearer historical context for understanding the Gospels.

Locating Jesus within his Jewish context for Christians goes beyond a deeper appreciation for how Jesus would have looked and sounded to those who initially saw his signs and heard his words. It also should both prompt questions about why people followed him and correct negative stereotypes about Jews and Judaism. Here again, the academic discussions can be helpful.

Concerning those Jews who followed Jesus, I am inclined to ask my first-year divinity students: When "Jesus came to Galilee, proclaiming the good news (*euangellion*) of God, and saying, 'The time is fulfilled, and the kingdom of God has come near; repent, and believe in the good news' (*euangelion*)" (Mark 1:14-15), what was the good news? One typical response: "He died for our sins." Another: "He conquered death." Both responses are quite fine (if at this educational stage somewhat undeveloped) and both find support in the New Testament. But both also presuppose that "the Jews" had no means of atoning for sins and that "the Jews" had no hope in an afterlife. Locating Jesus in his historical context shows both vigorous Jewish views of a forgiving G-d and the various options Jews had regarding life-after-death, from immortality of the soul to its transmigration to resurrection of the body.

Moreover, this "good news," at least for Mark 1:14-15 and, I think, for the historical Jesus, initially cannot have been his atoning death or resurrection: he had not mentioned either, and the people who followed him did not believe he was going to die. It is Jesus the Jew who provides the answer, whose teaching gives the content. Here Jesus the Jew can be recovered, with the notice that he does not have to be original in all places in order to be profound.

As for the details of this good news, a deeper understanding of Jesus' Jewish setting corrects the common stereotypes held by many Christians about Jews then and perhaps now. Among these are a concern for works righteousness to the point of legalism (noted by Professors Greenspoon and

Theissen and Dr. Winter), a xenophobia that restricted the divine word and divine concern to the Jewish people (a concern that has engaged Professor Lohr's study on election,[9] and underlies the "canard" as Professor Lerner puts it, that Jews typically referred to gentiles as "dogs"), the view that Temple was a domination system run by an undifferentiated mass of Jewish elites (see Professor Cook's study) and was by definition corrupt and co-opted by the state, as all forms of ancient institutionalized religions were (for an alternative view not only of Jesus' temple incident, but also of the Temple, see Professor Regev's study). The essays in this volume correct the stereotypes.

Dialogue

Professor Le Donne speaks of "allowing historical study to serve interfaith dialogue." As with my concerns for language above, again, I have a vocabulary concern. For many Jews involved in such dialogue, the issue is not a "faith" matter. To talk of "faith" or "faith communities" already skews the conversation toward Christian terms. Whereas one is a "Christian" because of some assent to Jesus' soteriological role (whether that soteriology is seen as ethical or eschatological), the vast majority of Jews today are Jews because their mothers are Jews.[10] A number of Jews who participate in dialogue do not do so because of a faith or a belief system.[11] Many enter because they want to correct negative Christian stereotypes, or because they want to understand what Christianity is about. They are not faith-identified (they may well be atheists or agnostics). The "faithful" Jews in the Orthodox spectrum do not typically engage in such dialogue, any more than do Evangelical Christians: they see no point in having religious conversations with those who are either wrong, or heretical, or at best in need of conversion. Rather than "interfaith," perhaps the descriptor "Jewish-Christian (or "Christian-Jewish") Dialogue" would more accurately capture the process and the participants.

Professor Le Donne also suggests that Jewish-Christian dialogue today does ask questions of Jesus and his placement in his Jewish context, and it does in fact use "this consensus [of the historical Jesus in his Jewish context] for contemporary Jewish-Christian dialogue." I would nuance the point: whereas the broad consensus is used in dialogue contexts (I know this in part because my *Misunderstood Jew* is being used in numerous dialogue groups), the general point about Jesus in his Jewish context is not being promoted to the extent that it should be among laity. I suggest one reason for this is that clergy in general, and especially Christian clergy, do not receive sufficient education on the topic, and thus they are ill-equipped to pass along recommendations to their congregants.

The Association for Theological Schools, the major accrediting organization of U.S. divinity schools and seminaries, does not require or even place in a "best practices" category its member institutions to provide instruction on how to avoid anti-Jewish teaching and preaching. I have personally requested that they make such a recommendation (e.g., a three-hour training program in which the negative stereotypes that clergy and congregants often hold would be named and corrected); they declined it. Until Christian clergy receive direct education in Jesus' Jewish context, dialogue among their parishioners will be hampered. Here Hebrew Union College (Cincinnati), which requires its students for rabbinical ordination to take a substantial course on New Testament methodology (taught by Michael Cook), sets the appropriate standard.

Professor Le Donne states, "Christians and Jews cannot check their religious identities at the door on their way to the roundtable discussion of history. Moreover, they should not be asked to do so." Amen. What then of the scholar? The introduction states that "the authors of this book write, not only as scholars of the history and legacy of Jesus, but also as Jews and Christians." Sort of. Today in the academy, especially in settings marked with post-modern sensibilities, it is *de rigeur* to begin an article with a confession of sorts: "I, as a white, well-educated, heterosexual, Jewish woman from Massachusetts . . ." and so on. The problem with such identifications is that they rarely tell the reader the information necessary to adjudicate the scholarship or determine the stakes. It is not enough to know that a person is a Jew: I would want to know, if the issue is the stake in the dialogue: Is he a theist? Is she *shomer shabbos*? Does he pray? How much of Jewish tradition does she know? How good is his Hebrew? Moreover, people sometimes sit uneasily in the pew (or behind the mechitzah), and there are inevitable disagreements internal to denominations: it was often noted, in the religiously affiliated university where I earned both my master's and doctoral degrees, that the term *United Methodist* was at best a wish, and more often an oxymoron.

In the dialogue context, once participants are sufficiently identified, parameters need to be established. Instead of hoping for a consensus result, where the dialogue agrees on a lowest common denominator and then everyone holds hands and sings *Kumbaya*, dialogue today requires acknowledgment and, more, celebration of differences. Professor Senior, citing the Pontifical Biblical Commission's document on the "Jewish People and their Sacred Scriptures in the Christian Bible," notes the following helpful statement: "This discord [i.e., the differing viewpoints between Judaism and Christianity] is not to be taken as 'anti-Jewish sentiment', for it is disagreement at the level of faith, the source of religious controversy between two human groups that take their point of departure from the same Old Testament faith basis, but are in disagreement on how to conceive the final development of that faith. Although profound, such disagreement in no way implies reciprocal hostility." The comment could be glossed by a number of

Jewish statements (here adapted from a focus on Talmudic discussions to an application to Jewish-Christian conversation).

Pirke Avot 5.17 records: "A controversy for the sake of Heaven will have lasting value, but a controversy not for the sake of Heaven will not endure. What is an example of a controversy for the sake of Heaven? The debates of Hillel and Shammai. What is an example of a controversy not for the sake of Heaven? The rebellion of Korach and his associates."

The Babylonian Talmud, *Eruvin* 13b, describes a three-year dispute between the schools of Hillel and Shammai over interpretation of Torah. Finally a voice from Heaven (a *bat qol*) proclaims, "Both are the words of the living G-d, but the Law is in agreement with the rulings of the School of Hillel." Why if both responses are divine, do the Hillelites receive approval? "Because they were kindly and modest, they taught their own rulings as well as those of the School of Shammai, and even more, they taught the rulings of the School of Shammai before their own. This should teach you that one who humbles oneself is exalted by the Holy One and one who exalts oneself is humbled by the Holy One" (a look at Matthew 23:12 and Luke 14:11; 18:14 would be appropriate).

The Maharal of Prague (sixteenth century) stated that "the multiplicity of views in themselves are all from G-d—and even if they are contradictory, nonetheless, in each of them there is a dimension of truth."

The idea of multiple interpretations of a single verse, or theological question, or historical understanding, is likely more at home in the dialogical setting of the synagogue than the confessional setting of the church. Jews may have an easier time at disputation since, at the end of the day, they are all still Jews. But for the Christian, determined not by birth but by being "born again," and thus by confession, disagreement more easily can put one on the outside. Jesus provides a helpful model here: he disagrees with fellow Jews over a lot—from family values to Temple action to personal authority—but he remains a Jew.

As for the subject of the dialogue, I return to the question of Jesus and, to conclude these reflections, to the text that prompted the Christian Scholars' Group statement with which this essay began. Professor Senior concludes, following Eugene Borowitz, "the fundamental difference between contemporary Judaism and Christianity is not a dispute about the Jewish character of the historical Jesus but the ultimate identity and mission attributed to Jesus by orthodox Christian faith." Why? Why not the fundamental Jewish view of peoplehood? Or the role of the Talmud in relation to the New Testament? Or the sense of the correct interpretation of the Scriptures of Israel? That is, why is the "fundamental difference" determined on Christian terms? Not only do Jews, in general, have a different view of the "ultimate identity and mission attributed to Jesus" by their Christian neighbors, it is also the case that the Christian neighbors may have a fundamental disagreement with their Jewish neighbors over the role of Talmud, the Jewish sense of peoplehood and election, distinctive ritual practice, the sense of "chosen people," and so on.

In September 2000, "*Dabru Emet* [Hebrew for 'Speak Truth'], A Jewish Statement on Christians and Christianity," signed by more than two hundred rabbis and Jewish scholars, began the new millennium's Jewish-Christian Dialogue. *Dabru Emet* made eight proposals. Along with statements on theology, Scripture, the Land of Israel, the Moral Principles of Torah, Christian responsibility for the Nazi atrocities, Jewish knowledge of Christianity, and eschatological redemption, only one proposal spoke to Jesus' role, and this in a gloss: "The humanly irreconcilable difference between Jews and Christians will not be settled until God redeems the entire world as promised in Scripture." The gloss states, "Christians know and serve God through Jesus Christ and the Christian tradition. Jews know and serve God through Torah and the Jewish tradition. That difference will not be settled by one community insisting that it has interpreted Scripture more accurately than the other, nor by exercising political power over the other. Jews can respect Christians' faithfulness to their revelation just as we expect Christians to respect our faithfulness to our revelation. Neither Jew nor Christian should be pressed into affirming the teaching of the other community." This statement both shows that Jesus is "a" center, but not necessarily "the" center to Jewish-Christian dialogue, even as it indicates the purpose of that dialogue: not to convert, but to learn.

Jesus holds a central place in Jewish-Christian dialogue, and historical study of his life, of the Gospels, and of the formative Judaism in which he lived and by which he was nourished has much to contribute to that dialogue. With careful uses of terminology, attention to problems of translation, recognition of the histories of how Jews and Christians over time have understood Jesus of Nazareth, awareness of the tendentious aspects of all historical sources and the presuppositions that necessarily enter even the most "objective" of scholarly writings, the conversation advances, the knowledge increases, and the answers, inevitably, lead to new questions.

Conclusion

Bruce Chilton and Jacob Neusner

In two vital ways, the study of ancient Judaism changed in the latter part of the twentieth century. Owing to the intrinsic relationship between ancient Judaism and early Christianity, those changes have influenced the understanding of the connections between these two religions, and have even altered the ways in which Judaism and Christianity themselves are conceived.

1. Seeing Texts Generatively

The first of these changes involved the appreciation that the sources of Rabbinic Judaism need to be approached generatively, within an understanding of how they unfolded over time.[1] Rabbinic Judaism is represented by legal and exegetical writings, specifically, four ancient law codes and a dozen compilations of exegesis of Scripture produced in the first six centuries CE by sages bearing the title *rabbi* meaning, "my lord." The Halakhic documents are the Mishnah, circa 200 CE; the Tosefta, a supplement, circa 250–300 CE; and two commentaries to the Mishnah as amplified by the Tosefta, the Talmud of the Land of Israel, also known as the Yerushalmi, circa 400 CE, and the Talmud of Babylonia, also known as the Bavli, circa 600 CE. The Aggadic documents present commentaries to Genesis, Exodus, Leviticus, Numbers, and Deuteronomy, that is, the Pentateuch, privileged in Rabbinic Judaism, as well as Song of Songs, Lamentations, Ruth, and Esther. The Bavli also contains a large component of Aggadic writing. These documents, all together forming the canon of formative Rabbinic Judaism, preserve the state of the Rabbinic system from the first through the seventh centuries CE and in continuator-writings define the norms of a single, uniform, universal Judaism from then to modern times.

The Targums are translations of the Hebrew Bible into Aramaic;[2] they developed for the most part during the Rabbinic period. The principal renderings of the Torah are Onqelos and Neophyti (both from the third century), but even Pseudo-Jonathan (seventh century) includes readings of interest to students of the New Testament. Targum Jonathan, the Aramaic version of the Prophets, Former and Latter, took shape principally during the second and fourth centuries, but there are also later additions. The Targums to the Writings are the latest addition, some date from the medieval period, as do some later renderings of the Pentateuch.

The New Testament was produced during the first century in primitive communities of Christians to prepare people for baptism, to order worship, to resolve disputes, to encourage faith, and similar communal purposes. As a whole, it is a collective document of primitive Christianity.[3] Once the New Testament was formed, it was natural to refer to the Scriptures of Israel as the "Old Testament." From thinkers as different from one another as Bishop Irenaeus in France and as Origen, the speculative teacher active first in Egypt and then in Palestine, a commonly Christian philosophy began to emerge.

The diversity involved inevitably produced disputes, notably between those theologians called "Catholic" and those called "Gnostic." Early Christianity cannot be understood in its history without reference to Gnostic thought, but for the purpose of comparison with the thought of ancient Israel and the Rabbis an obvious Christian counterpart is the Catholic and Orthodox Church, which embraced—in opposition to clearly stated Gnostic denials—both the Hebrew Scriptures and the biblical claim that God may be known through God's creation of a basically good earth.

Comparison with Judaic literature has been a matter of controversy, especially since the publication of *Kommentar zum Neuen Testament aus Talmud und Midrasch* by Hermann L. Strack and Paul Billerbeck.[4] The problems with Strack-Billerbeck have been rehearsed many times.[5] They tended to conceive of a single, unitary Judaism, represented in Rabbinic literature, and they treated the Gospels as a distinct entity outside the framework of that Judaism. Such an approach distorts the situation of Christianity in its earliest phase, which defined itself within—or in relation to—the Israel promised an inheritance by the Scriptures. Christianity as represented within the Gospels needs to be compared and contrasted with other Judaisms of its time, because they all belong to the same family of religious systems. In order to encourage study along critical lines, the intellectual task of understanding the Gospels in their Judaic contexts must be pursued in the work of comparison.

Strack-Billerbeck treat the literature of Judaism too much as an undifferentiated whole, without proper regard to issues of chronology and development. They contrasted their extensive construct of Rabbinica with the Gospels and Paul, in the interests of an obvious (and today largely abandoned) theological fashion. Strack-Billerbeck were pre-critical in their chronological treatment of Rabbinica; it is sometimes overlooked that they were also somewhat undifferentiated in their treatment of the New Testament itself.

Nearly a century after Strack-Billerbeck were in the process of research, a persistent tendency remains: to assume that, if the New Testament and another Judaic source speak about more or less the same subject, they must be referring to the same issues. Then they are contrasted without further reflection, as if they were having an argument or coming to agreement. "Parallelomania," in the memorable accusation of Sandmel,[6] has been the persistent companion of the trivialization of Judaism by Christian scholars since the Enlightenment.

The question of practical exegesis is this: if the quest for alleged parallels has proven to be an exercise in apologetics, what counsel for the interpreter can be offered apart from ignorance? To address this concern, a greater awareness of the nature of comparison needs to be developed. The critical task begins not with the finding of contacts among literatures but with the observations of analogies.[7] This is the approach that a generative appreciation of the literatures makes possible.

Analogies between the Gospels and Judaic literature might be of several types—simple, topical, interpretive, or close. Only the last type ("close") corresponds to the claim of a "parallel" according to the model of analysis that became fashionable during the last century. Even so, we do not hold that even close analogies in themselves demonstrate dependence, as a review of these categories, with illustrations drawn from analogies in the Targum Jonathan of Isaiah (the closest in time to the Gospels), will indicate.

Simple Analogy

The theme of the consequences of not attending to the voice of the prophets was shared by Jesus (according to the Gospels) with Judaic tradition, including the Isaiah Targum, but Jesus also formulated a demand based on the unique experience of his followers (Matt. 13:17; compare Luke 10:24): "Amen I say to you that many prophets and just people wished to see what you see and did not see, and hear what you hear and did not hear."

This conviction that a fresh experience of God brings with it new requirements of response is also reflected in the Isaiah Targum (48:6a, with *differentiae* from the Hebrew text in italics): "You have heard: *has what is revealed to you been revealed to any other people*; and will you not declare it?" Obviously, no case for dependence can be made here, but the coherence of pattern is nonetheless worthy of note.

Topical Analogy

The second type of analogy concerns characteristically Targumic phrases appearing within the New Testament. The best example is the central category of Jesus' theology: the kingdom of God, which also appears in the form "kingdom of the LORD" in the Targums (see Targum Onqelos, Exod. 15:18; Targum Jonathan, Isa. 24:23; 31:4; 40:9; 52:7; Ezek. 7:7; Obadiah 21; Zech. 14:9). The first usage in the Isaiah Targum (24:23) associates the theologoumenon of the kingdom of God with God's self-revelation on Mount Zion, where God's appearing is to occasion a feast for all nations (see 25:6-8). The association of the kingdom with a festal image is comparable to Jesus' promise in Matt. 8:11 and Luke 13:28-29, that many will come from the ends of the earth to feast with Abraham, Isaac, and Jacob in the kingdom of God.

The influence of Targumic usage on Jesus would help to account for one of the most striking features of his theology: his insistence that the kingdom is a dynamic, even violent intervention within human affairs. The Isaiah Targum provides a theological precedent for the sort of usage that Jesus developed further, opening the possibility that traditions later incorporated with the Targum were current in Jesus' time and had an impact on his theology. The Masoretic Text offers a picture of the Lord descending upon Mount Zion as a lion, which is not afraid of the shepherds who attempt to protect the prey. That arresting image is referred explicitly to the kingdom in the Isaiah Targum (31:4):

> As *a* lion, *a* young lion *roars* over its prey, and, when a band of shepherds *are appointed* against it, it is not *broken up* at their shouting or *checked* at their *tumult*, so *the kingdom of* the LORD of hosts will *be revealed to settle* upon *the* Mount *of Zion* and upon its hill.

This passage directly refutes the outworn generalization that the kingdom within Judaic usage was static in nature, and that the dynamic aspect was Jesus' innovation. The kingdom's dynamism was not original with Jesus; his particular contribution was in his portrayal of how the kingdom comes.

Interpretative Analogy

The third type of analogy does not involve sharing explicit wording, but it does presuppose a comparable understanding of the same biblical passage in the Targums and the New Testament. An example is Jesus' parable of the vineyard in Matt. 21:33-46; Mark 12:1-12; and Luke 20:9-19. After he has told his story of the abuse suffered by those the owner sends to acquire his share of the vintage, the Synoptic Gospels agree that the opposition to Jesus among the Jewish authorities hardened to the point that they wanted to seize him. When the symbolism of the vineyard in the Isaiah Targum 5:1-7 is considered, the opposition to Jesus becomes easily explicable. There, the vine is a primary symbol of the Temple, so that the tenants of Jesus' parable are readily identified with the leadership of the Temple. They knew he was telling the parable against them.

Both Matthew (21:33) and Mark (12:1) allude to Isa. 5:2, when they refer to a hedge set around the vineyard. Their allusion is to the Septuagintal version of Isa. 5:2, so that any conscious awareness of the Targum at the point of the composition of those Gospels cannot be claimed. The point is rather that the memory of allusion to Isaiah 5 is preserved; what the Targumic version of Isaiah explains, while other versions do not, is why the priestly opposition to Jesus would feel particularly engaged by his parable.

Close Analogy

The final verse of the book of Isaiah in the Targum identifies who will suffer—and specifies where they will suffer—at the end of time, when it says "*the wicked* shall be *judged in Gehenna until the righteous will say concerning them, We have seen enough*" (66:24). Gehenna is just what Jesus associates with the statement that "their worm will not die and their fire will not be quenched" (Mark 9:48, and see vv. 44 and 46 in many manuscripts), which is taken from the same verse of Isaiah. In the Targum, the first part of the phrase reads, "their *breaths* will not die." The term *Gehenna* refers in a literal sense to the Valley of Hinnom in the Kidron Valley, just across from the Temple in Jerusalem. But because that had been a place where idolatrous human sacrifice by fire had taken place (see 2 Kgs. 16:3; 21:6), the site was deliberately destroyed and desecrated by King Josiah as part of his cultic reform during the seventh century BCE (see 2 Kgs. 23:10). As a result, Gehenna came to be known as the place of the definitive punishment of the wicked.

A fundamental question confronted in the comparative reading of the New Testament and Judaic literature is the manner in which the sources unfolded. That development may be illuminated by greater clarity in the first instance concerning the type of analogy that appears to be at issue (and why). Beyond that, there must be sensitivity to the literary contexts of Judaic sources and far greater accuracy and specificity in regard to questions of dating.

2. Seeing Religions Systematically

The generation of these complex and sometimes interactive literatures took place within their religious systems, systems that the literatures themselves contributed towards producing.[8] For this reason, each system needs to be kept in mind, allowing for variations but also confronting an ineluctable fact that inter-faith discussion has often attempted to ignore: in their truth claims, classical expressions of Judaism and Christianity use their profound disagreement with one another as a standard of an exclusive claim to truth. An intrinsically adversarial self-understanding is built into the way that ideas, emotions, and behaviors relate within Judaism and Christianity as systems.

Judaism's Truth Claims

Judaism is true because it accurately translates the law and theology of the Torah into the design of the kingdom of priests and the holy people that God commands humanity to bring into being. By the criterion of Scripture, Judaism is true. That is the sole basis on which Judaism lays claim to truth.

Judaism and Christianity sustain theological comparison because they share a common Scripture and its narrative. They produce theological contrasts because each brings to Scripture a distinctive perspective. Judaism receives Scripture as the written record of revelation, along with the oral components of the same act of revelation at Sinai ultimately transcribed in the Rabbinic canon of the first six centuries CE. Scripture and tradition, formed into a systematic theology realized in the laws that set the norms of the Israelite social order, together define Judaism. They embody its claim to truth: God's will for humanity.

That claim points for justification to the character of the Torah, beginning with its written component. Judaism follows the narrative of Scripture from the beginning to the eschatological present; Christianity reads from present to past. Judaism finds in Scripture the story of holy Israel, the community called into being by God through Abraham and Sarah and realized at Sinai with the covenant of the Torah: "We shall do and we shall obey." That yields a community with no counterpart in humanity: not a race, not an ethnic group, not an extended family, but a social entity formed by a common affirmation, a shared response to God. That response takes the form of covenantal nomism: keeping the law of the Torah as the realization of Israel's covenant to be God's people. Christianity, coming after so much has happened and been learned, starts fresh and rewrites Scripture, imposing its story upon the eternal tale of the Torah. While concurring with Judaism in many details, Christianity misses the main point of Sinai from the point of view of Judaism: the regeneration of all humanity through the discipline of the Torah.

Christianity misses the point because it substitutes the individual for the community, Christ for Israel, the world to come that is attained through faith for this world that we know and endure in patience. It consequently centers on the notional and personal instead of on the public and the perpetual. And it imposes upon this world, in all its unredemption, the dimension of a now-realized salvation, as though the time had come, although it has manifestly not come. For the criteria set forth by the Torah for the realization of God's kingdom can be met only with the advent of the Messiah to raise the dead. Then comes the last judgment, and those who stand in judgment (having atoned for sin through death) will enter the world to come and live for eternity in Eden. That represents the restoration of humanity to the condition God intended to begin with.

Judaism and Christianity tell a story beginning in the same place—Eden—and ending in the same place—the resurrection of the dead. But while Judaism tells that story to the holy community Israel, defining Israel as those that take shelter under the wings of God's presence in the world and accept the Torah as God's will, Christianity stresses the individual relationship between God and person. To be sure, Judaism teaches that God wants the heart, and that the religious duties or commandments were given only to purify humanity's heart. And for its part Christianity acknowledges the social dimension. But the focus of the one—on that unique individual, Jesus Christ—differs in essence from the focus of the other, on God's people, meaning the community of those that know God in the Torah.

On that point of difference Judaism takes its stand. For Christianity the Torah *prepares* the way; for Judaism, the Torah *is* the way. In answering the question, *what is to be done about humanity?* the two traditions of ancient Scripture address the same problem, with different results. And the differences are many and complex. But they keep doubling back to the same point: Torah versus Christ.

Both traditions invoke the conception of a kingdom of God but differ on when that comes about and how it is conceived. Judaism conceives God's kingdom to come at the end of days. It views with astonishment the notion, not sustained in the everyday world, of a kingdom realized in the advent of Jesus. Easter has not yet come, and, when it does, it will encompass the entirety of humanity that knows God and seeks reconciliation with him. The notion that "all Israel has a portion in the world to come" promises resurrection and eternal life to those that have atoned through death and arisen from the grave, have been justified, and have entered into Eden. What are the Halakha's media for the reformation, regeneration, and renewal of humankind? Judaism legislates not for Eden but for the Kingdom of God, in the here and now—and therefore in the future.

For Sinai's answer to Eden's question both encompasses and transcends the matter of sin and atonement. After the reconciliation, what? That is the question that the Halakhic structure addresses: the conduct of the ordinary, everyday life lived under God's rule. That is because the normative deals with the normal and not just the exceptional: life made up of not only sinful, but also obedient, moments. From the perspective of Judaism, Christianity makes very little provision for the present tense of time, but only for that entry into God's intangible kingdom. As such, it seems as if there is little interest in the here and now. And so there also is no sacred community, only an individuated humanity, each person before God. But that is not how life is lived. That explains, also, why Christianity produces no coherent doctrine of resurrection, only a set of incoherent promises.

The three points at which Christianity in all its complexity has taken leave of God's truth as revealed in the Torah, therefore, are:

1. SCRIPTURE/TORAH: Christianity picks and chooses among the details of Scripture (its "Old Testament") without addressing its main point and principal message—that is that God yearns for the love of humanity, expressed in willing obedience to God's will *in the Torah*.

2. SOCIETY/INDIVIDUALITY: Christianity removes the individual from the social order and conceives of humanity one by one, not formed into a moral entity, a community called to form God's portion, God's kingdom here and now. That is the message of the prophets: God responds to the moral entity formed by the entire society, not just individual attitudes and actions.

3. HISTORY/ESCHATOLOGY: Christianity posits a caesura in the history of humanity, finding an end-time evidence for which the world has yet to reveal for all to see. Judaism, in contrast, accomplishes God's purpose in self-manifestation to humanity through the Torah. Judaism finds its definition in the Torah of Sinai. It focuses on the social order as the medium for serving God with the community as the arena of responsibility. Scripture is thereby replicated: the Torah, the Prophets, the Writings all fulfilled in the practicalities of a world not yet redeemed but susceptible of sanctification.

To Christianity, Judaism must say, not yet, not thus, not that one in particular. That is because Judaism affirms yes to the Torah, yes to the Prophets, yes to the writings—to which the Christian message is asymmetrical and awry.

Some would then ask, Has Christianity accomplished God's purpose? Does it not bring Israel's Scriptures to humanity? We find it difficult to share the view of some contemporary rabbis that Christianity forms the preparation for the Torah. That is not its intent, nor its record. It is a different religion from Judaism, and to the extent of the difference, it diverges from what God has instructed Israel to receive as God's will. Scripture—"the Old Testament" for Christianity, "the written part of the Torah" for Judaism—forms the arena for conflict between the competing heirs of Sinai—*sola Scriptura*. That conflict was joined at the very outset, in the language, "You have heard it said . . . but I say to you . . . ," and persists even in the pages of this labor of comparison and contrast. It would demean Christianity for Judaism to say anything less in response to Christianity's "why not," than Judaism's "why yes."

Christianity's Truth Claims

Christians implicitly endorse the claim of Judaism to the Torah by calling the Scriptures of Israel "the Old Testament." Those writings are cited as documents with a previous ownership. Christians believe in the durability of the covenant with Israel and locate themselves within that covenant's history.

But history's importance derives from the opportunity it offers; Christianity understands that the human condition transcends history. Where some people might see present reality as determined by the past, the Church sees it as defined by the future to which humanity is heading. So—in the case of defining the people of God—the only Israel that matters is the Israel we are all becoming, not the Israel that has been. Descent does not matter; heritage does not matter; the past is interesting but ultimately beside the point. Everything depends on where one is going.

Every single person who believes in the way that Abraham believed in God becomes a child of Abraham (Gal. 3:6-9), and therefore an Israelite. Paul said that, but in doing so he articulated a consensus of theology. Faith alone was Abraham's righteousness (Gen. 15:6), and that is a prophetic truth for Christianity as well. The whole issue of genealogical affiliation with Abraham and Sarah is set aside, because Jew and Greek, slave and free, male and female are explicitly rejected as yesterday's divisions, which are to be dissolved in the future glory of God's kingdom (Gal. 3:28).

As the Epistle to Diognetus (5.6) puts the matter, if the world is to be carved up between the race of the Greeks and the race of the Jews, then Christians are a third race, foreigners in every country and patriots of every land. Boundaries of race, class, and country are artificial structures of a corrupt world that is now in the process of passing away. "Israel" is the integer of salvation that emerges when the Spirit of God moves over one, a reality the Old Testament points to without mapping precisely.

So the Old Testament is every Christian's story, whether "Jew or Greek," because it is the record of how faith came to fruition, how it grew and developed like a plant, bobbed and weaved like a boxer, and broke through to the promise of a new heaven and a new earth in the poetry of vision that scholars call apocalyptic. That faith is the promise Christ fulfills, and for Christians the patriarchs and prophets and psalmists equally sing the Church's song—and sing it in their own words. But the melody, Christianity insists against Judaism, is that of prophecy rather than Torah.

In the Transfiguration Jesus appears to his disciples as he converses with Moses and Elijah; at the close of that discussion, a divine echo identifies him alone as God's own "child" (see Mark 9:2-8). Here we come to the heart of the matter. For the Church what Moses and Elijah and Jesus talk about is not the Torah, but the revelation of this special relationship to God.

The ways of fathers and sons, parents and their children, are remarkably constant. Many elemental features travel over time and across cultures. One stands out vividly in the memory of any first-time parent: children talk back. They interrupt. They get upset at you for no good reason. Remember that when the prophet Hosea (11:1) said, "Out of Egypt I called my son," he was talking about the Israelites, and in the same breath complaining graphically and bitterly about their lack of constancy. Simeon ben Shetach said something similar about Choni called the Circler, a worker of wonders (Taanit 23a): God listened to his prayers because he spoiled him like a child. Children behave like children, Jesus included.

The Spirit of God in Jesus' case brought a life of rigor and passion and vision and commitment, but also of doubt, anger, suffering, and loneliness. The Gospels do not conceal any of that; in fact they celebrate Jesus' weakness, although the celebration is too much for many pseudo-orthodox in the modern period. Tertullian went to the length of describing Jesus as short, squat, and ugly (*De carne Christi*). Why? This genuine humanity means that the sonship of Jesus, his intimacy with Spirit, is a model for our receiving of the Spirit, for all our own ugliness. At baptism, Paul says, the Spirit within us cries out to God, "Abba, Father" (Gal. 4:4-7; Rom. 8:14-17) as happened when Jesus was immersed by John the Baptist. Sonship belongs to humanity; it comes to us with our own immersion in Spirit, our own crosses to bear, our own transformation into eternal life.

Sonship belongs to humanity because it belongs to Jesus, and vice versa. Sonship is what the whole story of God with his people is about, first on Paul's list of Israel's gifts to all believers (with law-giving a distant fourth; Rom. 9:5). "I am sure," said Paul (Rom. 8:38-39), "that neither death nor life nor angels nor principalities nor things present nor things to come nor powers nor height nor depth nor anything else in all creation will be able to separate us from the love of God that is in Jesus Christ our Lord."

Christians believe the real content of revelation is the story of God's ceaseless longing to bring home his vagrant children in every time and place. As Saint Augustine, Bishop of Hippo, wrote in his longest treatise, *The City of God*, the whole of human history takes place in the dreadful caesura written in humanity's catastrophic confusion between passion and self-indulgence, between love of God and love of self (*City of God* 14.28):

> So two loves have constituted two cities—the earthly is formed by love
> of self even to contempt of God, the heavenly by love of God even to

contempt of self. For the one glories in herself, the other in the Lord. The one seeks glory from man; for the other God, the witness of the conscience, is the greatest glory. . . . In the one the lust for power prevails, both in her own rulers and in the nations she subdues; in the other all serve each other in charity, governors by taking thought for all and subjects by obeying.

By book 18, Augustine arrives at his own time, and repeats that the two cities "alike enjoy temporal goods or suffer temporal ills, but differ in faith, in hope, in love, until they be separated by the final judgment and each receive its end, of which there is no end" (*City of God* 18.54). That, for Christians, is the context of Scripture, its story of all time.

Augustine wrote while Genesis Rabbah was being compiled, and like the sages of that Midrash, Augustine synthesized Scripture with his view of the world and salvation as a whole. Unlike the Sages, his perspective was not one of a repeated pattern. Augustine teaches us something about Christianity that Christians themselves often have trouble seeing. To the naked eye, it can seem that Judaism and Christianity are fighting over words: one says the Scripture is about Torah, the other says it is about Christ. At some level, the disputation has to come down to that. But Augustine shows us plainly why the issue here is not merely a matter of words.

Jesus' sonship leads not to restoration, but to resurrection. This is not just a matter of afterlife somehow sometime, a wish for the pleasant parts of the status quo to keep on going or a return to nostalgia as it used to be. Rather, Jesus in the most ancient creed of the Church was raised to a new order of spiritual being at *God's right hand*, such that believers also strive for a transformation into life in the Spirit rather than the flesh. The focus of the Christian orientation expressed in the Apostles' Creed is precisely that resurrection of the spiritual bodies of believers (see Paul in 1 Cor. 15:12-54), a new and transformed life that the world has only glimpsed before in the case of Jesus.

So it must be the case that Christians read the Bible backward. When you are moving forward at great speed into unmapped territory, maps tell you where you have been, and provide only an inkling of where you are going. The heavenly Jerusalem that is humanity's true home is not objectively there in the text at all; intimacy with that Jerusalem, she who is our mother (Gal. 4:26), comes only with the Spirit that the Scriptures attest and awaken. Humanity's fate is determined not by patterns that always have been and will be, nor by any city ever on earth, but by directions to that city whose constitution is a kingdom not of this world. Christianity is true because it pleads its case on the basis of the Spirit of the God who will judge us all, just as God made us all and longs to reconcile us to Godself.

3. Applying the Generative and Systematic Principles

The generative approach to the sources of Judaism and Christianity, together with the systematic approach to those two religions, have changed the way we study our texts and attempt to define the relationship between Judaism and Christianity within the ancient period. The essays in the present volume press beyond those advances and seek to apply critical principles in the study of religion to relations between the two religions in the present. In doing so, they mark a transformative moment of study.

These essays put definitively behind them the model of Judaism and Christianity as static entities, and they treat the sources as developing expressions, rather than as fixed products. In both regards, they represent an approach that is not universal, but the older conventions, driven by confessional concerns, appear to be definitively on the wane. But if the generative and systematic principles have made their way into the mainstream of study and discussion, the means and methods by which they might be applied remain matters of debate because these are issues to be defined. Each of these essays contributes in its own way to that definition.

In both of his contributions, Anthony Le Donne marks out the shift in the ground under the feet of investigators occasioned by a change in the understanding of history. For the positivist historians, inspired by Leopold von Ranke during the nineteenth century, historical criteria produced findings of authenticity when applied to objective textual data. The humanist perspective, whose champion was R. G. Collingwood during the twentieth century, insists that historians of the ancient world cannot stand over their sources and find them right or wrong, because they do not have access to events except through those sources.[9] Rather, historians explain *how* their sources arose within their cultural environments, inferring the events that ultimately generated texts.

The irreducible place of inference in historical investigation brings to this entire volume a greater sense that findings are provisional or tentative than has been conventional in the study of Jewish and Christian origins. Given the diverse background of the contributors, that is helpful—but far from inevitable. Anthony Le Donne's interaction with the authors as the active editor of this volume put into practice his view of history.

Given this greater sense of provisionality on the part of contributors, the absolute claims of religious systems, especially claims to an exclusivity that militates against either the Jewish or the Christian side, are difficult to deal with. As Leonard Greenspoon shows in "Translating Jesus," there are no immediate cures for this problem, particularly because the cultural location of the translation, and its original text interact through the catalyst of rendering a new version. Judah ben Ilai said, "He who translates literally is a liar, while he who adds a word is a blasphemer" (*Tosefta Megillah* 3:41; *Bavli Kiddushin* 49). That judgment was applied to Exod. 24:10, where Moses and his companions "saw the God of Israel" according to the Hebrew text.[10] Since that is impossible, a literal translation would be a lie, while saying something like, "they saw the angel of the God of Israel," would blaspheme by replacing God with another figure. The Aramaic translation called Onqelos solved this conundrum by rendering that they "saw the glory of the God of Israel." How many failed attempts preceded that accommodation? As concerns anti-Semitism, in our time we are in a pre-Onqelon moment of rendering, and Greenspoon's acknowledgment that we should accept the pain of that predicament is wise.

Joel Lohr shows why the systems of religion we have to deal with in order to address Jewish-Christian relations involve this kind of discomfort. If eschatological judgment is irreducibly important for the understanding of Christianity—regardless of whether a given expression of that judgment may be attributed to Jesus—then statements of condemnation can scarcely be laundered out of exegesis without distorting the whole system of religion of which they are a part. When it is also acknowledged, as Lohr argues it must be acknowledged, that eschatological judgment was a part of the Judaism that informed earliest Christianity, the depth of this issue becomes plain.

In the case of the New Testament, the language of judgment against both "gentiles" and "Jews" is internalized, so that the system of religion can express judgment against either group. The implicit ambivalence of that position is made explicit in the story of the Syrophoenician or Canaanite Woman in Mark and Matthew, especially in the elegant treatment of Anne Lapidus Lerner. She seizes on the central feature of the story: that the anticipated pivot of the story, Jesus, turns out to serve an ancillary role as compared to the unnamed woman. That sends resonances through Matthew, Mark, and the community of readers, which continue to be heard.

A particular feature of this volume that takes up an implication of a generative approach to texts is that the place of sources within the Gospels is recognized. Until recently, source analysis was a refugee from a time of positivist historiography, although it would be a natural part of an approach inspired by the orientation of Collingwood in the study of Christian and Jewish origins. Michael J. Cook investigates the undoubted differences between Galilee and Jerusalem, taking up the approach of Ernst Lohmeyer[11] in parsing the significance of variations in how Jewish leaders are identified in Mark. Donald Senior devotes his attention to Matthew, showing how the emergence of sources into text needs to be taken into account for any understanding of the presentation of Jesus to form. In the case of both these articles, older approaches to source criticism are carefully and innovatively deployed, so as to avoid the piecemeal results of earlier efforts and to take account of issues of cultural location.

Earlier scholarship also inspires Eyal Regev to see Jesus' prophetic action in the Temple as a direct onslaught on the authority of the high priesthood that engaged the interests of Rome. This theme is anchored in the history of scholarship in the work of T. W. Manson, Cecil Roth, and Victor Eppstein, and was recently brought into prominence by a greater sensitivity to cultural location in the study of the Gospels.[12] This sensitivity is occasioned by the influence of anthropological and sociological approaches to exegesis, and has prompted a new attention to the place of ritual in Christianity, a topic that the dominance of Protestant approaches has tended to press into the background. In the present case, the relationship between Jesus' action in the Temple and his own ritual meals has proven to be an area of investigation not represented in the present volume.[13]

Dagmar Winter explicitly takes up the theme of Protestantism's inheritance in theology. In particular, she demonstrates that the concern to portray Jesus' as "dissimilar" from his environment, to the point of standing out as a genius part from his time, stoked the growing anti-Semitism of the period *after* the Enlightenment. When the relationship between Jesus and his environment is taken to be a working out of the place of grace in contrast to law, the results were predictable but no less disastrous. Rudolf Bultmann's crucial role in bringing the nexus of grace and law (or faith and works) to the lens of interpretation by means of dialectical theology naturally comes in for close scrutiny.

But then Gerd Theissen, in a searching analysis of what the Third Reich did to the study of Jesus, defends the place of Bultmann's existentialism within the politics of his time. Theissen uses this existentialism, in turn, to discover a principle of transcendence in the New Testament's criticism of Judaism that is nonetheless neither anti-Judaic nor anti-Semitic. In the process, he also explores the interesting question of the sometimes inadvertent consequences of positions taken for the best of motives.

The contemporary edge of the discussions in the present volume broadens the usual scope of the participants in scholarly dialogue and offers the prospect that the critical study of religion will have an increasing role to play in relations among religions. James D. G. Dunn brings that out at the close of his chapter and so summarizes the individual articles that there is no necessity to do so here.

At the same time, Dunn makes it plain that the experiments represented by this volume are just that; they apply principles of analysis whose execution will continue to arouse debate, together with the principles themselves. To take the most prominent example of Dunn's criticism (of the article by Eyal Regev), New Testament scholars persist in seeing the issue of "messiahship" as central to the death of Jesus to the exclusion of other issues. Although Dunn accepts that the Temple was crucial, he focuses on what Jesus allegedly said about the Temple while Regev is more concerned with what Jesus did, and how his action was perceived by both the authorities in the Temple and the Romans.

Dunn further criticizes Regev for not accepting the accounts in the New Testament to the extent that only elements mentioned in those texts should be accepted as historical. But then one purpose of Regev's essay (and several in this volume) is to extend the horizon of history beyond any one text or canon of texts, so as to include a wider number of perspectives within the construction of history. If historical study is to be limited to what one set of literatures says about a topic, its claim to be history—on either a positivist construction or the perspectival orientation represented by most essays in this volume—will be weak indeed.

Dunn's focalizing on Jesus' "messiahship" illustrates Amy-Jill Levine's complaint that the terms of reference of discussions of Judaism and Christianity tend to be defined within the Christian lexicon. Her criticism goes hand in hand with her plea to show more caution in using the word *marginal*. If post-modernism were a belief system (as may be the case), then "marginal" has acquired the confessional status of an attribute that must characterize a speaker for his or her assertion to be valid. At the same time, by observing the role of scholarship in recent efforts of understanding among Jews and Christians, Levine shows how the issue of the historical Jesus has been relativized within an assessment of Jesus' religious importance.

Levine's point is strengthened by keeping in mind the willingness of several contributors to the present volume to see the texts of the New Testament not as unitary compositions but as collaborative. Sources within them, written and/or oral, delivered themselves not only of different Christologies, but sometimes of barely any Christology at all, in pursuing commitments that were to them more pressing. Opening up the New Testament to inquiry involves not only moving from one page to another, but also seeing the variety within each page that is resonant with the diverse and rich world of discussion that is today seeing us beyond the repetitive disputes of an earlier time and into an era of mutual understanding.

Notes

Foreword

1. Christian Scholars Group on Christian-Jewish Relations, "A Sacred Obligation: Rethinking Christian Faith in Relation to Judaism and the Jewish People," http://www .jcrelations.net/A_Sacred_Obligation_-_Rethinking_Christian_Faith_in_Relation_to _Judaism_and_the.2372.0.html

2. National Jewish Scholars Project, "*Dabru Emet,*" http://www.jcrelations.net/ Dabru_Emet_-_A_Jewish_Statement_on_Christians_and_Christianity.2395.0.html

Introduction: Allowing Historical Study to Serve Interfaith Dialogue

1. Geza Vermes, *Jesus the Jew: A Historian's Reading of the Gospel*, 1st Fortress Press ed. (Minneapolis: Fortress Press, 1981), 19.

2. See chapter 7 in this book for my critique of the standard divisions of "Quests" in Jesus research. N. T. Wright coined the phrase "The Third Quest for the Historical Jesus" in his revision of Neill: S. Neill and N. T. Wright, *The Interpretation of the New Testament, 1861–1986,* 2nd ed. (Oxford: Oxford University Press, 1988), 379.

3. Of course, Vermes admitted that his was "a very Jewish book indeed" in so far as understanding Jesus requires a specialized knowledge of Second Temple Judaism (*Jesus,* 7). In other words, it was Vermes's commitment to do right by Second Temple Judaism that was most important. To be fair, the fact that his book was not simply a Jewish book written for Jews allowed for a greater impact—an impact for which I am grateful. More-over, there is nothing wrong with standing firmly within secular historiography as long as one admits that this brings its own prejudices with it.

4. Jon Levenson, "The Universal Horizon of Biblical Particularism," in *Ethnicity and the Bible,* ed. M. G. Brett (Leiden: Brill, 1996), 146; see also his "The Perils of Engaged Scholarship: A Rejoinder to Jorge Pixley," in *Jews, Christians, and the Theology of the Hebrew Scriptures,* eds. A. Ogden Bellis and J. S. Kaminsky (Atlanta: Society of Biblical Literature, 2000), 241. See the useful assessment of Levenson's method with an eye to the

question of election theology in Joel N. Lohr, *Chosen and Unchosen: Concepts of Election in the Pentateuch and Jewish-Christian Interpretation* (Winona Lake, IN: Eisenbrauns, 2009), 71–86.

5. Levenson argues that we must not confuse these two statements: "'We all have biases' and 'All we have is biases.' The first is true; the second is false" ["Perils of Engaged Scholarship," 241].

6. For an introduction to the relationship between history and memory, see my *The Historiographical Jesus: Memory, Typology, and the Son of David* (Waco: Baylor University Press, 2009), chs. 2–3; cf. P. Hutton, *History as an Art of Memory* (Hanover, NH: University Press of New England, 1993); Y. Zerubavel, *Recovered Roots: Collective Memory and the Making of Israeli National Tradition* (Chicago: University of Chicago Press, 1995).

7. Excerpt from *Zakhor: Jewish History and Jewish Memory* (Seattle: University of Washington Press, 1982) in *The Collective Memory Reader*, eds. J. Olick, V. Vinitzky-Seroussi, and D. Levy (Oxford: Oxford University Press, 2011), 206–7; Yerushalmi also quotes Eugen Rosenstock-Huessy: "The historian is the physician of memory. It is his honor to heal wounds, genuine wounds. As a physician must act, regardless of medical theories, because his patient is ill, so the historian must act under moral pressure to restore a nation's memory, or that of mankind." *Out of Revolution: Autobiography of Western Man*, (New York: William Morrow & Co. Reprints: 1964 [1938]), 696.

8. Richard Harries, Norman Solomon, and Tim Winter, eds. *Abraham's Children: Jews, Christians, and Muslims in Conversation* (New York: T&T Clark, 2006), 97, 87.

9. It should be mentioned that the vast majority of young Christians have never heard this phrase, much less used it. This only proves further ignorance, not necessarily the progress of enlightenment.

10. Cf. Edward Kessler, *An Introduction to Jewish-Christian Relations* (Cambridge: Cambridge University Press, 2010), 1–24.

11. Tikva Frymer-Kensky, et al., "Jewish-Christian Dialogue: Jon D. Levenson and Critics," *Commentary* 113, no. 4 (2002): 9.

12. J. Schröter argues, "If *every* historical construction represents the relationship between event and story (even those that are written within the rubric of the historical-critical consciousness) then a contemporary portrait of Jesus cannot simply set aside the narrative representations of the person of Jesus in the Gospels. On the contrary, this portrait has to be related to these representations and be reconstructed within the rubric of contemporary epistemology. The outcome is not the "real" Jesus behind the Gospels. The outcome is a historical construction which claims to be plausible within the rubric of contemporary epistemology." My translation from "Von der Historizität der Evangelien: Ein Beitrag zur gegenwärtigen Diskussion um den historischen Jesus," in *Der historische Jesus: Tendenzen und Perspektiven der gegenwärtigen Forschung*, eds. J. Schröter and R. Brucher; *BZNW* 114 (Berlin: De Gruyter, 2002), 205–6.

13. James D. G. Dunn, *Romans*, WBC 38A (Dallas: Word, 1988), 3–26, gives seven reasons to support this.

14. Luke, thought by most to be a gentile author, portrays the child Jesus teaching in his "Father's house"—the Jerusalem Temple (Luke 2:49).

Chapter 1: Translating *Jesus* and *the Jews*

1. On this and related issues, see Leonard Greenspoon, "Jewish Translations of the Bible" in *The Jewish Study Bible*, eds. Adele Berlin and Marc Zvi Brettler (New York: Oxford, 2003), 2005–20.

2. Willis Barnstone, *The Poetics of Translation: History, Theory, Practice* (New Haven: Yale University Press, 2003), 62.

3. Ibid., 64.

4. Willis Barnstone, *Restored New Testament: A New Translation with Commentary, Including the Gnostic Gospels Thomas, Mary, and Judas* (New York: W. W. Norton, 2009), 16f.

5. Barnstone, *Poetics,* 65.

6. Barnstone, *Restored,* 16–17.

7. Barnstone, *Poetics,* 66.

8. Ibid., 65–66.

9. Ibid., 74–75.

10. Ibid., 75–77.

11. Ibid., 77–78.

12. Ibid., 78.

13. Ibid., 78–79.

14. Ibid., 80.

15. Barnstone, *Restored,* 14.

16. For full publication information, see note 4 above.

17. Everett Fox, *The Five Books of Moses. A New Translation with Introductions, Commentary, and Notes,* vol. 1 of *The Schocken Bible* (New York: Schocken, 1995 [earlier versions of Genesis and Exodus also appeared]).

18. Barnstone, *Restored,* 1058.

19. Ibid., 100.

20. David H. Stern, trans., *Jewish New Testament* (Jerusalem: Jewish New Testament Publications, 1989); *Complete Jewish Bible* (Messianic Jewish Resources International, 2007).

21. Ibid., ix.

22. Ibid., x.

23. Ibid., xi.

24. Ibid., xix.

25. Ibid., xx.

26. Barnstone, *Restored,* 73–74.

27. *Contemporary English Version* (New York: American Bible Society, 1995).

28. Barclay M. Newman, "CEV's Chief Translator: We Were Faithful to the Intention of the Text [Counterpoint]," *Bible Review* 12 (1996): 43.

29. David J. Burke, "Translating the Jews *(hoi Ioudaioi)* in the New Testament: Comparing the Pertinent Passages in Recent English Versions," in *Removing the Anti-Judaism from the New Testament,* eds. Howard Clark Kee and Irvin J. Borowsky (Philadelphia: American Interfaith Institute/World Alliance, 1998 and 2000), 63–64.

30. Ibid., 64–65.

31. Newman, "CEV's Chief Translator," 43.

32. Burke, "Translating," 65.

33. Newman, "CEV's Chief Translator," 43, 51.

34. Burke, "Translating," 79–80.

35. Ibid., 78–79.

36. Ibid., 70, 82–84; publication information on the NLT: *New Living Translation* (Wheaton, IL: Tyndale House, 1996).

37. James A. Sanders, "The Hermeneutics of Translation," in *Removing the Anti-Judaism from the New Testament,* eds. Howard Clark Kee and Irvin J. Borowsky (Philadelphia: American Interfaith Institute/World Alliance, 1998 and 2000), 59.

38. Ibid., 61.

39. For Borowsky's views, see Irvin J. Borowsky, "Removing the Anti-Judaism from the New Testament," in *Removing the Anti-Judaism from the New Testament,* eds. Howard Clark Kee and Irvin J. Borowsky (Philadelphia: American Interfaith Institute/World Alliance, 1998 and 2000), 9–20.

40. Joseph Blenkinsopp, "The Contemporary English Version: Inaccurate Translation Tries to Soften Anti-Judaic Sentiment [Point]," *Bible Review* 12 (1996): 51.

41. Barnstone, *Restored,* 16.

42. Ibid., 18.

43. Gerald S. Sloyan, *John* (Interpretation; Atlanta: John Knox, 1988), xiv. Cited by Marilyn J. Salmon, *Preaching without Contempt: Overcoming Unintended Anti-Judaism,* Fortress Resources for Preaching (Minneapolis: Fortress Press, 2006), 120–21.

Chapter 2: A Jewish Teaching

1. Lamar Cope, "Matthew 25:31-46: 'The Sheep and the Goats' Reinterpreted," *NovT* 11 (1969): 32. I have altered Cope's original spelling of *concensus* to *consensus.*

2. Recent works arguing for the authenticity of the core of the passage include Craig S. Keener, *A Commentary on the Book of Matthew* (Grand Rapids: Eerdmans, 1999), 602–6, and John Nolland, *The Gospel of Matthew: A Commentary on the Greek Text,* NIGTC (Grand Rapids: Eerdmans, 2005), 1023–37. Theirs is a minority position, however.

3. Cope, "Reinterpreted," esp. 41–42. Compare the similar discussion of Rudolf Bultmann, *The History of the Synoptic Tradition* (New York: Harper and Row, 1963), 123–24.

4. I refer to Matt. 25:31-46 as the "Sheep and the Goats story" for the sake of convenience, and to avoid the term *parable* (for reasons why, see, e.g., R. T. France, *The Gospel of Matthew,* NICNT [Grand Rapids: Eerdmans, 2007], 960). Also out of convenience, I refer to the author of the gospel as "Matthew" and occasionally "he." This is not intended as a statement about the authorship of the gospel.

5. *Jesus and Judgment: The Eschatological Proclamation in Its Jewish Context* (Minneapolis: Fortress Press, 1997), esp. 19–163. For our purposes, I am forced to truncate Reiser's discussion and gloss over important specifics of his work. For helpful summaries of ancient judgment texts that specifically parallel, or should be considered in reading, Matt. 25:31-46, see W. D. Davies and Dale C. Allison, *A Critical and Exegetical Commentary on the Gospel According to Saint Matthew* (Edinburgh: T&T Clark, 1997), 418–19; Klyne R. Snodgrass, *Stories with Intent: A Comprehensive Guide to the Parables* (Grand Rapids: Eerdmans, 2008), 544–49; and Graham N. Stanton, "Once More: Matthew 25:31-46," in *A Gospel for a New People: Studies in Matthew* (Louisville: Westminster John Knox, 1993), 207–31, esp. 21–30.

6. Ibid., 156.

7. Such a statement is not meant as a challenge to covenantal nomism per se, though it is interesting how strongly E. P. Sanders reacted to texts like 4 Ezra in which fidelity to the Torah forms the basis of judgment. See his *Paul and Palestinian Judaism* (London: SCM, 1977), 409–28, and for discussion, Reiser, *Judgment,* 111–23, esp. 116–17.

8. Ibid., 157.

9. Ibid., 157.

10. Ibid., 161-62.

11. Joel S. Kaminsky makes just this point in surveying late biblical and Second Temple texts dealing with the "other," conversion, and gentile judgment. See his "Israel's Election and the Other in Biblical, Second Temple, and Rabbinic Thought," in *The "Other" in Second Temple Judaism: Essays in Honor of John J. Collins,* ed. Daniel C. Harlow, et. al. (Grand Rapids: Eerdmans, 2011), 17–30, esp. 22–23.

12. Franz Delitzsch, *The New Testament Translated into Hebrew* (London: British Bible Society, 1885). Compare the identical translation of Salkinson and Ginsburg (1886).

13. Aelred Cody, "When Is the Chosen People Called a Gôy?" *VT* 14 (1964): 1–6. He notes that although *goy* is used of Israel in the Hebrew Bible on occasion (usually as a note of divine rejection or in judgment) such usage ends by the Hellenistic period.

14. Douglas R. A. Hare and Daniel J. Harrington, "'Make Disciples of All the Gentiles' (MT 28:19)," *CBQ* 37 (1975): 359–69.

15. John P. Meier, "Nations or Gentiles in Matthew 28:19," *CBQ* 39 (1977): 94–102.

16. Although I am not sure I would translate *ethnei* as *gentile* in Matt. 21:43, I am not convinced this passage is as clear as Meier suggests. For instance, Meier's reading does not adequately account for Matthew's insertion of the term over and against Mark and Luke's use of *allois* ("others"). Part of this also relates to the fact that I read Matthew quite differently with respect to the book's view of gentiles and Jews (see discussion below), and I think the use of *ethnei* in 21:43 is a rhetorically powerful term given the Jewish-gentile conflict at hand. At a minimum, it is not clear why Meier thinks the onus lies on interpreters to prove that *ethnē* refers to gentiles, not nations, in Matt. 25:32 ("the responsibility for proving otherwise lies on the side of those who favor a restriction" [100]). Even after having read his work carefully a number of times, I am still baffled by this assertion. To my mind, ancient Jewish usage of *ethnē* as gentiles (something Meier does not dispute) *alone* suggests the opposite to be true when encountering the word in contemporary Jewish literature like Matthew.

17. See Stanton, "Once More," 214, and Ulrich Luz, "Anti-Judaism in the Gospel of Matthew as a Historical and Theological Problem: An Outline," in *Studies in Matthew* (Grand Rapids: Eerdmans, 2005), 249. Examples of those who assume, or provide little or no argument to show, that *ethnē* means all humankind in Matt. 25:32 abound. Two characteristic examples suffice: Dan O. Via claims that the passage "clearly suggests that Israel is included" without substantiating this idea ("Ethical Responsibility and Human Wholeness in Matt. 25:31-46," *HTR* 80 [1987]: 91), while Donald A. Hagner uses a circular argument, appealing to Matt. 28:19 to conclude that because Matt. 28:19 includes all humans without distinction, Matt. 25:32 must as well (*Matthew 14–28* [Dallas: Word, 1995], 742).

18. R. C. H. Lenski, *The Interpretation of St. Matthew's Gospel* (Minneapolis: Augsburg, 1961), 988.

19. Leon Morris, *The Gospel According to Matthew* (Leicester: Apollos, 1992), 635, n. 58.

20. David L. Turner, *Matthew* (Grand Rapids: Baker Academic, 2008), 605. Compare Snodgrass, *Stories with Intent*, 555, who calls it "the determinative issue."

21. The case is made most clearly by Stanton, "Once More," 207–31. See also Hagner, *Matthew 14-28*, 744–45; Robert H. Gundry, *Matthew: A Commentary on His Literary and Theological Art* (Grand Rapids: Eerdmans, 1982), 514–15; and Turner, *Matthew*, 605–7.

22. Douglas Hare, *The Theme of Jewish Persecution of Christians in the Gospel According to St. Matthew* (Cambridge: Cambridge University Press, 1967).

23. Although we did not cover the idea of treatment-of-Israel as the criterion for final judgment of gentiles in our above survey, it does feature from time to time. See especially 4 Ezra 7:37-38; 2 Bar. 72:2—73:1; 1 Enoch 62; 103–4 and for discussion, consult Stanton, "Once More," 224–28. Also, I've placed the term "true Israel" in scare quotes because the term, though rhetorically useful for my discussion, is not altogether accurate. Consult Amy-Jill Levine, *The Social and Ethnic Dimensions of the Matthean Salvation History: 'Go nowhere among the Gentiles . . .' (Matt. 10:5b).* (Lewiston, NY: Edwin Mellen, 1988), 241–71, esp. 270–71.

24. The most comprehensive study is Sherman W. Gray, *The Least of My Brothers: Matthew 25:31-46: A History of Interpretation* (Atlanta: Scholars, 1989). Compare Ulrich Luz, *Matthew 21-28: A Commentary* (Minneapolis: Fortress Press, 2005), 267–74.

25. Snodgrass, *Stories with Intent*, 556.

26. Ibid., 556.

27. Pace Stanton, who implies that these textual variants support his least-as-disciples interpretation ("Once More," esp. 215, 230–31).

28. Francis Watson, "Liberating the Reader: A Theological-Exegetical Study of the Parable of the Sheep and the Goats (Matt. 25.31-46)," in *The Open Text: New Directions for Biblical Studies?*, ed. Francis Watson (London: SCM, 1993), 65.

29. Ibid., 69. Compare the similar conclusions of Davies and Allison, *Matthew*, 429; and David Wenham, *The Parables of Jesus* (Downers Grove, IL: InterVarsity, 1989), 89–93.

30. J. Ramsey Michaels, "Apostolic Hardships and Righteous Gentiles: A Study of Matthew 25:31-46," *JBL* 84 (1965): 28–29. Compare the similar, more recent, words of Keener: "The king thus judges the nations based on how they have responded to the gospel of the kingdom already preached to them before the time of his kingdom . . ." (*Matthew*, 605).

31. Morris, *Matthew*, 634, 637.

32. Graham Foster, "Making Sense of Matthew 25:31-46," *Scottish Bulletin of Evangelical Theology* 16 (1998): 139. Compare Turner, *Matthew*, 604. The passage's "distinctive teaching," according to Foster, is one of consolation for the persecuted church.

33. Luz, "Anti-Judaism"; translation of "Der Antijudaismus des Matthäusevangeliums als historisches und theologisches Problem," *EvT* 53 (1993): 310–28. In what follows, I draw freely from and add to this material. I have also been influenced by the insightful overviews of Terence L. Donaldson, *Jews and Anti-Judaism in the New Testament: Decision Points and Divergent Interpretations* (Waco: Baylor University Press, 2010), esp. 30–54, and Amy-Jill Levine, "Anti-Judaism and the Gospel of Matthew," in *Anti-Judaism and the Gospels*, ed. William R. Farmer (Harrisburg, PA: Trinity International, 1999), 9–36.

34. David Levenson, "Anti-Judaism in the Gospel of Matthew" (paper presented at International Symposium on the Interpretation of the Bible as a Force for Social Change, Goethe Universität Frankfurt, 2001).

35. Consult Luz, "Anti-Judaism," esp. 260, who reflects on Matthew's tendency to ignore Jesus' teaching of love of enemy and forgiveness regarding the scribes and Pharisees.

36. Luz notes the particularly grotesque nature of this scene, unique to Matthew, given that "the gentile Pilate [is] observing a Jewish-Biblical expiation ritual" ("Anti-Judaism," 247–48).

37. The debates regarding whether this mission still includes Israel are heated. The strongest, most compelling case that it still does is by Levine, *Social and Ethnic Dimensions*. Compare also her "Anti-Judaism and Matthew," esp. 30, as well as her more recent "'To All the Gentiles': A Jewish Perspective on the Great Commission," *RevExp* 103 (2006): 139–58, esp. 147. In the latter Levine acknowledges, however (through a favorable citation of Brendan Byrne's work), that "the overall impression gained from the gospel is that, for the Matthean community, the mission to Israel is factually finished."

38. This point is brought out particularly well by Levine, "AntiJudaism and Matthew," 31–33. Our conclusions move in slightly different directions, however.

39. For more on election theology of Israel more generally, as derived from the Hebrew Bible and in conversation with Jewish interpretation, see my *Chosen and Unchosen: Conceptions of Election in the Pentateuch and Jewish-Christian Interpretation* (Winona Lake, IN: Eisenbrauns, 2009).

40. Here is it not difficult to see an analogy between the Pharisees and other characters in the Hebrew Bible who lose their elect status, those Joel Kaminsky has termed "anti-elect" (e.g., Achan in Joshua 7). See further his *Yet I Loved Jacob: Reclaiming the Biblical Concept of Election* (Nashville: Abingdon, 2007), especially 111–12.

41. I am entirely unconvinced by David C. Sim, "The Gospel of Matthew and the Gentiles," *JSNT* 57 (1995): 19–48, who argues that Matthew's Gospel should be understood to have, at best, a neutral view of gentiles, certainly not positive, and that a vision of a gentile mission is not in view. While I agree that Matthew's view of gentiles is complex, it seems that Sim overlooks the development of Matthew's Gospel that culminates in the Great Commission. His view that "A glance at the Gospel's missionary references reveals that the greater part of them refer to the Jewish mission. . . . By contrast, the references to the Gentile mission are sparse and very general in nature" (41–42) really does not prove anything, unless the criterion for determining such things is a tallying system in which

the idea with the most references wins. That most references in Matthew point to a Jewish mission makes one to the gentiles at the end of the gospel all the more striking.

42. Marc Hirshman recently argued that although first-century Judaism appears to be divided on the issue, in the second and third century the Jewish group associated with Rabbi Ishmael appears to have welcomed and encouraged gentiles who were involved with Torah, even if that person did not convert. See his "Rabbinic Universalism in the Second and Third Centuries," *HTR* 93 (2000): 101–15. Compare the insightful essay by John M. G. Barclay, "Universalism and Particularism: Twin Components of Both Judaism and Early Christianity," in *A Vision for the Church: Studies in Early Christian Ecclesiology in Honour of J.P.M. Sweet*, eds. Markus Bockmuehl and Michael B. Thompson (Edinburgh: T&T Clark, 1997), 207–24.

43. For more on this latter idea, consult the study by David Novak, *The Image of the Non-Jew in Judaism: An Historical and Constructive Study of the Noahide Laws* (New York: Edwin Mellen, 1983).

44. Luz, "Anti-Judaism," esp. 250–57.

45. Ibid., 258, n. 50. Luz's quotation here is that of an oral comment made by Rabbi Marcel Marcus of Bern.

46. Of course many studies point out that Matthew's rhetoric was simply the convention as far as first-century inter-Jewish polemics were concerned. Luke T. Johnson's seminal article ("The New Testament's Anti-Jewish Slander and the Conventions of Ancient Polemic," *JBL* 108 [1989]: 419–41) is characteristic of this approach. Although there is little to debate regarding whether Matthew's vehement rhetoric was unique (it was *not*), studies like Johnson's are only really helpful if we decide (as he does for the purposes of his article) "not to worry about what to do with this language so much as what the language was doing" (419). The same holds true for the NT and its teaching on the subordination of women.

47. David Novak, *The Election of Israel: The Idea of a Chosen People* (Cambridge: Cambridge University Press, 1995), 14 and note 43 above. For discussion, see Lohr, *Chosen and Unchosen*, 46–59.

48. Modern Catholic teaching on the matter seems to have changed with the Second Vatican Council. Though not entirely relieved of potential problems, see, for instance, *Lumen Gentium*, section 16.

Chapter 3: A Dogmatic Jesus

1. Throughout I have used the text as presented in English in Joel Marcus, *Mark 1–8: A New Translation with Introduction and Commentary* (New York: Doubleday, 2000), unless otherwise indicated.

2. Throughout I use the translation in Ulrich Luz, *Matthew 8–20*, trans. James E. Crouch; ed. Helmut Koester (Minneapolis: Fortress Press, 2001), unless otherwise indicated.

Matthew has introduced a number of elements into this story that do not appear in Mark. "Especially in vv. 22-25 and 28 the text has been completely rewritten by Matthew. In these verses the redactional characteristics are extraordinarily heavy. Matthew used only a few of Mark's words here; in addition one can see the influence of Mark 10:47-48" (Luz, 336).

3. Amy-Jill Levine suggests that the centurion in Matthew 8:5-13 also requests a cure for his son. Amy-Jill Levine, "Canaanite Woman" in *Women in Scripture: A Dictionary of Named and Unnamed Women in the Hebrew Bible, the Apochrypha/Deuterocanonical Books, and the New Testament,* eds. Carol Meyers, Toni Craven, and Ross S. Kraemer (Boston: Houghton Mifflin, 2000), 412.

4. For example, Mark 5:24-29.

5. For example, Mark 5:1-20.

6. Although I have followed the capitalization of "lord" and "son (of David)" in the translations, I have not used capital letters in my text as a reminder that both words are subject to a variety of interpretations in this story.

7. Claudia Setzer, "Three Odd Couples: Women and Men in Mark and John," in *Mariam, the Magdalen, and the Mother*, ed. Deirde Good (Bloomington & Indianapolis: Indiana University Press, 2005), 77; Hal Taussig, "Dealing under the Table: Ritual Negotiation of Women's Power in the Syro-Phoenician Woman Pericope," in *Reimagining Christian Origins: A Colloquium Honoring Burton L. Mack*, eds. Eliabeth A. Castelli and Hal Taussig (Valley Forge, PA: Trinity Press International, 1996), 264.

8. See map "Palestine in New Testament Times," Marcus, ix.

9. Although the route of Jesus' journey of many days from the region of the Sea of Galilee to the region of Tyre and Sidon is not specified, his return is described in Mark in most curious fashion. It has him heading north to Sidon and then east beyond the western shore of the Sea of Galilee to Decapolis, finally coming southeast of the Sea of Galilee. The suggestion has been made that this reflects not geographical ignorance, but an attempt to fulfill the prophecy in Isaiah 8:23 (9:1 in the Christian versions). Anson E. Rainey and R. Steven Notley, *The Sacred Bridge: Carta's Atlas of the Biblical World* (Jerusalem: Carta, 2006), 361–62.

10. Luz argues that "[. . .] the 'gentile' expression 'the region of Tyre and Sidon' shows that Matthew was not interested in the idea of the 'biblical' Holy Land." Thus, although some argue that the area designated as Tyre at the time might have included a few Jewish villages, that was of little interest to Matthew, whose focus is the people rather than the place (Luz, 338).

11. E.g., "First, it is noteworthy that Jesus' circuitous journey in Mark 6:45—8:26 is the only report of Jesus' ministry outside of the borders of the Land of Israel" (Rainey and Notley, *Sacred Bridge*, 361).

12. Luz, 336.

13. Amy-Jill Levine suggests that the woman meets Jesus in a "public space." Levine, "Canaanite Woman," 412.

14. Cf., Mark 7:36; 9:9.

15. Anthony Le Donne suggested to me that "origin" might be a better translation than "race."

16. Marcus, 462. An indication of class seems more significant to me than having that information serve merely as an indication that the dialogue was conducted in Greek.

17. There were different groups of Phoenicians, as Marcus indicates, but he does not ascribe significance to her belonging to one group or another.

18. Luz, 337.

19. Levine, "Canaanite Woman," 412.

20. Matthew's identification of Jesus with the son of David who has healing powers and may be the Messiah is explored in detail by Wayne Baxter, who connects it with Ezekiel 34 (Wayne Baxter, "Healing and the 'Son of David': Matthew's Warrant," *Novum Testamentum* 48, no. 1 [2006], 40 et passim). A broader survey of the implications of the term *son of David* in both Judaism and Christianity in the time when Matthew was written may be found in Richard Van Egmond, "The Messianic 'Son of David' in Matthew," *Journal of Greco-Roman Christianity and Judaism* 3 (2006): 41–71.

21. Luz, 337.

22. Ibid., 339.

23. Jesus had previously directed his disciples to go to "the lost sheep of the house of Israel" (Matt. 10:6).

24. Nanos also questions whether Jesus' response is directed at the disciples or intended for the woman. Mark D. Nanos, "Paul's Reversal of Jews Calling Gentiles 'Dogs' (Phil.

3:2): 1600 Years of an Ideological Tale Wagging an Exegetical Dog?" in *Biblical Interpretation* 17 (2009): 471.

25. Luz, 336.

26. Marcus suggests that Jesus' words reflect the ambient socioeconomic setting in which the Jews of the Galilee suffered from deprivation while the produce they grew was eaten by the gentiles in Tyre (Ibid., 462 note to 7:24).

27. BT *Baba Metzi'a* 71a.

28. Nanos suggests that "Jesus' challenge is based on a zero-sum game." In other words, if the food is fed to the dogs, there will be none for the children. While Nanos correctly analyzes Jesus' premise, the premise is flawed. Nanos, "Paul's Reversal," 471.

29. Marcus, 464.

30. There has been considerable discussion of the source of the "dog" taunt. The claim has been made that Jews had a long history of calling gentiles "dogs," and that justifies the reversal in which Christians call Jews "dogs." Mark D. Nanos stresses the absence of evidence for the Jewish use of "dogs" to refer to gentiles. Nanos also looked into this matter most carefully and concludes: "Yet there is no evidence predating Paul that Jews called Gentiles dogs." Nanos, "Paul's Reversal," 452 et passim.

31. None of the references to "dog" in the Concordance to the Mishnah refers to gentiles.

32. If one links Jesus' two statements in the Matthean text, one can imagine the gentile dogs bringing the lost sheep of Israel back to the fold.

33. Levine, "Canaanite Woman," 412.

34. Matt. 18:10-14.

35. For a parsing of this text see Nanos, 470.

36. Marcus, 464.

37. Luz, 341, n. 62.

38. Marcus, 465.

39. Elizabeth Struthers Malbon's assertion that the woman's persistence, as recorded in Mark, stems from her sensing "the fuller implications of Jesus' ministry of healing: he heals what is broken—broken bodies, broken spirits, and broken relationships" reads into the text a great deal that I do not find there. Elizabeth Struthers Malbon, "Syrophoenician Woman," in *Women in Scripture: A Dictionary of Named and Unnamed Women in the Hebrew Bible, the Apochrypha/Deuterocanonical Books, and the New Testament,* eds. Carol Meyers, Toni Craven, and Ross S. Kraemer (Boston: Houghton Mifflin, 2000), 427.

40. Luz, 341. "A substantial part of the manuscript tradition seeks to portray the woman as an example of humble submissiveness by inserting 'yes' into the text, and therefore downplaying the 'but' of the woman: 'But the woman answered and said, yes Lord.'" Elisabeth Schüssler Fiorenza, *But SHE Said: Feminist Practices of Biblical Interpretation* (Boston: Beacon, 1992), 12.

41. Contra Malbon, who claims that "Jesus gracefully reacts with the maturity that empowers change and enables inclusivity." Malbon, "Syrophoenician Woman," 427.

42. Malbon, "Daughter of the Syrophoenician Woman," *Women in Scripture: A Dictionary of Named and Unnamed Women in the Hebrew Bible, the Apochrypha/Deuterocanonical Books, and the New Testament,* eds. Carol Meyers, Toni Craven, and Ross S. Kraemer (Boston: Houghton Mifflin, 2000), 428.

43. Marcus, 465. I am grateful to Anthony Le Donne for drawing my attention to the variety of translations of *logos* in this text found in contemporary English-language Bibles.

44. Luz considers this "concluding assurance of healing [. . .] very brief" in comparison with other stories that involve healing from a distance (Luz, 335).

45. Levine, "Canaanite Woman," 412.

46. Schüssler Fiorenza, *But SHE Said*, 13.

47. Levine, "Canaanite Woman" 412.

48. Ibid.

49. See Amy-Jill Levine, "Putting Jesus Where He Belongs: The Man from Nazareth in His Jewish World," in *Perspectives in Religious Studies* 27, no. 2 (Summer 2000): 167–77.

50. Even in the absence of a name, he might have addressed her as he did a woman whom he had healed earlier: "Daughter, your faith has saved you. Go in peace and be well from your scourge" (Mark 5:34; Matt. 9:22).

51. The notion that Jesus has learned a lesson here is widespread, e.g., "It is the only first-century text where Jesus is corrected and instructed by someone else" (Taussig, 264).

Chapter 4: The Distribution of Jewish Leaders in the Synoptic Gospels

1. Michael J. Cook, *Modern Jews Engage the New Testament* (Woodstock: Jewish Lights, 2008), 176–91.

2. Biblical quotations are primarily from The Revised Standard Version (any italics are added).

3. Bart Ehrman, *The New Testament: A Historical Introduction to the Early Christian Writings* (New York: Oxford, 2000), 74.

4. Conjoined in Mark 8:31; 11:27; 14:43, 53; 15:1; sometimes "elders" are missing: 10:33; 11:18; 14:1; 15:31.

5. Conjoined in Mark 3:6 and 12:13 (possibly 8:15).

6. Mark 7:5 continues with "the Pharisees and the scribes."

7. For instance, T. A. Burkill, "Anti-Semitism in St. Mark's Gospel," *Novum Testamentum* 3 (1959): 39 n. 3.

8. Rudolf Bultmann, *Die Geschichte der synoptischen Tradition* (Göttingen: Vandenhoeck & Ruprecht, 1931), 16, cited by W. L. Knox, *The Sources of the Synoptic Gospels: I* (Cambridge: Cambridge University Press, 1953), 14.

9. See Mark 8:31; 11:27; 14:43, 53; 15:1.

10. Chief priests in Mark 14:10 remain in concert with scribes (vv. 1-2). In 14:55, bracketed with "the whole council," they remain joined with elders and scribes (14:53). Mark 15:3 continues 15:1, so scribes and elders remain with chief priests (this applies also to 15:10-11).

11. T. A. Burkill, *New Light on the Earliest Gospel* (Ithaca: Cornell University Press, 1972), 219 n. 49; cf. 218ff.

12. Scribes' appearances: Mark 1:22; 2:6, 16; 3:22; 7:1, 5; 8:31; 9:11, 14; 10:33; 11:18, 27; 12:28, 32, 35, 38; 14:1, 43, 53; 15:1, 31. Chief priests: 8:31; 10:33; 11:18, 27; 14:1, 10, 43, 53, 55; 15:1, 3, 10, 11, 31. Pharisees: 2:16, 18, 24; 3:6; 7:1, 3, 5; 8:11, 15; 10:2; 12:13. Elders: 8:31; 11:27; 14:43, 53; 15:1 (disqualified is 7:3 since "elders" here denotes not the first-century group but former generations of teachers). Herodians: 3:6; 12:13; cf. 8:15. Sadducees: 12:18.

13. Pharisees and scribes are implied.

14. Martin Albertz, *Die synoptischen Streitgespräche* (Berlin: Trowitzsch & Sohn, 1921), 5–36; Burton Easton, "A Primitive Tradition in Mark," *Studies in Early Christianity*, ed. S. J. Case (New York: Century, 1928), 83–101; ibid., *The Gospel before the Gospels* (New York: Charles Scribner's and Sons, 1928), 71–72, 114–15; Paul Winter, *On the Trial of Jesus* (Berlin: Walter De Gruyter, 1961), 111–28 passim, 206, 209–10 nn. 25, 27.

15. Because it displays camaraderie inconsistent with a controversy collection?

16. My own reconstruction is detailed in chapter 12 of *Modern Jews Engage the New Testament*, 133–48. Crucial is the determination that the triad of "chief priests + scribes + elders" was ensconced in this earliest stratum—since, indeed, no viable Passion storyline could support itself without such opposition forces to drive the plot. Surveying

thirty-four reconstructions of putative pre-Markan Passion renditions is Marion Soards, "The Question of a Premarcan Passion Narrative," *The Death of the Messiah 2*, ed. Raymond Brown (New York: Doubleday: 1994), 1492–1524.

17. Excluding Mark 9:12b if one believes that all Mark's uses of "Son of Man" are redactional (except 13:26). As noted, the Elijah pericope, in chapter 9, appears shifted there by Mark (from what is now chapter 12).

18. Excluding Mark 2:28 if one believes that all Mark's uses of "Son of Man" are redactional (except 13:26).

19. On Mark's general pronounced reverse-thrust editing throughout his Gospel, see Cook, *Modern Jews Engage the New Testament*, 139, 144–48, 181–85 passim.

20. Bultmann, *The History of the Synoptic Tradition* (New York: Harper & Row, 1963 [1921]), 53.

21. This, the *lectio difficilior*, is more likely what Luke received.

22. Luke paralleled Paul's Sanhedrin trial to that of Jesus. Since Mark 14:53 placed scribes in Jesus' Sanhedrin, Luke wished scribes present for Paul's. Luke based Paul's trial on the Pharisaic precept of resurrection which Mark 12:28 had identified also as a scribal teaching. Hence Luke identified Sadducean opponents as both Pharisees and scribes. Rather than an unwieldy two groups, Luke would opt for Mark 2:16's one-group ("scribes of the Pharisees")—generating Luke's "scribes of the Pharisees' party."

23. Cf. Sanhedrin 88b; Kiddushin 17b, 39a, possibly 30a; Sukkah 28a; Rosh Hashanah 19a; Yevamoth 20a.

24. Matt. 9:11; 17:14; 21:23; 26:3, 47; 27:1. Matthew's use of "scribe" in 13:52 is unrelated to the Scribal group whom Mark derived from his two primitive strata.

25. Winter, *Trial*, 209–10 n. 25.

26. See Cook, *Modern Jews Engage the New Testament*, 90f., 121–22, 133–48, 150–54, 176–91, 273–74; cf. 109–20.

Chapter 5: Viewing the Jewish Jesus of History through the Lens of Matthew's Gospel

1. Donald Senior, "Matthew at the Crossroads of Early Christianity: An Introductory Assessment," in *The Gospel of Matthew at the Crossroads of Early Christianity*, ed. Donald P. Senior, Bibliotheca Ephemeridum Theologicarum Lovaniensium 243 (Louvain: Peeters, 2011), 3–24.

2. See Donald Hagner, "The Sitz in Leben of the Gospel of Matthew," in *Treasures New and Old: Contributions to Matthean Studies*, eds. David R. Bauer & Mark Allan Powell (Atlanta: Scholars, 1996), 47; see also, D. Hagner, *Matthew 1-13*, Word Biblical Commentary Vol. 33a (Dallas: Word, 1993), lxv–lxxi.

3. Dennis C. Duling, "Ethnicity, Ethnocentrism, and the Matthean Ethos," in *Biblical Theology Bulletin* 35 (2005): 125–43.

4. On the relationship with Roman context see, for example, Warren Carter, *Matthew and Empire: Initial Explorations* (Harrisburg, PA: Trinity International, 2001); John Riches and David C. Sim, eds., *The Gospel of Matthew in Its Roman Imperial Context* (London: T & T Clark International, 2005).

5. Richard Bauckham has challenged the assumption that the gospels were written specifically for a limited local audience. He suggests that the evangelists may have assumed that their works would be widely circulated and therefore had a broader audience in mind. See Richard Bauckham, ed., *The Gospels for All Christians: Rethinking the Gospel Audiences* (Grand Rapids: Eerdmans, 1998). When referring to "Matthew" as the author of the Gospel in this essay I do not imply that Matthew is one of the twelve mentioned in the Gospel is the actual author of the Gospel text as we have it. No doubt the Gospel went through a complex process of composition before reaching its final form. Ultimately

it was not written by a "committee" but a single author in concert with his community brought the text to its final form; that anonymous final redactor or editor is referred to here as "Matthew."

6. For a discussion of the question of Matthew's context in recent scholarship, see D. Senior, "Directions in Matthean Studies," in *The Gospel of Matthew in Current Study*, ed. D. Aune (Grand Rapids: Eerdmans, 2001), 5–21; also, D. Senior, "Between Two Worlds: Gentile and Jewish Christians in Matthew's Gospel," *CBQ* 61 (1999): 1–23.

7. Ulrich Luz, *Matthew 21–28. A Commentary* (Minneapolis: Augsburg Press, 2005), 637–44; also, U. Luz, *Studies in Matthew* (Grand Rapids: Eerdmans, 2005), 3–17; see also his *The Theology of the Gospel of Matthew*, New Testament Theology (Cambridge: Cambridge University Press, 1995), esp. 17–21.

8. See a fine scan of this evidence in E. P. Sanders, "Jesus in Galilee," in *Jesus: A Colloquium in the Holy Land*, ed. Doris Donnelly (New York: Continuum, 2001), 5–26.

9. On this point see the discussion in Martin Hengel, *Studies in the Gospel of Mark* (Philadelphia: Fortress Press, 1985), esp. 1–30.

10. See D. Gurtner, "Matthew's Theology of the Temple and the 'Parting of the Ways': Christian Origins in the First Gospel," in *Built upon Rock: Studies in the Gospel of Matthew*, eds. D. Gurtner and J. Nolland (Grand Rapids: Eerdmans, 2008), 128–53.

11. On this passage, see chapter 3 and the essay written by Anne Lapidus Lerner.

12. The question continues to be debated whether in directing the apostles to "the nations" the Matthean community was thereby turning away from the mission to Israel. I share the view of those who believe that Matthew's community was extending its mission to the nations but not abandoning its connection to Israel, of which it considered itself a rightful part. See the discussion in U. Luz, *Matthew 21–28*, 628–61. He concludes that "all nations" in 28:20 does not mean simply "gentiles" are now the object of the Christian mission to the exclusion of Israel, particularly in the light of Matt. 10:23 that seems to assume that the mission to Israel will continue to the end of time. However, Luz believes that because of rejection and persecution "Matthew probably no longer has great hopes for it" (631).

13. John P. Meier, *A Marginal Jew. Rethinking The Historical Jesus*, 4 vols. (New Haven: Yale University Press, 2009).

14. Ibid., 4:4–5.

15. Ibid., 4:293–97.

16. Ibid., 4:413–15.

17. Ibid., 4:124–28.

18. Ibid., 4:198–06.

19. See the references in U. Luz, *Matthew 1–7*, Heremeneia (Minneapolis: Fortress Press, 2007), 262–64.

20. See the comment of Luz: "Christian interpretation should not try to defend the originality of Jesus' demand at all costs. Taken by itself it is not original. . . . It fits well with the sharpened interpretation of the seventh (sixth) commandment that we can observe in the context of Judaism's purity idea in that day." *Matthew 1–7*, 245.

21. *Marginal*, 4:528–51.

22. These statements which place Jesus' teaching alongside other prevailing interpretations are in the main not truly "antithetical" (e.g., condemning murder is not antithetical to the warning that anger itself can lead to violence) but rather "contrasting" one stance with a more radical position—both of which deal with the same moral issue. See Donald Senior, *Matthew*, Abingdon New Testament Commentaries (Nashville: Abingdon, 1998), 73–74.

23. The Greek term *teleios* used here in Matthew, the adjectival form of the noun *telos*, meaning the end or goal (contrast the parallel in Luke, "merciful" [*oiktirmones*]) has the connotation of being "complete" rather than statically "perfect."

24. *Marginal,* 4:499–528.

25. Ibid., 4:480.

26. "Beyond all the individual legal pronouncements Jesus issued during his public ministry, did he ever give an indication of his stance vis-à-vis the Law as a whole? The answer this chapter [on the love commandments] gives is a qualified yes. I say "qualified" because the answer is not the full programmatic type of answer that we get—and would prefer—from Matt. 5:17-20 or from Matthew's reworking of Mark's pericope on the double commandment. But at least the bare-bones tradition behind Mark 12:28-34 shows us that the historical Jesus did not simply issue ad hoc halakic pronouncements on scattered topics like divorce, oaths, or the Sabbath. He did reflect on the totality of Torah and did extract from that totality the love of God and the love of neighbor as the *first* and *second* commandments of the Torah, superior to all others. Love—of God first and of our neighbor second, in that pointed order—is supreme in the Law. Other statutes—while by no means rejected or denigrated—are of lesser importance." Meier, *A Marginal Jew,* 4:575–76.

27. In Matthew's Gospel, for example, see the exhortations not to scandalize or "despise" the "little ones" and the parable of the lost sheep in 18:1-14, and the famous parable of the sheep and the goats in 25:31-46 where the disciples are judged on their care for the "least," namely, the hungry, the naked, the sick, and the imprisoned.

28. This dimension of the Gospel is the subject of a respectful and engaging dialogue between Pope Benedict XVI and Rabbi Jacob Neusner in the Pope's book, *Jesus of Nazareth* (New York: Doubleday, 2007), 103–27. Neusner contends that this "universalizing" tendency of Jesus' presented in the Gospels and particularly the attention given to Jesus' own singular authority ultimately undermine Judaism's focus on obedience to God's Torah and the social bond of the family and the people Israel. Joseph Ratzinger (as he prefers to refer to himself as the author of this book) contends that the universal dimension of the Christian mission based on the teaching of Christ as the Son of God fulfills the historic destiny of Israel as a light to the nations.

29. See James D. G. Dunn, who uses the image of the concave and convex to describe the impact of the historical Jesus (his teaching, his healing, the charismatic force of his person, etc.) on the earliest disciples. The force of the historical Jesus' person and mission leaves an imprint on the collective memory of the first generation of disciples that ultimately is given intense theological interpretation and expansion in the light of resurrection faith in *Christianity in the Making: Vol. I, Jesus Remembered* (Grand Rapids: Eerdmans, 2003).

30. See D. Senior, "*Nostra Aetate* and the Catholic Biblical Renewal: A New Understanding of Judaism and the Jewish Roots of Early Christianity," in *"Perché stessero con Lui" Scritti in onore di Klemens Stock SJ nel suo 75° compleanno,* eds. Lorenzo De Santos and Santi Grasso (Rome: Gregorian and Biblical Institute, 2010), 27–41.

31. This was pointed out by Eugene B. Borowitz in one of the earliest works supporting the Christian Jewish dialogue: "Nothing so divides Judaism and Christianity as the Christian doctrine of the Christ. If Jews and Christians are to talk together for more than pragmatic reasons, they must confront this area of their radical disagreement." Eugene B. Borowitz, *Contemporary Christologies: A Jewish Response* (New York: Paulist, 1980), 1.

32. Several recent works from both Jewish and Christian scholars have emphasized this point; see, for example, Gabriele Boccaccini, *Middle Judaism: Jewish Thought, 300 B.C.E. to 200 C.E.* (Minneapolis: Fortress Press, 1991); Mary Boys, *Has God Only One Blessing? Judaism as a Source of Christian Self-Understanding* (New York: Paulist, 2000); and Daniel Boyarin, *Border Lines: The Partition of Judaeo-Christianity* (Philadelphia: University of Pennsylvania Press, 2005). In his recent work, *Jesus and the God of Israel* (Grand Rapids: Eerdmans, 2008), Richard Bauckham explores the compatibility of the Christian Trinitarian notion of the divine with the Jewish context of early Christianity.

33. See the Pontifical Biblical Commission, *The Jewish People and Their Sacred Scriptures in the Christian Bible* (Vatican City: Libreria Editrice Vaticano, 2002).

34. Ibid.

Chapter 6: The Trial of Jesus and the Temple

1. For several possibilities and their background, see S. McKnight, *Jesus and His Death: Historiography, the Historical Jesus, and Atonement Theory* (Waco: Baylor University Press, 2005), esp. 93–99.

2. W. Wrede, *The Messianic Secret* (London and Cambridge: James Clarke; Greenwood S. CR: Attic, 1971 [1901]). J. Weiss, *Jesus' Proclamation of the Kingdom of God* (London: SCM, 1971 [1892]) concluded that Jesus ultimately regarded himself as becoming a messiah only after his death. A. Schweitzer, *The Mystery of the Kingdom of God* (London: A&C Black, 1925 [1901]) argued that Jesus did not reveal to his disciples his recognition that he is the Messiah.

3. This is a simplification of the views of the following studies, among many others: J. Blinzler, *The Trial of Jesus*, trans. I. and F. McHugh (Westminster: Newman, 1959), 102–11, 125–27, 188–93, 290–92; D. Catchpole, *The Trial of Jesus: A Study in the Gospels and Jewish Historiography from 1770 to the Present Day* (Leiden: Brill, 1971), 71–148; D. L. Bock, *Blasphemy and Exaltation in Judaism* (Tübingen: Mohr-Siebeck, 1998); see also his "The Son of Man Seated at God's Right Hand and the Debate over Jesus Blasphemy,'" in *Jesus of Nazareth, Lord and Christ*, eds. J. B. Green and M. Turner (Eugene, OR: Eardmans, 1999), 181–91; D. Flusser, *Jesus* (Jerusalem: Magnes 2001), 131–32, 141, 152–55, 166, 274–27; N. A. Dahl, *Jesus the Christ. The Historical Origins of Christological Doctrine* (Minneapolis: Fortress Press, 1991), 27–47; P. Fredriksen, *Jesus of Nazareth, King of the Jews: A Jewish Life and the Emergence of Christianity* (New York: Vintage, 1999), 244–59; C. Meyers, *Binding the Strong Man: A Political Reading of Mark's Story of Jesus* (Maryknoll, NY: Orbis, 1988), 369–82. See also E. P. Sanders, *Jesus and Judaism* (London: SCM, 1985), 69–71, 296–306, discussed below.

4. J. B. Green, *The Death of Jesus: Tradition and Interpretation in the Passion Narrative* (Tübingen: Mohr Siebeck, 1988); H. Koester, *Ancient Christian Gospels: Their Origins and Development* (London and Philadelphia: Trinity, 1990), 220–40; A. Yarbo-Collins, "The Passion Narrative of Mark," in *The Beginnings of the Gospel: Probing of Mark in Context* (Minneapolis: Fortress Press, 1992), 92–118.

5. For the messianic and Christological characteristics as well as Mark's purposes, see D. Juel, *Messiah and Temple: The Trial of Jesus in the Gospel of Mark* (Atlanta: Scholars, 1977), 46–116. The lack of historical perspective is apparent in Mark's failure (14: 54, 61, 63) to mention the name of the high priest who questioned Jesus. His identity was noted by the three other evangelists. See P. Winter, *On the Trial of Jesus*, rev. ed. (Berlin and New York: de Gruyter, 1974), 44–59.

6. Compare B. Mack, *A Myth of Innocence: Mark and Christian Origins* (Philadelphia: Fortress Press, 1988), 263, 288–90.

7. J. D. Crossan, *Who Killed Jesus? Exposing the Roots of Anti-Semitism in the Gospel Story of the Death of Jesus* (New York: HarperCollins, 1995), 106–8.

8. Sanders, *Jesus and Judaism*, 297-98. For suggestions how early Christians knew what happened in those hearings, see Bock, "The Son of Man," 183–84.

9. E. Bickerman, "Utilitas crucis," *Revue de l' Histoire des Religions* 112 (1935), repr. in *Studies in Jewish and Christian History* (Leiden: Brill, 1986), 3.82–138.

10. Apart from those expressed by different Jewish authors, I would mention the one attributed to Judah Maccabee in 2 Macc. 2:18. For other examples, see E. Regev, *Sectarianism in Qumran: A Cross-Cultural Perspective* (Berlin: de Gruyter, 2007), 58–64.

11. None of the anti-Roman so-called messianic prophets and popular movements mentioned by Josephus are designated as such. For these, see R. A. Horsley and J. S. Hanson, *Bandits, Prophets and Messiahs: Popular Movements in the Time of Jesus* (Harrisburg: Trinity, 1985), 88–134. Theudas and the Egyptian were "prophets" (*Ant.* 20.97, 169–70; *War* 2.261; cf. Acts 5:36-37).

12. James D. G. Dunn (*Jesus Remembered* [Grand Rapids: Eerdmans, 2003], 697–702) commented that "teacher" is the most common title used for Jesus in the Jesus traditions (e.g., Matt. 10:24-25; Luke 6:40). See also Luke 7:35. Note that Josephus (*Ant.*18.63) calls him "a wiseman" (*sophos aner*). For the authenticity of this part in Josephus' account, see J. P. Meier, "Jesus in Josephus: A Modest Proposal," *CBQ* 52 (1990): 76–103; *A Marginal Jew: Rethinking the Historical Jesus, I: The Problem and the Person* (New York: Doubleday, 1991), 56–88.

13. See Mark 6.4; 11:32; Luke 4:24; 13:33; John 4:44; cf. Dunn, *Jesus Remembered*, 660–66. I leave the controversial question of the Son of Man designation out of the discussion.

14. Luke 7:26; Matt. 11:9; cf. Luke 11:32; Matt. 12:41.

15. N. T. Wright, *Jesus and the Victory of God* (Minneapolis: Fortress Press, 1996), 543–52, realized the crux of the problem and concluded that the high priest's Sanhedrin and Pilate were aware of this difference but used the messianic charge only as an excuse to get rid of Jesus. The fact is that they did not arrest his followers.

16. Horsley and Hanson, *Bandits, Prophets and Messiahs*.

17. S. G. F. Brandon, *Jesus and the Zealots: A Study in the Political Factor in Primitive Christianity* (Manchester: Manchester University Press, 1967); R. A. Horsley, *Jesus and Empire: The Kingdom of God and the New World Disorder* (Minneapolis: Fortress Press, 2003), 98–104.

18. M. Hengel, *Was Jesus a Revolutionist?* (Philadelphia: Fortress Press, 1971); C. Bryan, *Render to Caesar: Jesus, the Church and the Roman Superpower* (New York: Oxford University Press, 2005). See also Sanders, *Jesus and Judaism*, 231, 295, 317–18, 329.

19. M. J. Borg, "A Temperate Case for a Non-eschatological Jesus," *Forum* 2 (1986): 81–102; *Jesus in Contemporary Scholarship* (Valley Forge, PA: Trinity, 1994), 18–43 [=*HTR* 84 (1991): 1-22]; S. J. Patterson, "The End of Apocalypse: Rethinking the Eschatological Jesus," *Theology Today* 52 (1995): 29–48; J. D. Crossan, *The Historical Jesus: A Life of a Mediterranean Jewish Peasant* (New York: HarperCollins, 1991), esp. 265–302; R.W. Funk and R.W. Hoover, eds., *The Five Gospels* (New York: HarperSanFrancisco, 1993); D. R. A. Hare, *The Son of Man Tradition* (Minneapolis: Fortress Press, 1990).

20. C. Tuckett, "Q and Thomas: Evidence of a Primitive 'Wisdom Gospel'?" *ETL* 67 (1991): 346–60; "On the Stratification of Q: A Response," *Semeia* 55 (1992): 213–22; E. P. Meadors, "The "Messianic" Implications of the Q Material," *JBL* 118 (1999): 253–77; Meier, *Marginal*, 1:124-139; Meier, *A Marginal Jew, II: Mentor, Message and Miracles* (New York: Doubleday, 1994), 2:289–397; D. C. Allison, "A Plea for Thoroughgoing Eschatology," *JBL* 113 (1994): 651–68; *Jesus of Nazareth: Millenarian Prophet* (Minneapolis: Fortress Press, 1998).

21. See R. J. Miller, ed., *The Apocalyptic Jesus: A Debate* (Santa Rosa, CA: Polebridge, 2001), featuring Allison, Borg, Crossan, and Patterson. For my own view on this debate, see E. Regev, "Temple or Messiah: On the Trial of Jesus, the Temple and the Roman Policy,'" *Cathedra* 119 (2006): 14–25 (Hebrew).

22. Crossan, *Who Killed Jesus?*, 82–107. Some combined the temple charge with Jesus eschatological message: H. K. Bond, *Caiaphas. Friend of Rome and Judge of Jesus?* (Louisville: Westminster John Knox, 2004), 64–72. Some saw the temple issue as the reason behind his arrest, but not the execution. See Sanders, *Jesus and Judaism*, 69–71, 296–306; R. A. Horsley, *Jesus and the Spiral of Violence: Popular Jewish Resistance in Roman Palestine*

(San Francisco: Harper & Row, 1987), 292–300, 321. Cf. the studies cited in Blinzler, *The Trial of Jesus*, 101 n. 26.

23. Tomas, 71. Translation follows J. M. Robinson (ed.), *The Nag Hammadi Library in English*, revised ed. (Leiden: Brill, 1996), 134. The weight of this evidence depends on whether one regards Thomas as preserving an earlier version of Jesus' saying or merely a later reworking of the saying in the canonical gospels. Cf., e.g., Tucket, "Q and Thomas."

24. Jesus son of Ananias and Rabbi Yohanan ben Zakkai only foresaw the coming destruction. See *War* 6.301-309; b. Yoma 39b. The eschatological tone of the saying notwithstanding, the time-span of three days for its rebuilding is too short for an eschatological prophecy.

25. For positive early Christian approaches towards the Temple, see below.

26. For a bibliographic survey on scholars who think that Mark regarded the temple charge as true or false, see Juel, *Messiah and Temple*, 120–22.

27. John is thus referring to Jesus' resurrection three days after his crucifixion; hence John portrayed Jesus as *analogous* to the Temple. See R. Brown, *The Gospel According to Saint John I-XII*, AB 29 (New York: Doubleday 1966), 122–25.

28. Mark 11:15-16. See Matt. 21:12-13; Luke 19:45-46; John 2:13-22.

29. E.g., R. Bultmann, *History of the Synoptic Tradition*, trans. John Marsh (New York: Harper & Row, 1963) 36, 120; Sanders, *Jesus and Judaism*, 363–64 and passim; Crossan, *The Historical Jesus*, 356–60.

30. J. Klausner, *Jesus of Nazareth: His Life, Times and Teachings*, trans. H. Danby (Boston: Beacon, 1925), 313–16; Flusser, *Jesus*, 138–39; B. Chilton, *The Temple of Jesus* (University Park: Pennsylvania State University Press, 1992), 100–159; P. Richardson, "Why Turn the Tables? Jesus' Protest in the Temple Precincts," *SBL Seminar Papers* 31 (1992): 507–23. See John 2:16.

31. H. D. Betz, "Jesus and the Purity of the Temple (Mark 11:15-18): A Comparative Religion Approach," *JBL* 116 (1997): 455–72; J. Knight, *Luke's Gospel* (London and New York: Routledge, 1998), 182–83; Horsley, *Jesus and the Spiral of Violence*, 289–91, 298–317.

32. C. A. Evans, "Jesus' Action in the Temple: Cleansing or Portent of Destruction," *CBQ* 51 (1989): 237–70; M. Hengel, *The Zealots* (Edinburgh: T & T Clark, 1989), 216; S. G. F. Brandon, *Jesus and the Zealots* (New York: Charles Scribner's Sons, 1967), 331–35.

33. Sanders, *Jesus and Judaism*, 69–71; R. H. Hiers, "Purification of the Temple: Preparation for the Kingdom of God," *JBL* 90 (1971): 82–90; J. D. G. Dunn, *The Parting of the Ways* (London and Philadelphia: SCM and Trinity, 1991), 47–49; *Jesus Remembered*, 639–40, 650; Wright, *Jesus and the Victory of God*, 413–28.

34. E. Regev, "Moral Impurity and the Temple in Early Christianity in Light of Qumranic Ideology and Ancient Greek Practice," *HTR* 79, no. 4 (2004): 383–411, here 297–402.

35. Note that whereas Mark 12:40 rebukes the scribes' treatment of the widows, Jesus' exhortations are general, with no specific rebuking of priestly immorality. I think that Evans "Jesus' Action in the Temple" exaggerates regarding the relevance of the Jewish polemic against the corruption of the high priests to understanding of the Jesus' traditions. For lack of evidence for Jesus' criticism of the priesthood see Sanders, *Jesus and Judaism*, 66. The view of Jesus' protest against the high priests' behavior is usually based on the parable of the wicked tenants (Mark 12:1-12 and parallels, including Thomas 65). The allegory, however, pertains to the leaders' rejection of Jesus and not to their general immorality. The argument that the parable's anti-priestly stance was grounded in first-century Targums is unsound. Compare J. C. De Moor, "The Targumic Background of Mark 12:1-12: The Parable of the Wicked Tenants," *JSJ* 29 (1998): 63–80.

36. For a different approach that also links cult, money, and righteousness see B. Chilton, *The Temple of Jesus* (University Park: Pennsylvania State University Press, 1992), 128–30, who suggested that Jesus argued that the sacrifice should be one's own property and not bought with money.

37. The references are collected and discussed in Regev, "Moral Impurity and the Temple," 386–90. See also Luke's parables of mercy 7:41-43, 10:30-37; 13:6-9; 15:3-7; 15:8-10 (//Matt. 18:10-14); 15:11-32; 18:9-14. Crossan, *The Historical Jesus*, 292, 294, characterized Jesus' message as "ethical Kingdom."

38. See, e.g., Q 12:16-20, 22-31; Matt. 5:3-6//Luke 6:20-31; Matt. 6:19-21//Luke 12:33-34; Matt. 23:23//Luke 11:42; Mark 10:17-25//Matt. 19:16-24//Luke 18:18-25 ("Rich Man Entering Kingdom"); Mark 10:21; Luke 14:33; Thomas 63-65; Crossan, *The Historical Jesus*, 268–82.

39. For the moral corruption of money, see 1 Tim. 6:10; Richard H. Hiers, "Friends by Unrighteous Mammon," *JAAR* 38 (1970): 30–36. For wealth as corrupting, see E. Regev, "Wealth and Sectarianism: Comparing Qumranic and Early Christian Social Approaches," in *Echoes from the Caves: Qumran and the New Testament*, ed. F. Garcia Martinez, *STDJ* 85 (Leiden: Brill, 2009), 211–30.

40. 1QpHab 8:11-12 and 12:19 (both quoted above); 1QS 6:19-20, 22; cf. 1QS 9:22/4QS^d 2 III 6; 1QH^a 19:25-26 (Sukenik 10:22-23). For the more abstracted sense of "evil wealth" see also CD 8:5, 8.

41. [To] "separate (themselves) from the sons of the pit and to refrain from the wicked wealth (which is) *impure due to oath(s) and dedication(s) and to (being) the wealth of the sanctuary*, (for) they (the sons of the pit) steal from the poor of his people, preying upon wid[ow]s and murdering orphans." See Regev. *Sectarianism in Qumran*, 111. A similar claim that corrupted money polluted the Temple is mentioned in Jub. 23:21.

42. One of the most recent examples is G. Theissen and A. Merz, *The Historical Jesus: A Comprehensive Guide* (London: SCM, 1998), 432–36. Compare also Crossan, *The Historical Jesus*, 355, 360.

43. See E. Regev, "The Temple in Mark: A Case Study about the Early Christian Attitude toward the Temple," in *Studies in Rabbinic Judaism and Early Christianity. Text and Context*, ed. D. Jaffé; Ancient Judaism and Early Christianity Series 74 (Leiden: Brill 2010), 139–59, where the following evidence and other arguments for Jesus' rejection of the Temple are dismissed.

44. See Mark 11:15, 27-28; 12:35-44; 14:48-49. Luke and John mentioned additional visits.

45. J. Klawans, "Interpreting the Last Supper: Sacrifice, Spiritualization, and Anti-Sacrifice." *NTS* 48 (2002): 1–17, who also discussed the authenticity of the Eucharist words, their different variations, and previous scholarship.

46. A. L. A. Hogeterp, *Paul and God's Temple* (Leuven: Peeters, 2006); J. Lieu, "Temple and Synagogue in John," *NTS* 45 (1999): 51–69; K. S. Fuglseth, *Johannine Sectarianism in Perspective: A Sociological, Historical, and Comparative Analysis of Temple and Social Relationships in the Gospel of John, Philo, and Qumran*, Sup. NT 119 (Leiden: Brill, 2005); E. Regev, "Temple Concerns and High Priestly Persecutions from Peter to James: Between Narrative and History," *NTS* 56, no. 1 (2010): 64–89. It seems that only Hebrew and Revelation reject the Temple. See E. Regev, "A Kingdom of Priests or a Holy (Gentile) People: The Temple in Early Christian Life and Thought," *Cathedra* 113 (2004): 5–34 (Hebrew).

47. For the present purpose, I disregard Mark 11:17 (in which Isa. 56:7 and Jer. 7:11 are attributed to Jesus) since it probably derives from Markan redaction. See Sanders, *Jesus and Judaism*, 61–76, esp. 66–67; J. Marcus, "The Jewish War and the *Sitz im Leben* of Mark," *JBL* 111 (1992): 448–49.

48. Bond, *Caiaphas*, 40–63. Caiaphas served as a high priest in 18/19–37 CE, throughout the whole period of Pilate's governorship. The leading role of the high priest in all the variants of the Passion Narrative and his later identification with Caiaphas by Matthew and John are commonly accepted as authentic, despite the non-historical character of the Passion. See Winter, *Trial of Jesus*, 44–59, 66–67.

49. His identification as a Sadducee is based on Acts 5:17: "the high priest and all who were with him, that is, the sect of the Sadducees" (NRSV). J. A. Fitzmyer, *The Acts of the Apostles*, AB 18C (New York: Doubleday, 1998), 334, translated *kai pantes oi sun autō* "and all his colleagues." While the name of the high priest is not mentioned here, Luke's chronology makes it clear that the high priest was Caiaphas who served in ca. 18–37 CE. Caiaphas is also mentioned in Acts 4:6. See Bond, *Caiaphas*, 7–8, 13, 24; Fitzmyer, *Acts*, 299; Joachim Jeremias, *Jerusalem on the Time of Jesus* (Philadelphia: Fortress Press, 1969), 229; J. Le Moyne, *Les Sadducéens* (Paris: Gabalda, 1972), 345; D. Flusser, "Caiaphas in the New Testament," *Atiqot* 21 (1992): 82, 84.

50. E. Regev, *The Sadducees and Their Halakhah: Religion and Society in the Second Temple Period* (Jerusalem: Yad Izhak ben Zvi, 2005), esp. 46–48, 318–19 (Hebrew). Cf. *Ant.* 13.298; 18.17; 20.199.

51. A. F. J. Klijn, "Scribes, Pharisees, High-Priests and Elders,'" *Novum Testamentum* 3 (1959): 259–67; M. Smith, *Jesus the Magician* (London: V. Gollancz, 1978), 153–58. This indeed may be a result of not only a lack of interest, but also a lack of power. For the attitudes of the Sadducees and Pharisees towards the early Christians, see Regev, "Temple Concerns."

52. E.g., the burning of the red heifer m. *Parah* 3.7; t. *Parah* 3.8 (ed. Zuckermandel, 632).

53. Regev, *Sadducees and Their Halakhah*, 132–81, 226–41, 383–85; "The Sadducees, the Pharisees and the Sacred: Meaning and Ideology in the Halakhic Controversies between the Sadducees and the Pharisees." *Review of Rabbinic Judaism* 9 (2006): 126–40. I have defined the Sadducees' approach as "dynamic holiness" as opposed to the Pharisees' "static holiness." Another example is the Sadducees' opposition to the pharisaic regulation of the annual half-shekel donation to the Temple which would have undermined the priestly exclusive cultic status (Regev, *Sadducees and Their Halakhah*, 132–39).

54. T. *Ḥahiagah* 3.35 (ed. Lieberman, 394). In early, non-rabbinic penal code, Sancta trespassing required a death penalty, which was probably practiced by stoning, which was the most common way of execution in pre-rabbinic halakha. The early rabbis, however, left such transgressions to divine punishment (*karet*) with no human intervention. Compare Philo, *Leg. ad Gaium* 307; Temple Scroll 35:1-8; 4QD^a 6ii 9-10, with m. *Keritot* 1:1; t. *Sanhedrin* 14:16 (ed. Zuckermandel, 437).

55. *Ant.* 20.189-195. Ishmael followed the Sadducean laws of purity in t. *Parah* 3.6 (ed. Zuckermandel, 632). See Regev, *Sadducees and Their Halakhah*, 176–79. On the religious objection for Agrippa's watchings, cf. Daniel R. Schwartz, "Viewing the Holy Utensils (P. Ox. V, 840)," *NTS* 32 (1986): 153–59. Unnamed high priests were involved in demanding that the high priest's garments of the Day of Atonement be kept in the temple instead of in the custody of the Roman governor, and succeeded in their application to Claudius in that matter (*Ant.* 20.6-14). A quite different, but nevertheless relevant case is the desperate call of Ananus son of Ananus the Sadducee (*Ant.* 20.199) for the defense of the temple from the violent Zealots, protesting the Zealots' pollution of the temple with bloodshed (*JW* 4.318-325, 151, 162–206). Ananus also declared that he is willing to die for the sake of "God and the Sanctuary" (*JW* 4.191). Although the speech was probably created by Josephus, it may represent Ananus's approach, since Josephus knew him personally.

56. *Annales* 15. 44. Compare the early Christian apologetic attempts to put the blame on the Jewish leaders rather than on Pilate. See H. K. Bond, *Pontius Pilate in History and Interpretation* (Cambridge: Cambridge University Press, 1998), 129–37, 150–62.

57. Josephus and Philo mention several incidents in which Pilate did not respect Jewish religious taboos, although Bond tries to explain these as resulting from attempts to demonstrate Roman rule rather than anti-Judaism. See Bond, *Pontius Pilate*, xv–xvi, 39–45, 79–81, 93, 204.

58. The claim that the Jews were not allowed to execute (e.g., Catchpole, *The Trial of Jesus*, 221–60, following John 18:31) was disproved by Winter, *Trial of Jesus*, 18–23. This conclusion is also followed by P. Segal "The Penalty of the Warning Inscription from the Temple of Jerusalem," *IEJ* 39 (1989): 79–84.

59. M. Hengel, *Crucifixion* (Philadelphia: Fortress Press, 1977), 26, 34, 36–38, 40, 46–50.

60. *JW* 6.301–9.

61. Compare E. P. Sanders, *The Historical Figure of Jesus* (London: Allen Lane, 1993), 265, 270–74.

62. *Ant.* 18.90-95; 20.6-14.

63. Philo, *Leg.* 157, 317; *War* 2.197; *Against Apion* 2.77. Special sacrifices were also offered for the sake of the emperor on specific occasions. See *Leg.* 356.

64. M. D. Goodman, *The Ruling Class in Judaea* (Cambridge: Cambridge University Press, 1987), 42–43. For the Romanization of the Temple, see Betz, "Jesus and the Purity of the Temple," 462–65. The Roman patronage was also practiced by the manner in which the Roman rulers honored the Temple. See *Ant.* 16.14-15; Philo, *Leg.* 157, 295–97, 310, 319. In fact, the Herodian Temple even looked like a Roman one. See D. Jacobson, "The Jerusalem Temple of Herod the Great," in *The World of the Herods; The World of the Herods and the Nabataeans, Vol. 1*, ed. N. Kokkinos (Stuttgart and Munich: Franz Steiner, 2007), 145–76.

65. S. R. F. Price, *Rituals of Power: The Roman Imperial Cult in Asia Minor* (Cambridge: Cambridge University Press, 1984).

66. J. E. Taylor, "Pontius Pilate and the Imperial Cult in Roman Judaea," *NTS* 52 (2006): 555–82.

67. For the more general role of religion in provincial revolts against Rome, see M. Goodman, "Opponents of Rome: Jews and Others," in *Images of Empire* (ed. L. Alexander, JSOT Sup 122; Sheffield: Sheffield Academic, 1991), 222–38. See also the studies by Dyson cited below.

68. Tacitus, *Annales*, 1.57; cf. ibid., 39.

69. Ibid., 14.31–32.

70. Tacitus, *Histories*, 4.54; S. L. Dyson, "Native Revolt Patterns in the Roman Empire," *ANRW* II.3 (1975): 157–59.

71. *War* 2.409–410. For the denial to accept sacrifices from gentiles, see D. R. Schwartz, "On Sacrifice by Gentiles in the Temple of Jerusalem," in *Studies in the Jewish Background of Christianity* (Tuebingen: Mohr-Siebeck, 1992), 102–16.

72. See G. W. Bowersock, "The Mechanics of Subversion in the Roman Provinces," in *Opposition et Résistances a l'empire d'Auguste a Trajan* (eds. A. Giovanini and D. van Berchem; Geneva: Foundation Hardt, 1987), 291–317; M. Beard, J. North, and S. Price, *Religions of Rome: A History* (Cambridge: Cambridge University Press, 1998), 1.347–348. The Romans responded in violating the native cults (such as in Wales during Boudica's revolts) and establishing the imperial cult more firmly. See S. L. Dyson, "Native Revolts in the Roman Empire," *Historia* 20 (1971): 258–59, 260–61. Compare also the reestablishment of Galba's statues in response to the revolt in the late 60s CE in northwest Anatolia (Tacitus, *Histories* 3.7).

73. Dio 54: 34: 5-7.

74. G. Webster, *Boudica: The Roman Conquest of Britain* (London: Batsford, 1993), 86–89. Note that Claudius prohibited Druidism (Suetonius, *Claud.* 25.5).

75. Tacitus, *Histories*, 4.61.

76. Dio 72.4.

77. R. MacMullen, *Enemies of the Roman Order* (Cambridge, MA: Harvard University Press, 1966), 128–62.

78. For confrontations between Vespasian with Apollonius, Hadrian with a philosopher, and Caracalla with a Gnostic, see G. Anderson, *Sage, Saint and Sophist. Holy Men and Their Associates in the Early Roman Empire* (London and New York: Routledge, 1994), 151–66.

79. All were directed by Sadducean high priests. See Regev, "Temple Concerns."

Chapter 7: Remapping Schweitzer's Quest through Jewish-Christian Polemic, Apology, and Dialogue

1. This chapter is based on the research presented in A. Le Donne, "The Quest for the Historical Jesus: A Revisionist History through the Lens of Jewish-Christian Relations." *Journal for the Study of the Historical Jesus* 10, no. 1 (2012): 63–86. I also offer my thanks to Michael J. Cook and Gerd Theissen for critiquing an earlier form of this chapter. Of course, any deficiencies herein are my own.

2. *The Interpretation of the New Testament 1861-1961* (New York: Oxford University Press, 1966), 192.

3. For a recent survey of this intellectual history see J. K. Beilby and P. R. Eddy, eds., *The Historical Jesus: Five Views* (Downers Grove, IL: InterVarsity, 2009), 9–54. The editors take their lead from N. T. Wright in exposing the roots of the "First Quest" in English Deism. However, as is typical in most Jesus books, there is little more than a paragraph on the period before Lessing and Reimarus (11–12).

4. Among the growing number of caveats and nuances of the tripartite division of Quests, see the compelling studies of Fernando Bermejo Rubio, "The Fiction of the 'Three Quests': An Argument for Dismantling a Dubious Historiographical Paradigm," *JSHJ* 7 (2009): 211–53; Dale C. Allison, *Resurrecting Jesus: The Earliest Christian Tradition and Its Interpreters* (London: T & T Clark, 2005), 1–18; cf. also Stanley E. Porter, *The Criteria for Authenticity in Historical-Jesus Research: Previous Discussion and New Proposals*, JSNTSup 191 (Sheffield: Sheffield Academic, 2000), 28–62.

5. For example, J. G. Herder, J. P. F. Richter, W. von Humboldt. See Albert Reble, *Geschichte der Pädagogik* (Stuttgart: Klett-Cotta, 1989), 190–94. This idea of the "hero" in history, however, is at least as old as Giambattista Vico (1668–1744). See especially *The New Science of Giambattista Vico,* trans. Thomas Goddard Bergin and Max Harold Fisch (Ithaca, NY: Cornell University Press, 1968), 331. Vico, however, associated the "heroic" with a particular stage in (pre)history while Carlyle located particular heroes that began successive stages of history.

6. Thomas Carlyle, *On Heroes, Hero-Worship, and the Heroic in History*, vol. 5 of *The Works of Thomas Carlyle*, ed. H.D. Traill, 30 vols. (London: Chapman & Hall, 1896–1901).

7. *The Quest of the Historical Jesus*, trans. W. Montgomery and F. C. Burkitt (Mineola, NY: Dover, 2005), 13.

8. Reimarus's portrait of Jesus was published posthumously by Gotthold Ephraim Lessing among the group of publications between 1774 and 1778 titled "Fragments."

9. *Quest*, 15.

10. Ibid., 3.

11. Ibid., 14.

12. One is tempted to see Schweitzer's comments in terms of race here, although such an association would be hasty at this point. I will discuss the concept of "race" as an Enlightenment preoccupation below. It is also noteworthy that Schweitzer attempts to qualify his enthusiastic *enkomion* of German theology in the preface to his sixth edition.

13. *Antiquities* 18.63–64: "Now there was about this time Jesus, a wise man, if it be lawful to call him a man; for he was a doer of wonderful works, a teacher of such men as receive the truth with pleasure. He drew over to him both many of the Jews and many of the Gentiles. He was [the] Christ. And when Pilate at the suggestion of the principal men amongst us, had condemned him to the cross, those that loved him at the first did not

forsake him; for he appeared to them alive again the third day; as the divine prophets had foretold these and ten thousand other wonderful things concerning him. And the tribe of Christians, so named from him, are not extinct at this day" (trans. from William Whiston, *The New Complete Works of Josephus* [Grand Rapids: Kregel Academic, 1999], 662).

14. *A Marginal Jew: Rethinking the Historical Jesus*, 4 vols. (New York: Doubleday, 1991), 1:64.

15. "Jesus of Nazareth: A Magician and False Prophet Who Deceived God's People?" in *Jesus of Nazareth Lord and Christ: Essays on the Historical Jesus*, eds. J. Green and M. Turner (Grand Rapids: Eerdmans, 1994), 164–80, here 169–71.

16. In *b.Sanh.* 107b, Jesus is accused of being a false teacher, "and the master said: Yeshu practiced magic [כישף] and deceived and led Israel astray." Similarly *b.Sanh.* 43a recounts an execution where Yeshu [ישו] "is going to be stoned for practicing magic [כישוף] and leading Israel astray." The designation "magician" should be understood as a polemic in this context; cf. the much later *Athanasius and Zacchaeus* 79.1.

17. T. Shab 11:15; T. Sanh 10:11; M. Yeb 4:13; T. Yeb 3:3,4; Yeb 49ab; Yom 66b; Sanh 43a; Ket 51b; Sanh 106ab. Shab 104b; J. Shab 13d; Sanh 107b; Sot 47a; Git 90a.; Sanh 43a; cf. M. Abot 2:8; Sanh 14a; A.Z. 8b; T. Sanh 9:7; T. Hul 2:22–24; Shab 116ab; Sanh 43a, 67a, 103a, 107b; Sot 47a; A.Z. 16b–17a. Sanh 43a; cf. T. Sanh 10:11; J. Sanh 25cd.

18. Michael J. Cook, *Modern Jews Engage the New Testament: Enhancing Jewish Well-Being in a Christian Environment* (Woodstock: Jewish Lights, 2008), 15.

19. *Jesus in the Talmud* (Princeton: Princeton University Press, 2007), 15–19. As mentioned, Cook is much less optimistic about reconstructions of Jesus based on the Talmud.

20. Both traditions presuppose Jesus' identity as a magician who studied in Egypt. However, these traditions are sufficiently different in both content and proper nouns so that direct dependence is unlikely.

Also worth noting is the Neo-Platonist philosopher Porphyry (ca. 234–305 CE). Porphyry criticized the reliability of the historical accounts given in the Gospels. Porphyry is clearly dependent on Celsus's earlier criticism but praises Christ's wisdom rather than accusing him of magic (Augustine, *De Civ.* 19.22–23). Cf. Robert L. Wilken, *The Christians as the Romans Saw Them* (New Haven: Yale University Press, 1984), 126–63, here 130, 145, 159–60.

What is further interesting for my thesis is that Porphyry questions Christian particularity of salvation through Christ and acknowledges that this particularity stems from Jewish particularity via Jewish law. Augustine reflects Porphyry's objection that salvation through Christ would naturally be of little use for those who died before Christ was born. Assuming that Christians might point to Jewish salvation via law, Porphyry argues that this is equally problematic because this law was never extended to Italians, Romans, or Latins. Thus Christians have no recourse to appeal to the ancient Jewish means of salvation to validate their own. He suggests that the innumerable souls of the non-Jews who died before the coming of Christ are not accounted for within Christian soteriology (Augustine, *Ep.* 102.8). Thus, for Porphyry, Christianity was an unreasonable system of belief for both historical and theological deficiencies.

21. *Augustine and the Jews* (New York: Doubleday, 2008), esp. 213–34, 290–352.

22. No doubt, there are other notable Christian writers who have the topic of Jewish-Christian debate in mind (e.g., Justin's *Dialogue with Trypho* and Tertullian's *Aduersus Iudaeos*—the authorship of the latter is disputed). Normally these take the form of Christian apologetic against (perceived) Jewish objections to Christianity. See the helpful treatment of this literature in William Horbury, *Jews and Christians in Contact and Controversy* (Edinburgh: T & T Clark, 1998), esp. 180–99.

23. Because my focus is on Jesus and not Paul, I cannot treat this subject with any depth. However, I would argue that Paul never intended his polemic to be parroted by non-Jews (Rom. 11:17-22).

24. St. Augustine, *The City of God* (Garden City: Doubleday, 1985), XVIII, chs. 46, 47. My gratitude to Steve Cone for looking over this portion of my chapter.

25. Fredriksen, *Augustine and the Jews*, xi–xx.

26. The history of Jewish and Christian relationship is complex and cannot be dealt with adequately here. For a recent attempt to emphasize the commonalities and inter-relational dynamics of these evolving identities, see Leo Duprée Sandgren, *Vines Inter-twined: A History of Jews and Christians from the Babylonian Exile to the Advent of Islam* (Peabody: Hendrickson, 2010).

27. John Rousmaniere, *A Bridge to Dialogue* (New York: A Stimulus Book, 1991), 54.

28. For a recent introduction to this literature see Lawrence Lahey, "Evidence for Jewish Believers in Christian-Jewish Dialogues through the Sixth Century (excluding Justin)," in *Jewish Believers in Jesus*, ed. O. Skarsaune and R. Hvalvik (Peabody, MA: Hendrickson, 2007), 581–639. I am also grateful for Lahey's personal correspondence on this topic.

29. The Greek text can be found in Eduard Bratke, *Das sogenannte Religionsgespräch am Hof der Sasaniden*, TUGAL 4.3 (Leipzig: J. C. Hinrichs, 1899), 1–45. Bratke simply calls this story "Das sogenannte Religionsgespräch am Hof der Sasaniden"; Lahey shortens this unwieldy title to "*EP*" (from: The Explanation of the Events in Persia).

30. The Persian king's name is disputed, but he is called "Arrinatus" in some accounts.

31. Andreas Külzer suggest that this story was authored during the reign of Justinian, in the mid-sixth century (*Disputationes graecae contra Judaeos: Untersuchungen zur byz-antinischen antijüdischen Dialogliteraur und ihrem Judenbild*; Byzantinisches Archiv. Bd. XVIII [Stuttgart and Leipzig: Teubner, 1999], 142–47).

32. Lahey also discusses parallel accounts of formal debates that included third-party moderators in Persia during this period ("Evidence," 608).

33. I agree with Lahey that this story should not be summarily dismissed as fiction ("Evidence," 607).

34. Cook, *Modern*, 16.

35. Shlomo Eidelberg, *The Jews and the Crusaders: The Hebrew Chronicles of the First and Second Crusades* (Madison: University of Wisconsin Press, 1977), 121–22; Fredrickson, *Augustine and the Jews*, xi.

36. On this point, see my "Jesus and Jewish Leadership," in *Jesus among Friends and Enemies*, eds. L. W. Hurtado and C. Keith (Grand Rapids: Baker Academic, 2011), forthcoming.

37. See Luther's *On the Jews and Their Lies* (1543); on Luther's anti-Semitic legacy see Robert Michael, *Holy Hatred: Christianity, Antisemitism, and the Holocaust* (New York: Palgrave Macmillan, 2006), 105–54.

38. On the relationship between Nazism and the so-called "German Christians" see the magnificent work by Susannah Heschel, *The Aryan Jesus* (Princeton: Princeton University Press, 2008); Heschel (7) translates this summary statement by Wolf Meyer-Erlach: "In the Nazi treatment of the Jews and its ideological stance, Luther's intentions, after centuries, are being fulfilled" (Juden, Mönche und Luther [Weimar: Deutsche Christen, 1937], 60). See also the treatment of this topic in Gerd Theissen's chapter in this book.

39. Martin Luther, "That Jesus Christ Was Born a Jew," in *Luther's Works*, trans. W. I. Brandt (Philadelphia: Fortress Press, 1962), 201, 229.

40. This segment is indebted to Harvey Falk, *Jesus the Pharisee* (Mahwah, NJ: Paulist, 1985), esp. 13–23. Falk's still useful work had an unfortunate deficiency of timing. Had the Dead Sea Scrolls been more available in 1985, Falk's work might have avoided several debilitating pitfalls. However his treatment of Emden and the Shabbateans is valuable.

41. Falk, *Jesus the Pharisee*, 13–15.

42. See A. Le Donne, *Historiographical Jesus*, 18–22.

43. The so-called *Jefferson Bible* was first published in 1895 (posthumously) by Jefferson's grandson, although earlier drafts circulated during his lifetime.

44. Via personal correspondence, Gerd Theissen has suggested that Hugo Grotius (1583–1645) should be mentioned alongside Spinoza as a parallel voice in early critical study.

45. So as not to duplicate previous studies, I will not recount the "liberal lives of Jesus" movement in this section. To fill out this portrait, see Susannah Heschel, *Abraham Geiger and the Jewish Jesus* (Chicago: University of Chicago Press, 1998), 127–61; for a recent and succinct introduction to Reimarus's Jesus, see J. D. G. Dunn, *Jesus Remembered: Christianity in the Making, Vol. 1* (Grand Rapids: Eerdmans, 2003), 29–32.

46. Cf. H. B. Nisbet, *Lessing: Eine Biographie* (Munich: Beck 2008), 708. For a general account of this friendship see V. Forester, *Lessing und Moses Mendelssohn: Geschichte einer Freundschaft* (Darmstadt: Schneider, 2010).

47. See description in Arno Schilson, "Lessing and Theology," in *A Companion to the Works of Gotthold Ephraim Lessing*, eds. B. Fischer and T. C. Fox (Rochester, NY: Camden House, 2005), 157–84; esp. 170–74.

48. I am grateful to Gerd Theissen for suggesting that this question might be an important one.

49. Cook, *Modern*, 17.

50. For example, Abraham Geiger, *Das Judenthum und seine Geschichte* (Breslau: Schletter, 1864); Heinrich Graetz, *Sinai et Golgotha* (Paris: Michael Lévy frères, 1867).

51. A fuller discussion of Jewish scholarship on Jesus would have to include the following: Isaac of Troki (c. 1533–1594), Leon of Modena (1571–1648), Joseph Klausner (1874–1958), C. G. Montefiore (1858–1938), and Robert Eisler (1882–1949). For a brief survey see G. Theissen and A. Merz, *The Historical Jesus: A Comprehensive Guide* (Minneapolis: Fortress Press, 1996), 8–10. Attention to D. F. Strauss's influence on Leopold Zunz is also warranted (cf. Luitpold Wallach, *Liberty and Letters: The Thoughts of Leopold Zunz* (London: Leo Baeck Institute, 1959), 65.

52. Heschel, *Geiger*, 4.

53. There is a prominent thread in the field of ethnic studies that argues that the very idea of race is an invention of the Enlightenment; see Michael Omi and Howard Winant, *Racial Formation in the United States* (New York: Routledge, 1986). This field is heavily influenced by Stuart Hall [for example, "Cultural Studies: Two Paradigms," *Media, Culture and Society* (1980), 2:57–72]; however, one does not need to be convinced of this thesis to acknowledge that the *science of* race was an Enlightenment construct.

54. Rousmaniere, *Bridge to Dialogue*, 108–9.

55. Heschel, *Aryan*, 37; in fact, Gobineau accused Renan of plagiarizing his research.

56. To be fair, Renan saw well the consequences of using racial identity to impose nationhood at the expense of external provincial identities. In an essay published in 1882, Renan describes what he understands as a theoretical error: "The Germanic family, according to the theory I am expounding here [of Renan's opponents], has the right to reassemble the scattered limbs of the Germanic order. . . . The right of the Germanic order over such-and-such a province is stronger than the right of the inhabitants of that province over themselves." Renan thus sees the problems that the elevation of racial identity creates and argues that if this theory is taken too far, it might "destroy European civilization" (Ernest Renan, "What Is a Nation?" in *The Collective Memory Reader*, eds. J. Olick, V. Vinitzky-Seroussi, and D. Levy [Oxford: Oxford University Press, 2011], 80–83, here 81).

57. Cf. Heschel, *Aryan*, 32.

58. Ernest Renan, *The Life of Jesus*, trans. C. E. Wilbour (London: Trübner & Co., Paternoster Row, 1864), 168.

59. It might be worth noting here that Renan's idea was also echoed by Jewish historian Joseph Klausner (cf. the discussion of Klausner in Gerd Theissen's chapter within this book).

60. Indeed, perhaps we should follow Allison's suggestion that we call this period in German Jesus research the "no biography" years (*Resurrecting*, 5; cf. F. Bermejo Rubio, "Fiction," 244). I will further qualify this problematic moniker below.

61. Martin Kähler, "Against the Life-of-Jesus Movement," in *The Historical Jesus in Recent Research*, ed. S. McKnight and J. D. G. Dunn, *The Historical Jesus in Recent Research; Sources for Biblical Research and Theological Study, Vol. 10* (Winona Lake, IN: Eisenbrauns, 2005), 67–86; Kähler credits Schweitzer for this observation of Luther (67–68).

62. Bultmann, *Jesus*; more popularly known as R. Bultmann, *Jesus and the Word* (New York: Scribner's, 1934 [1926]).

63. My thanks to John Barclay for this insight.

64. Cf. also Konrad Hammann, *Rudolf Bultmann: Eine Biographie* (Teubingen: Mohr Siebeck, 2009), 255–74.

65. Ernst Käsemann, "Das Problem des historischen Jesus," *ZThK* 51 (1954): 125–53.

66. See Dagmar Winter's chapter in this book for more on this topic.

67. Theissen and Merz, *Comprehensive Guide*, 6–11. As suggested already, I am persuaded that we must move away from the tripartite division of most Quest surveys. For lack of better terminology, "Third Quest" is used here to provide continuity with the block quotation of Dunn in what follows.

68. For the development of the traditional criteria see A. Le Donne, "The Rise of the Quest for an Authentic Jesus: An Introduction to the Crumbling Foundations of Jesus Studies," in *Jesus, Criteria, and the Demise of Authenticity: The 2012 Lincoln Christian University Conference* (New York: Continuum, 2012), forthcoming.

69. See Richard A. Horsley, *Jesus and Empire: The Kingdom of God and the New World Disorder* (Minneapolis: Fortress Press, 2003); William Herzog II, *Jesus, Justice and the Reign of God: A Ministry of Liberation* (Louisville: Westminster John Knox, 1999); John Dominic Crossan, *Jesus: A Revolutionary Biography* (San Francisco: HarperSanFrancisco, 2009).

70. However, see, for example, Donald Hagner, *The Jewish Reclamation of Jesus: Analysis and Critique of the Modern Jewish Study of Jesus* (Grand Rapids: Zondervan, 1984), 23–39; Michael J. Cook, "How Credible Is Jewish Scholarship on Jesus?" in *The Jewish Jesus: Revelation, Reflect, Reclamation*, ed. Zev Garber (West Lafayette: Purdue University Press, 2011), 251–70. Hagner argues that Jewish scholarship has tended to emphasize Jesus' Jewishness at the expense of the Gospel's witness concerning Jesus and his relationship to Christianity in general. However, within particular Gospel episodes that betray ancient Jewish culture, Jewish scholarship has tended to ascribe more historical reliability (67). Cook has recently suggested that Jewish scholarship has tended to accept the historicity of the Gospels, bordering on uncritical appraisal. He argues that much of Jewish scholarship has tended toward ignorance of Christian scholarship by Gospel specialists.

71. Dunn, *Jesus Remembered*, 86.

72. Dunn writes, "Schweitzer's own account of the quest simply failed to take account of the substantial debate between Jewish and Christian scholarship on the theme of Jesus the Jew" (*Remembered*, 87; cf. Heschel, *Abraham Geiger*, 127).

Chapter 8: The Dissimilar Jesus

1. For a very useful one-page systematic summary of the phases of Jesus research, see G. Theissen and A. Merz, *The Historical Jesus: A Comprehensive Guide* (Minneapolis: Fortress Press, 1998), 12.

2. T. Morgan *The Moral Philosopher*, vols. 1–3. London, 1738–1740. Facsimile Reprint in One Volume, ed. G. Gawlick (Stuttgart: Fromman, 1969), 1:439–41.

3. D. F. Strauss, *The Life of Jesus Critically Examined*, trans. G. Eliot (London: SCM, 1973).

4. For relating Jesus to Judaism in this period, see D. Wünsche, *Neue Beiträge zur Erläuterung der Evangelien aus Talmud und Midrasch* (Göttingen: Vandenhoeck & Ruprecht, 1878), and G. Dalman: *The Words of Jesus: Considered in the Light of Post-Biblical Jewish Writings and the Aramaic Language*, trans. D. M. Kay (Edinburgh: T & T Clark, 1909), orig. German 1898. The problems of the hero/personality in history and anti-Judaism/anti-Semitism form the main part of this essay further down.

5. A. Schweitzer *The Quest of the Historical Jesus*, trans. W. Montgomery (London: A. & C. Black, 1910), orig. German 1906.

6. R. Bultmann *Theology of the New Testament*, trans. K. Grobel (New York: Charles Scribner's Sons, 1951). J. Wellhausen, *Einleitung in die ersten drei Evangelien* (Berlin: G. Reimer, 1911), 102.

7. On this point, also see Gerd Theissen's chapter in this book.

8. E. Käsemann, "The Problem of the Historical Jesus," in *Essays on New Testament Themes*, SBT 41 (London: SCM, 1964). First published in *ZThK* 51 (1954): 125–53.

9. See B. Kellermann, *Kritische Beiträge zur Entstehungsgeschichte des Christentums* (Berlin: Poppelauer, 1906), and J. Klausner, *Jesus of Nazareth: His Life, Times and Teaching*, trans. H. Danby (Boston: Beacon, 1925). In the years following there were also C. G. Montefiore, *The Synoptic Gospels*, 2 vols. (London: Macmillan, 1909), and R. Eisler *Iesus basileus u basileusas*, 2 vols. (Heidelberg: Winter, 1927/30). Forerunners to the Third Quest are D. Flusser, *Jesus in Selbstzeugnissen und Bilddokumenten*, 9th ed. (Reinbek: Rowohlt, 1978), and G. Vermès, *Jesus the Jew: A Historian's Reading of the Gospels* (London: Collins, 1973).

10. Among the best known Third Quest scholars are: J. Riches, *Jesus and the Transformation of Judaism* (London: Darton, Longmann & Todd, 1980), M. J. Borg, *Conflict, Holiness and Politics in the Teaching of Jesus,* SBEC 5 (New York: E. Mellen, 1984), E. P. Sanders, *Jesus and Judaism* (London: SCM, 1985), D. Crossan, *The Historical Jesus. The Life of a Mediterranean Jewish Peasant* (Edinburgh: T & T Clark, 1991), J. H. Charlesworth, *Jesus within Judaism. New Light from Exciting Archaeological Discoveries* (New York: Doubleday, 1988); but also G. Theissen, *The Shadow of the Galilean: The Quest of the Historical Jesus in Narrative Form*, trans. J. Bowden (Philadelphia: Fortress Press, 1987).

11. G. Theissen and D. Winter, *The Quest for the Plausible Jesus: The Question of Criteria*, trans. M. E. Boring (Louisville and London: Westminster John Knox, 2002).

12. A. Le Donne, *The Historiographical Jesus: Memory, Typology, and the Son of David* (Waco: Baylor University Press, 2009); also see his more popular introduction, *Historical Jesus. What Can We Know and How Can We Know It?* (Grand Rapids: Eerdmans, 2011).

13. For a comprehensive study, see Theissen and Winter, *The Quest for the Plausible Jesus.*

14. E. Käsemann, "The Problem of the Historical Jesus," in *Essays on New Testament Themes*, SBT 41 (London: SCM, 1964), 37.

15. See the comprehensive work by Susannah Heschel, *The Aryan Jesus: Christian Theologians and the Bible in Nazi Germany* (Princeton: Princeton University Press, 2008).

16. For the latest encyclopedic study, see Robert S. Wistrich's epic work *A Lethal Obsession: Anti-Semitism from Antiquity to the Global Jihad* (New York: Random House, 2009).

17. M. Luther "The Jews and Their Lies," in *Luther's Works*, vol. 47, trans. W. I. Brandt (Philadelphia: Fortress Press, 1971), 137–76.

18. See Rudolf Seydel, *Die Buddhalegende und das Leben Jesu nach den Evangelien* (The Buddha Legend and the Life of Jesus after the Gospels) (Weimar: Felber, 1884), and other works.

19. Ernest Renan, *The Life of Jesus*, trans. C. E. Wilbour (London: Trübner, 1864), orig. French 1863.

20. Ibid., 100.

21. E. Schürer, *Geschichte des jüdischen Volkes im Zeitalter Jesu Christi*, vol. 2, 2nd ed. (Leipzig: Hinrich, 1886). H. S. Chamberlain *Die Grundlagen des Neunzehnten Jahrhunderts*, 1. Hälfte, 4th ed. (Munich: Bruckmann, 1903). See also G. F. Moore, "Christian Writers on Judaism," *HTR* 14 (1921): 197–254.

22. See S. Heschel, *The Aryan Jesus*, for detailed analysis.

23. Ibid., 27.

24. J. Wellhausen, *Die Pharisäer und die Sadducäer. Eine Untersuchung zur inneren jüdischen Geschichte*, (1874), 17; J. Wellhausen, "Abriss der Geschichte Israels und Juda's," in *Skizzen und Vorarbeiten, Vol. 1* (Berlin: Reimer, 1884), 5–102, here 98.

25. Published in 1870 in the *Allgemeine evangelisch-lutherische Kirchenzeitung*; cf Moore, "Christian Writers on Judaism," 228.

26. W. Bousset, *Das Wesen der Religion. Dargestellt an ihrer Geschichte*, 4th ed. Lebensfragen 28 (Tuebingen: Mohr, 1920), 105.

27. A. Kalthoff, *Das Christusproblem. Grundlinien zu einer Sozialtheologie* (Leipzig: Diederichs, 1902), 12–13.

28. G. Bornkamm, *Jesus von Nazareth*, 13th ed., UB 19 (Stuttgart: Kohlhammer, 1983). Significant changes occur in the 10th edition (unchanged thereafter), for instance: the Talmud is described in much less hostile tones (24), the Pharisees are described more favorably, warning of a summary caricature of them (34ff.), the chapter on Jesus and the law and the new righteousness (85–97) has been completely revised, and small significant changes are made such as "In contrast to Jewish thought" becomes "In contrast to vulgar thought" (125; that is, no longer identified with Jewish thought!).

29. Ibid., 92.

30. Ibid., 124–26.

31. Ibid., 35.

32. J. Burckhardt, "Das Individuum und das Allgemeine," in *Weltgeschichtliche Betrachtungen. Über geschichtliches Studium*, Collected Works 4 (Darmstadt: Wiss. Buchges, 1956), 166.

33. T. Carlyle, *The Works of Thomas Carlyle*, Vol. 5, ed. H. D. Traill (London: Chapman & Hall, 1896–1901).

34. See G. Theissen and D. Winter, *The Quest for the Plausible Jesus*, 44–56.

35. A. Weiss, "Das Problem der Entstehung des Christentums," *ARW* 16 (1913): 515, 427. Cf also the discussion of Spinoza in the Introduction.

36. R. Bultmann, *Jesus and the Word*, trans. L. P. Smith and E. Huntress Lantero (New York: Charles Scribner's Sons, 1958).

37. Ibid., 158–59.

38. Bultmann wants to lead the reader of his Jesusbook to "a highly personal *encounter* with history." Ibid., 6.

39. G. Bornkamm, *Jesus of Nazareth*, trans. Irene and Fraser McLuskey with James M. Robinson (New York: Harper & Row, 1960), 56.

40. Käsemann, "The Problem of the Historical Jesus," 39.

41. I include here the works of Jewish scholars.

42. J. R. Rosenbloom, *Conversion to Judaism: From the Biblical Period to the Present* (Cincinnati: Hebrew Union College Press, 1978), 63.

Chapter 9: Jesus within Judaism

1. Wolfgang Fenske, *Wie Jesus zum "Arier" wurde: Auswirkungen der Entjudaisierung Christi im 19. und zu Beginn des 20* (Jahrhunderts, Darmstadt: Wiss. Buchgesellschaft, 2005); Susannah Heschel, *The Aryan Jesus: Christian Theologians and the Bible in Nazi Germany* (Princeton: Princeton University Press, 2008), 26–66. The thesis that Jesus was not

Jewish by birth was popularized by H. St. Chamberlain, *Die Grundlagen des neunzehnten Jahrhunderts*, 2 vols. (Munich: F. Bruckmann, 1899); *The Foundations of the Nineteenth Century*, 2 vols. (New York: John Lane, 1910). Academic theologians also argued for such a hypothesis: Reinhold Seeberg (1859–1935) developed the thesis that Mary was a gentile woman, "Die Herkunft der Mutter Jesu," in *Theologische Festschrift* (Leipzig: G. N. Bonwetsch, 1918), 13–24. Emanuel Hirsch, *Das Wesen des Christentums* (Weimar: Deutsche Christen, 1939), 158–65, claimed that Jesus with all probability was not of Jewish origin ("nach aller Regel wissenschaftlicher Wahrscheinlichkeit ist Jesus nichtjüdischen Blutes gewesen"). Cf. also Walter Grundmann, *Jesus der Galiläer und das Judentum* (Leipzig: Georg Wigand, 1940), 196.

2. G. Theissen, *Sociology of Early Palestinian Christianity* (Philadelphia: Fortress Press, 1978), 1.

3. J. Klausner, *Jesus von Nazareth: Seine Zeit, Sein Leben und seine Lehre* (Berlin: Jüdischer, 1934), 574; ET: *Jesus of Nazareth: His Life, Times, and Teaching* (London: Allen & Unwin, 1929, orig. Hebrew 1907). Klausner underscores that there must be some contradiction between the convictions of Jesus and Judaism in order to explain the origin of the Christian religion that contradicts the spirit of Judaism (*Jesus von Nazareth*, 9).

4. A good history of the church and theology in the Third Reich is Klaus Scholder, *Die Kirchen und das Dritte Reich: Vorgeschichte und Zeit der Illusionen, 1918–1934* (Frankfurt and Berlin: Propyläen, 1977/1980); *Das Jahr der Ernüchterung, 1934* (Frankfurt and Berlin: Propyläen, 1985); Gerhard Besier, *Die Kirchen und das Dritte Reich: Spaltungen und Abwehrkämpfe 1934–1937* (Berlin and Munich: Propyläen, 2001).

5. Cf. the excellent book of S. Heschel on the "Eisenacher Insitut," in *The Aryan Jesus*, (2008).

6. Cf. Annette B. Merz, "Philhellenismus und Antisemitismus: Zwei Seiten einer Medaille in den akademischen Publikationen von Carl Schneider," *Kirchliche Zeitgeschichte* 17 (2004): 314–30.

7. Cf. Rudolf Bultmann, "Hirsch's Auslegung des Johannes-Evangeliums," *EvTh* 4 (1937): 115–42, cf. 126 with R. Bultmann, *Theologie als Kritik* (Tuebingen: Mohr, 2002), 353–77, esp. 364.

8. Konrad Hammann, *Rudolf Bultmann: Eine Biographie* (Tuebingen: Mohr, 2009).

9. Rudolf Bultmann, "Die Aufgabe der Theologie in der gegenwärtigen Situation," *Theologische Blätter* 12 (1933): 161–66; R. Bultmann, *Neues Testament und christliche Existenz*; Theologische Aufsätze, ed. A. Lindemann (Tuebingen: Mohr, 2001), 172–80.

10. Gerd Theissen, *Neutestamentliche Wissenschaft vor und nach 1945: Karl Georg Kuhn und Günther Bornkamm* (Schriften der Philosophisch-historischen; Klasse der Heidelberger Akademie der Wissenschaften 47; Heidelberg: Winter 2009), 195–221.

11. Rudolf Bultmann, *Jesus* (Berlin: Deutsche Bibliothek, 1926).

12. Ernst Käsemann, "Das Problem des historischen Jesus," *ZThK* 51 (1954): 125–53; *Exegetische Versuche und Besinnungen, I* (Göttingen: Vandenhoeck & Ruprecht, 1960), 187–214; cf. Ernst Käsemann, *The Problem of the Historical Jesus: Essays in New Testament Themes* (London: SCM, 1964), 15–47.

13. Cf. the booklet of G. Bornkamm against the "German Christians" where he asks [Did Paul spoil Christianity?]: *Hat Paulus das Christentum verdorben?* (Berlin: Heliand 46, 1937).

14. Z. Bauman, "Allosemitism: Premodern, Modern, Postmodern," in *Modernity, Culture and "the Jew,"* eds. B. Cheyette and L. Marcus (Cambridge: Polity, 1998), 143–56.

15. Günther Bornkamm, "Wandlungen im alt- und neutestamentlichen Gesetzesverständnis," in *Geschichte und Glaube II* (Ges. Aufs. Bd. 4; BEvTh 53; Munich: Kaiser, 1971), 73–119.

16. R. Walter, "Ernst Käsemanns Wirken als Gemeindepfarrer im Kirchenkampf in Westfalen 1933–1946," *KZG* 12 (1999): 199–224.

17. See Dagmar Winter's chapter in this book.

18. Ernst Käsemann, "Die neue Jesus-Frage," in *Jésus aux origines de la christologie*, ed. J. Dupont; *Bibliotheca Ephemeridum theologicarum Lovaniensium* 40 (Leuven: Leuven University Press, 1975), 52.

19. For a more extended discussion of this problem cf. Gerd Theissen, "Jesus im Judentum. Drei Versuche einer Ortsbestimmung," in *Jesus als historische Gestalt: Beiträge zur Jesusforschung*, ed. G. Theissen (Göttingen: Vandenhoeck & Ruprecht, 2003), 35–56.

20. The definition of Judaism as "covenantal nomism" is due to E. P. Sanders, *Paul and Palestinian Judaism: A Comparison of Patterns of Religion*, (Philadelphia: Fortress Press, 1977). E. P. Sanders is dealing with Palestinian Judaism. If we take into regard also Diaspora Judaism we should add the attribute "Monotheism" to the basic structure of Judaism. On the one side it was a distinguishing feature of Jewish faith; on the other side the faith into a creator included a universalism.

21. E. P. Sanders, *Jesus and Judaism* (London: SCM, 1985).

22. Cf. Gerd Theissen, "Jünger als Gewalttäter (Mt 11:12ff.; Lk 16:16): Der Stürmerspruch als Selbststigmatisierung einer Minorität," in *Jesus als historische Gestalt: Beiträge zur Jesusforschung*, ed. Gerd Theissen (Göttingen: Vandenhoeck & Ruprecht, 2003), 153–68.

23. Gerd Theissen and Annette Merz, *The Historical Jesus: A Comprehensive Guide* (Minneapolis: Fortress Press, 1998), 130–46, give a survey on the plurality of groups and movements.

24. L. Wittgenstein, *Philosophische Untersuchungen* (Berlin: Akademie, 1998), 66.

25. Gerd Theissen, "Sadduzäismus und Jesustradition: Zur Auseinandersetzung mit Oberschichtmentalität in der synoptischen Überlieferung," in G. Theissen, *Jesus als historische Gestalt: Beiträge zur Jesusforschung*, ed. G. Theissen (Göttingen: Vandenhoeck & Ruprecht, 2003), 111–31.

26. Think of the impressive work of John P. Meier, *A Marginal Jew: Rethinking the Historical Jesus*, 4 vols. (New York: Doubleday, 1991; 1994; 2001; New Haven: Yale University Press, 2009).

27. Gerd Theissen, "Das Reinheitslogion Mk 7,15 und die Trennung von Juden und Christen," in G. Theissen, *Jesus als historische Gestalt: Beiträge zur Jesusforschung*, ed. G. Theissen (Göttingen: Vandenhoeck & Ruprecht, 2003), 73–89.

28. E. P. Sanders, *Judaism: Practice and Belief 63 BCE–66 BCE* (London: SCM, 1992), coined the term "Common Judaism."

29. This theory was developed by F. G. Downing, "Cynics and Christians," *NTS* 30 (1984): 584–93; see also his *Christ and the Cynics*, JSOT Manuals 4 (Sheffield: JSOT, 1988). The most prominent representative of this cynic interpretation of Jesus is J. Dominic Crossan, *The Historical Jesus: The Life of a Mediterranean Jewish Peasant* (Edinburgh: T & T Clark, 1991). The most convincing interpretation of Jesus as a Cynic is according to my view Bernhard Lang, *Jesus der Hund. Leben und Lehre eines jüdischen Kynikers* (Munich: C. H. Beck, 2010).

30. Cf. Gerd Theissen, "Jesus as an Itinerant Teacher, Reflections from Social History on Jesus' Roles," in *Jesus Research. An International Perspective: The First Princeton-Prague Symposium on Jesus Research*, eds. J. H. Charlesworth and P. Pokorný (Grand Rapids: Eerdmans, 2009), 98–122. I think that Judas Galilaios may have been an itinerant teacher who was influenced in a superficial way by Cynicism and could have used a Cynic outfit (a bag, staff, and so on) in order to spread his rebellious message in Palestine as an itinerant teacher. Jesus stressed the difference to such Cynic-like itinerant teachers when he forbade a Cynic outfit to his disciples (Luke 10:4; Matt. 10:9ff.). He did not want his disciples to evoke memories of Judas Galilaios. But such a contrast does not exclude the possibility of a certain influence.

31. Our thanks to scholar and poet Aaron Michael Moe for his English rendering of this verse.

Chapter 10: The Importance of a Jewish-Christian Dialogue on Jesus

1. Ernst Käsemann, *Commentary on Romans* (Grand Rapids: Eerdmans, 1980), 87.

Chapter 11: Jesus in Jewish-Christian Dialogue

1. http://www.bc.edu/dam/files/research_sites/cjl/sites/partners/csg/Sacred_Obligation.htm.

2. See Peter Schäfer, *Jesus in the Talmud* (Princeton: Princeton University Press, 2009).

3. Amy-Jill Levine, "Review Essay: Evangelical Biblical Scholarship," *Journal for the Study of the Historical Jesus*, forthcoming.

4. See the various scholarly depictions of this woman, usually made to enhance her abjection, and the means by which these depictions feed into an anti-Jewish agenda in my "Matthew's Advice to a Divided Readership," in *The Gospel of Matthew in Current Study*, ed. David E. Aune (Grand Rapids: Eerdmans, 2001).

5. G. Theissen, *Sociology of Early Palestinian Christianity* (Philadelphia: Fortress Press, 1978), 1.

6. See Jacob Neusner and Bruce D. Chilton, eds., *The Quest of the Historical Pharisees* (Waco: Baylor University Press, 2007).

7. See discussion in my *The Misunderstood Jew: The Church and the Scandal of the Jewish Jesus* (San Francisco: HarperOne, 2006).

8. See Mark Kinzer, "Messianic Jews and the Jewish World," in *Introduction to Messianic Judaism: Its Ecclesial Context and Biblical Foundation*, ed. David Rudolph and Joel Willitts (Grand Rapids: Zondervan, forthcoming); I thank Dr. Kinzer for sharing with me his chapter.

9. Joel N. Lohr, *Chosen and Unchosen: Concepts of Election in the Pentateuch and Jewish-Christian Interpretation* (Winona Lake, IN: Eisenbrauns, 2009).

10. I am bracketing here the "Jew by choice"; the Reform movement also recognizes as a Jew a child of a Jewish father.

11. Kate McCarthy, *Interfaith Encounters in America* (New Brunswick, NJ: Rutgers University Press, 2007), 202, notes that theological questions of truth, soteriology, particularity, and universality were "remarkably irrelevant" in the effort to understand how people experienced "religious others."

Conclusion

1. For an application of the principle of generation to the relationship between ancient Judaism and early Christianity, see Jacob Neusner, Baruch A. Levine, and Bruce Chilton, *Torah Revealed, Torah Fulfilled: Scriptural Laws in Formative Judaism and Earliest Christianity* (London and New York: T & T Clark, 2008).

2. See Paul V. M. Flesher and Bruce Chilton, *The Targums: A Critical Introduction* (Waco: Baylor University Press, 2011).

3. For an introduction to the New Testament from a generative point of view, see Bruce Chilton and Deirdre Good, *Studying the New Testament: A Fortress Introduction* (Minneapolis: Fortress Press, 2010).

4. Brought out between 1922 and 1961 by Beck in Munich.

5. See Bruce Chilton, "Reference to the Targumim in the Exegesis of the New Testament," *Society of Biblical Literature: 1995 Seminar Papers*, ed. L. H. Lovering (Atlanta: Scholars, 1995), 77–82, and "Jesus and Judaism," *The Encyclopedia of Judaism*, eds. J. Neusner, A. J. Avery-Peck, and W. S. Green (Leiden: Brill, 2000), 2:534–46.

6. Samuel Sandmel, "Parallelomania," *Journal of Biblical Literature* 81 (1962): 1–13.

7. The application of analogies is essayed in Bruce Chilton (General Editor), with Darrell Bock (Associate Editor), Daniel M. Gurtner (Editor for the Pseudepigrapha, Josephus, and Philo), Jacob Neusner (Editor for Rabbinic Literature), Lawrence H. Schiffman (Editor for the Literature of Qumran), and Daniel Oden (Assistant Editor), *A Comparative Handbook to the Gospel of Mark: Comparisons with Pseudepigrapha, the Qumran Scrolls, and Rabbinic Literature*, The New Testament Gospels in their Judaic Contexts 1 (Leiden: Brill, 2010).

8. For the development of the statements that follow, see Bruce Chilton and Jacob Neusner, *Classical Christianity and Rabbinic Judaism: Comparing Theologies* (Grand Rapids: Baker Academic, 2004).

9. Collingwood's abiding influence within the study of religion was marked by the publication of Bernard J. F. Lonergan's *Method in Theology* (New York: Herder and Herder, 1972).

10. See Willem F. Smelik, *The Targum of Judges*, Oudtestamentische studiën 36 (Leiden: Brill, 1995), 649–56.

11. See Ernst Lohmeyer, *Galiläa und Jerusalem*: Forschungen zur Religion und Literatur des Alten und Neuen Testaments 34 (Göttingen: Vandenhoeck and Ruprecht, 1936).

12. Some of this work is cited by Regev; further discussion and application is available in Bruce Chilton, *Rabbi Jesus: An Intimate Biography* (New York: Doubleday, 2000), 213–30, 305.

13. See Bruce Chilton, *A Feast of Meanings. Eucharistic Theologies from Jesus through Johannine Circles*, Supplements to *Novum Testamentum* 72 (Leiden: Brill, 1994), and Bernhard Lang, *Sacred Games: A History of Christian Worship* (New Haven: Yale University Press, 1997).

Bibliography

Albertz, Martin. *The Gospel before the Gospels*. New York: Charles Scribner's and Sons, 1928.

―――. *Die synoptischen Streitgespräche*. Berlin: Trowitzsch & Sohn, 1921.

Allison, Dale C. "A Plea for Thoroughgoing Eschatology." *Journal of Biblical Literature* 113 (1994): 651–68.

―――. *Jesus of Nazareth: Millenarian Prophet*. Minneapolis: Fortress Press, 1998.

―――. *Resurrecting Jesus: The Earliest Christian Tradition and Its Interpreters*. London: T & T Clark, 2005.

Anderson, Graham. *Sage, Saint and Sophist: Holy Men and Their Associates in the Early Roman Empire*. London: Routledge, 1994.

Augustine. *The City of God*. Garden City: Doubleday, 1985.

Barclay, John M. G. "Universalism and Particularism: Twin Components of Both Judaism and Early Christianity." In *A Vision for the Church: Studies in Early Christian Ecclesiology in Honour of J.P.M. Sweet*. Edited by Markus Bockmuehl and Michael B. Thompson, 207–24. Edinburgh: T & T Clark, 1997.

Barnstone, Willis. *The Poetics of Translation: History, Theory, Practice*. New Haven: Yale University Press, 2003.

―――. *Restored New Testament: A New Translation with Commentary, Including the Gnostic Gospels Thomas, Mary, and Judas*. New York: W. W. Norton, 2009.

Bauckham, Richard, ed. *The Gospels for All Christians: Rethinking the Gospel Audiences*. Grand Rapids: Eerdmans, 1998.

―――. *Jesus and the God of Israel*. Grand Rapids: Eerdmans, 2008.

Bauman, Zygmunt. "Allosemitism: Premodern, Modern, Postmodern." In *Modernity, Culture and "the Jew."* Edited by B. Cheyette and L. Marcus, 143–56. Cambridge: Polity, 1998.

Baxter, Wayne. "Healing and the 'Son of David': Matthew's Warrant." *Novum Testamentum* 48, no. 1 (2006): 36–50.

Beard, Mary, John North, and Simon Price. *Religions of Rome: A History.* Cambridge: Cambridge University Press, 1998.

Beilby, J. K., and P. R. Eddy, eds. *The Historical Jesus: Five Views.* Downers Grove, IL: InterVarsity, 2009.

Benedict XVI. *Jesus of Nazareth.* New York: Doubleday, 2007.

Betz, H. D. "Jesus and the Purity of the Temple (Mark 11:15-18): A Comparative Religion Approach." *Journal of Biblical Literature* 116 (1997): 455–72.

Bickerman, Elias. "Utilitas crucis." In *Studies in Jewish and Christian History*, 82–138. Leiden: Brill, 1986.

Blenkinsopp, Joseph. "The Contemporary English Version: Inaccurate Translation Tries to Soften Anti-Judaic Sentiment [Point]." *Bible Review* 12 (1996): 42, 51.

Blinzler, Josef. *The Trial of Jesus.* Translated by Isabel and Florence McHugh. Westminster: Newman, 1959.

Boccaccini, Gabriele. *Middle Judaism: Jewish Thought, 300 B.C.E. to 200 C.E.* Minneapolis: Fortress Press, 1991.

Bock, Darrell L. *Blasphemy and Exaltation in Judaism.* Tübingen: Mohr-Siebeck, 1998.

———. "The Son of Man Seated at God's Right Hand and the Debate over Jesus' Blasphemy." In *Jesus of Nazareth, Lord and Christ.* Edited by Joel B. Green and M. Turner, 181–91. Eugene: Eerdmans, 1999.

Bond, Helen K. *Caiaphas: Friend of Rome and Judge of Jesus?* Louisville: Westminister John Knox, 2004.

———. *Pontius Pilate in History and Interpretation.* Cambridge: Cambridge University Press, 1998.

Borg, Marcus J. *Conflict, Holiness and Politics in the Teaching of Jesus.* SBEC 5. New York: Edwin Mellen, 1984.

———. *Jesus in Contemporary Scholarship.* Valley Forge: Trinity Press International, 1994.

———. "A Temperate Case for a Non-eschatological Jesus." *Forum* 2 (1986): 81–102.

Bornkamm, Günther. *Hat Paulus das Christentum verdorben?*, Heft *46;* Berlin: Evangelischen Bundes *Berlin, 1937.*

———. *Jesus of Nazareth.* Translated by Irene and Fraser McLuskey with James M. Robinson. New York: Harper & Row, 1960.

———. *Jesus von Nazareth.* 13th ed., UB 19. Stuttgart: Kohlhammer, 1983.

———. "Wandlungen im alt- und neutestamentlichen Gesetzesverständnis." In *Geschichte und Glaube II*, Vol. 4, BEvTH 53, 73–119. Munich: Kaiser, 1971.

Borowitz, Eugene B. *Contemporary Christologies: A Jewish Response.* New York: Paulist, 1980.

Borowsky, Irvin J. "Removing the Anti-Judaism from the New Testament." In *Removing the Anti-Judaism from the New Testament.* Edited by Clark Kee and Irvin J. Borowsky, 9–20. Philadelphia: American Interfaith Institute/ World Alliance, 1998 and 2000.

Bousset, Wilhelm. *Das Wesen der Religion. Dargestellt an ihrer Geschichte.* 4th ed. Lebensfragen 28. Tübingen: Mohr Siebeck, 1920.

Bowersock, G. W. "The Mechanics of Subversion in the Roman Provinces." In *Opposition et Résistances a l'empire d'Auguste a Trajan.* Edited by A. Giovanini and D. van Berchem, 291–317. Geneva: Foundation Hardt, 1987.

Boyarin, Daniel. *Border Lines: The Partition of Judaeo-Christianity.* Philadelphia: University of Pennsylvania Press, 2005.

Boys, Mary. *Has God Only One Blessing? Judaism as a Source of Christian Self-Understanding.* New York: Paulist, 2000.

Brandon, S. G. F. *Jesus and the Zealots: A Study in the Political Factor in Primitive Christianity.* Manchester: Manchester University Press, 1967.

Bratke, Eduard. *Das sogenannte Religionsgespräch am Hof der Sasaniden.* TUGAL 4.3. Leipzig: J. C. Hinrichs, 1899.

Brown, Raymond. *The Gospel According to Saint John I–XII.* Anchor Bible 29. New York: Doubleday, 1966.

Bryan, Christopher. *Render to Caesar: Jesus, the Church and the Roman Superpower.* New York: Oxford University Press, 2005.

Bultmann, Rudolf. "Die Aufgabe der Theologie in der gegenwärtigen Situation." In *Theologische Blätter* 12 (1933): 161–66.

———. "Hirsch's Auslegung des Johannes-Evangeliums." *Evangelische Theologie* 4 (1937): 115–42.

———. *History of the Synoptic Tradition.* Translated by John Marsh. New York: Harper & Row, 1963.

———. *Jesus.* Berlin: Deutsche Bibliothek, 1926.

———. *Jesus and the Word.* New York: Scribner's, 1934.

———. *Jesus and the Word.* Translated by L. P. Smith and E. Huntress Lantero. New York: Charles Scribner's Sons, 1958.

———. *Theology of the New Testament.* Translated by K. Grobel. New York: Charles Scribner's Sons, 1951.

Burckhardt, Jacob. "Das Individuum und das Allgemeine." In *Weltgeschichtliche Betrachtungen. Über geschichtliches Studium.* Collected Works 4, 151–80. Darmstadt: Wiss. Buchges, 1956.

Burke, David J. "Translating the Jews (*hoi Ioudaioi*) in the New Testament: Comparing the Pertinent Passages in Recent English Versions." In *Removing the Anti-Judaism from the New Testament.* Edited by Howard Clark Kee and Irvin J. Borowsky, 63–87. Philadelphia: American Interfaith Institute/ World Alliance, 1998 and 2000.

Burkill, T. A. "Anti-Semitism in St. Mark's Gospel." *Novum Testamentum* 3 (1959): 34–53.

———. *New Light on the Earliest Gospel.* Ithaca: Cornell University Press, 1972.

Carlyle, Thomas. *On Heroes, Hero-Worship, and the Heroic in History.* Vol. 5 of *The Works of Thomas Carlyle.* Edited by H. D. Traill. London: Chapman & Hall, 1896–1901.

———. *The Works of Thomas Carlyle.* 30 vols. Edited by H. D. Traill. London: Chapman & Hall, 1896–1901.

Carter, Warren. *Matthew and Empire: Initial Explorations.* Harrisburg: Trinity Press International, 2001.

Catchpole, David. *The Trial of Jesus: A Study in the Gospels and Jewish Historiography from 1770 to the Present Day.* Leiden: Brill, 1971.

Chamberlain, H. S. *Die Grundlagen des neunzehnten Jahrhunderts.* 2 vols. Munich: F. Bruckmann, 1899.

———. *Die Grundlagen des Neunzehnten Jahrhunderts.* 1. First Half, 4th ed. Munich: Bruckmann, 1903.

Charlesworth, James H. *Jesus within Judaism: New Light from Exciting Archaeological Discoveries.* New York: Doubleday, 1988.

Chilton, Bruce. *A Feast of Meanings. Eucharistic Theologies from Jesus through Johannine Circles.* Supplements to *Novum Testamentum* 72. Leiden: Brill, 1994.

———. "Jesus and Judaism." Vol. 2 of *The Encyclopedia of Judaism.* Edited by J. Neusner, A. J. Avery-Peck, and W. S. Green. Leiden: Brill, 2000.

———. *Rabbi Jesus: An Intimate Biography.* New York: Doubleday, 2000.

———. "Reference to the Targumim in the Exegesis of the New Testament." In *Society of Biblical Literature: 1995 Seminar Papers.* Edited by L. H. Lovering, 77–82. Atlanta: Scholars, 1995.

———. *The Temple of Jesus: His Sacrificial Program within a Cultural History of Sacrifice.* University Park: Pennsylvania State University Press, 1992.

———, Darrell Bock, Daniel M. Gurtner, Lawrence H. Schiffman, and Daniel Oden, eds. *A Comparative Handbook to the Gospel of Mark. Comparisons with Pseudepigrapha, the Qumran Scrolls, and Rabbinic Literature.* The New Testament Gospels in their Judaic Contexts 1. Leiden: Brill, 2010.

———, and Deirdre Good, *Studying the New Testament: A Fortress Introduction.* Minneapolis: Fortress Press, 2010.

———, and Jacob Neusner, *Classical Christianity and Rabbinic Judaism: Comparing Theologies.* Grand Rapids: Baker Academic, 2004.

Christian Scholars Group on Jewish-Christian Relations. "A Sacred Obligation: Rethinking Christian Faith in Relation to Judaism and the Jewish People." http://www.jcrelations.net/A_Sacred_Obligation_-_Rethinking_Christian_Faith_in_Relation_to_Judaism_and_the.2372.0.html.

Cody, Aelred. "When Is the Chosen People Called a Gôy?" *Vetus Testamentum* 14 (1964): 1–6.

Cook, Michael J. *Modern Jews Engage the New Testament: Enhancing Jewish Well-Being in a Christian Environment.* Woodstock: Jewish Lights, 2008.

Cope, Lamar. "Matthew 25:31-46: 'The Sheep and the Goats' Reinterpreted." *Novum Testamentum* 11 (1969): 32–44.

Crossan, John Dominic. *The Historical Jesus: The Life of a Mediterranean Jewish Peasant.* Edinburgh: T & T Clark, 1991.

————. *The Historical Jesus: A Life of a Mediterranean Jewish Peasant*. New York: HarperCollins, 1991.

————. *Who Killed Jesus? Exposing the Roots of Anti-Semitism in the Gospel Story of the Death of Jesus*. New York: HarperCollins, 1995.

Dahl, Nils Alstrup. *Jesus the Christ. The Historical Origins of Christological Doctrine*. Minneapolis: Fortress Press, 1991.

Dalman, Gustaf. *The Words of Jesus: Considered in the Light of Post-Biblical Jewish Writings and the Aramaic Language*. Translated by D. M. Kay. Edinburgh: T & T Clark, 1909.

Davies, W. D., and Dale C. Allison. *A Critical and Exegetical Commentary on the Gospel According to Saint Matthew*. 3 vols. International Critical Commentary. Edinburgh: T & T Clark, 1997.

Delitzsch, Franz. *The New Testament Translated into Hebrew*. London: British Bible Society, 1885.

De Moor, J. C. "The Targumic Background of Mark 12:1-12: The Parable of the Wicked Tenants." *Journal for the Study of Judaism in the Persian, Hellenistic, and Roman Periods* 29 (1998): 63–80.

Donaldson, Terence L. *Jews and Anti-Judaism in the New Testament: Decision Points and Divergent Interpretations*. Waco: Baylor University Press, 2010.

Downing, F. G. "Cynics and Christians." *New Testament Studies* 30 (1984): 584–93.

————. *Christ and the Cynics*. JSOT Manuals 4. Sheffield: JSOT Press, 1988.

Duling, Dennis C. "Ethnicity, Ethnocentrism, and the Matthean Ethos." *Biblical Theology Bulletin* 35 (2005): 125–43.

Dunn, James D. G. *Jesus Remembered*. Vol. 1 of *Christianity in the Making*. Grand Rapids: Eerdmans, 2003.

————. *A New Perspective on Jesus: What the Quest for the Historical Jesus Missed*. Grand Rapids: Baker Academnic; London: SPCK, 2005.

————. *The Parting of the Ways*. London: SCM; Philadelphia: Trinity Press International, 1991.

————. *Romans*. 2 vols. Word Biblical Commentary 38A-B. Dallas: Thomas Nelson, 1988.

Dyson, S. L. "Native Revolt Patterns in the Roman Empire." *Aufstieg und Niedergang der römischen Welt: Geschichte und Kultur Roms im Spiegel der neueren Forschung* II.3 (1975): 157–59.

————. "Native Revolts in the Roman Empire." *Historia* 20 (1971): 258–59.

Ehrman, Bart. *The New Testament: A Historical Introduction to the Early Christian Writings*. New York: Oxford University Press, 2000.

Eidelberg, Shlomo. *The Jews and the Crusaders: The Hebrew Chronicles of the First and Second Crusades*. Madison: University of Wisconsin Press, 1977.

Eisler, Robert. *Iesus basileus u basileusas*. 2 vols. Heidelberg: Winter, 1927–1930.

Evans, Craig A. "Jesus' Action in the Temple: Cleansing or Portent of Destruction." *Catholic Biblical Quarterly* 51 (1989): 237–70.

Falk, Harvey. *Jesus the Pharisee*. Mahwah: Paulist, 1985.

Fenske, Wolfgang. *Wie Jesus zum "Arier" wurde*. Auswirkungen der Entjudaisierung Christi im 19 und zu Beginn des 20 Jahrhunderts. Darmstadt: Wiss. Buchgesellschaft, 2005.

Fitzmyer, Joseph A. *The Acts of the Apostles*. Anchor Bible 18C. New York: Doubleday, 1998.

Flesher, Paul V. M., and Bruce Chilton. *The Targums: A Critical Introduction*. Waco: Baylor University Press, 2011.

Flusser, David. "Caiaphas in the New Testament." *Atiqot* 21 (1992): 81–87.

———. *Jesus*. Jerusalem: Magnes, 2001.

———. *Jesus in Selbstzeugnissen und Bilddokumenten*. 9th ed. Reinbek: Rowohlt, 1978.

Forester, Vera. *Lessing und Moses Mendelssohn: Geschichte einer Freundschaft*. Darmstadt: Schneider, 2010.

Foster, Graham. "Making Sense of Matthew 25:31-46." *Scottish Bulletin of Evangelical Theology* 16 (1998): 128–39.

Fox, Everett. *The Five Books of Moses: A New Translation with Introductions, Commentary, and Notes*. Vol. 1 of *The Schocken Bible*. New York: Schocken, 1995.

France, R. T. *The Gospel of Matthew*. New International Commentary on the New Testament. Grand Rapids: Eerdmans, 2007.

Fredriksen, Paula. *Augustine and the Jews*. New York: Doubleday, 2008.

———. *Jesus of Nazareth, King of the Jews: A Jewish Life and the Emergence of Christianity*. New York: Vintage, 1999.

Frymer-Kensky, Tikva, David Novak, Peter Ochs, and Michael Signer. "*Dabru Emet*: A Jewish Statement on Christians and Christianity." Jewish-Christian Relations. http://www.jcrelations.net/Dabru_Emet_-_A_Jewish_Statement_on_Christians_and_Christianity.2395.0.html.

———. "Jewish-Christian Dialogue: Jon D. Levenson & Critics." *Commentary* 113, no. 4 (2002): 8–21.

Fuglseth, K. S. *Johannine Sectarianism in Perspective: A Sociological, Historical, and Comparative Analysis of Temple and Social Relationships in the Gospel of John, Philo, and Qumran*. Sup. NT 119. Leiden: Brill, 2005.

Funk, Robert W., and R. W. Hoover, eds. *The Five Gospels*. San Francisco: HarperSanFrancisco, 1993.

Geiger, Abraham. *Das Judenthum und seine Geschichte*. Breslau: Schletter, 1864.

Goodman, Martin. "Opponents of Rome: Jews and Others." In *Images of Empire*. Edited by L. Alexander. JSOT Sup 122, 44–51. Sheffield: Sheffield Academic, 1991.

———. *The Ruling Class in Judaea*. Cambridge: Cambridge University Press, 1987.

Graetz, Heinrich. *Sinai et Golgotha*. Paris: Michael Lévy frères, 1867.

Gray, Sherman W. *The Least of My Brothers: Matthew 25:31-46: A History of Interpretation*. Atlanta: Scholars, 1989.

Green, Joel B. *The Death of Jesus: Tradition and Interpretation in the Passion Narrative*. Tübingen: Mohr Siebeck, 1988.

Greenspoon, Leonard. "Jewish Translations of the Bible." In *The Jewish Study Bible*. Edited by Adele Berlin and Marc Zvi Brettler, 2005–20. New York: Oxford, 2003.

Grundmann, Walter. *Jesus der Galiläer und das Judentum*. Leipzig: Georg Wigand, 1940.

Gundry, Robert H. *Matthew: A Commentary on His Literary and Theological Art*. Grand Rapids: Eerdmans, 1982.

Gurtner, Daniel. "Matthew's Theology of the Temple and the 'Parting of the Ways'": Christian Origins in the First Gospel." In *Built upon Rock: Studies in the Gospel of Matthew*. Edited by D. Gurtner and J. Nolland, 128–53. Grand Rapids: Eerdmans, 2008.

Hagner, Donald A. *Matthew 1–13*. Word Biblical Commentary 33a. Dallas: Word, 1993.

———. *Matthew 14–28*. Word Biblical Commentary 33b. Dallas: Word, 1995.

———. "The Sitz in Leben of the Gospel of Matthew." In *Treasures New and Old: Contributions to Matthean Studies*. Edited by David R. Bauer and Mark Allan Powell, 27–68. Atlanta: Scholars, 1996.

Hall, Stuart. "Cultural Studies: Two Paradigms." *Media, Culture and Society* 2 (1980): 57–72.

Hammann, Konrad. *Rudolf Bultmann: Eine Biographie*. Tübingen: Mohr Siebeck, 2009.

Hare, Douglas R. A. *The Son of Man Tradition*. Minneapolis: Fortress Press, 1990.

———. *The Theme of Jewish Persecution of Christians in the Gospel According to St. Matthew*. Cambridge: Cambridge University Press, 1967.

Hare, Douglas R. A., and Daniel J. Harrington. "'Make Disciples of All the Gentiles' (MT 28:19)." *Catholic Biblical Quarterly* 37 (1975): 359–69.

Harries, Richard, Normon Solomon, and Tim Winter, eds. *Abraham's Children: Jews, Christians, and Muslims in Conversation*. New York: T & T Clark, 2006.

Hengel, Martin. *Crucifixion*. Philadelphia: Fortress Press, 1977.

———. *Studies in the Gospel of Mark*. Philadelphia: Fortress Press, 1985.

———. *Was Jesus a Revolutionist?* Philadelphia: Fortress Press, 1971.

———. *The Zealots*. Edinburgh: T & T Clark, 1989.

Heschel, Susannah. *Abraham Geiger and the Jewish Jesus*. Chicago: University of Chicago Press, 1998.

———. *The Aryan Jesus: Christian Theologians and the Bible in Nazi Germany*. Princeton: Princeton University Press, 2008.

Hiers, Richard H. "Friends by Unrighteous Mammon." *Journal of the American Academy of Religion* 38 (1970): 30–36.

———. "Purification of the Temple: Preparation for the Kingdom of God." *Journal of Biblical Literature* 90 (1971): 82–90.

Hirsch, Emanuel. *Das Wesen des Christentums*. Weimar: Deutsche Christen, 1939.

Hirshman, Marc. "Rabbinic Universalism in the Second and Third Centuries." *Harvard Theological Review* 93 (2000): 101–15.

Hogeterp, Albert L. A. *Paul and God's Temple*. Leuven: Peeters, 2006.

Horbury, William. *Jews and Christians in Contact and Controversy*. Edinburgh: T & T Clark, 1998.

Horsley, Richard A., *Jesus and Empire: The Kingdom of God and the New World Disorder*. Minneapolis: Fortress Press, 2003.

———. *Jesus and the Spiral of Violence: Popular Jewish Resistance in Roman Palestine*. San Francisco: Harper & Row, 1987.

Horsley, Richard A., and J. S. Hanson. *Bandits, Prophets and Messiahs: Popular Movements in the Time of Jesus*. Harrisburg: Trinity Press International, 1985.

Hutton, Patrick H. *History as an Art of Memory*. Hanover: University Press of New England, 1993.

Jacobson, David. "The Jerusalem Temple of Herod the Great." Vol. 1 of *The World of the Herods*. Edited by N. Kokkinos, 145–76. Stuttgart: Franz Steiner, 2007.

Jeremias, Joachim. *Jerusalem on the Time of Jesus*. Philadelphia: Fortress Press, 1969.

Johnson, Luke T. "The New Testament's Anti-Jewish Slander and the Conventions of Ancient Polemic." *Journal of Biblical Literature* 108 (1989): 419–41.

Juel, Donald. *Messiah and Temple: The Trial of Jesus in the Gospel of Mark*. Atlanta: Scholars, 1977.

Kähler, Martin. "Against the Life-of-Jesus Movement." In *The Historical Jesus in Recent Research*. Edited by Scot McKnight and James D. G. Dunn. Vol. 10 of *The Historical Jesus in Recent Research; Sources for Biblical Research and Theological Study*, 67–86. Winona Lake, IN: Eisenbrauns, 2005.

Kalthoff, Albert. *Das Christusproblem: Grundlinien zu einer Sozialtheologie*. Leipzig: Diederichs, 1902.

Kaminsky, Joel. S. "Israel's Election and the Other in Biblical, Second Temple, and Rabbinic Thought." In *The "Other" in Second Temple Judaism: Essays in Honor of John J. Collins*. Edited by Daniel C. Harlow, Matthew Goff, Karina Martin Hogan, and Joel S. Kaminsky, 17–30. Grand Rapids: Eerdmans, 2011.

———. *Yet I Loved Jacob: Reclaiming the Biblical Concept of Election*. Nashville: Abingdon, 2007.

Käsemann, Ernst. "Das Problem des historischen Jesus." *Zeitschrift fur Theologie und Kirche* 51 (1954): 125–53.

———. "Die neue Jesus-Frage." In *Jésus aux origines de la christologie*. Edited by J. Dupont. Bibliotheca Ephemeridum theologicarum Lovaniensium 40, 47–57. Leuven/Gembloux: University Press, 1975.

———. "The Problem of the Historical Jesus." In *Essays on New Testament Themes* (SBT 41; London: SCM, 1964). Originally "Das Problem des historischen Jesus," *ZThK* 51 (1954): 125–53.

Keener, Craig S. *A Commentary on the Book of Matthew*. Grand Rapids: Eerdmans, 1999.

Kellermann, Benzion. *Kritische Beiträge zur Entstehungsgeschichte des Christentums*. Berlin: Poppelauer, 1906.

Kessler, Edward. *An Introduction to Jewish-Christian Relations*. Cambridge: Cambridge University Press, 2010.

Kinzer, Mark. *Introduction to Messianic Judaism: Its Ecclesial Context and Biblical Foundation.* Grand Rapids: Zondervan, forthcoming.

Klausner, Joseph. *Jesus of Nazareth: His Life, Times and Teachings.* Translated by Herbert Danby. Boston: Beacon, 1925.

———. *Jesus von Nazareth: Seine Zeit, sein Leben und seine Lehre.* Berlin: Jewish, 1934.

Klawans, Jonathan. "Interpreting the Last Supper: Sacrifice, Spiritualization, and Anti-Sacrifice." *New Testament Studies* 48 (2002): 1–17.

Klijn, A. F. J. "Scribes, Pharisees, High-Priests and Elders." *Novum Testamentum* 3 (1959): 259–67.

Knight, Jonathan. *Luke's Gospel.* London: Routledge, 1998.

Koester, Helmut. *Ancient Christian Gospels: Their Origins and Development.* Philadelphia: Trinity Press International, 1990.

Külzer, Andreas. *Disputationes graecae contra Judaeos: Untersuchungen zur byzantinischen antijüdischen Dialogliteraur und ihrem Judenbild.* Byzantine Archive Bd. XVIII. Stuttgart-Leipzig: Teubner, 1999.

Lahey, Lawrence. "Evidence for Jewish Believers in Christian-Jewish Dialogues through the Sixth Century (excluding Justin)." In *Jewish Believers in Jesus.* Edited by O. Skarsaune and R. Hvalvik, 581–639. Peabody: Hendrickson, 2007.

Lang, Bernhard. *Jesus der Hund: Leben und Lehre eines jüdischen Kynikers.* Munich: C. H. Beck, 2010.

———. *Sacred Games: A History of Christian Worship.* New Haven: Yale University Press, 1997.

Le Donne, Anthony. *Historical Jesus: What Can We Know and How Can We Know It?* Grand Rapids: Eerdmans, 2011.

———. *The Historiographical Jesus: Memory, Typology, and the Son of David.* Waco: Baylor University Press, 2009.

———. "Jesus and Jewish Leadership." In *Jesus among Friends and Enemies.* Edited by L.W. Hurtado and C. Keith. Grand Rapids: Baker Academic, 2011.

———. "The Quest for the Historical Jesus: A Revisionist History through the Lens of Jewish-Christian Relations." *Journal for the Study of the Historical Jesus* 10, no. 1 (2012): 63–86.

Le Moyne, Jean. *Les Sadducéens.* Paris: Gabalda, 1972.

Lenski, R. C. H. *The Interpretation of St. Matthew's Gospel.* Minneapolis: Augsburg Fortress, 1961.

Levenson, David. "Anti-Judaism in the Gospel of Matthew." Paper presented at International Symposium on the Interpretation of the Bible as a Force for Social Change, Goethe University, Frankfurt, 2001.

Levenson, Jon. "The Perils of Engaged Scholarship: A Rejoinder to Jorge Pixley." In *Jews Christians, and the Theology of the Hebrew Scriptures.* Edited by A. Ogden Bellis and J. S. Kaminsky, 239–46. Atlanta: Society of Biblical Literature, 2000.

———. "The Universal Horizon of Biblical Particularlism." In *Ethnicity and the Bible*. Edited by M. G. Brett, 143–69. Leiden: Brill, 1996.

Levine, Amy-Jill. "Anti-Judaism and the Gospel of Matthew." In *Anti-Judaism and the Gospels*. Edited by William R. Farmer. Harrisburg: Trinity International, 1999.

———. "Canaanite Woman." In *Women in Scripture: A Dictionary of Named and Unnamed Women in the Hebrew Bible, the Apochrypha/Deuterocanonical Books, and the New Testament*. Edited by Carol Meyers, Toni Craven, and Ross S. Kraemer. Boston: Houghton Mifflin, 2000.

———. "Matthew's Advice to a Divided Readership." In *The Gospel of Matthew in Current Study*. Edited by David E. Aune, 22–41. Grand Rapids: Eerdmans, 2001.

———. *The Misunderstood Jew: The Church and the Scandal of the Jewish Jesus*. San Francisco: HarperOne, 2006.

———. "Putting Jesus Where He Belongs: The Man from Nazareth in His Jewish World." *Perspectives in Religious Studies* 27, no. 2 (2000): 167–77.

———. "Review Essay: Evangelical Biblical Scholarship." *Journal for the Study of the Historical Jesus* (forthcoming).

———. *The Social and Ethnic Dimensions of the Matthean Salvation History: 'Go nowhere among the Gentiles . . .' (Matt. 10:5b)*. Lewiston: Edwin Mellen, 1988.

———. "'To All the Gentiles': A Jewish Perspective on the Great Commission." *Review and Expositor* 103 (2006): 139–58.

Lieu, Judith. "Temple and Synagogue in John." *New Testament Studies* 45 (1999): 51–69.

Lohmeyer, Ernst. *Galiläa und Jerusalem*. Research on the Literature of the Old and New Testaments 34. Göttingen: Vandenhoeck and Ruprecht, 1936.

Lohr, Joel N. *Chosen and Unchosen: Conceptions of Election in the Pentateuch and Jewish-Christian Interpretation*. Winona Lake, IN: Eisenbrauns, 2009.

Lonergan, Bernard J. F. *Method in Theology*. New York: Herder and Herder, 1972.

Luther, Martin. "That Jesus Christ Was Born a Jew." Vol. 45 of *Luther's Works*. Translated by W. I. Brandt, 201–29. Philadelphia: Fortress Press, 1962.

———. "The Jews and Their Lies." Vol. 47 of *Luther's Works*. Translated by W. I. Brandt, 137–76. Philadelphia: Fortress Press, 1971.

Luz, Ulrich. "Anti-Judaism in the Gospel of Matthew as a Historical and Theological Problem: An Outline." In *Studies in Matthew*, 243–63. Grand Rapids: Eerdmans, 2005.

———. *Matthew 1–7: A Commentary*. Hermeneia. Minneapolis: Fortress Press, 2007.

———. *Matthew 8–20: A Commentary*. Hermeneia. Minneapolis: Fortress Press, 2001.

———. *Matthew 21–28: A Commentary*. Hermeneia. Minneapolis: Fortress Press, 2005.

———. *Studies in Matthew*. Grand Rapids: Eerdmans, 2005.

————. *The Theology of the Gospel of Matthew.* New Testament Theology. Cambridge: Cambridge University Press, 1995.

Mack, Burton. *A Myth of Innocence: Mark and Christian Origins.* Philadelphia: Fortress Press, 1988.

MacMullen, Ramsay. *Enemies of the Roman Order.* Cambridge, MA: Harvard University Press, 1966.

Malbon, Elizabeth Struthers. "Daughter of the Syrophoenician Woman." In *Women in Scripture: A Dictionary of Named and Unnamed Women in the Hebrew Bible, the Apochrypha/Deuterocanonical Books, and the New Testament.* Edited by Carol Meyers, Toni Craven, and Ross S. Kraemer. Boston: Houghton Mifflin, 2000.

————. "Syrophoenician Woman." In *Women in Scripture: A Dictionary of Named and Unnamed Women in the Hebrew Bible, the Apochrypha/Deuterocanonical Books, and the New Testament.* Edited by Carol Meyers, Toni Craven, and Ross S. Kraemer. Boston: Houghton Mifflin, 2000.

Marcus, Joel. *Mark 1–8: A New Translation with Introduction and Commentary.* Anchor Bible. New York: Doubleday, 2000.

————. "The Jewish War and the *Sitz im Leben* of Mark." *Journal of Biblical Literature* 111 (1992): 448–49.

McCarthy, Kate. *Interfaith Encounters in America.* New Brunswick: Rutgers University Press, 2007.

McKnight, Scot. *Jesus and His Death: Historiography, the Historical Jesus, and Atonement Theory.* Waco: Baylor University Press, 2005.

Meadors, E. P. "The 'Messianic' Implications of the Q Material." *Journal of Biblical Literature* 118 (1999): 253–77.

Meier, John. "Jesus in Josephus: A Modest Proposal." *Catholic Biblical Quarterly* 52 (1990): 76–103.

————. *Law and Love.* Vol. 4 of *A Marginal Jew: Rethinking the Historical Jesus.* New Haven: Yale University Press, 2009.

————. *A Marginal Jew: Rethinking the Historical Jesus.* 4 vols. New York: Doubleday, 1991–2009.

————. *Mentor, Message, and Miracles.* Vol. 2 of *A Marginal Jew: Rethinking the Historical Jesus.* New Haven: Yale University Press, 1994.

————. "Nations or Gentiles in Matthew 28:19." *Catholic Biblical Quarterly* 39 (1977): 94–102.

————. *The Problem and the Person.* Vol. 1 of *A Marginal Jew: Rethinking the Historical Jesus.* New Haven: Yale University Press, 1991.

Merz, Annette B. "Philhellenismus und Antisemitismus: Zwei Seiten einer Medaille in den akademischen Publikationen von Carl Schneider." *Church History* 17 (2004): 314–30.

Meyer-Erlach, Wolf. *Juden, Mönche und Luther.* Weimar: Deutsche Christen, 1937.

Meyers, Ched. *Binding the Strong Man: A Political Reading of Mark's Story of Jesus.* Maryknoll: Orbis, 1988.

Michael, Robert. *Holy Hatred: Christianity, Antisemitism, and the Holocaust.* New York: Palgrave Macmillan, 2006.

Michaels, J. Ramsey. "Apostolic Hardships and Righteous Gentiles: A Study of Matthew 25:31-46." *Journal of Biblical Literature* 84 (1965): 25–37.

Miller, R. J., ed. *The Apocalyptic Jesus: A Debate.* Santa Rosa: Polebridge, 2001.

Montefiore, C. G. *The Synoptic Gospels.* 2 vols. London: Macmillan, 1909.

Moore, George Foot. "Christian Writers on Judaism." *Harvard Theological Review* 14 (1921): 197–254.

Morgan, Thomas, *The Moral Philosopher.* Vols. 1–3. London: printed for the author, 1738–1740. Facsimile reprint in one volume. Edited by G. Gawlick. Stuttgart: Fromman, 1969.

Morris, Leon. *The Gospel According to Matthew.* Pillar New Testament Commentary. Leicester: Apollos, 1992.

Nanos, Mark D. "Paul's Reversal of Jews Calling Gentiles 'Dogs' (Philippians 3:2): 1600 Years of an Ideological Tale Wagging an Exegetical Dog?" *Biblical Interpretation* 17 (2009): 448–83.

Neill, Stephen. *The Interpretation of the New Testament 1861–1961.* New York: Oxford University Press, 1966.

Neill, Stephen, and Tom Wright. *The Interpretation of the New Testament.* 2nd ed. Oxford: Oxford University Press, 1988.

Neusner, Jacob, Baruch A. Levine, and Bruce Chilton. *Torah Revealed, Torah Fulfilled: Scriptural Laws in Formative Judaism and Earliest Christianity.* London: T & T Clark, 2008.

Neusner, Jacob, and Bruce J. Chilton, eds. *The Quest of the Historical Pharisees.* Waco: Baylor University Press, 2007.

Newman, Barclay M. "CEV's Chief Translator: We Were Faithful to the Intention of the Text [Counterpoint]." *Bible Review* 12 (1996): 43, 51.

Nisbet, H. B. *Lessing: Eine Biographie.* Munich: Beck, 2008.

Nolland, John. *The Gospel of Matthew: A Commentary on the Greek Text.* New International Greek Testament Commentary. Grand Rapids: Eerdmans, 2005.

Novak, David. *The Election of Israel: The Idea of a Chosen People.* Cambridge: Cambridge University Press, 1995.

———. *The Image of the Non-Jew in Judaism: An Historical and Constructive Study of the Noahide Laws.* New York: Edwin Mellen, 1983.

Omi, Michael, and Howard Winant. *Racial Formation in the United States.* New York: Routledge, 1986.

Patterson, S. J. "The End of Apocalypse: Rethinking the Eschatological Jesus." *Theology Today* 52 (1995): 29–48.

Pontifical Biblical Commission, The. *The Jewish People and Their Sacred Scriptures in the Christian Bible.* Vatican City: Libreria Editrice Vatican, 2002.

Porter, Stanley E. *The Criteria for Authenticity in Historical-Jesus Research: Previous Discussion and New Proposals.* JSNTSup 191. Sheffield: Sheffield Academic, 2000.

Price, S. R. F. *Rituals of Power. The Roman Imperial Cult in Asia Minor.* Cambridge: Cambridge University Press, 1984.

Rainey, Anson E., and R. Steven Notley. *The Sacred Bridge: Carta's Atlas of the Biblical World.* Jerusalem: Carta, 2006.

Reble, Albert. *Geschichte der Pädagogik.* Stuttgart: Klett-Cotta, 1989.

Regev, Eyal. "A Kingdom of Priests or a Holy (Gentile) People: The Temple in Early Christian Life and Thought." *Cathedra* 113 (2004): 5–34.

———. "Moral Impurity and the Temple in Early Christianity in Light of Qumranic Ideology and Ancient Greek Practice." *Harvard Theological Review* 79, no. 44 (2004): 383–411.

———. *The Sadducees and Their Halakhah: Religion and Society in the Second Temple Period.* Jerusalem: Yad Izhak ben Zvi, 2005.

———. "The Sadducees, the Pharisees and the Sacred: Meaning and Ideology in the Halakhic Controversies between the Sadducees and the Pharisees." *Review of Rabbinic Judaism* 9 (2006): 126–40.

———. *Sectarianism in Qumran: A Cross-Cultural Perspective.* Berlin: de Gruyter, 2007.

———. "Temple Concerns and High Priestly Persecutions from Peter to James: Between Narrative and History." *New Testament Studies* 56, no. 1 (2010): 64–89.

———. "The Temple in Mark: A Case Study about the Early Christian Attitude toward the Temple." In *Studies in Rabbinic Judaism and Early Christianity: Text and Context.* Ancient Judaism and Early Christianity Series 74. Edited by D. Jaffé, 139–59. Leiden: Brill, 2010.

———. "Temple or Messiah: On the Trial of Jesus, the Temple and the Roman Policy." *Cathedra* 119 (2006): 14–25.

———. "Wealth and Sectarianism: Comparing Qumranic and Early Christian Social Approaches." In *Echoes from the Caves: Qumran and the New Testament.* Studies on the Texts of the Desert of Judah 85. Edited by F. Garcia Martinez, 211–30. Leiden: Brill, 2009.

Reiser, Marius. *Jesus and Judgment: The Eschatological Proclamation in Its Jewish Context.* Minneapolis: Fortress Press, 1997.

Renan, Ernest. *The Life of Jesus.* Translated by C. E. Wilbour. London: Trübner, Paternoster Row, 1864.

———. "What Is a Nation?" In *The Collective Memory Reader.* Edited by J. Olick, V. Vinitzky-Seroussi, and D. Levy, 80–83. Oxford: Oxford University Press, 2011.

Richardson, Peter. "Why Turn the Tables? Jesus' Protest in the Temple Precincts." *SBL Seminar Papers* 31 (1992): 507–23.

Riches, John, and David C. Sim, eds. *The Gospel of Matthew in Its Roman Imperial Context.* London: T & T Clark International, 2005.

Riches, John Kenneth. *Jesus and the Transformation of Judaism.* London: Darton, Longmann & Todd, 1980.

Robinson, J. M., ed. *The Nag Hammadi.* Library in English. Rev. ed. Leiden: Brill, 1996.

Rosenbloom, Joseph R. *Conversion to Judaism: From the Biblical Period to the Present.* Cincinnati: Hebrew Union College Press, 1978.

Rousmaniere, John. *A Bridge to Dialogue.* New York: A Stimulus Book, 1991.

Rubio, Fernando Bermejo. "The Fiction of the 'Three Quests': An Argument for Dismantling a Dubious Historiographical Paradigm." *Journal for the Study of the Historical Jesus* 7 (2009): 211–53.

Salmon, Marilyn J. *Preaching without Contempt: Overcoming Unintended Anti-Judaism.* Minneapolis: Fortress Press, 2006.

Sanders, E. P. *The Historical Figure of Jesus.* London: Allen Lane, 1993.

———. "Jesus in Galilee." In *Jesus: A Colloquium in the Holy Land.* Edited by Doris Donnelly, 5–26. New York: Continuum, 2001.

———. *Jesus and Judaism.* London: SCM 1985.

———. *Judaism: Practice and Belief 63 BCE–66 BCE.* London: SCM, 1992.

———. *Paul and Palestinian Judaism.* London: SCM, 1977.

Sanders, James A. "The Hermeneutics of Translation." In *Removing the Anti-Judaism from the New Testament.* Edited by Howard Clark Kee and Irvin J. Borowsky, 43–62. Philadelphia: American Interfaith Institute/World Alliance, 1998 and 2000.

Sandmel, Samuel. "Parallelomania." *Journal of Biblical Literature* 81 (1962): 1–13.

Schäfer, Peter. *Jesus in the Talmud.* Princeton, NJ: Princeton University Press, 2009.

Schilson, Arno. "Lessing and Theology." In *A Companion to the Works of Gotthold Ephraim Lessing.* Edited by B. Fischer and T. C. Fox, 170–74. Rochester: Camden House, 2005.

Schürer, Emil. *Geschichte des jüdischen Volkes im Zeitalter Jesu Christi.* 3 vols. 2nd ed. Leipzig: Hinrich, 1886.

Schüssler Fiorenza, Elisabeth. *But SHE Said: Feminist Practices of Biblical Interpretation.* Boston: Beacon, 1992.

Schwartz, Daniel R. "On Sacrifice by Gentiles in the Temple of Jerusalem." In *Studies in the Jewish Background of Christianity*, 102–16. Tuebingen: Mohr-Siebeck, 1992.

———. "Viewing the Holy Utensils (P. Ox. V, 840)." *New Testament Studies* 32 (1986): 153–59.

Schweitzer, Albert. *The Mystery of the Kingdom of God.* London: A. & C. Black, 1925.

———. *The Quest of the Historical Jesus.* Translated by W. Montgomery. London: A. & C. Black, 1910.

———. *The Quest of the Historical Jesus.* Translated by W. Montgomery and F. C. Burkitt. Mineola: Dover, 2005.

Seeberg, Reinhold. "Die Herkunft der Mutter Jesu." In *Theologische Festschrift für G. N. Bonwetsch zu seinem 70 Geburtstag*, 13–24. Leipzig: Deichert, 1918.

Segal, Peretz. "The Penalty of the Warning Inscription from the Temple of Jerusalem." *Israel Exploration Journal* 39 (1989): 79–84.

Senior, Donald. "Between Two Worlds: Gentile and Jewish Christians in Matthew's Gospel." *Catholic Bible Quarterly* 61 (1999): 1–23.

———. "Directions in Matthean Studies." In *The Gospel of Matthew in Current Study.* Edited by David E. Aune, 5–21. Grand Rapids: Eerdmans, 2001.

———. *Matthew.* Abingdon New Testament Commentaries. Nashville: Abingdon, 1998.

———. "*Nostra Aetate* and the Catholic Biblical Renewal: A New Understanding of Judaism and the Jewish Roots of Early Christianity." In *"Perché stessero con Lui" Scritti in onore di Klemens Stock SJ nel suo 75° compleanno.* Edited by Lorenzo De Santos and Santi Grasso, 27–41. Rome: Gregorian & Biblical, 2010.

Setzer, Claudia. "Three Odd Couples: Women and Men in Mark and John." In *Mariam, the Magdelen, and the Mother.* Edited by Deirde Good. Bloomington: Indiana University Press, 2005.

Seydel, Rudolf. *Die Buddhalegende und das Leben Jesu nach den Evangelien.* Weimar: Felber 1884.

Sim, David C. "The Gospel of Matthew and the Gentiles." *Journal for the Study of the New Testament* 57 (1995): 19–48.

Smelik, Willem F. *The Targum of Judges.* Oudtestamentische studiën 36. Leiden: Brill, 1995.

Smith, Morton. *Jesus the Magician.* London: V. Gollancz, 1978.

Snodgrass, Klyne R. *Stories with Intent: A Comprehensive Guide to the Parables.* Grand Rapids: Eerdmans, 2008.

Soards, Marion. "The Question of a Premarcan Passion Narrative." In *The Death of the Messiah* 2. Edited by Raymond Brown. New York: Doubleday: 1994.

Stanton, Graham. "Jesus of Nazareth: A Magician and False Prophet Who Deceived God's People?" In *Jesus of Nazareth Lord and Christ: Essays on the Historical Jesus.* Edited by Joel B. Green and M. Turner, 169–71. Grand Rapids: Eerdmans, 1994.

Stanton, Graham N. "Once More: Matthew 25:31-46." In *A Gospel for a New People: Studies in Matthew,* 401–3. Louisville: Westminster John Knox, 1993.

Stern, David H., trans. *Complete Jewish Bible.* Messianic Jewish Resources International, 2007.

———, trans. *Jewish New Testament.* Jerusalem: Jewish New Testament Publications, 1989.

Strauss, David Friedrich. *The Life of Jesus Critically Examined.* Translated by G. Eliot. London: SCM, 1973.

Taussig, Hal. "Dealing under the Table: Ritual Negotiation of Women's Power in the Syro-Phoenician Woman Pericope." In *Reimagining Christian Origins: A Colloquium Honoring Burton L. Mack.* Edited by Eliabeth A. Castelli and Hal Taussig. Valley Forge: Trinity Press International, 1996.

Taylor, Joan E. "Pontius Pilate and the Imperial Cult in Roman Judaea." *New Testament Studies* 52 (2006): 555–82.

Theissen, Gerd. "Das Reinheitslogion Mk 7,15 und die Trennung von Juden und Christen." In *Jesus als historische Gestalt: Beiträge zur Jesusforschung.* Edited by Gerd Theissen, 73–89. Göttingen: Vandenhoeck & Ruprecht, 2003.

———. "Jesus as an Itinerant Teacher: Reflections from Social History on Jesus." In *Jesus Research: An International Perspective, The First Princeton-Prague Symposium on Jesus Research.* Edited by J. H. Charlesworth and P. Pokorný, 98–122. Grand Rapids: Eerdmans, 2009.

————. "Jesus im Judentum: Drei Versuche einer Ortsbestimmung." In *Jesus als historische Gestalt: Beiträge zur Jesusforschung*. Edited by Gerd Theissen, 35–56. Göttingen: Vandenhoeck & Ruprecht, 2003.

————. "Jünger als Gewalttäter (Mt 11:12f ; Lk 16:16). Der Stürmerspruch als Selbststigmatisierung einer Minorität." In *Jesus als historische Gestalt: Beiträge zur Jesusforschung*. Edited by Gerd Theissen, 153–68. Göttingen: Vandenhoeck & Ruprecht, 2003.

————. *The Historical Jesus: A Comprehensive Guide*. London: SCM, 1998.

————. *Neutestamentliche Wissenschaft vor und nach 1945: Karl Georg Kuhn und Günther Bornkamm*. Schriften der Philosophisch-historischen Klasse der Heidelberger Akademie der Wissenschaften 47, Seite(n) 5–260. Heidelberg: Universitätsverlag C. Winter, 2009.

————. "Sadduzäismus und Jesustradition. Zur Auseinandersetzung mit Oberschichtmentalität in der synoptischen Überlieferung." In *Jesus als historische Gestalt: Beiträge zur Jesusforschung*. Edited by Gerd Theissen, 111–31. Göttingen: Vandenhoeck & Ruprecht, 2003.

————. *Sociology of Early Palestinian Christianity*. Philadelphia: Fortress Press, 1978.

————. *The Shadow of the Galilean: The Quest of the Historical Jesus in Narrative Form*. Translated by J. Bowden. Philadelphia: Fortress Press, 1987.

Theissen, Gerd, and Annette Merz. *The Historical Jesus: A Comprehensive Guide*. Minneapolis: Fortress Press, 1996.

Theissen, Gerd, and Dagmar Winter. *The Quest for the Plausible Jesus: The Question of Criteria*. Translated by M. E. Boring. Louisville: Westminster John Knox, 2002.

Tuckett, Christopher M. "Q and Thomas: Evidence of a Primitive 'Wisdom Gospel'?" *Ephemerides theologicae lovanienses* 67 (1991): 346–60.

————. "On the Stratification of Q: A Response." *Semeia* 55 (1992): 213–22.

Turner, David L. *Matthew*. Baker Exegetical Commentary on the New Testament 1. Edited by Robert W. Yarbrough and Robert H. Stein. Grand Rapids: Baker Academic, 2008.

Van Egmond, Richard. "The Messianic 'Son of David' in Matthew." *Journal of Greco-Roman Christianity and Judaism* 3 (2006): 41–71.

Vermes, Geza. *Jesus the Jew: A Historian's Reading of the Gospel*. 1st Fortress Press ed. Minneapolis: Fortress Press. 1981.

————. *Jesus the Jew: A Historian's Reading of the Gospels*. London: Collins, 1973.

Via, Dan O. "Ethical Responsibility and Human Wholeness in Matthew 25:31-46." *Harvard Theological Review* 80 (1987): 79–100

Vico, Giambattista. *The New Science of Giambattista Vico*. Translated by Thomas Goddard Bergin and Max Harold Fisch. Ithaca: Cornell University Press, 1968.

Walter, Richard. "Ernst Käsemanns Wirken als Gemeindepfarrer im Kirchenkampf in Westfalen 1933–1946." *KZG* 12 (1999): 199–224.

Watson, Francis. "Liberating the Reader: A Theological-Exegetical Study of the Parable of the Sheep and the Goats (Matt. 25.31-46)." In *The Open Text:*

New Directions for Biblical Studies? Edited by Francis Watson. London: SCM, 1993.

Weber, Ferdinand. "Das System des jüdischen Pharisäismus und des römischen Katholizismus. Eine religionsgeschichtliche Parallele." *Allgemeine evangelisch-lutherische Kirchenzeitung* 3, 1870, col. 805–9 (no. 44); col. 823–28 (no. 45); col. 845–48 (no. 46).

Webster, Graham. *Boudica: The Roman Conquest of Britain.* London: Batsford, 1993.

Weiss, A. Johannes. *Jesus' Proclamation of the Kingdom of God.* Translated by Richard H. Hiers and D. Larrimore Holland. London: SCM, 1971. Originally *Die Predigt Jesu von Reiche Gottes.* Göttingen: Vandenhoeck & Ruprecht, 1892.

———. "Das Problem der Entstehung des Christentums." *Archiv für Religionswissenschaft* 16 (1913): 423–515.

Wellhausen, Julius. "Abriss der Geschichte Israels und Juda's." In *Skizzen und Vorarbeiten.* Volume 1, 5–102. Berlin: Reimer, 1884.

———. *Einleitung in die ersten drei Evangelien.* Berlin: G. Reimer, 1911.

———. *Die Pharisäer und die Sadducäer: Eine Untersuchung zur inneren jüdischen Geschichte,* 1874.

Wenham, David. *The Parables of Jesus.* Downers Grove, IL: InterVarsity, 1989.

Whiston, William. *The New Complete Works of Josephus.* Grand Rapids: Kregel Academic, 1999.

Wilken, Robert L. *The Christians as the Romans Saw Them.* New Haven: Yale University Press, 1984.

Winter, Paul. *On the Trial of Jesus.* Berlin: de Gruyter, 1961.

———. *On the Trial of Jesus.* Rev. ed. Berlin: de Gruyter, 1974.

Wistrich, Robert S. *A Lethal Obsession: Anti-Semitism from Antiquity to the Global Jihad.* New York: Random House, 2009.

Wittgenstein, Ludwig. *Philosophische Untersuchungen.* N. 66. Berlin: Academy, 1998.

Wrede, William. *The Messianic Secret.* Translated by J. O. G. Greig. London and Cambridge: James Clarke, 1971.

Wright, N. T. *Jesus and the Victory of God.* Minneapolis: Fortress Press, 1996.

Wünsche, Karl August. *Neue Beiträge zur Erläuterung der Evangelien aus Talmud und Midrasch.* Göttingen: Vandenhoeck & Ruprecht, 1878.

Yarbo-Collins, Adele. "The Passion Narrative of Mark." In *The Beginnings of the Gospel: Probing of Mark in Context,* 92–118. Minneapolis: Fortress Press, 1992.

Zerubavel, Yael. *Recovered Roots: Collective Memory and the Making of Israeli National Tradition.* Chicago: University of Chicago Press, 1995.

Index of Modern Authors

Index of Ancient Sources

New Testament

Matthew